PUBLISHED UNDER THE AUSPICES OF
THE CENTER FOR JAPANESE AND KOREAN STUDIES,
UNIVERSITY OF CALIFORNIA, BERKELEY

JAPANESE URBANISM

GARY D. ALLINSON

JAPANESE URBANISM

Industry and Politics in

Kariya, 1872–1972

UNIVERSITY OF CALIFORNIA PRESS

BERKELEY · LOS ANGELES · LONDON

University of California Press
Berkeley and Los Angeles, California
University of California Press, Ltd.
London, England

Copyright © 1975, by
The Regents of the University of California

ISBN 0-520-02842-2
Library of Congress Catalog Card Number: 74-84141
Printed in the United States of America

FOR PAT

CONTENTS

TABLES

ABBREVIATIONS
USED IN THE FOOTNOTES

Atn   Aichi ken. *Aichi ken tōkei nenkan* [Statistical Annual of Aichi Prefecture]. 23 vols. Nagoya, 1950–1972.

Ats   Aichi ken. *Aichi ken tōkei sho* [Statistical Handbook of Aichi Prefecture]. 51 vols. Nagoya, 1884–1893, 1907–1942, and 1946–1949.

Kcs   Kariya machiyakuba. *Kariya chō shi* [History of the Town of Kariya]. Kariya, 1932.

Kss   Kariya shiyakusho. *Kariya shi shi* [History of the City of Kariya]. Kariya, 1960.

30-nen shi   Shashi henshū iinkai, ed. *Toyota jidōsha 30-nen shi* [A History of 30 Years of Toyota Motors]. Toyota, 1967.

40-nen shi   Shashi henshū iinkai, ed. *Toyota jidō shokki seisakusho 40-nen shi* [A History of 40 Years of the Toyota Automatic Loom Works]. Kariya, 1967.

ACKNOWLEDGMENTS

In the course of preparing this book, I have incurred many debts on both sides of the Pacific. In addition to those named in person below, my sincerest appreciation goes out to the people of Kariya. Their willingness to provide materials and sit for interviews made our visits to Kariya a great pleasure and helped immeasurably in bringing the history of their city to light.

First and foremost I want to thank my wife Pat for her indispensable role in making this book. She had to manage households in Japan on two occasions, to conduct the family's diplomacy, to rear an active son, and to cater to the often impossible demands of a husband during the years this book was in progress. As she so effortlessly does, she handled all these tasks with skill, grace, and compassion. Dedicating this book to her does not begin to express the sincere appreciation she deserves.

Pat and I both owe a very special debt to Inagaki Toyomi and his wife Hiroko, two friends in Kariya who accepted us into their home and made our visits there in 1970 and 1972 experiences which we shall always value. We are indebted to many other teachers and friends in Japan for a great variety of assistance. To Andō Seiichi, Nagai Michio, and Sawa Shun'ichi go my personal thanks for their guidance as *sensei*. To Abe Osamu, Hara Toshio, Hattori Masayoshi, Inaba Etsuzō, Kataoka Masako and Hachirō, Masaki Kazuo, Murase Masayuki, Nishimura Kiyoshi, Ōta Ichizō, Satō Seizaburō, and Tamura Kenshō go our joint thanks for their many favors.

A number of teachers, colleagues, and friends in the United States helped bring this book to fruition. Thomas Smith inspired the conception of this study at Stanford in the late 1960s and assisted its development in many ways thereafter. Kurt Steiner also lent his cultivated and incisive talents to the making of the book. To both of them I owe my fondest appreciation. Keith Brown, Gorden Berger, Ellis Krauss, Richard Smethurst, and Gabriel Tortella all read parts of the manuscript in draft form. They deserve special thanks for interrupting their own work to help mine. I also wish to thank Samuel Hays and Douglas Johnson for conversations which decisively shaped the content and concerns of this book.

Several organizations funded this study over a period of years. National Defense Foreign Language Fellowships awarded by the Department of

Health, Education and Welfare supported my graduate studies, while a grant from the Foreign Area Fellowship Program underwrote research in Japan. I am particularly grateful for their generosity and for the unfettered freedom they allowed me in pursuing my interests. The Center for Research in International Studies at Stanford University and the University Center for International Studies at the University of Pittsburgh both provided funds for typing purposes, and the Faculty of Arts and Sciences at the University of Pittsburgh provided support for a visit to Japan in 1972. I want to express my appreciation to these organizations, also.

Mrs. Carol Riley typed the final manuscript and handled the task with exceptional competence. At the University of California Press the manuscript was skillfully edited by Severn Towl, and John Enright guided it through the production processes at a highly professional pace. To all of them I extend my warmest gratitude.

I alone bear responsibility for the errors which inevitably remain.

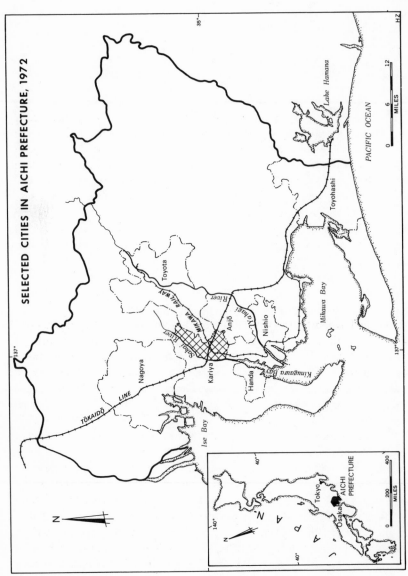

SELECTED CITIES IN AICHI PREFECTURE, 1972.

1

INTRODUCTION

Two hours from Tokyo, Japan's Bullet Train skirts the broad expanse of Lake Hamana and shortly after crosses into Aichi Prefecture. On a clear day it is possible to glimpse off to the right the outline of the jagged mountains which fill the northeastern quarter of the prefecture and form the southern extremity of the Japan Alps. In a few moments the flat dinginess of the prefecture's second largest city, Toyohashi, comes into view. Spread across the coastal headlands of Mikawa Bay, it is the social focus for the people on the plain and in the towns up the valley. Its appearance as it flits past the train windows conveys little sense of vitality, however. The tightly packed, low-lying, and unpainted buildings which are the homes and shops of Toyohashi become a gray blur from the train. Only a few high concrete buildings in the distance rise above it, making a mute plea for recognition as the symbols of a modern city.

Leaving Toyohashi, the train hugs the shore of Mikawa Bay momentarily before gliding northwestward. The next twenty minutes carry it through lush farmland situated in the foothills that skirt the mountains. Here and there the skyline is dotted with a cluster of dwellings, which identify a rural market town, or a clump of trees shading a small temple in a blanket of green. Occasionally the train passes a city rimmed with new apartment houses, which have the appearance of endless rows of matchboxes. A white haze flows upward from the chimney of a spinning factory, almost, it seems, in the middle of nowhere.

Before one realizes it, the train slows for a stop in the sprawling metropolis of Nagoya. Situated about midway between Tokyo and Osaka, Nagoya has long been among Japan's three or four largest cities. It rules over the Nōbi Plain, the only broad, open area on the rugged coast that lies along the shore between Osaka and Tokyo. Settled since the earliest periods of Japanese history, this area has long functioned as a catch point for men, culture, and ideas. The crush of people in the station and the rush of shoppers who flow in and out of the prosperous department stores nearby attest to its continued importance as a magnet for men and business. Ten minutes from Nagoya, the train begins the ascent toward Sekigahara when it enters Gifu Prefecture and leaves Aichi behind.

I

Forty-five minutes suffice to cross the prefecture. Although it is one of Japan's largest, its 2,000 square miles make it only half again the size of Rhode Island. Autos on the new tollway take only an hour to cross it.

The mountains and foothills of the east and the Nōbi Plain on the west of Aichi were once separate political regions. Most of the plain lay within the province (*kuni*) of Owari, while the foothills and mountains were in the province of Mikawa. During the Tokugawa Period (1600–1868) all of Owari was part of a single fief governed by a branch of the Tokugawa family, the ruling house of Japan. Owari was one of the nation's largest domains, and it emerged by the late Tokugawa Period as a region of active commerce and industry. Unlike Owari, Mikawa was divided and disunited politically. During the Tokugawa hegemony many groups shared authority in the Mikawa area. These included numerous hereditary lords (*fudai daimyo*), retainers of the Tokugawa house (*hatamoto*), the ruling house itself, and a number of temples and shrines. Until the end of the Tokugawa era, Mikawa remained an area of considerable diversity, hampered economically by its lack of political coherence.

Following the Meiji Restoration of 1868, the Japanese government ordered numerous changes in the administrative make-up of the two provinces. It abolished the domains in 1871. In 1872 it consolidated Owari and Mikawa to form the present prefecture of Aichi. Two decades later it established a system of local government, according to which the prefecture was divided into one urban area (Nagoya) and some eighteen counties (*gun*), which were further divided into a number of towns (*machi*) and villages (*mura*).[1] Villages were clusters of residential units in the countryside; towns differed only by being a bit larger and more diversified. In the 1920s the districts were abolished. In the meantime, many towns had grown much larger, to become cities (*shi*).[2] Aichi had seven by 1945. In the next two decades, with population growth and consolidation programs, it witnessed the emergence of fourteen more.

[1] One of these counties, Hekikai *gun*, is discussed in this study. Hekikai was one of eighteen counties created in 1878. Between 1891 and 1923 it enjoyed some administrative authority, but for most of the period covered in this book it was merely a geo-political area. Hekikai rested on the westernmost border of old Mikawa. It was twenty miles long from north to south and nine miles wide from east to west. At the turn of the century, there were five towns and ten villages in Hekikai. By 1972 the district had for all purposes disappeared, obliterated by consolidations which had made cities of its entire area.

[2] To avoid confusion, I employ in this study the Japanese definition of city (*shi*), which is an essentially administrative usage. Cities were first defined in codes of local government promulgated in 1888 as entities of larger size and slightly greater autonomy than towns and villages (*chōson*). Requirements for elevation to city status have varied over the last eight decades, but those which prevailed in 1954 convey a sense of the key provisions. In that year a settlement qualified as a city if it had: (1) 50 percent of its work force engaged in non-agricultural pursuits; (2) houses 60 percent of which were contiguous; and (3) a population exceeding 40,000, 60 percent of which was in the city center. (The population minimum has often varied, ranging from 25,000 to 50,000.)

By 1972 Aichi was an almost entirely urban prefecture. In addition to Nagoya, it embraced twenty-eight other cities. Some, such as Toyohashi and Okazaki, were former castletowns. Others, such as Handa and Seto, were once handicraft centers. Still others, such as Kasugai and Komaki, were commuter suburbs serving metropolitan Nagoya. These twenty-nine cities covered almost half of the prefectural land area and housed 85 percent of the prefecture's inhabitants. They ranged in size from the massive 2 million of Nagoya to the modest 31,000 of Takahama. Three had populations in the 200,000's and two in the 100,000's, but the majority were small cities between 30,000 and 90,000. This book deals in detail with one of those cities, Kariya, and in lesser detail with several of the others.[3]

Kariya was a thriving industrial center of almost 90,000 people in 1972. Each day some 15,000 of its inhabitants bustled off to work in one of the city's 400 factories. They were joined by another 15,000 who poured into Kariya from surrounding cities by car, bus, bike and train. Most of those people finally filtered through the gates of seven giant firms, where they spent their days making piston rings, headlamps, seat springs, and auto bodies. Some of them made different items—food products, household furniture, sewing machines, roof tiles—but the vast majority engaged in the production of automobiles. For nearly a quarter-century, Kariya had been at the center of Japan's auto industry. Thousands of persons settled there to staff factories, man production lines, or to serve the local populace. They made Kariya one of Japan's most active and prosperous industrial cities.

The city was shaped in the form of a crescent running eight miles from north to south and four from east to west. It covered an area of slightly more than nineteen square miles. Hugging the shore of Kinugaura Bay and the east bank of the Sakai River, it was divided into three segments by two other rivers which flowed westward into the bay. The northern part of the city was high and hilly. Much of it remained paddy land or scrub forest. Some of it was being developed for residences; the new teachers' college had made it a high-status location. The southern third of the city was a mixed zone of farmland and factories, spread across a flat plateau about 100 feet above sea level. From the midst of its drab horizon a set of radio towers thrust skyward to mark it for miles. The center segment formed the heart of the city. In this section were most of its houses, shops and factories, as well as its new shopping center, its schools, hospitals and

[3] In order to place Kariya in a specific urban context, I draw comparisons in this study with four nearby communities, when materials permit. They are Toyota (before 1959 the community of Koromo), Anjō, Nishio and Handa. Koromo and Nishio originated in the sixteenth century and were castletowns during the Tokugawa Period. Handa was a port town and commercial settlement then. Anjō developed as an agricultural frontier town after the Tōkaidō Line went through Aichi in 1889. The four communities thus represent a range of urban types against which to compare Kariya's history.

government offices. For more than four centuries, this had been the focal point of urban Kariya.

Kariya's origins as an urban settlement date from 1533, when the Mizuno family constructed a castle at the head of Kinugaura Bay. Perched on a low bluff overlooking the Sakai River, with an expansive view of Owari Province in the distance, this was an ideal location for the castle of a minor lord. The lord's retainers settled in homes built to encircle the castle and merchants arrived to serve their commercial needs. In time a small castletown developed, with a population composed of samurai, merchants, craftsmen, and peasants. After four generations the Mizuno family left Kariya, but they were succeeded by other families, the last of which was most permanent. Beginning in 1747, nine generations of the Doi family ruled Kariya until the new Meiji government abolished the domain in 1871.

During the Doi reign, Kariya enjoyed a putative allotment of 23,000 koku (or almost 115,000 bushels of unhulled rice), which made it one of the smallest of the approximately 270 fiefs in Japan. Governing from the domain center in Kariya, the Doi house gathered its revenues from twenty-one villages surrounding the castle, and from fourteen villages in northeastern Japan. Among the twenty-one local villages were nineteen which had since become a part of the contemporary city.

Although people inhabited the area around Kariya as early as the fourth century B.C., most of Kariya's nineteen settlements date from the Tokugawa Period. During that era there were two hamlets with special functions.[4] One was a rest stop on the Tōkaidō and the other was a residential community for Kariya's samurai. The remaining hamlets housed the peasantry and rural overlords whose agricultural activities were the foundation of the region's economy. Until the 1870s these hamlets were units of taxation, through which the lord exercised financial and political control over his domain. But under the Meiji government, they underwent changes designed to bring them into the administrative web of the central state.

Consolidations made Kariya physically what it was in 1972. One program, carried out in 1906, fully alerted the status of the settlements in the Kariya area, by producing larger entities enjoying a measure of self-government. Six historic settlements, lying in the center of the nineteen, became the town of Kariya, or Kariya machi. These were Moto Kariya, Kariya, Kuma, Takatsunami, Oyama, and Shigehara. Four hamlets to the south of these and nine to the north became Yosami mura and Fujimatsu mura, respectively. For a half-century these town and

[4] Hamlet, or buraku in Japanese, is a term which refers to the smallest unit of settlement in the countryside. Hamlets have long since been incorporated into larger governing bodies such as administrative villages (mura), towns (machi), or cities (shi).

village units survived unaltered, save for a slight change when Kariya *machi* passed the 30,000 mark in 1950 and became a city. In 1955, however, Fujimatsu and Yosami were formally incorporated with Kariya to form the contemporary city. The area within this municipality is the geographic focus of this study.[5]

The purpose of this study is to analyze the social and political consequences of industrialization in Kariya over a one-century period. To fulfill this objective this book employs a multi-faceted approach, so that it actually encompasses three studies in one. The first traces the development of one of the world's largest industrial concerns, the Toyota enterprise. The second describes the social and political history of the community of Kariya. The third analyzes Kariya's political response to industrialism. This third analysis, which explores the complex interrelationships between industrialization and political change, is the focal point of the book as a whole.

In relating Kariya's history, this study presents materials which portray economic, social, and political aspects of the city. Economic materials bear heavily on the evolution of the Toyota enterprise, illustrating how a small textile maker became a complex, heavy industrial concern. Other economic subjects treated include agricultural change in the nineteenth century, the growth of the textile industry in Aichi Prefecture after the Meiji Restoration, and the industrialization of the western Mikawa region between the 1870s and the 1970s. In addition, the study deals with many problems which bridge the gap between the social and economic spheres. It portrays the conditions of workers in the two industries which have been so important in Aichi: the textile industry before the war and the auto industry after. This study also traces the evolution of employment practices in the major firms in this area and examines the backgrounds of both workers and managers in order to illuminate the full scope of industry's social impact on this community and the region of which it is a part. Finally, the study examines how social changes fostered by industrial growth undermined the status of established groups in the community, and how their claims to leadership were overshadowed by the claims of new groups tied to the city's factories.

[5] These administrative changes pose serious problems of terminology. To insure consistency in the text, I employ the following usages. This study tries, whenever possible, to examine changes which have taken place in the area of the enlarged post-1955 city; I refer to this as "the Kariya city area" or simply as "Kariya." Between 1906 and 1955 this area was divided into a town and two villages. I refer to the town as "Kariya *machi*" or the "town of Kariya," and to the villages by name ("Fujimatsu" and "Yosami") or simply as "the villages." During this same period, Kariya *machi* was divided into six wards (*ku*) which coincided with the six former historical settlements which formed the town. I refer to these wards by their names, listed in the text above. Finally, before 1906 there were altogether nineteen separate residential clusters in the present city area. I refer to the thirteen of these not accounted for by previous definitions as "the hamlets."

In dealing with political aspects of Kariya's history, a key task was to determine "who governed," in the manner of Robert Dahl's investigation of community power in New Haven, Connecticut.[6] Consequently, this study focuses, first, on the backgrounds of men who served as mayors, prefectural assemblymen, and Diet members in this area, and second, on several "issues" in local politics, to the extent that written materials permitted. The study also examines how the public in general participated in the political process, and how its level of participation and its preferences affected political change. Finally, the sharpest light is cast on the relationship between industrial growth and political change, in order to illuminate how the people of Kariya, the workers in its factories, and the managers of its industrial enterprises resolved the problems of conflict and competition. The final chapter compares Kariya's solutions with those adopted in Britain and the United States.

The format selected to present this material is that of a local history. Local history can serve valuable intellectual purposes, because communities and regions are workable subjects for intensive, empirical analysis. Exposed to the light of close scrutiny, the experiences of a small city clarify the complex processes of historical change witnessed in the past century. The historian can feel some degree of assurance when dealing with a fixed number of industrial enterprises, a small group of local politicians, a population of modest size, and a community with a sense of continuity. Even in the face of highly mobile populations, far-reaching trade networks, and rapid communication, the permanence of industrial firms, social institutions, and family groups provides a continuous subject for historical inquiry. Close analysis of historical events in such a setting promises to illuminate—as sharply as a national study does—our understanding of the complex processes of modern history.

This is especially true if the locale reflects in microcosm essential aspects of the history of the nation itself. In other words, local history is most valuable when it isolates for intensive analysis changes inherent in the nation's history and therefore, often, in modern world history. The best local studies examine specific areas in order to analyze major trends of broad, general significance. Success in this task rests heavily on one's choice of subject.

Kariya recommended itself for study for many reasons, but the first and most important reason was its history as an industrial community. In the past century, the Japanese economy passed through three phases of change, characterized by handicraft production, light industry (especially textiles), and heavy industry. Kariya participated in these changes at a pace and intensity which very nearly duplicated the national norm. Its

[6] Robert A. Dahl, *Who Governs?* (New Haven, 1961).

industrial evolution presented in microcosm the salient features of Japan's modern economic development. Kariya thus satisfied the need for a city with a reasonably typical industrial history.

The location of the city also favored its choice. Since the late nineteenth century, four areas have dominated the Japanese economy: the Tokyo-Yokohama region, the Osaka-Kobe region, northern Kyushu, and the Tōkai region, an area midway between Tokyo and Osaka which is formed by the prefectures of Shizuoka, Aichi, Gifu, and Mie. Less industrial before the war than the other areas, the Tōkai region developed rapidly after the early 1950s to become a center of both light and heavy industry. Since Kariya was directly involved in this expansion, its growth illustrates the historical forces at work in shaping the political economy of a major industrial zone in twentieth-century Japan, one, moreover, which is seldom treated in English-language sources.

The nature of the city's history provided a third reason for studying Kariya. Kariya originated as a castletown, as did many major Japanese cities at the turn of the seventeenth century. From then until the end of the nineteenth century, the castletown was the modal form of urban settlement in Japan. In the twentieth century the industrial city came to dominate the urban scene, and Kariya, by 1972, enjoyed undisputed membership in this group. Kariya's evolution from castletown to industrial city thus embraces the two most important categories of urbanism in modern Japan.

Kariya's size further recommended its choice. Metropolitan areas, such as Tokyo, Osaka, and Nagoya, were simply too large to study. They raised complex problems of data, scope, and analysis too difficult for an initial study of this sort. Medium-sized cities were unsuitable because they were often regional centers of administration and/or commerce, not industrial cities. A small city afforded the best opportunities for study. It provided a subject that was significant and manageable as well. Like three of every four Japanese cities in 1970, Kariya had a population of less than 100,000. In that year, nearly a quarter of Japan's total population and almost one in every three urban dwellers lived in a city of comparable size. Since virtually nothing has been written in English about such communities, Kariya's selection enjoys unique significance.

The final consideration justifying Kariya's choice had to do with documentation. Despite some gaps in the evidence, there was material available to do a historical study spanning the past century. Both local and national scholars in Japan have recognized the city's growing importance and have collected a valuable body of historical data. Other sources were also accessible in the form of prefectural and central government documents, monographs, company and union histories, general reference works, local memorabilia, and ephemeral publications. Although gaps in the material forced me to dispense with some problems, documentation relevant to my central concern existed in abundance.

Foregoing comments may have hinted at Kariya's typicality. No one studying a single city, however, would wish to claim that it was perfectly "representative." Kariya was no exception. It met criteria imposed by my interests, abilities, and time. It was not a normal city situated neatly on an optimum spot in an "ideal" continuum. Rather, it was a friendly, and somewhat dumpy, little industrial center with its own characteristics. It is worth noting some of them here, in order to define Kariya's image as a city a bit more sharply.

Kariya was unusual because of the structure and ownership of its major industry. After the mid-1920s the machine industry dominated the local economy, with the manufacture first of textile equipment and later of automobiles. The largest firms in this industry were all a part of the Toyota concern, which originated as a textile enterprise and later turned to auto making. Many of the other industrial firms in Kariya were affiliated with Toyota as partly-owned subsidiaries or as subcontractors. Given this heavy emphasis on machine manufacture and a high concentration of ownership in local industry, Kariya resembled a one-industry, company town.

Exactly how unconventional this made the city is difficult to judge, because one-industry and company towns are numerous in Japan. There are two major ones just thirty minutes away: Toyota (headquarters for the auto firm) and Tōkai (site of a huge works recently established by New Japan Steel). There are many others: Hitachi, home of the electrical manufacturer; Fuji, with its pulp and paper factories; Suzuka, headquarters for another auto firm; and Niihama, where there is a major Sumitomo works, to note just four. The same phenomenon prevailed in the prewar period; the Ōhara enterprise in Kurashiki is one well-known example. As a proportion of all Japanese cities, such towns comprise only a modest share of the total. But they form an important category among Japanese industrial cities. Kariya was, therefore, unusual because of its domination by a single industry and one major firm; but it was not unique.

Kariya was also unusual because of its very high rate of industrialization. In 1966 Kariya's population ranked 176 among all Japanese cities, but its factory labor force ranked 29 in the nation. At that time a larger share of its resident population (57 percent) was engaged in manufacturing than was common in either the prefecture (45 percent) or the nation (32 percent). Since Kariya's firms drew many commuters from the surrounding area, even this relatively high level of factory employment understated its industrial stature. The city was thus atypical for it was more heavily industrialized than most cities its size.

Finally, even though it was a castletown turned industrial center,

Kariya entered the mainstream of Japanese urban growth only in the 1950s. With its modest allotment, Kariya was among the smallest of the nation's approximately 150 castletowns by the late 1800s. As settlements grew during the Meiji and Taishō Periods, Kariya remained a small commercial town. When war broke out with China in 1937, there were nearly 150 cities in Japan, but Kariya was not one of them. Numbered among them were the largest former castletowns, the major handicraft centers, the ports of the land, twentieth-century industrial towns, religious centers, and administrative cities. Those were Japan's largest cities, the ones with the longest urban histories, serving the most critical urban functions.

Only after the Pacific War did Kariya claim a population large enough to warrant designation as a city. By acquiring city status in 1950, Kariya did precede almost 70 percent of Japan's present cities, most of which gained urban status as a result of consolidation in the 1950s or of administrative provision during the early 1970s. Kariya, therefore, ranked among the oldest third of Japan's contemporary municipalities; but readers should bear in mind the relative novelty of its urbanism.

Four historiographical aims underlay this study and shaped its format. The first aim was to cast fresh empirical light on a problem central to Japan's modern history, and in a larger sense also, to modern world history. Ever since England "unbound Prometheus," as David Landes put it, forces of economics and technology have worked constantly to reshape man's social and political environment.[7] Viewing those complex processes under the rubric of "modernization," many scholars in the past two decades have asserted that we were all becoming more alike. They invoked the "convergence theory" to claim that simple "traditional" societies, through a process of "modernization," would one day evolve toward a common—and implicitly optimum—end. This end looked suspiciously like America in the 1950s, or, more accurately, like the image of American society which the smug confidence of the early postwar period had produced. But events of the 1960s sorely tested the intellectual viability of those claims. In recent years some social scientists have issued a call for more sophisticated views of the potentialities of social change.[8] This study tries to heed that injunction by seeking sound empirical answers to the question "What are the social and political consequences of industrialization?"

A second aim was to illuminate the process of Japan's urbanization by

[7] David Landes, *The Unbound Prometheus* (Cambridge, 1969).

[8] For instance, S. N. Eisenstadt in "Post-Traditional Societies and the Continuity and Reconstruction of Tradition," *Daedalus* (Winter 1973), pp. 1-27; and Reinhard Bendix, "Tradition and Modernity Reconsidered," *Comparative Studies in Society and History* 9:3 (April 1967), pp. 292-346.

composing a history of a single city over the past century. Japan has long been a nation of great cities. As early as the ninth century, a distinctive urban culture flourished in Kyoto. In the eighteenth century, Tokyo (then known as Edo), with a population nearing one million, may have harbored twice the population of any of Europe's largest cities. In the past century, Japan has become one of the world's most urban nations. Three in every four Japanese now live within the bounds of a city, and more than half the nation's population lives in densely inhabited zones where rates of concentration approximate those of metropolitan New York. Yet, surprisingly, no scholarly histories of Japanese cities exist in English. There are books, surveys, and articles on aspects of the city. But at the very time that Japan has emerged prominently on the world scene, at the very time we need to know more about that highly urban society, there are no urban histories. This book responds to that need.

The third historiographical goal was to contribute to the small store of knowledge available in English on Japanese communities. There are several fine works in this field. The most important publications are John Embree's record of *Suye Mura*, Ronald Dore's analysis of *City Life in Japan*, Richard Beardsley's account of *Village Japan*, and Ezra Vogel's portrait of *Japan's New Middle Class*.[9] These books appeared at fitful intervals, however. Embree observed his central Kyushu settlement in the mid-1930s. Dore studied his "ward" in Tokyo, and the Beardsley group its Okayama village, in the early 1950s. Vogel's book is the most recent, but even he conducted his field work in the late 1950s. These books all deal, moreover, with communities of two specific types: small rural villages or the metropolitan capital, Tokyo. They are all seminal works, and they have rightly become irreplaceable social documents. But despite their merits, they now convey an outdated image of a nation which has undergone exceedingly rapid change in the past decade. This study was composed in part, therefore, to provide a more timely sketch of city life in Japan, and to portray conditions in a community of a type which has not been treated in English sources.

Fourth, and last, this work was intended to demonstrate the merits of a novel approach to the study of modern Japan, one referred to elsewhere as a "new social history." [10] American historiography on modern Japan has focused on two areas of inquiry: national political problems and individual intellectual anxieties. Historians have seldom dealt with people behaving under normal circumstances as members of groups, communities, or social classes. As a result, we have created an image of Japan's modern history which confines itself to the highest social strata and to the political center.

[9] Full citations appear in the bibliography.
[10] See Gary D. Allinson, "Modern Japan: A New Social History," *Historical Methods Newsletter* 6:3 (June 1973), pp. 100–110.

We know very little about the collective behavior of the Japanese people in everyday settings. To alleviate this shortcoming, historians should make more fruitful use of concepts and methods from the social sciences in order to promote a more holistic vision of Japanese history.

Others have recognized this need before, although few have tried to satisfy it. In the mid-1960s John W. Hall wrote:

> The aspects of Japanese history from 1868 to 1918 which have been less well studied are sociological. . . . What is most needed is a better understanding of the relationship between social change and political events on the one hand and economic developments on the other. So far such an organic view of the rise of the Japanese state is lacking even in the works of Japanese scholars.[11]

Hall confined his remarks to the Meiji Period, but they also apply to the years since, because we still have no "organic view" of Japan's history for the years after 1868. This book was designed to satisfy that need by demonstrating what a new social history for modern Japan could be.

The first step in that direction carries us back to Kariya in the second half of the nineteenth century. The following two chapters portray the social, economic, and political history of Kariya between the 1870s and the 1910s, before it became an industrial city. They provide a tangible background against which to evaluate the changes which took place in Kariya after 1922. In that year the first of many Toyota firms which would locate in the city arrived, and the community underwent its first decade of industrialization, the consequences of which chapter 4 examines. Between 1932 and 1945 Kariya and the Toyota enterprise both witnessed penetrating changes which shaped the form and content of postwar history. Chapter 5 analyzes those changes. Following the war Kariya experienced several years of sharp economic and political conflict which only began to pale in the 1950s as the Toyota enterprise began a period of unprecedented expansion. Chapters 6 and 7 deal with the rapidly shifting texture of economic and political life between 1945 and 1967. Chapter 8 sketches conditions in Kariya at the end of a half-century of industrialization, leaving a final portrait of a community still very much in search of its future. The ninth and concluding chapter analyzes, in the light of some international comparisons, the significance of Kariya's political experience as an industrial city.

[11] John W. Hall, *Japanese History* (Washington, D.C., 1966), p. 54.

2

RECAPITULATING THE PAST,
1872–1889

In 1872 the cities of new Japan were bursting with the exuberance of the Meiji Restoration. Thousands of new residents descended on Tokyo, Yokohama, and Kobe annually, some curious to behold changes wrought by the Restoration, others eager to seize opportunities it offered. Occupations unknown a decade before opened daily. There were jobs for newspaper reporters, rail conductors, bricklayers, tram drivers, and many others. Fostered by the enthusiasm to make Japan a model of the West overnight, progress was especially visible in the economic sphere. The Meiji government was already hard at work creating a modern armaments industry, sponsoring experimental textile plants, and subsidizing gas companies which would light the way to the industrial future. The driving force behind these changes was a small group of men from the old ruling class who had purportedly given up their privileges as samurai to build a modern nation for all the people. It was still too early to chart the significance of the political changes brought by the Restoration, but they appeared in 1872 to be quite pervasive.

Outside the cities and away from the foreign enclaves, however, a much different scene persisted. Stability characterized most of the country's villages while its castletowns lapsed in a state of decay. Even in large ones like Nagoya and Kanazawa, thousands of people left in the early 1870s to taste the promise of the capital or the new port cities. Those who remained eked out a living as they had for centuries. Farm families continued to dominate the population, and efforts at industrial growth, so conspicuous in the cities, barely materialized in most rural areas. The vigorous, expansive spirit of Meiji found its expression in such places as Tokyo and Yokohama; it barely penetrated the towns and villages of the countryside.

This was particularly true of Kariya and its vicinity. During the first two decades of the Meiji Period, the community remained small and stable. Most of its occupants earned a living by farming. A few entrepreneurs tried their hand at industrialization, but the major economic change was the construction of a canal system which benefitted farmers, not townsmen. Leading rural families, of the kind whose househeads organized support for the canal, were influential figures in the

12

community. Together with a few prominent merchants and descendants of high-ranking samurai families, they formed a social triumvirate which retained its secure grip on customary privileges and exercised a form of paternal authority over the area.

This chapter serves two purposes. It provides a tangible baseline from which to evaluate subsequent changes in the social, economic, and political life of Kariya, and it appraises the impact of the Meiji Restoration on one small area in central Japan. The chapter opens with a short sketch of Kariya's physical layout in 1872. It then discusses in brief detail Kariya's demographic trends, economic character, social make-up, and political structure during the three-decade period preceding 1889.

Journeying back a century in time would put us in Kariya shortly after the restoration of the Meiji emperor. We might rely on a young boy from the community to show us around, if we could find one not working. Someone about ten or eleven might still be evading the need to help his family full-time with tasks around the farm or in the shop, an occupation he will probably follow till death. He might be studying, casually with a tutor, or in one of the private schools scattered around town. More than likely he is not, since only one of every two or three boys spends much time at formal learning and almost none of the girls. His dress is simple, only a rough cotton garment draped robe-like around him, with bare feet, or a pair of reed sandals. He stands under four feet now, but he could stretch to five feet or more as an adult. Now that he has passed the dangerous early years, when death is common, he can look forward to two or three full decades of active life. He could even become one of the venerable old men of the community and survive into his sixties.

Our guide joins us at the riverbank, on the western edge of town. This is a natural playground for him and his friends. The Sakai River, which flows along here, produces Kariya's whitebait. They are a delicacy which breed only in the cleanest water. A famous local product, the daimyo once presented them as gifts to the shogun in Edo. Before turning toward town, our guide points out the warehouses at Ichibara landing where dock workers bustle about unloading oils and fertilizers. The Ōta family brings these goods to Kariya from as far away as Hokkaido; most heavy shipments moving in and out of Kariya pass through their wharf. A low marshy area separates the river from the town, strung across the low, flat tableland beyond.

From our vantage point at Ichibara landing, we can see three distinct settlements spread along the eastern horizon. To the north is Kuma, a hamlet which traces its origins to the Kamakura Period (1185–1333), when the shrine of Kumano was founded. During the Tokugawa Period, lower-ranking samurai from the Kariya domain lived there. Many of their

descendants still reside in the hamlet in the squat homes that clump
together among scraggly trees. To the south is the hamlet of Moto Kariya.
Lords of the Mizuno family dominated this area during the Warring
States Period from military headquarters located in this hamlet. Here also
the mother of Tokugawa Ieyasu grew to maturity under the eye of Mizuno
Tadamasa. It was Mizuno who made the decision to build a castle farther
upriver and to abandon Moto Kariya during the 1540s. Thereafter Moto
Kariya survived as a farming village. Amidst dingy peasant huts, the
spacious residences of wealthy farm families catch our eye now. So also do
several Buddhist temples perched on a low crest of land overlooking the
valley which divides Moto Kariya from its successor, the castletown of
Kariya.

To reach the castletown, our guide leads us up the dusty road from the
landing to the first homes about a quarter-mile away. At the point where
the road ascends a slight incline, we begin to pass the dwellings which once
housed the leading officials and highest-ranking samurai of the domain.
Those with spacious courtyards in front even now suggest the presence of a
family of status, if not wealth, for the homes are commonly in need of
patchwork and repair. At an opening near the end of this path, we bear
sharply left and in a few moments enter onto a broad area cut here and
there by the remnants of defensive moats. Ten years earlier our view
would have been blocked by the gate which guarded this spot, for we now
stand on what was once the main entry to the castle of Kariya.

Our guide speaks with childlike awe about the castle, reciting legends
which he had heard at his grandfather's knee. In fact, Kariya's castle was
a modest affair, even by comparison with others which stood in Mikawa
and especially by comparison with the one which still stands in Himeji
today. The Kariya castle had no stuccoed walls forming an endless
labyrinth of defensive barriers. Nor did it have a five-storied lookout tower
from which to command a view of the countryside. Instead, there were
mud and stone walls, shaped to the contours of the knoll on which the
castle stood. These walls stretched about one-half mile in length, their
battlements dividing the castlegrounds into a main citadel to the north
and two other zones forming defensive arcs to the south. The highest point
of the castle was a watchtower which rose a mere forty-two feet into the
Mikawa skies. Spread over twenty-one acres, the castle encompassed
within its walls, in addition to the citadel and the lord's dwelling, a
number of office buildings, a granary, other storage sites, a large
equestrian area, and many tree-covered slopes. These all disappeared
quickly following the Restoration. Now a new elementary school sits where
office buildings once stood, and a small brick factory operates where
samurai once displayed their skills at horsemanship. A small crest of land

poking into the western horizon is the only reminder that from this site the lord of the castle once exercised his authority.

Turning and retracing our steps, a few minutes' walk carries us away from the castle site into the former *chōnin* quarter, where the merchants and artisans of the town worked and lived. Their descendants are still here, cramped into shops which hug the narrow street; walking abreast with arms extended two people can almost touch the buildings on either side. Bearing left at the corner to continue up the path we took from the river through the samurai area, we enter Sakana-machi. This is the site of fish merchants (from whose produce the block took its name) and a variety of other shopkeepers who serve the daily needs of the populace: green grocers, fruit dealers, bean curd makers, rice sellers, and peddlers making boiled vegetables and fish balls. Sakana-machi covers only a short block which lies parallel to another, called Hom-machi, which we enter by turning left at the end of the street and walking north a few paces.

Hom-machi is Main Street. It is the physical axis of the civil community, its shops lining the road that travels eastward out of Kariya. Settled during the seventeenth century, Hom-machi is the oldest section of the community. Peering westward down the street, we can make out the long front of the Ōta family's business and residence. Its dinginess hides the tranquil garden with its pond and landscaped terraces, occupying nearly an entire block behind the home. Moving to the right the road carries us through the heart of the business district, an area fairly jumping with activity. In several shops workers squat over benches on the floor making wooden clogs. Confectioners busy themselves over small fires to produce stacks of sweets and biscuits. A cooper adds finishing touches to a sake barrel for one of the nearby brewers. There are shops selling yard goods, umbrellas, candles, used clothes, and storage chests. Beyond the mat-covered reception areas at the front of the better shops, families are eating in the dim interiors. Some live above the shops, and enjoy sunlight through the sliding doors of a mock veranda where bedding is often left to air. Messengers and carriers trot along the street, boxes strung on poles resting on their shoulders. From one of the windows above the street a young mother with a child strapped to her back calls down to her son, our guide. Before running off, he points out the road which will carry us to the edge of town.

In ten minutes we have passed through Naka-machi and Suso-machi, roughly Central Block and Terminal Block, leaving the bustling *chōnin* quarter behind. If we followed the tree-lined path which stretches ahead, it would eventually carry us to the post town an hour or so away. In the distance the midday haze shrouds from view the foothills in which nestle Koromo and Okazaki, other castletowns adjusting to the new era of Meiji.

Turning for one final view of the town, we can make out to the south a cluster of residences for the low-ranking samurai of the Yoshiike group, and beyond it, the settlement of Shigehara. In the distance to our right, trees mark the rural villages of Oyama and Takatsunami. These three villages, along with the three settlements just passed through, will become the town of Kariya in just four short decades.

Had these villages been joined in 1876, they would have made a settlement of modest size. In that year the castletown had a population of 658 households numbering about 2,500 persons. The other five settlements were all smaller. Kuma had a population of 255 households; Moto Kariya, 392; Takatsunami, 91; Oyama, 253; and Shigehara, 164. Altogether the six settlements numbered slightly over 1,800 households, for a population approximating 7,500.[1]

This figure changed very little through the end of the century. The castletown population itself appears to have been quite stable from the 1840s through the 1890s. Surveys for the 1840s, the 1860s, and the 1880s all enumerated about 2,500 persons. The last count for the century, taken in 1896, found 2,676 persons in the castletown and 7,918 in the six villages.[2] There was a slight increase in population at the end of the century, but on the whole the Kariya town area remained a small settlement of somewhat less than 10,000 people.

In comparison with other settlements in the vicinity, the Kariya castletown was quite small. A prefectural census for 1879 listed six named villages in Hekikai County. Kariya ranked fourth among them, following Ōhama (a port with nearly 10,000 persons), Tanao (a marketing village of 5,000) and Chiryū (a former post town). Kariya did little better by comparison with the other urban settlements in Mikawa. Throughout the 1870s and the 1880s, it remained the smallest of these. In those years Okazaki enjoyed first place with about 12,000 persons, followed by Toyohashi with 9,000, Nishio with 5,500, and Koromo with 2,600. All of these communities were in turn dwarfed by Nagoya, across the border in old Owari, with its population of 115,000.[3]

Although the size of these communities remained steady during the late nineteenth century, the populations living in them were not permanent and immobile. Recent studies have revealed the folly of accepting periodic census counts as a sensitive picture of demographic trends.[4] Census reports

---

[1] The information on Kariya's population in 1876 comes from Kariya shiyakusho, *Kariya shi shi* (Kariya, 1960), p. 315 (hereafter cited as Kss). Please see List of Abbreviations for other works cited in short-form in this study. For English translations of Japanese titles, please consult the bibliography.

[2] Tanaka Keizaburō, *Aichi ken Hekikai gunkai shi* (Kariya, 1923), pp. 54–55.

[3] Aichi ken, *Aichi ken tōkei gaihyō: 1879* (Nagoya, 1880), p. 20.

[4] See especially Peter R. Knights, *The Plain People of Boston* (New York, 1971); also, Peter Laslett, ed., *Households and Family in Past Time* (Cambridge, 1972).

provide us only with a series of still lives, conveying a static image of a community at one moment in time and neglecting entirely the flux which occurs in intervening years. Although it is not possible to trace the mobility of populations at town and village levels in Aichi during this period, random statistics do permit brief comment on the stability of populations at the prefectural and county levels between 1880 and 1893.[5] During those years Aichi witnessed a sharp, persistent rise in the number of people moving in and out of the prefecture. Newcomers totaled 11,455 in 1880; 23,222 in 1885; 124,907 in 1890; and 143,940 in 1893. Outmigrants were fewer: 4,876 in 1880; 21,804 in 1885; 106,029 in 1890; and 127,535 in 1893. Such movements produced a net annual gain in prefectural population ranging from a low of 1,500 to a high of nearly 19,000. These gains helped to boost Aichi's population from 1.3 to 1.5 million during the decade of the 1880s.

Within the prefecture, these moves were distributed unevenly among rural and urban areas. Many primarily agrarian regions, such as the county of Hekikai, experienced a loss in population as a result of migration. During this thirteen-year period, outmigrants consistently exceeded inmigrants in Hekikai, usually by a portion of two to one. On the other hand, urban areas such as Nagoya grew quickly due to immigration. In 1885, 7,983 newcomers entered Nagoya while only 4,311 persons left the city. The same pattern continued at an accelerated rate in later years. In 1890 and 1893, 49,215 and 59,662 persons entered the city while only 10,855 and 14,607 left, respectively. As a result of such migration, Nagoya grew from 115,000 in 1879 to over 200,000 by the mid-1890s. Population movements thus stimulated growth in the prefecture's major city and in rural areas active commercially and industrially, but they retarded growth in primarily agrarian counties. On balance, population movements, in combination with natural increases, contributed to an overall rise in the prefectural population.

Two things about these figures are striking. First, migration accelerated very sharply during the middle years of the Meiji era. In 1880 migrants accounted for less than 1 percent of the prefectural population, but by 1893 they accounted for nearly 10 percent. The timing of this increase suggests that people needed a decade or two to overcome the psychological impediments to mobility which several generations of its political curtailment under the Tokugawa shogunate had caused.[6] The human rush to

[5] This information on population mobility comes from *Aichi ken tōkei gaihyō: 1880* (Nagoya, 1881), pp. 2–3; and from Aichi ken, *Aichi ken tōkei sho: 1885* (Nagoya, 1886), pp. 19–20 (hereafter referred to as Ats, followed by a date indicating year of coverage); Ats: 1892, p. 20; and Ats: 1892–3, pp. 19–20. The data in these sources are very crude, but they are adequate to convey some impression of the sharp differences between the mobile urban areas and the stable rural areas.

[6] Psychological barriers may not have been the only impediments to widespread travel. Murase Masayuki has discovered that Kariya citizens, as late as 1882, were still making

seek new opportunities in the Meiji Period did not follow immediately
upon the Restoration; in this area at least, it followed the Restoration by a
decade or more.

The second striking aspect of these figures concerns the high rate of
movement in or out of Nagoya. People moving in and out of the city
numbered about 10 percent of the population in 1885. By 1893, when the
city had become a commercial and textile center, turnover in the city's
population affected the equivalent of 40 percent of its residents each year.
Nagoya was having to deal with vast numbers of newcomers, who needed
jobs, housing, and social moorings. This created a social atmosphere in
Japan's largest cities, just three decades after the Restoration, far different
from the one which prevailed in the country's towns and villages.[7]

If mobility characterized the cities, stability characterized the countryside. In the decade following the Restoration, the Japanese economy was
overwhelmingly agrarian. Tsuchiya Takao has estimated that 80 percent
of Japanese workers were engaged in agriculture in 1873.[8] The remaining
20 percent of the workers divided their efforts between commerce,
manufacturing, day labor, or a combination of all of these. Both Aichi
Prefecture and Hekikai County conformed closely to the national norm.
Farmers accounted for a bit more than 80 percent of the work force in
Aichi and Hekikai in 1869, followed by merchants and clerks, artisans and
others, in that order. With the passage of a decade, the percentage of
farmers in Aichi declined to 63, while commercial and other occupations
increased commensurately. But through the end of the century, farming
continued to occupy most of the workers in the prefecture and the county
around Kariya.

Kariya itself was a bit more diversified occupationally than the
prefecture, but not by much. A simple breakdown based on the 1876
household registers listed 1,360 farm households among the 1,813 in the
town area, a ratio of three in every four. Wide diversity existed among the
settlements, however. In the old castletown only one-half of the households
participated in farming. The remainder engaged in a variety of commercial and industrial pursuits or provided services of one kind or another to
the surrounding villagers. Non-farm households were also prominent in

formal application to the local authorities, just as they would have during the Tokugawa
Period, in order to travel for a few weeks outside the prefecture. See his *Bakumatsu-Ishin no
Kariya* (Kariya, 1969), p. 78.

[7] This only substantiates what we already know about the high rates of mobility in
Japanese cities even before 1868. Robert J. Smith, for example, has discovered that as many
as one-half of the urban households in his sample from Nishinomiya and Osaka may have
moved at seven year intervals during the late 1700s and early 1800s. See his article, "Small
Families, Small Households, and Residential Instability: Town and City in 'Pre-Modern'
Japan," on pages 429–473 in the study by Laslett above.

[8] Tsuchiya Takao, "Meiji shonen no jinkō kōsei ni kansuru ichi kōsatsu," *Shakai keizai
shigaku* 1:1 (May 1931), p. 160.

Kuma, where a third of the families found a livelihood away from agriculture, due in large part to its history as a samurai settlement. In the four remaining villages virtually all households engaged in farming, the ratios ranging from 89 to 98 percent. In 1876 Kariya was thus a tiny haven for merchants and artisans amidst a sea of farmers.[9]

We have long since learned that farmers in a pre-industrial society are not an undifferentiated mass of peasants just tilling the soil. Thomas Smith's writings have shown this to be especially true of Japan.[10] Nor is the agricultural sector the scene of an unchanging traditional order. Vast changes took place in Japan's agrarian economy, even before the advent of the Meiji government. Following its stabilization, the new government concentrated attention on agrarian problems, as well it should have in a society still predominantly rural. It is thus not unusual that one of the most important economic changes of this period in the area around Kariya was one which affected primarily farmers. This was the creation of the Meiji canal, an irrigation works opened in 1880. Originally envisioned as a small system to serve villages in what are now Anjō and Nishio, the canal ultimately brought water to a three-county area and served a farm population numbering in the tens of thousands. The canal had a pervasive impact on this area, socially and politically as well as economically. Frequent mention later in the study attests to this. At this point, the early history of the canal warrants attention, illustrating, as it does so effectively, aspects of the political economy of this area in the nineteenth century.[11]

The conception for the Meiji canal originated with a man named Tsuzuki Yakō, the scion of a wealthy, landholding family engaged in commerce and sake brewing. During his last twenty-one years, Tsuzuki was a steward (*daikan*) for one of the Matsudaira lords overseeing villages in what is now Anjō City. Early in his tenure, he recognized the need for a water system in the region, most of which was dry tableland suitable only for raising grasses. Tsuzuki spent more than a decade developing his plans, surveying land in the area, and formulating his petition. In 1828 he presented it to the *bakufu* (the Tokugawa government), which, after some investigation and delay, approved his petition in 1832. He had crossed a major hurdle.

Unfortunately, *bakufu* approval was only the first step in gaining political assent for his project. Since Tsuzuki's system encompassed lands which lay in several domains, it was necessary to win the agreement of the lords and overseers of all of them. This Tsuzuki could not do. Some lords refused cooperation because they did not want to sacrifice grass and forest

<hr/>

[9] Kss, p. 315.

[10] See especially his major study, *Agrarian Origins of Modern Japan* (Stanford, 1963).

[11] The following account relies primarily on Meiji yōsui shishi hensan iinkai, ed., *Meiji yōsui*, 2 vols. (Anjō, 1953), 1: 378–396, 459, and 556.

lands from which they derived cash incomes. Others refused because the canal system, whose waterworks were to fall under *bakufu* authority, would reduce the lands in their domains. Each of the many small holdings in western Mikawa represented an impediment to political consensus, a dilemma which the *bakufu* was powerless to overcome. Tsuzuki was no more successful himself. He could not persuade many distant lords and obstinate local peasants of the benefits of increased paddy land. Having virtually destroyed his family financially, Tsuzuki died in 1833, his unremitting efforts to bring the canal to life ending in failure.

Knowledge of the project survived, however, and in the 1860s two more advocates of the canal system appeared. These men, Iyoda Yohachirō and Okamoto Hyōmatsu, arrived at advocacy of the program by different routes but eventually joined to work for a common goal. Rural overseer (*shōya*) for thirty-three villages in the Okazaki domain, Iyoda first conceived of a canal system to solve drainage problems in his area caused by the Yahagi River. He worked alone from the early 1860s through the early 1870s to promote his project, first through the domain government and the *bakufu* and after the Restoration through the new, and often shortlived, agencies of the Meiji government. Unsettled administrative conditions at all levels of government impeded interest in and approval of his project. At the same time, Okamoto was also undertaking efforts to promote a canal system. Once a prosperous and influential merchant, he became interested in Tsuzuki's project in the late 1860s when he moved to a large plot of reclaimed land and turned to full-time farming. His location (in the northern Hekinan City area) encouraged adoption of the same type of program Tsuzuki had envisaged, one which would bring water from the Yahagi to irrigate the tablelands along Kinugaura Bay. Despite his diligent efforts in the early 1870s, Okamoto's proposals, like Iyoda's, went unheeded, victim of the general instability of government at the local level.

Finally, in 1874, the two men joined together to promote the canal works. Adopting a plan very similar to Tsuzuki's, they set out to persuade their opponents and to raise funds for the project. Both hoped to benefit personally from the system, by winning administrative control over the completed irrigation channels and by assuming ownership of strategic plots of land. As Iyoda sought funds, Okamoto overcame opposition. Within a short period of time, they had raised enough funds and attracted enough support so that the project could begin.

The work of Iyoda and Okamoto was important, but lying behind their cooperation was the influence of the new prefectural government. Its authority was the motive force that brought the canal to completion. A thirty-year-old prefectural official named Kurokawa took great interest in the Iyoda-Okamoto proposals and lent them his support. Staying in the background, Kurokawa waited for them to do the essential groundwork for the canal before committing the prefecture to assist them. But once their work was done, Kurokawa stepped forward decisively with administrative and financial support. In 1879 workers began construction of the canal. One year later, Iyoda, Okamoto, and the prefectural government celebrated its completion. Private individuals had generated support for the project, but it came to fruition only after the prefectural government acted vigorously to provide direction and funding. In the process, the government also assumed control of the canal system. Okamoto, his influence relegated to that of a minor official, saw his dreams of wealth disappear and died an impoverished and bitter man. Iyoda, his status already far more secure than Okamoto's, accepted the government's role more sanguinely. He recognized the long-range benefits that would flow from this achievement.

The canal brought three improvements to the farmers of southern Hekikai County. First, it increased the amount of land under cultivation. Between 1881 and 1920 arable land in Hekikai increased by 50 percent. In the three-county area served by the canal (Hekikai, Hazu, and Nishi Kamo), some 6,200 chō of new and converted paddy land became available. This was the equivalent of an average holding for 5,000 farm families. In one Yosami settlement alone arable land increased ten-fold after the canal opened.[12] Second, it permitted a change in the diet of the local population. For some time local residents had existed on lesser cereal grains, such as millet (awa) and deccan grass (hie). Now they were able to eat rice more frequently. This may not have been a nutritional improvement, but it probably enhanced their self-esteem greatly. Finally, the canal offered an opportunity for independent owners to establish themselves in the area. Owner-cultivators, rather than landlords, predominated in the canal area, thanks to general allotment of small, equal-sized plots of land and the grant of a long tax holiday. This had singular effects on the political character of the region.[13] Although it required fifty frustrating years to become a reality, the canal brought considerable improvements to the locale. Largely because of the canal, Hekikai would become one of the largest rice-producing counties in Aichi, an achievement that benefitted farmers and merchants alike.

Local merchants benefitted from agricultural advances because in 1875 they were still intimately tied to the rural economy. Among the 400 merchant and artisan families in the Kariya town area, a very large portion depended on farm products and rural customers. Many shops in the old castletown provided an outlet for basic farm commodities such as

[12] Tonoki Yoshio, "Sangyōka ni tomonau chihō toshi shūhen no henjō," Shakai kagaku tō kyū 11:1 (June 1965), p. 113.
[13] Chapter 4 will treat this subject in greater detail.

rice, cereal grains, cotton, vegetables, and beans. Other shops sold goods to the farmer, such as seed and fertilizer. Many of the artisans depended heavily on farmers for their raw materials: sake brewers for rice, *tōfu* makers for soya beans, ginners for cotton, mat makers for reeds, and paper makers for pulp and paper base. In return, farmers depended on artisans for some of their needs, especially the blacksmiths and coopers, and no doubt a good many of the carpenters and cabinet makers as well. During this period, merchants and artisans in town lived in close, often dependent, harmony with the vast numbers of farm families surrounding them. Their lives still dictated by the necessities of an agrarian economy, few, probably, of Kariya's residents in the last quarter of the nineteenth century would even have realized the potential of urban industry.

Industry did thrive in several areas of the prefecture, but it occupied only a small portion of all working families. Only 4 or 5 percent of all households were engaged full time in making or processing goods for sale around 1875. This still sufficed, however, to make Aichi one of the most important manufacturing areas in Japan. It ranked especially high in the output of soy sauce, sake, vinegar, pottery, textiles, and candles, with sake and pottery among its most famous products.[14]

During the late eighteenth and early nineteenth centuries, Owari and Mikawa together followed the Osaka region as one of the country's major sake-producing areas. Between 1784 and 1836 the two provinces produced more than 10 percent of the sake sold annually in Edo (Tokyo), the largest domestic market.[15] Sake makers were situated throughout Owari and Mikawa. The largest were located in or around Handa, a small port south of the castletown of Nagoya. Many other establishments were in the villages of the area, but some were also located in the small towns of Mikawa. Kariya was one town with a number of sake makers, and a closer examination of its firms will reveal the central characteristics of the sake industry in Aichi.

Sake manufacturing has been an enduring industry, but sake firms often had short, volatile histories. Sake making began in Kariya about 1650 with the arrival of a member of the Konoike family, a large Osaka merchant house. By the 1690s there were seven sake makers in the castletown. In succeeding centuries firms were often undermined financially by forced loans to domain lords in economic difficulty and by *bakufu* policies which intermittently limited the quantity of sake sold in Edo. Failures were common and few firms survived beyond two or three generations. All of the firms in Kariya in 1690 had sold their production licenses and disappeared by 1775. The makers which succeeded them in

[14] Chihōshi kenkyū kyōgikai, ed., *Nihon sangyōshi taikei,* 8 vols. (Tokyo, 1959-1961), 1: 273-374.

[15] Yunoki Manabu, *Kinsei Nadazake keizaishi* (Kyoto, 1965), p. 350.

the early nineteenth century were no longer very prosperous by the 1860s. Of twenty-seven firms which joined a sake maker's association in western Mikawa in 1837, only three remained by 1850. Subsequently, two major concerns were established in Kariya, in 1869 and 1895; but only one—the Inatoku Company—remained active into the 1970s.[16]

Inaba Tokuzaburō founded the Inatoku Sake Company in 1869.[17] Leadership of his firm remained under family control thereafter, passing through three generations to a grandson of the founder by 1970. The Inaba plant was a small one, and produced approximately the same amount of sake annually as Kariya's largest firm produced in the 1850s. The manufacturing process used by the company in 1970 differed only slightly from that employed by local firms 100 years before. Sake was made during the four to five coldest months of the year, usually between October and early April, because the fermentation process must occur at a constant low temperature if superior quality is to be achieved. Consequently, all steps in the sake-making process—save one—took place in a set of large, unheated buildings. Some mechanized equipment was used, but wooden vats, storage tanks, plant site and raw materials were the primary capital needs.

The labor force was small and disciplined. Nine or ten men worked at the Inaba factory. All of them were farmers in Fukui Prefecture on the Japan Sea coast who traveled to Kariya annually, leaving their families at home, to earn cash incomes during the winter off-season. The men formed a work association overseen by one leader, about forty-five years of age, who had been coming to Kariya for twenty years. He was responsible for organizing the group and for full supervision of the production process within the factory. For this he received double pay. Other members of the group were younger. They were assigned specific tasks, such as grinding, washing, stirring, or pressing, and had titles which derived from their respective duties. With experience at all tasks, a young man could eventually rise to assist the leader, called the *tōji*, and in time could become a *tōji* himself. A dormitory on the factory site housed the workers until late March or early April, when they returned to their villages after the sake production was completed to prepare their fields for the growing season. Crops planted, grown, and harvested, they returned in October for the following sake season.

Management in this firm was composed of two members of the Inaba family. They were permanent residents of Kariya, and on occasions in the past their predecessors had assumed positions of leadership in local economic and social organizations. The family assigned full responsibility

[16] Kss, pp. 189–192.

[17] This description is based on an interview with Inaba Etsuzō conducted in Kariya on January 20, 1970.

for production to the *tōji,* but did all the purchasing, marketing, and accounting itself. Raw materials came mainly from the local area, but some special materials were purchased near Osaka, where much of the final product was sold. There have been considerable changes in Japan's sake industry in the past century, but this small, local firm still retained many of the organizational and work patterns which identified Kariya's sake firms during the nineteenth century.

In addition to its sake breweries, the potteries of Aichi enhanced the prefecture's importance as a manufacturing region in the nineteenth century. Two major products were made: pottery for eating utensils and clay tiles for roofing. The former was made in the small community of Seto, northeast of Nagoya. The availability of special clays attracted artists and potters to the area as early as the thirteenth century, and by the nineteenth century, Seto was an important center of ceramics manufacture. In the 1930s one in every four workers engaged in pottery making in Aichi was employed in Seto. In 1970, 85 percent of the city's workers still followed this historical occupation.

The clay tile industry was located in the western Mikawa area. Most producers were clustered in a small settlement south of Kariya, but they spread over an area that stretched from Kariya to Hekinan. Many tile makers sprang up in the early 1870s when new construction in Tokyo held promise of large markets for roofing materials. Firms were nearly always small, family ventures, sometimes operated as a seasonal adjunct to the regular occupation of farming. Workers were family members or part-time laborers temporarily free of duties on their farms. Capital needs were low, for simple kilns were easily built by hand and raw materials were readily available nearby. Very commonly a family's tile-making operation simply integrated itself into the existing order. A small shed was appropriated for storing and molding clays, the farmyard was used as a drying area, and wives and children were assigned still another household task. The sight remained familiar into the 1970s.

Not all of the firms established then were tiny family operations. Occasionally, large organizations were founded. Among them was Kariya's first large factory, which arose under the stimulus of new markets.[18] In the 1870s two members of the nobility approached Kariya's leading political figure, a former samurai named Ōno Sadame, and offered him funds with which to build a brick factory to supply army garrisons. Ōno accepted the offer, on the condition that the organization provide jobs for former samurai in difficult financial circumstances. A factory was built on land which Ōno possessed and his younger brother was appointed manager. After an unsteady first decade, during which a prefectural loan

[18] Aichi ken, *Aichi ken shi,* 4 vols. (Nagoya, 1938–1939), 2: 117–118.

was needed to sustain the company and failure seemed always imminent, some success was achieved. A contract to supply bricks for the national railway was concluded in the 1880s. Assured of this reliable customer, the company grew to employ a regular staff of thirty-five to fifty workers in the years between 1880 and 1925. The first manager's eldest son inherited control of the firm in the 1920s, but it soon fell on bad times and finally closed in the 1930s. Kariya's first experiment in modern industry had lasted only half a century.

That experiment was undertaken to assist what before the Meiji Restoration had been Japan's privileged urban group, the samurai. Members of a hereditary, arms-bearing class, the samurai had dominated the country, and this community, socially and politically for three centuries before 1868. During the first decade of the Meiji government, policies were adopted which altered dramatically the status of the samurai. No class, however, which enjoys the political and social status that Japan's samurai did during the Tokugawa Period is swept easily from the historical scene. Nor were the samurai in the years following Restoration. Since the samurai comprised the key social group in Kariya during the nineteenth century, an evaluation of their fate in the 1870s and 1880s is essential. To understand how they adjusted to the Meiji order, it is first necessary to know something of this area's political life in the years preceding the Restoration.[19]

In the early 1860s a Kariya samurai named Matsumoto Keidō was party to an incident which colored both national and local events for a decade thereafter. By his acts Matsumoto posed a stark choice for other samurai between their support of the *bakufu* or their loyalty to the throne. Matsumoto was born in 1831. While he was still an adolescent, officials promoted him over his peers for special training at the Shōheikō in Edo.[20] He was thus in the capital at the height of the furor over the coming of Perry and the other "barbarians." These experiences must have whetted his political appetites, isolated as he had been from national events, because henceforth he was not content in his home domain. After teaching in the domain school for a short time, he left Kariya to open his own academy in Nagoya. In 1861 he moved to Osaka where he renewed his acquaintance with former classmates at the Shōheikō. These men were deeply involved in political activities which would bring an early end to Matsumoto's life.

The men he met in Osaka became members of the Tenchūgumi, a

---

[19] The most readable account of Kariya's pre-Restoration politics is Murase's *Bakumatsu-Ishin no Kariya*.

[20] Established in 1630 as an academy under the direction of Hayashi Razan, this school trained prospective bakufu officials in the Confucian orthodoxy. After the Restoration it became a part of Tokyo University.

group of imperial loyalists responsible for the Yamato revolt of 1863.[21] This was one of the first direct acts of opposition to the *bakufu*, one which foreshadowed the impending chaos of the next five years. The members of the Tenchūgumi intended to revolt against the *bakufu* in the name of the emperor, using as a pretext the imperial visit to the Grand Shrine at Ise. When a minor coup d'etat occurred in the capital, the imperial visit was cancelled, but the group proceeded with its plans undeterred. Joined by some 100 supporters in late September 1863, forty members of the Tenchūgumi attacked the headquarters of a *bakufu* steward at Gojō (in the present prefecture of Nara), beheaded him, and claimed the land in the emperor's name. They then called on other samurai to join them in casting off the allegedly improper authority of the *bakufu*. Support failed to materialize. Within days some 10,000 loyalists responded to the *bakufu*'s pleas for assistance and routed the Tenchūgumi. Only a handful of its members escaped; most were killed. In the midst of the rout, Matsumoto Keidō pledged his loyalty to the emperor and committed suicide by disembowelment.

His dedication to the imperial cause did not go unheeded in his former domain. Already there was contention among the Kariya samurai dividing advocates of continued *bakufu* support from the alleged "radicals" who sought imperial restoration. Those divisions came to a head inadvertently, shortly after Matsumoto's death, when a Chōshū extremist was discovered with Kariya samurai in Edo. The domain lord responded by incarcerating four samurai at his family's domain in the Kantō and imprisoning seven others in Kariya. At the same time he replaced his highest officials with men who were not implicated in restorationist plots, men who were thus also advocates of pro-*bakufu* policies. These officials assumed their posts in late 1863 and kept a conservative hand on the rudder of domain politics throughout the stormy 1860s.

Kariya's administration restrained imperial loyalists for more than six years, but it finally gave way before the forces of the Restoration. Increasingly during the 1860s, young samurai became disenchanted with local policies. Many of them left, going to Kyoto and other areas. By 1867 there were many samurai living outside the domain, and some still living in it, who wished ardently for a change of leadership. By early 1868 they could wait no longer; they took violent action. On the very night that the lord's councillors decided to join the imperial cause, eighteen young activists rushed the castle and beheaded the three highest-ranking officials. Now the lord had no choice. Forced to appoint new councillors, he selected one of the former dissidents and three of the men who had been imprisoned. By late 1868 Kariya was enthusiastically in the camp of the

[21] An account of the Tenchūgumi and the Yamato revolt appears in W. G. Beasley, *The Meiji Restoration* (Stanford, 1972), pp. 166–168, 218–220.

Restoration leaders. Its samurai now faced the need for adjustment to the new era.

The samurai formed an important social class, but they were only a small part of the total population. In Japan as a whole, samurai and their family members comprised about 5 to 6 percent of the population at the end of the Tokugawa Period. This percentage varied among domains. In some, samurai families accounted for as much as 27 percent of the population; in others, for as little as 4 percent.[22] Members of the samurai class in Kariya numbered about 5 percent of the domain population. In 1870 there were 335 samurai households with just over 1,200 persons.[23] They comprised about one-half the population of the castletown. Within Mikawa, the Kariya samurai contingent was one of the smallest. It ranked behind the large domains, such as Toyohashi (which had 3,243 samurai and dependents), Nishio (3,176), and Okazaki (3,119), but ahead of the two smallest, Koromo (907 persons) and Tawara (894).

Materials that might portray the samurai class in more social detail are unavailable for this period, but even the scant statistical data which do survive reveal one point of interest. In all of these domains there was a marked difference in size between samurai households and commoner households, and between households within the samurai class itself. In all of the domains for which data exist, samurai families averaged three to four members, usually about three. Commoner households, on the other hand, consistently averaged four to five members, five as often as four. Within the samurai class, which for this count in 1870 was broken down into two ranks, there was a disparity between the higher *shizoku* households and the lower *sotsu*. The former ranged in size from an average of 3.6 persons per family to a high of 4.8. The latter were consistently smaller, ranging from a low of 2.2 in Koromo to a high of 3.3 in Kariya.

These figures reflect the economic conditions which by 1870 differentiated commoners from samurai and, within the samurai class, higher-ranking families from lower.[24] The relative deprivation of the samurai vis à vis the commoner impelled him to limit the size of his family as a matter of economic necessity. Declining stipends and proscriptions against outside work made population control prudent, if not inevitable. For the same

[22] Tsuchiya, p. 163.

[23] The following information on samurai comes from Ōtsuka Takematsu, *Hansei ichiran*, 2 vols. (Tokyo, 1928). Mikawa domains appear in volume one.

[24] The question of household size raises issues which are important, controversial, and difficult to resolve. One might, for example, explain the differences in size among *shizoku*, *sotsu*, and merchant households by noting that many *sotsu* households may have been formed by young, unmarried males, or by pointing out that many merchant households may have had a clerk or two living in. Such explanations would easily account for the differences in average size between a *sotsu* and a merchant household. Unfortunately, until local authorities release nineteenth-century household registers for scholarly investigation, it will be impossible to resolve this issue for the city of Kariya.

reason, the foot soldier on a marginal stipend was forced to limit the size of his family, even more so than his superior who might at least draw a supplementary stipend for official duty. One result of such choices was that many samurai families in this area were so small by the beginning of the Meiji Period that they could well have found it difficult to reproduce enough offspring to sustain themselves beyond one generation. This undoubtedly contributed to the decline in the number of samurai families witnessed in the Mikawa domains between 1870 and the mid-1880s.[25]

While the number of samurai families in Kariya declined after 1875, as in other Mikawa domains, samurai descendants who remained adapted flexibly to the needs of the Meiji era. They actually found themselves liberated from a rather stagnant existence, once social classes were abolished and domain rule eliminated. In response to these changes, the Kariya samurai collectively resigned their commissions in 1875. In return the national government made them an outright gift (it would have been a severance allotment) of ¥167,000.[26] They invested this sum in a money-lending enterprise which they organized themselves. There were shops in Kariya, Heisaka (a village south of Kariya), and Yokohama. Two shops prospered, but the Heisaka branch fell into debt. In 1880 they abandoned the enterprise, dividing net proceeds among the remaining participants. Having accepted their allotment early, Kariya's samurai were not eligible for the stipend commutation allotments which the government made in 1876; but they were not left hapless victims of the new order.

On the contrary, samurai were particularly well-suited to survive in the Meiji era, by the possession of skills developed during the past two centuries. They were primarily administrators and soldiers. But they were also educators, clerks, financial agents, artists, physicians, and writers. In the wake of the Restoration the samurai class formed a reservoir of talent which governments and institutions did not hesitate to tap. Former educators taught in the new schools, clerks occupied posts in government and business, financial agents became bankers, artists and writers formed a modern intelligentsia, and physicians created a new medical profession.

This was true at the local level as well as the national. In Kariya the samurai shed their archaic status as warriors to adopt a variety of new roles. A number of them became teachers in the local elementary school, where the son of a former councillor was principal between 1881 and 1912, and where half the faculty as late as 1901 was made up of samurai descendants.[27] Some became clerks in the town office; in fact, virtually all

[25] Samurai populations in the Mikawa towns declined for two other reasons, also: (1) because a government directive in 1872 removed many of those in the *sotsu* rank from the list of samurai, and (2) because many samurai left to settle elsewhere.

[26] *Aichi ken shi*, 2:117.

[27] Kariya machiyakuba, *Kariya chō shi* (Kariya, 1932), pp. 88–93 (hereafter cited as Kcs).

of the assistant mayors between 1906 and 1930 were samurai descendants.[28] Others undertook jobs in the brick factory, the post office, and commercial enterprises. They found an outlet for their talents in a society more expansive and secular than they had known before. It was a society which differed radically on the surface from the one left behind, but it created a number of comfortable positions for the old privileged class. These functioned as strong points of continuity linking the old order and the new. Nowhere was this more true than in the realm of politics.

The structure of political authority in this domain during the Tokugawa Period followed the normal pattern. Kariya enjoyed virtual autonomy under the leadership of the daimyo. He was reasonably free to establish laws, collect revenues, and adjudicate disputes as he saw fit. He organized his domain administration along functional and spatial lines to govern his household, his contingent of samurai and its military tasks, the castletown, and the rural villages. To administer the domain he relied on representatives from three social groups: samurai, townsmen or *chōnin*, and peasants. Samurai staffed offices which oversaw the lord's household, the affairs of the samurai class, and the general governance of the castletown and the villages. Townsmen held office as *shōya* in the castletown. *Shōya* were in charge of counting population, collecting taxes, and resolving minor legal disputes, under the direction of a samurai magistrate (*machi bugyō*). In the villages of the domain, wealthy peasant families served as *shōya*. They discharged the same tasks as their townsmen counterparts, also under the supervision of a samurai magistrate, the *gun bugyō*. The formal political structure of the Tokugawa Period thus functioned under the ultimate authority of the daimyo while relying on delegates from three social groups to staff key offices.

In actual practice, the daimyo was less the supreme figure of authority he was alleged to be and more a political figurehead. Two factors operated in Kariya to dilute daimyo power and to transmit significant power into the hands of his subordinates. The first of these was biological. Eight of the nine lords of the Doi family were only teenagers when they assumed office; their average age was sixteen. Moreover, they had brief lives. Only two lived beyond their mid-thirties; average age at death was thirty-three.[29] This meant that their reigns were short, enduring normally for about thirteen years. On these counts the Doi house measured up rather poorly against other ruling houses. The fifteen Tokugawa shogun were on the average twenty-eight years old at succession. They lived into their early fifties and reigned an average of eighteen years. Their youth meant that the Kariya daimyo were quite inexperienced when they assumed authority. Their short reigns, half of which had to be spent in Edo (because of the

[28] Ibid., p. 41.
[29] I am indebted to Sawa Shun'ichi for this information on the dates of Kariya's daimyo.

alternate attendance system), prevented them from becoming wholly familiar with conditions in the locale. For both these reasons, the lords of Kariya were reliant to a large degree on the advice and council of their high-ranking subordinates, who exercised a significant measure of power in the domain.

Finances were a second factor constraining daimyo authority. Leaders of some large domains, such as Satsuma, had undertaken comprehensive reform programs in the 1830s. These resulted in revenues that financed innovative policies, such as the creation of modern factories using imported machinery. Small, relatively poor domains such as Kariya found such initiatives difficult, if not impossible, hampered as they were by severe financial problems. Kariya's financial dilemma dated to 1794 when the *bakufu*, in punishment for a peasant revolt which Kariya had not handled properly, removed twenty-one villages in western Mikawa from the Kariya register and replaced them with fourteen in northeastern Japan. Distant from the domain and less productive than local lands, these exchange villages posed a critical administrative and financial problem for the domain until its demise in 1871. Although revenues declined as a result of this transfer, outlays did not. The domain still had to finance attendance on the shogun in Edo, to maintain the post station at Chiryū, and to offer up forced loans to the shogun. Squeezed by low income and high expenses, the Kariya domain enjoyed no financial margin which the daimyo might have exploited to display their powers of leadership and initiative. In fact, the domain's inability to resolve its financial problems bespoke an outright lack of leadership—if not authority—on the part of the daimyo.

The Kariya daimyo shared power with a small number of leading samurai families. The most important of these families were the ones among which rotated the office of councillor (*karō*). Permanently resident in the castletown, these families were well informed about local conditions, in a way that the young daimyo, often absent in Edo, could not be. Such knowledge put them in a position to exercise significant power in making domain policies. Moreover, these persons, rather than the daimyo himself, were often the tangible symbol of domain authority in the eyes of the local populace. For this reason, the Ono, Tame, Hamada, Kuroda, Odani, and Endō families enjoyed both real power and a reputation for power only slightly less exalted than the daimyo himself.

Merchants and farmers who served as *shōya* were indispensable associates of local samurai administrators. Merchants occupying this post were usually among the wealthiest in the castletown. Some of them were purveyors to the lord (*goyōtashi shōnin*) who enjoyed the right to bear a sword and to possess a surname. Others were sake makers, cotton merchants, money lenders, and prominent family heads from among the general shopkeepers. Farmers who became *shōya* were heads of families which had resided in the area for several generations and controlled amounts of land larger than normal. By the end of the Tokugawa Period, these families were often active in supplementary endeavors, such as sake brewing, money lending, and cotton dealing. Both town and village *shōya* were thus men of wealth and status who worked in close association with samurai administrators to govern the affairs of the locale.

Despite its apparently thoroughgoing impact, the Meiji Restoration did remarkably little to change this system of political authority. There *were* dramatic changes: the emperor restored to authority, a new government formed in Tokyo, domains abolished, and prefectures created. But the novelty of these changes should not obscure the continuities which lay beneath them. In virtually all cases in the Kariya area, men who filled positions in the new government were drawn from the three social groups which had governed before. Samurai served in the highest, supervisory posts (as they had previously) at the prefectural (*ken*), county (*gun*), and district (*ku*) levels. Prominent merchants and rural househeads were the new subdistrict leaders (*kochō*) and town and village mayors (*chōsonchō*). Even the new elective institutions drew their members from these social groups. At all levels of government, prominent men from the social groups which had exercised power in the locale for several decades continued to do so following the Restoration.

Indeed, in most cases it was not just prominent representatives of the samurai, *chōnin*, and the peasantry; it was the very same individuals themselves. We have already seen in the discussion of the Meiji canal how men like Iyoda Yohachirō enjoyed political influence which spanned the Restoration. In the late Tokugawa Period Iyoda had been a steward overseeing a number of villages for the lord of the Okazaki domain. In the early Meiji Period he served as a subdistrict head (*kochō*). Examples of similar continuity in Kariya are numerous. The first county superintendent (*gunchō*) was a former samurai from the neighboring domain. Kariya's first representative to the prefectural assembly was Ōno Sadame, the descendant of a leading councillor family and himself a former *karō*. The spotty data which survive also indicate that the men who oversaw the town and the villages after 1868 were former samurai, wealthy farmers, or prominent businessmen, in most cases bearing surnames of the same families which had occupied those posts before 1868. On the local political scene following Restoration, leadership—at the very least—was characterized by a strong measure of continuity.

This chapter has sketched conditions in Kariya during the thirty years before 1889. Those were years which spanned the Meiji Restoration, an event of seminal importance for modern Japanese history. The portrait of

Kariya which has emerged from those years reveals that the early Meiji Period in essence recapitulated the past. Demographically, Kariya remained much the way it had been before 1868. Like the other urban settlements in Mikawa, it was for most of the nineteenth century a commercial center whose population did not surpass 10,000. Economically, few changes occurred to revise conditions which had prevailed before 1868. Most local residents derived a living from the land. The Meiji canal brought benefits to some of them, and surely stimulated a more lively commerce in the old castletown. Some innovative activities were tried, largely to resolve the plight of the samurai, as was so often the case in the early Meiji Period. One, the commercial enterprise, folded within five years of its inception. Another, the brick factory, survived into the twentieth century, but it operated on such a small scale that it exerted little impact on the local economy. Sake brewing continued to be the most prosperous industry in town. It was an established industry, however, with a small, seasonal, and itinerant labor force, so it stimulated only marginal economic expansion.

One cannot escape the conclusion that even by the standards of the time Kariya was by no means prosperous during the late nineteenth century. A prominent local observer writing in 1894 said of the old castletown, "In general the people are frugal and preserve old customs; the area lacks an air of progressiveness." [30] If banking was a sign of progress, this was certainly the case. There were thirteen chartered banks in the prefecture in 1884, but not one in Kariya. Nagoya and Toyohashi had four each, followed by Handa with two, and three other settlements with one each. Moreover, among the 2,107 shareholders in those banks, none came from Kariya and only fourteen came from Hekikai.[31] If there was capital in the community, it clearly was not being invested locally in new financial institutions. Modes of transport in the city raised doubt that there was even much capital.[32] Most towns in Aichi in 1884 could at least boast of a few horse-drawn carriages, but Kariya had none at all. Nor did it have any animal-drawn carts, just one hundred carts that provided a means of hand-drawn transport for about one family in every seven. The picture is one which justified a comment made by prefectural survey makers in 1883: "In general, the people in the southwestern portion of Hekikai are modestly well off while those in the northeastern portion are rather poor." [33] Economically, Kariya lived into the 1890s under the heavy stamp of the past.

[30] *Kariya chō shi* (Kariya, 1894), p. 10. This is a draft history, composed by an anonymous author, in the possession of the head librarian at the Kariya Public Library.

[31] Ats: 1884, pp. 3–5.

[32] Ibid., p. 2.

[33] *Aichi ken shi*, 2: 326.

It was in the area of politics especially that the early Meiji Period recapitulated the past. For two-and-one-half centuries the nation had drawn its political leaders from a privileged group which comprised a minute percentage of the total population, and from small numbers of key families living in the towns and villages. Through the first two decades of the Meiji era, political leaders continued to rise out of these same groups. They ingratiated themselves into a structure which was radically different from its predecessor on the surface, but one which adapted nicely to the social realities of Japanese politics. Samurai and their descendants filled the top posts at the national and prefectural levels. In the towns and villages, prominent merchants and landlords continued to govern, as they had during the Tokugawa Period. New structures evoked new images, but in substance and operation they remained remarkably constant.

This had a telling effect on the way power was exercised. Even the most "westernized" of the Meiji officials retained a striking fidelity to former modes of political authority, as Ivan Hall's study of Mori Arinori so eloquently demonstrates.[34] Those at the top disposed of their power as they saw fit, and they expected to do so unopposed. Far from liberating political forces, the Restoration actually squeezed political power away from local areas, placing it in a central depository where national leaders drew on it as they wished, to achieve their aspirations for the modern Japanese state. In the years after 1889, a major task on Kariya's agenda was to integrate itself with that state, a subject which will be taken up in the following chapter.

[34] Ivan P. Hall, *Mori Arinori* (Cambridge, Mass., 1973), pp. 295–323.

3

JOINING THE NATION-STATE, 1889–1921

Joining the nation-state was essentially a process by which local communities grasped opportunities offered by the center. In societies developing along an expanding frontier, the motive force of change stems from private initiatives at the boundary. This fosters traits of self-reliance, voluntarism, and political independence, at least it seemed to in the United States. In societies with long-established historical traditions which abruptly confront the need for sweeping reform, the political center becomes a primary force of change. This was very much the case in Japan during the Meiji Period. Under the pressures of central direction, traits emerged which were far different from those on the American frontier. The salient trait could be characterized as one of dependence.

In both their political and economic relationships, local communities were especially dependent on the center. [Politically, the central government enjoyed a visible monopoly on the basic resources necessary to promote, or impede, change: political power, ideas, coercive force, and material goods. Cities, towns, and villages could not carry out substantial reforms themselves; they were dependent on the center for the allocation of resources.] Economically, also, the center—that is, the capital and primary metropolis of Tokyo—was a dominant force. It commanded the largest single share of the nation's financial resources. It was also the home of Japan's major business enterprises and often the point of entry for new technology and managerial practices. Local communities often depended on the center in its economic, as well as its political, capacity.

Communities which were successful at joining the nation-state were characterized by the trait of responsive dependence. They knew how to take advantage of political and economic opportunities offered by the center. A political opportunity might take the form of financial assistance for a new school. An economic opportunity might appear when a Tokyo firm needed land for a new factory. The center had resources to share, but local communities had to undertake a range of initiatives if they were to benefit from those resources. If a community sat passively by, it withered. If, on the other hand, it was responsive to central inducements and energetic in bargaining for them, the community flourished. The respon-

34

siveness of a town to its dependent status thus determined its progress in integrating itself with the nation-state.

Three links with the center were essential in order to achieve full integration. One was the communications link. Within a few decades of the Restoration, railroads replaced coastal shipping as the basic means of transport in Japan. Access to a rail system thus had a decisive impact on a community's fate. A second link was economic. The years between 1890 and 1920 witnessed Japan's industrial revolution. Communities which rode the crest of change found themselves integrated with the national economy. Those which failed to catch the tide drifted in a backwater. The final tie to the state was political. Although power resided in the center and flowed outward from it, local communities could work to channel central resources in their direction. This required practice in political organization as well as the ability to bargain, especially in the ministries of the central government. The following pages portray the history of Kariya in the years between 1889 and 1921, paying special attention to its ability to establish these three links with the center.

The first tangible link between Kariya and the Japanese state occurred with the opening of the Tōkaidō Line. Long the object of dispute within the government, this rail system began operations in 1889 and immediately became the main transportation route between Tokyo and Osaka. In that year the once-daily train from Tokyo required twenty hours and five minutes to reach Kobe. This may seem slow to those used to making that trip in three hours on the Bullet Train. But to their ancestors, who waited four days for a letter to reach Kyoto from Tokyo by rapid express, and who set aside two weeks or more to make the trip themselves, this must have seemed an awesome improvement. For the people of Kariya, it meant that a trip to Nagoya or the capital could be made far more easily than before, and it meant that local merchants had access to a relatively cheap, rapid means of transport.

Kariya's location on the Tōkaidō Line was due to a combination of good luck and local effort. The community itself was situated only a few miles from the old Tōkaidō Road, the primary route for land transport between Edo and Osaka during the Tokugawa Period. Due as much to good fortune as any reason, therefore, Kariya was located in the natural corridor which the new rail line was virtually obliged to follow, once the coastal route was chosen. This did not guarantee it a station, however. At first, it appeared that Anjō, then only a small hamlet, would become the site of the station simply because it was centrally located. Fearing damage to Kariya if that were to happen, two prominent citizens undertook a campaign to establish a Tōkaidō stop in Kariya. They were Ōno Kaizō, a descendant of the former councillor family, and Ōta Heiuemon, head of

the town's largest commercial enterprise. Exploiting the political contacts
of the Ōno family and the business contacts of the Ōta house, they were
successful. In 1888, three years before Anjō, Kariya saw its station on the
Tōkaidō Line go up.

Having the station was not the boon they had anticipated. To begin
with, it was located well away from the center of the old castletown. One
had to walk nearly half an hour to reach it, and goods moving in and out
had to be transferred by carts from town to station. For some time this
discouraged both riders and shippers. Moreover, as other stations sprang
up along the new Tōkaidō Line, merchants and agents around those
stations began drawing off business which had once come to Kariya by
water, through the port at Ichibara. Consequently, many years passed
before Kariya was able to exploit the new line to its full potential.[1]

As important to Kariya's subsequent economic fate as the Tōkaidō Line
was a small private railroad.[2] It was called the Mikawa Railway, and it
had a checkered history lasting just twenty-nine years. Miura Ippei and a
man from Osaka first conceived the idea for the railway in 1910. Miura
had already made a name for himself as an advertiser in Tokyo, but he
had been born in Kariya and retained an interest in its development; he
was about to stand for the Diet from this district. Miura and his friend
sought financial and managerial assistance from Osaka financiers, and
political aid from prominent Kariya businessmen. In 1912 they won
approval for their plans, quickly incorporated, and set about building the
line.

Construction began in January 1913, and continued, for purposes of
extending the route, through 1936. The new line was clearly a boon to
local transport, but at some cost to its passengers: engines were so weak in
the early years that riders often had to get off and push when they faced an
incline! Freight, passengers, and revenues all increased steadily after the
line opened in 1914, but financial and managerial problems plagued the
firm until 1916, when Kamiya Dembei became president and majority
stockholder. Born in Mikawa, Kamiya had gone to Tokyo at an early age.
In an Alger-like tale so characteristic of the Meiji era, he had struggled
with a number of odd jobs before finally making a fortune by producing a
popular honey wine. Kamiya nursed the Mikawa Railway to prosperity,
but it fell on bad times again with his death in 1921. Managers tried to
resolve the firm's problems with a merger, which they finally concluded in
1941, when government policy virtually imposed consolidation with the
Nagoya Railway. With that merger, the Mikawa Railway disappeared,

[1] Data on passengers and freight moving through the Tōkaidō station in Kariya appear in
Kcs, pp. 248–249.
[2] This account is based on Shashi hensan iinkai, ed., *Nagoya tetsudō shashi* (Nagoya, 1961),
pp. 225–226, 293–300, and on Sakamoto Shin'nosuke, *Kamiya Dembei* (Tokyo, 1921).

but in name only. Its old lines still flourished in 1972 as part of the Meitetsu system, Kariya's major commuter connection with Nagoya.

The circumstances under which the Mikawa Railway was organized warrant brief mention, because they were characteristic of a pattern which came to identify Kariya's economic processes. A native son pursuing a business career in Tokyo conceived the idea for the railroad. Acquaintances from Osaka assisted him. Men from outside the community provided most of the capital to fund the corporation, although some locals along its route made small investments, too. Virtually all of the members of the board and the managing directors were outsiders with little or no contact with Kariya. The only roles which local citizens played were those of promoters and nominal directors. Serving neither as organizers, investors, nor managers, their purpose was to make the firm acceptable to local interests.

Local citizens directly associated with the Mikawa Railway were members of Kariya's Enterprise Council.[3] Formed in 1908, this council was organized to foster morality, encourage industry, and increase local prosperity. Its early presidents were men from leading samurai and *chōnin* families in the old castletown. Acting through this council they fostered a small-time local boosterism designed to attract new firms and promote progress. Their first major effort was exerted on behalf of the Mikawa Railway. In subsequent years, they undertook several similar efforts as well, after the organization changed its articles of federation in 1925 to become the Kariya Chamber of Commerce.

The pattern adopted by the Enterprise Council in its relations with the Mikawa Railway was repeated again and again. Outside interests with plans and capital would approach leading local businessmen for support in their ventures. Eager to oblige, the council members would mediate on the local scene, helping perhaps to raise funds, to buy land, or to overcome opposition. Once the firm was securely established, they would retreat from the scene. They seldom if ever became employees, managers, or investors. Out of this process developed a mode of relationship between the local community and large outside enterprises which persisted into the 1970s. It characterized not only Kariya, but many other Japanese cities as well. The term responsive dependence conveys the essence of the relationship. Lacking its own resources to construct a railroad, Kariya depended on outsiders to raise capital and form a company, acting responsively to the inducements once they appeared.

Operation of the Mikawa Railway brought a number of specific benefits to Kariya. When the first section of the line opened in 1914, it connected Kariya with the port and pottery town of Ōhama (part of the city of

[3] Kcs, pp. 202–203.

Hekinan). One year later, the line was extended to Chiryū, and five years later, to a village near Koromo. This opened a route for trade and commerce between Kariya and Koromo, and also gave Kariya ready access to the clay pits of the Koromo region. The Mikawa Line also encouraged much greater use of the Tōkaidō Line. People in Kariya could now hop a Mikawa train in town and ride it to the Tōkaidō Station. This eliminated the one-mile walk to the station from town and brought Nagoya much closer—both actually and psychologically. The Mikawa Line also fed goods, passengers, and customers into Kariya from the communities north and south of town. With completion of the Mikawa Railway, Kariya found itself strategically located at the hub of a transport system perfectly suited to industrial use.

The first firms to exploit this salutary location were brick and tile manufacturers.[4] Two years after assuming the presidency of the Mikawa Railway, Kamiya Dembei took further steps to insure its profitability. He and his Tokyo associates raised ¥1 million to establish the Tōyō Taika Renga Corporation. This firm manufactured heat-resistant bricks, using clays available near the rail line in Koromo. In a short time this firm employed over 100 workers. Taking advantage of its proximity to the national rail line, it soon established a nationwide market. In subsequent years the company underwent numerous reorganizations and steady expansion. In 1943 it became a part of the Tōshiba concern. It subsequently built a new factory, located south of the city center, which employed nearly 500 workers in 1970. Seven years after the Tōyō firm was established, a second Tokyo organization built a factory nearby. This factory, part of the Japan Tile Corporation, employed in 1970 some 600 workers on its original site near the Tōkaidō Station. These were small concerns when they formed, but they provided jobs for several hundred workmen by the late 1920s. They also created a lasting reputation for tile manufacturing and they fostered closer ties with the national economy.

In addition to the brick and tile firms, a handful of other factories appeared in Kariya during these years. A second sake brewery joined the Inaba company in 1895. By 1907 it employed sixteen workers. Two textile factories opened at the turn of the century. One spun silk, the other wove cotton. They employed about 100 female operatives. In 1908 the Ōta interests established a plant in the town center to produce paper bags. This firm relied on nearly 2,000 workers in 650 homes in Kariya and other nearby settlements to fold and glue the bags, which it then marketed at a handsome profit.[5] These four firms, along with the Tōyō company and three other firms established before 1890, were Kariya's "factories" in

[4] Ibid., pp. 217–220.
[5] Aichi ken nōkai, *Aichi ken no fukugyō* (Nagoya, 1920), pp. 195–198.

1920. Together they employed about one-third of its industrial workers. The remaining two-thirds found jobs in small firms, where they made clogs, processed foods, fired roof tiles, wove cloth, or caulked barrels.

The new firms stimulated very little population growth.[6] Between 1892 and 1920, the city-area population expanded only 10 percent, from 19,130 to 21,200. Growth was a bit more rapid in the town area, where population expanded 14 percent, from 7,585 to 8,648. In the same period, however, the national population shot up 37 percent. Had Kariya grown at national rates, it would have had a population exceeding 25,000 by 1920. It was simply failing to keep pace demographically.

Emigration contributed to the slow rates of growth. There was a conspicuous drop in the village populations, for instance, between 1916 and 1919, when people left farms to work in city factories during the wartime boom. But a more general flow of population out of the community had been going on for some time. Young people were leaving the community in large numbers. A general lack of opportunity at home fed their wanderlust, and the appeal of jobs in large cities and booming towns drew them away. This skewed the age structure, leaving Kariya with relatively more infants and elderly than there were in nearby towns. By 1920 it was becoming a haven in which to grow or die, but not a place in which to seek work.

It still suffered badly by comparison with other prefectural towns. Even in the largely rural county of Hekikai, Kariya ranked well down the list of settlements. The towns of Anjō (18,520), Yahagi (11,055), and Takahama (10,831) and the village of Meiji (10,951) all surpassed it, thanks to pronounced expansion in the textile and pottery trades. Other towns in the region, which would later become Kariya's friendly urban rivals, also surpassed it. These included Koromo with 11,924 people in 1920, Nishio with 15,150, and Handa with 17,805.

Slow rates of growth left the make-up of the labor force virtually unchanged. In 1920 fully one-half of the workers in Kariya *machi* were still farmers. Two in every ten persons engaged in manufacturing, another two in ten in commerce and trade, and the final one in ten in other activities, most of them as officials or teachers. Adding Fujimatsu and Yosami to this picture further affirms Kariya's agrarian character at this time. In those two villages, 83 percent of the work force was engaged in farming. In the city area as a whole, therefore, three in four workers were still farmers, a ratio which had changed hardly at all since 1876. On this count, Kariya differed little from the county of which it was a part, for two of three workers in Hekikai were still employed in agriculture in 1920.

[6] The following comments on population are based on Naikaku tōkei kyoku, *Kokusei chōsa hōkoku: 1920, Aichi ken* (Tokyo, 1925).

A portrait of what life in the villages was like emerges from a survey of
Hitotsuki at the turn of the century.[7] One of the hamlets which became a
part of Fujimatsu in 1906, 'Hitotsuki lay several miles northeast of the
contemporary city center. At the time of the survey it was a settlement of
247 households and 1,343 persons, most of them farmers. They tilled
almost 75 percent of the 320 *chō* in the village, each family working an
average plot of 1.25 *chō* (about 3 acres). Some families (41 percent) worked
less than a *chō*, but a majority (59 percent) worked more.

By comparison with nearby villages, land ownership in Hitotsuki was
well distributed. Only 10 percent of all households were pure tenants with
no land of their own. This was well below the rate in a village near
Okazaki, where 25 percent were tenants, and in another village near
Nishio, where 36 percent were tenants. Large landlords were also
relatively uncommon in Hitotsuki. There were only two families owning
more than 5 *chō* (12.5 acres) of land. As a result, ownership of village land
was less concentrated than elsewhere. In Hitotsuki, one-third of the
families possessed 75 percent of all village land. But in the Okazaki village,
where there were four large landlords, only 17 percent of the families
exercised control over 77 percent of the land. The survey commented that
landlords were uncommon in Hitotsuki, and that it was one of the good
fortunes the village enjoyed.

Tenants with no land of their own might well have differed with that
view. Farming a hypothetical 1.1 *chō* of land, they would have earned
¥286 from it in 1902. But their expenses, of which rent amounted to more
than half, would have exceeded those of a landlord working the same
amount of land by nearly 100 percent. Their net return was thus much
smaller, ¥58 by comparison with the landlord's ¥165. Land distribution
may have been more even here than elsewhere, but it still led to sharp
differences among family incomes in the hamlet.

To eke out their living, farmers put in a full day the year around. The
hardest season ran from April to July, when they rose at five in the
morning and toiled until seven at night, with about three to four hours off
in between. After eleven or twelve hours in the fields, they must have
retired early, with no pangs of guilt over a leisure schedule. At other times
of the year, although the work day ran only six to eight hours, they
managed to put in another two hours after supper, repairing tools, winding
rope, or hauling goods for a local merchant.

Farming occupied 90 percent of the families. Rice was the major crop,
but by no means the only one. Many raised barley; some still grew cotton;
a few raised tobacco and fruit. By-employments occupied a portion of the

[7] This account is based on the following sources: Nakashima Yokichi, ed., *Aichi ken, Hekikai
gun, Hitotsuki sonze* (Nagoya, 1906); *Aichi ken, Nukata gun, Fujikawa sonze chōsa* (n.p., 1902);
Aichi ken, Hazu gun nōkai, ed., *Aichi ken, Hazu gun, Nishinomachi mura sonze* (Nishio, 1903).

families, in such tasks as cocoon raising, cotton weaving, rope making, and drayage. Ten percent of the families earned their living from manufacturing, sales, or wages. Farm earnings, however, dominated the income of the village. Sale of farm products and animals brought in 84 percent of the village income; sale of cocoons, rope and textiles another 10 percent. Wages and commercial profits added only 6 percent to the total income of the village.

How affluent people were in this hamlet is difficult to judge, because subjective factors color any conclusion. A farmer put in twelve hours a day during the busy season; eight to ten hours a day during the off-season. He worked outside; he was his own boss (usually); and he set his own schedule. Factory workers at the time averaged twelve to sixteen hours a day, six to seven days a week. They toiled in stuffy, dark buildings under the eye of a foreman, at the behest of the company and the machine. They earned fairly little, but so did the farmer. The average farm family in Hitotsuki took in about ¥200 annually. A cooper in Nagoya working six days a week could have earned ¥220 in a year. Stone masons, roofers, and brick makers could have earned a little more; clog makers would have earned less.[8] If we overlook disparities in allocation of income and accept the average figures, these farmers' earnings compared favorably with those of their urban counterparts at the turn of the century.

That so many of Kariya's residents were entrenched in the agrarian economy was one measure of its industrial backwardness in 1920. It was not alone. Other nearby towns such as Koromo, Anjō, and Nishio remained agrarian communities, too. Well out of the industrial mainstream, those towns had less than a quarter of their labor force employed in manufacturing positions in 1920. Industrial centers were of two types: large urban areas and medium-sized rural towns. The boom in textile spinning, which underlay industrial expansion in Aichi, redounded first to the benefit of Nagoya, Toyohashi, and Okazaki. By 1920 industrial laborers in those cities comprised a bit over 40 percent of the labor force. Even more industrial than these cities, however, were the old centers of handicraft production. Those included Handa, where sake brewing and cotton spinning had flourished for more than a century; Ichinomiya, which prospered from the weaving trades; and Seto, for several centuries a pottery center. Industrial workers numbered 66 percent of the work force in Handa, 47 percent in Ichinomiya, and 63 percent in Seto.[9] In 1920 these were the most heavily industrialized communities in Aichi.

The differences between Kariya and towns such as Handa and Seto were the product of thoroughgoing changes which were taking place in the industrial economy of the nation and the prefecture. The three decades

[8] Aichi ken, *Aichi ken shi*, 4:738–739.
[9] *Kokusei chōsa hōkoku: 1920*, pp. 24–42.

between 1890 and 1920 witnessed what can rightly be called Japan's industrial revolution. During those years the economy achieved a rate of sustained growth which transformed a still agrarian state into an embryonic industrial nation. As in England a century before, the textile trades dominated the emergent industrial sector. In the nation itself, almost one-half the factories in 1918 spun cotton, reeled silk, or wove cloth, and more than one-half of the factory laborers were textile operatives. In Aichi, textiles were even more dominant. Eighty-one percent of the factory workers, toiling in 60 percent of the factories, were engaged in the textile trades. To understand the larger economic setting in which Kariya found itself in the first decades of this century, a sketch of the textile industry in Aichi is essential.

Cotton was probably first raised in Aichi in the seventeenth century. By the nineteenth century two areas within the prefecture were large producers of raw cotton: the Bisai plain, northwest of Nagoya, and western Mikawa, in an arc extending from Kariya through Nishio to Gamagōri. These two areas remained large producers through the 1880s, when a combination of poor harvest and high demand led to importation of foreign cotton. For a decade thereafter, a political struggle was waged by agrarian and industrial interests to determine the source of Japan's cotton supply. Industry prevailed and import duties on foreign cotton were abolished in 1896. As a result, domestic cotton producers virtually disappeared.

Before this happened, however, financial need, easy availability of cotton, and the presence of a dependable market had encouraged textile manufacturing in the home. Women and children in rural areas learned to process, spin, and weave cotton for sale to travelling merchants connected with distant markets and dealers. This system of manufacturing and exchange was widespread in both Owari and Mikawa by the early nineteenth century. It remained largely unchanged in Mikawa until the 1880s, but underwent significant revisions in Owari after 1830 which resulted in a more differentiated and complex system of production and sale.[10]

During the 1880s textile manufacturing began to undergo a major transformation, one that required nearly fifty years to complete. At the instigation of a national government anxious to avoid fatal reliance on foreign goods, several model spinning factories were established in Japan between 1880 and 1884.[11] One of these opened in 1881 near Okazaki. Two

[10] Tamaki Hajime, "Mikawa chihō ni okeru sangyō hattatsushi gaisetsu," *Aichi daigaku chūbu chihō sangyō kenkyūjo kenkyū hōkoku*, no. 1 (Toyohashi, 1955). See also, Hayashi Hideo, "Kinsei makki ni okeru Bisai men orimono no hatten katei," *Shakai keizai shigaku* 22:5 and 6 (April 1956), pp. 44–74.

[11] *Aichi ken shi*, 4:425–432.

other large factories were constructed in Nagoya in 1885 and 1887. These were funded with private capital, utilized machinery imported from Britain, and employed 114 and 738 workers, respectively. The Okazaki factory soon passed into private hands, and disappeared entirely after a fire in 1895. The other two remained, however, and were later joined by more spinning mills. These were established first in the large cities and spread, during the 1920s and 1930s, to smaller cities and towns in the prefecture.

Early expansion was very slow, however, and the large spinning mill remained a comparative rarity for three decades. At the end of the nineteenth century, small plants with a few spindles and only ten or twenty workers were far more numerous. Characteristic of these were factories established in the Okazaki area in the 1880s, using low-cost domestic equipment invented by an ex-Buddhist priest from Nagano.[12] The machines—whose clackety operation gave their name to the threads produced, garabō—spun heavy yarns used by weavers in Mikawa and on the Chita Peninsula. The same machine was also used in small factories built on old boats; these were placed on the rivers of western Mikawa and relied on paddle wheels for a source of power. They flourished briefly until the turn of the century, along with the Okazaki factories. But garabō yarns did not compete well against the uniform, sturdy yarns of the steam-powered, foreign-equipped spinning mills in Osaka, Tokyo and Nagoya. When the Chita weavers turned to the latter in the 1890s, the garabō industry collapsed.

An abundant supply of spun cotton produced by the modern factories eliminated one task of the former cottage producers. Many of them turned at that point, from the late 1890s onward, to weaving. By 1903, Aichi had more weavers than any prefecture in the country.[13] Nearly seventy thousand weavers worked at hand-powered looms in their own homes, or in small weaving sheds with several other operatives. Two-thirds of the workers were located in Owari, especially around Ichinomiya. There were many in Mikawa as well. Hekikai County itself employed over four thousand in 1907.

Most of the weaving was done in villages characterized by relative poverty where the normal plot of land was smaller than elsewhere and was less fertile, due to acidic soils, rocky terrain, or poor drainage systems.[14] In such villages, families exploited the land to its limits, but still found themselves short financially. They undertook weaving as a by-employment

[12] Murase Masayuki, *Gaun Tatsuchi* (Tokyo, 1965).

[13] Nōshōmu shō, shōkō kyoku, *Shokkō jijō* (Tokyo, 1967), p. 218 (hereafter referred to as *Shokkō jijō*).

[14] The data to support these claims are exhaustive. My comments here are based primarily on a comparative analysis of three Mikawa villages around 1902. See footnote 7, above.

to boost incomes. Those who did the weaving were women and girls from the poorest families, the ones owning little or no land and cultivating only small plots. These persons were driven to the work by economic necessity or by the pressure of their landlord. They wove when they had time: in the evenings, on rainy days, during the cold months. It was a tedious task, but it kept slightly above the poverty line many who would otherwise have dropped below.

The implications of this system are important for an understanding of processes of economic development. Early expansion in the textile trades occurred at the expense of the poorest rural class. This is no revelation, but the social meaning of the assertion is significant. Japan was able to utilize underemployed pools of labor at low costs to build the foundations of an industrial economy. In time, the capital expansion which accompanied this process created better jobs for some of the underemployed. In the meantime, persons of low income earned supplements which enabled them to survive, not in any luxury but probably a step or two above the poverty line. Developing countries which immediately import the most advanced technology erase this phase of transition. This creates an explosive social environment in which a large group of poverty stricken under- or un-employed persons nurse silent grievances against a small group of fortunate experts, technicians, and friends who find remunerative employment in the "modern" factory. Japan was fortunate to experience neither the calamities of the English nor the woes of the developing countries. She paid a price, or rather those working the looms did, but she reaped the benefits of a smooth political transition from agrarianism to industrialism.

Indeed, the political quietism of factory workers is one of the most striking aspects of those years in Aichi Prefecture. Labor disputes of any kind were exceedingly rare; most of them involved men in the pottery trade in Nagoya and Seto. Labor organization was weak. Only 8 percent of Japan's entire labor force was organized at the peak of prewar union activity. In key trades, such as textiles, the figure was much lower. Nor did opposition parties arise which sought to give voice to the demands of an industrial working class. The reasons for this quiescence have long been attributed to government oppression, an oversupply of labor, or collusion between management and police. These explanations all have some validity, but there are deeper reasons which are embedded in the social character of the textile labor force.

Women and girls have nearly always dominated the textile labor force in Japan. Traditionally, spinning and weaving were household tasks undertaken by wives and children, often during winter months when farm duties were slack. This practice stamped textile workers with a permanent character. At the turn of the twentieth century, for example, 95 percent of the weavers in Aichi Prefecture were women.[15] The rate was lower in some areas than others; men composed 15 percent of the weavers in Ichinomiya. Generally men were less numerous, however, and women dominated the work force, usually numbering eight or nine in every ten workers. This distribution of workers by sex persisted virtually unchanged throughout the prewar period in Aichi. As late as 1932, 80 percent of the textile operatives were still women.[16]

More accurately, they were young women. Adolescent girls consistently occupied a majority of the positions in cottage establishments, weaving sheds, and spinning factories. At the turn of the century, 15 percent of the weavers around Ichinomiya were under thirteen; 53 percent were between fourteen and nineteen; and 29 percent were nineteen to twenty-four. Only 3 percent were over twenty-five.[17] At this time operatives in spinning factories tended to be somewhat older, although girls under nineteen still constituted a majority. As late as 1932 one in four textile workers was a young girl under the age of sixteen.[18] The second obvious trait of Aichi's textile force was then its extreme youth; it was dominated by young girls in their teens, virtually all of whom were single.

These girls generally received only modest educations before entering employment. Prior to the first decade of this century, textile laborers were likely to have received little or no formal education before starting work. A survey of several factories in 1898 revealed that 70 percent of the female employees had never attended school, athough 75 percent of the male workers had. The experience was less than satisfactory, however, even for those who had received schooling: only 9 percent of the girls and 25 percent of the boys were able to read *katakana*, the commonest of the Japanese written scripts at that time.[19]

After 1905 an effective system of compulsory education saw to it that most children received six years of schooling. Nevertheless, only 60 percent of Aichi's textile operatives had done so by 1920, according to a prefectural survey. Of the remainder, 32 percent left before finishing and 7 percent were without any formal education.[20] By the early 1930s nearly 70 percent of the workers had completed a six-year education and another 16 percent could boast of a higher elementary certificate, proof of eight years' training in all.[21] By this time, however, a middle school degree (signifying thirteen years of training) was expected by many; and the best students

[15] *Shokkō jijō*, p. 218.
[16] Aichi ken, keisatsu bu, kōba ka, *Aichi ken kōba yōran* (Nagoya, 1933), pp. 9-12 (hereafter abbreviated as *Kōba yōran*).
[17] *Shokkō jijō*, pp. 222-223.
[18] *Kōba yōran*, pp. 36-38.
[19] *Shokkō jijō*, pp. 133-135.
[20] Nagoya joseishi kenkyūkai, ed., *Haha no jidai: Aichi no joseishi* (Nagoya, 1969), p. 94.
[21] *Kōba yōran*, p. 39.

were readily able to finish studies at a technical college or a university. Those with a simple elementary education were an unquestioned majority in this society, but they were clearly at the bottom of the educational ladder among their peers. Even with their six years of schooling, the textile workers of 1932 probably enjoyed no higher social esteem than their unlettered predecessors had three decades earlier.

Their minimum educational achievements reflected their humble social origins. Throughout the prewar period most textile hands were recruited from farm villages. At first the villages were those near factories, many of which were situated in former castletowns or port cities. As time progressed and labor demands increased, companies sought workers in wider areas. By the 1920s they hired half their workers from outside the prefecture, within a regional labor market. Always, however, one thing remained true: workers came from isolated rural areas. In the 1890s they came from prefectural villages ill-served or wholly unserved by rail lines or water routes. In the 1930s they came from villages in the mountain areas of western, central, and northeastern Japan.[22] One conclusion must be drawn from this evidence. These girls most certainly came from very poor settlements, and within those settlements, no doubt from the poorest households. They were thus members of the lowest rural class.

In every crucial respect, textile hands were social subordinates. They were manual laborers in an economy which rewarded mental labor. They were poor in a society which esteemed wealth. They were unlettered among people who cherished scholarship. They were minor subjects in a state which was coming to revere its leaders. Finally, they were youth in a culture accustomed to gerontocracy, and women in a social order infused with masculine superiority. In short, they had severe disabilities which left them in a very deferential social status. Under such conditions they were subject to sometimes unmerciful exploitation.

Working demands left textile operatives exhausted physically, and living conditions demoralized them psychologically. The working day was exceedingly long. At the turn of the century, eleven- and twelve-hour days were the norm in the new spinning factories. In the small rural weaving sheds work days were longer. Many began operations at five or six in the morning and did not close until ten or twelve at night—nineteen hours at worst, sixteen at best.[23] Factory laws enacted begrudgingly during the 1910s and 1920s did little to reduce such extended hours, and eleven-hour days prevailed as a minimum well into the 1930s.

Respite from such demanding hours was generally inadequate. In the early part of this century, one or two days off in every thirty must have seemed a generous vacation. The only extended holidays came during the

[22] Handa shi, *Handa shi shi*, 3 vols. (Handa, 1969–1972), 2:416–617.
[23] *Shokkō jijō*, p. 233.

mid-year *obon* season and during the arrival of the new year. In the 1910s and 1920s some relaxation of work demands occurred, often under pressure from international opinion. By the mid-1920s the exhausting and demoralizing practice of night shifts was abolished, although evasions were numerous. At the same time, concessions were granted for more frequent holidays; four Sundays off each month became the usual practice. The work day itself was little diminished, however, and eleven hours continued as the norm.

Food and housing which textile hands received was meager compensation for the hours they put in. The basic fare provided by textile factories was distinguished by its small quantity and low protein content, even by comparison with the prevailing Japanese diet. A morning meal, generally served during the third hour of work, included *misoshiru* (bean paste soup) and rice. Noon meals provided *tōfu* (bean curd), sometimes *tsukemono* (pickled vegetables), infrequently fish, and rice. Evening meals were more varied, but inexpensive foods—*tōfu, daikon* (Japanese-style white radish), *konyaku* (a vegetable product), or sweet potatoes—were predominant. Fish or meat were served only at two- or three-day intervals. The rice provided with every meal was often downgraded by additions of lesser grains, a practice which workers found especially galling.

Housing, increasingly provided in the form of company dormitories after 1900, was notable for its overcrowding.[24] At the turn of the century, eight-mat rooms (144 square feet) housed ten workers. Conditions improved somewhat as companies remodeled old dorms or built new ones, but in 1921 most textile hands in Nagoya still lived in ten-mat rooms (180 square feet) with seven other persons.[25] Each girl then enjoyed 50 percent more space than her predecessor had two decades earlier, but she still had access to a private area only as large as a closet.

This combination of long hours, brief rest, poor diet, and crowded living produced a breeding ground for ill health and spiritual despair. Textile hands were constantly prone to tuberculosis and other respiratory diseases. There was no escaping the discomfort of the steamy, oily factory or the cold, drafty dormitories in winter. They were also victims of mechanical hazards within the factories, the more so because of their fatigue. Many girls returned home with damaged hands or missing fingers as a result of their inadvertent negligence or a faulty machine. Coupled with this physical sacrifice was the affront to dignity that came with small wages, often sharply below those of her male counterparts. Even in their meagerness the wages were sometimes discounted for food, bedding, and travel expenses. Little wonder then a malaise of helplessness settled over these young women and left them rootless, physically and emotionally.

[24] Ibid., pp. 139–151.
[25] *Haha no jidai*, p. 106.

The following comments, related by a former weaver in 1902, probably bespeak the plight of innumerable textile hands.

> I was born in Toyama Prefecture. At the age of eight I left my father's knee and was taken by a labor recruiter to some spinning factory in Tokyo. I worked there for about two years, but not one bit of what I earned in salary entered my hands. I suppose some middle man made off with it. Shiftless for a while, I was contacted by someone from Urawa and agreed—for ¥11 a year—to work in the home of someone from northern Ashikaga County, where I would be the only maid. Every bit of my ¥11 annual salary was taken by the Aimi Employment Agency which had found the job for me; I didn't get a thing. After working there for about three years, I was hired by someone who operated a weaving shed. Again, there was no agreement about wages beforehand, and I was more or less taken in by what he told me. I earned nothing there. I guess I'd been hired for three years, but a bowl of rice in that place was mixed with nine parts of cheap grain and the soup had nothing in it; you couldn't even call that stuff food. Also, we started work at five in the morning and in bad times we had to work until twelve at night. If you didn't produce your quota, well, slackers get the strap, and, oh I don't know, there just wasn't anything I could do about it.[26]

She finally found a solution: escape. At the time of her interview she had just fled from the weaving shed mentioned, only to be sent back by the local police. She returned to an incensed master who beat her and stripped her nearly naked. Almost delirious with fear she ran off again. She related her story to a government official while sitting in an employment agency awaiting her next job.

Other young girls in similar circumstances struck upon the same solution. As a result, textile concerns in the late nineteenth and early twentieth centuries were subjected to a startling instability in their labor forces. It was not unusual for a factory to lose its entire staff in a single year.[27] At the turn of the century seldom more than 50 percent of the workers in a textile factory had been there for over one year, and only 30 percent for more than two. This was due in part to the newness of many factories, but there is little doubt that a highly mobile labor force was also responsible for such low rates of tenure.

Challenged by such unsettling turnovers, managers responded with numerous incentives to retain workers for longer periods. In the following decades they developed a number of techniques, some negative and some positive, to insure a stable labor supply. On the negative side, they reverted to blunt oppression. Factory grounds were heavily patrolled and dormitories and buildings generally locked—from the outside! In addition, girls were forbidden to leave company grounds during their holidays. And

[26] *Shokkō jijō*, app., pp. 284–285.
[27] Ibid., pp. 66–67.

just in case someone conquered these obstacles, wages were often retained until resignation, to insure that no one could pay train fare home if she did escape.[28]

On the positive side, material and cultural improvements were offered to induce workers into longer stays. Better sanitary facilities were added, new dorms built, hospitals established, personnel divisions formed, and classroom work offered. The young girl could now hope to develop the domestic skills of flower arranging and Japanese cooking in her off hours. A recent study has treated these changes as the positive effects of a laudable market mechanism.[29] They were too contrived for selfish gain to be printed in such favorable colors. Evidently the workers felt this, too, for even though rates of turnover gradually fell, the declines were not terribly dramatic. In Aichi in 1932, 35 percent of the factory hands were new to their jobs in that year (compared with 50 percent around 1900), and only 40 percent had been in their jobs for more than two years (compared with 30 percent in 1900).[30]

Escape from exacting duties was not the only cause of high turnover, of course. Most girls entered the labor force with the intention of fulfilling a short, terminal contract. For some of them the job was undertaken as something of a lark, at least originally. It offered a chance to see the city, to earn some money, and to get away from home before settling into the ordained routines of married life. Increased knowledge of factory conditions eliminated this naive approach to jobs, but girls took them nevertheless. A small dowry was better than none at all and brief exposure to the city was preferable to a lifetime of isolation. Always, however, the stay was short; three-year contracts were standard in most areas, with five-year contracts common in some.

This phenomenon—high labor turnover—further impeded the organizational potential of textile workers. Most girls realized that they were short-term workers. If jobs became too demanding they could always attempt escape. Or, conversely, they could hitch up their determination— an attitude highly esteemed by Japanese under such circumstances—and stick it out. Many did this, resigning themselves to a period of personal and physical misery to attain their final rewards: a small nest egg, a clear name, and the dignity that accompanies survival. Whichever choice they made, they ignored the possibility of organization for political purposes. Physical and social conditions were ripe for such a response, but cultural and personal inclinations carried workers toward other ends.

Those who fled the factories were, of course, conducting a primitive form of political protest. In a society where collective political action was

[28] Hosoi Wakizō, *Jokō aishi* (Tokyo, 1954), pp. 140–180.

[29] See Koji Taira, *Economic Development and the Labor Market in Japan* (New York, 1970), p. 145.

[30] *Kōba yōran*, pp. 40–41.

uncommon, perhaps the private, retreatist act of escape was the clearest expression of a desire for reform. Only a very few workers chose the demanding alternative of giving voice to their desire for reforms, then organizing and agitating from within to secure them. The threshold of political action in Japan was historically high, and textile workers did little to lower it.

Men in the textile establishments shared many attributes in common with the girls. They came from poor families in rural areas and they had little schooling. But they were treated much differently. They often received higher salaries than women for comparable work. Generally men's wages were only 10 to 20 percent greater, but on occasion they were 50 percent higher than women's salaries. Men also carried out different tasks within the factory. While women tended spindles or staffed the weaving sheds, most men held technical and supervisory positions.[31]

In such posts they could wield considerable arbitrary power over the young operatives.[32] Having risen from menial jobs on the factory floor, many technicians were conditioned to expect abuse from seniors. Finding themselves in the senior position, they were naturally disposed to repeat the behavior of their superiors. This was an obvious way of endorsing their new status and a logical reaction to their new responsibilities. The young operatives, single and vulnerable, were open targets for personal whims and sexual abuse by these low-ranking supervisors, and provocations led to constant tension between the textile hands and their overseers. Given this tension, a dividing wedge was driven between female operatives and male technicians at precisely the point where a tenable political alliance might have formed.

This assertion is better explained by comparison with England's textile plants. There the family often served as a laboring unit, even after spinning and weaving were concentrated in factories. Male househeads, personal witnesses to the harsh circumstances under which their wives and children worked, played a critical role as organizers seeking to improve working conditions. As occupants of technical posts within the factory, they were able to conduct strategic work stoppages designed to assist labor's cause and to nurture organized action.[33]

In Japanese factories this intimate bond, linking male technical specialists with the unskilled operative on the factory floor, was missing. Young girls were psychologically separated from the older males who were supervisors, mechanics, and steam room attendants. The tensions that developed between these two groups, based on distrust and fear, ruptured a natural bond of collusion that could have been used to win mutual

[31] Hosoi, *Jokō aishi*, pp. 31–47.

[32] *Shokkō jijō*, app., pp. 250–256.

[33] See Neil Smelser, *Social Change in the Industrial Revolution* (Berkeley, 1959).

benefits. The Japanese working class was thus divided at a critical point where unity based on family ties had aided the cause of labor in England. This is another, and final, instance in which the social features of the Japanese factory impeded organized political protest.

In summary, there are obviously numerous reasons why the young girls who formed a majority of the industrial labor force in Aichi Prefecture were not fitted to be a vanguard for political dissent. First, they were closely watched by governments anxious to avoid a socialist holocaust, and by employers eager to win profits—whatever their social cost. But more importantly, they were subject to crass exploitation, exacting duties, and onerous working conditions because of their deferential social status. They were thus too exhausted physically and too demoralized spiritually to organize for reform. Many ignored protest, resigning themselves to a sorry life in an act of loyalty. Some protested privately by exiting, an act which brought some changes eventually. Very few, however, sought political reform through collective action. Already victims of long-standing inequities, the textile workers saw these reinforced in the context of industrial life, and this encouraged their adherence to traditional forms of political behavior.

Indeed, the formal structure of political life after 1889 was designed to nurture traditional modes of behavior. Domestic peace and national security were primary considerations for the men who ruled Japan after 1868, and especially for the men who drew up the laws which framed political activity after 1889. They tried to insure a stable system of authority by limiting political participation sharply, and by expanding the franchise only gradually. In this way, they shaped a political consensus whose purpose was to sanction choices made at the center. They did not create a competitive policy in which varying interest groups sought resolution of their conflicts.

Meiji leaders limited political participation by restricting the franchise severely. They relied on age, sex, wealth, and length of residence in a community to cut down the size of the electorate. As a result, in the first decade after promulgation of the Meiji Constitution in 1889, only 1 percent of the Japanese populace enjoyed the right to elect members to the Diet, the nation's popular representative body. The suffrage was limited to males over twenty-five years of age, registered in the prefecture where they lived, who had paid either ¥15 in land tax for one year or ¥15 in income tax for three years. These requirements were revised in 1900, 1919, and 1925. Each revision increased the size of the electorate by relaxing tax requirements, the residency requirements, or both. Thus, voters increased to about 2 percent of the populace in 1900; to about 6 percent in 1919; and to over 20 percent in 1925. But, until 1947, only males over twenty-five enjoyed the right to elect Diet members in Japan.

There were limits on the franchise at the prefectural and local levels, also. The same criteria were used to limit the electorate, with the purpose of granting political participation only to stable property owners. Consequently, even the voters who could elect members to the prefectural assembly or the town council comprised only a small portion of the populace. In Handa, for example, electors for the town council comprised about 8 percent of the population and represented four in every ten households before 1925.[34] Similar ratios prevailed in Kariya, making the right to vote and participate in the political process the privilege of an exclusive minority.

The degree of political participation was almost as closely controlled as the number of participants. Those who enjoyed the vote could exercise its benefits only to a certain point. In the centralized, bureaucratic state which the Meiji leaders constructed, ultimate power usually resided in appointive positions such as the cabinet at the national level or the governorships at the prefectural level. The central government jealously guarded the prerogatives of those positions and prevented popular election of their occupants. The government did grant the electorate the right to select delegates to legislative bodies, such as the Diet, the prefectual assembly, and the town council. They also allowed voters to elect their mayors, with Home Ministry approval before 1925, but freely thereafter. In this way, the Meiji leaders confined popular political participation to those parts of the political arena which seemed least likely to disrupt stable government.

To insure smooth operation of the centralized polity, Meiji leaders needed central bureaucrats, prefectural governors, and town and village mayors who were both accustomed to taking orders and loyal to the government's aims. Creation of an appointive central bureaucracy achieved this goal at the national and prefectural levels. At the local levels, the central government made it appear that it was taking a risk by offering a measure of self-government to cities, towns, and villages. In fact, and in practice, it took no risk at all. It restricted requirements for candidacy so severely that only men from the upper strata of local society could hold office in the first decades after 1889. In the Kariya area, the results would have occasioned considerable satisfaction among Meiji leaders, because Kariya's voters consistently chose their mayors from the town's traditional ruling circle.

Although men from other families held office on occasion, twelve families dominated local politics in the *machi* between 1889 and 1921. They were all drawn from the ruling group sketched in the preceding chapter. Five of them were descended from Kariya samurai families; four

---

[34] *Handa shi shi*, 3:883.

were prominent as merchants in the old castletown; and three were large landholders from Oyama. These twelve families provided all of the mayors of Kariya *machi*, all of the prefectural assembly delegates, and nine of fourteen of the county assembly delegates from the *machi* between 1889 and 1921. They also provided four out of six of the presidents of the Kariya Enterprise Council between 1908 and 1931. In short, less than 1 percent of the town's families occupied more than 75 percent of its leadership positions during this three-decade period. Sketches of some of these leaders will illuminate the social context of local politics at the beginning of this century.

During the seventeen years after 1889, when Kariya *machi* encompassed only the area of the old castletown, three men served as mayor: Murai Shin'ichirō, Takano Shōjirō, and Masaki Tsūhei. Murai was a former samurai who had once been a steward (*daikan*) on the Kariya lands in northeastern Japan.[35] In the early years of the Meiji Period, he served as a district official in the county. After 1875 he was one of the directing officers of the commercial enterprise undertaken by Kariya samurai. He became mayor of Kariya in 1889. Takano was also a former samurai.[36] In the two decades after the Restoration, he taught in the elementary school, a position which attests to his learning and his status. By the turn of the century he was a key figure in the community. He was a guiding force behind the Enterprise Council and first president, he was an officer in the Kariya Samurai Society, and he was elected to both the county and the prefectural assemblies. Both of these men were direct successors in the line of samurai officials who had governed local affairs before 1868. Now, three decades after the ostensible abolition of that class, they still exercised authority through the highest political office in Kariya.

It was not mere coincidence that Murai and Takano, as former samurai, played important political roles in town. From 1877 onward descendants of that group sustained their identity through an organization called the Kariya Samurai Society.[37] Originally formed to celebrate the memory of the Doi lords and their ancestors, the Society eventually took on other purposes as well. These came to include: maintaining the samurai spirit and commemorating martyrs of the national cause; caring for the memorial tablet to Matsumoto Keidō and fostering his memory through publications; sponsoring lecturers to raise the intellectual level of the local populace; raising money to support samurai descendants with fellowships; and caring for the graves of the Doi family at their local temple. This group underwent many changes after its foundation, but it

[35] Kcs, p. 572; Kss, p. 624.
[36] Kcs, p. 202; Kss, p. 626; Tanaka, *Aichi ken Hekikai gunkai shi*, pp. 91–92.
[37] Kcs, pp. 127–131. Sawa Shun'ichi provided information on recent activities of the Kōwa Society.

still functioned in 1972, having been known since 1947 as the Kōwa Society. It still took the last duty seriously, but its other activities were confined largely to historical investigations.

At the turn of this century, the Kariya Samurai Society played a central role in local affairs. In fact, well-informed local historians believe it may have been the most important organization in the town. This is impossible to prove, but the belief is supported by some evidence. Between 1877 and 1931 men from twenty-one families served on the Society's board of directors. Among them were five town council members, three mayors, two county assembly representatives, four school principals, and four presidents of the Enterprise Council. If the Society itself did not exercise a collective influence on local institutions, its members did play instrumental roles—as individuals—in strategic political, economic, and educational posts.

Perhaps equally important was the psychological effect of a continued samurai consciousness. Although it ebbed and flowed and took many forms, this kept the samurai and their values prominently positioned before the public eye. Their values celebrated military endeavor and often resulted in dramatic action at times of nationalist excitement. For instance, in 1904, at the time of the Russo-Japanese War, 135 samurai descendants in Kariya petitioned the governor to allow them to again use the designation samurai (*shizoku*). They had abandoned that usage in a small fit of egalitarianism at the beginning of the Meiji era, but here they were thirty years later seeking public endorsement of their special social pedigree. Again, in 1915, as Japan was flexing its muscles in China, they dispensed with the previous informality of their group and organized themselves as a corporate body. Their own annual celebration of Tokugawa values before the daimyo's temple in the center of town, coupled with their efforts at education and the prominent activities of individual members, nurtured a climate in which Kariya's residents accepted a continuing samurai influence in local affairs.

Samurai did not monopolize local office. As before, they shared political responsibility with prominent merchants and landlords. Masaki Tsūhei, who held office twice, personified the social traits and personal achievements of the townsmen.[38] His family originated in the settlement of Takasu, now a section of the city lying about a mile south of the urban center. A branch house—allegedly of samurai extraction—moved to the castletown sometime during the seventeenth century, where the first-generation head of the family died in 1700. Eventually, the family resigned samurai status to assume *chōnin* rank. During the eighteenth and

---

[38] Kcs, p. 411; and Kss, p. 619. I am indebted to Masaki's granddaughter for an interview in Kariya on February 16, 1970, where she provided me with much of the information recorded above.

nineteenth centuries it was a distinguished commercial and political house in the castletown. Landownership, trade, and primitive banking constituted the basis of the family's economic well-being. It developed rice lands south of the castletown, lent money, and owned rice warehouses and weaving sheds on a parcel of land near the castle. In 1972 family descendants continued to live on that land in an area of the city still known as Masaki-machi.

The Masaki house was also an active participant in the political affairs of the castletown. As early as 1716 a member of the family served in the office of *shōya*, an official post with the responsibility for overseeing legal affairs and exercising social control in the civilian section of town. Throughout the eighteenth and nineteenth centuries, the names of the Masaki householders appeared repeatedly in *shōya* records. Masaki Tsūhei's father was *shōya* from 1839 to 1843. In the 1870s he also served as *fukukochō*, an office comparable under the legal structure of the period to that of assistant mayor in Japan today (although it did not have the same practical importance).

Young Tsūhei was destined for political office by virtue of his family's status and his father's position. In 1878, at the age of twenty-six, he became secretary to the head of the county government. He was secretary for thirteen years until he returned to Kariya as assistant mayor in 1891. Nearing the acceptable age for leadership, Tsūhei was elected mayor of Kariya *chō* in 1904. When the town combined with five surrounding settlements in 1906, Katō Shin'uemon became the new mayor, but Masaki was elected to office again in 1908. He served for three years, but resigned in 1911, shortly before his term of office expired.

Two other mayors possessed social backgrounds similar to Masaki's. They were Katō Shin'uemon, mayor from 1906 to 1908, and Okamoto Hirotarō, mayor on two occasions between 1915 and 1923. Katō was a member of the thirteenth generation of his family to live in Kariya.[39] His family name appears frequently in *shōya* lists, indicating that the family was an important merchant house during the last forty years of the Edo Period. Shin'uemon was the manager of a commercial establishment located in the center of the old castletown. Kariya's largest downtown department store—still a family property—flourished on the site in 1972. In addition to serving as mayor between 1906 and 1908, Katō was also a member of the town assembly between 1906 and 1911, a representative to the prefectural assembly between 1890 and 1893, and a member of the county assembly from 1897 to 1899. Okamoto was descended from a distinguished merchant family, also, being the seventh-generation head of

[39] This account is based on Tanaka, pp. 91–92; Kss, pp. 624–625; and Kumai Yasumasa, *Mikawa chimei jinshi roku* (Tokyo, 1939), p. 108.

his house.[40] His grandfather was an important sake brewer in the community during the Edo Period. As one of the wealthiest houses in the castletown, the Okamoto house served the domain ruler as *goyōtashi* (purveyors); they were also *shōya* on several occasions during the nineteenth century. Hirotarō was a sake dealer and distributor during his lifetime. He was mayor of Kariya twice, once between 1915 and 1919 and again between 1921 and 1923, a city council member for nine years, and a county assemblyman for three years. Masaki, Katō, and Okamoto were all descendants of old *chōnin* families that enjoyed high social status and preserved comfortable wealth into the twentieth century; they were appropriately qualified for high local political office.

The five rural settlements, after 1906, also provided some of Kariya's political leaders. In explanation for this, two arguments can be cited, both entirely speculative. First, given the composition of the assembly, it was possible for delegates from rural areas to vote en bloc against Kariya to nominate their candidate for mayor. He might be expected, for example, to listen more sympathetically to requests for farm roads or drainage improvements than a resident of the castletown area. To insure his candidacy, either several rural hamlets voting together, or a coalition between a few Kariya delegates and others from the hamlets, could have produced the majority necessary for nomination. Given the Japanese penchant for unanimity in decision making, however, a second explanation for the rise of rural mayors seems more plausible. Rural candidates may have been elected simply because they were equally as well—or even better—qualified for office than their peers from the old castletown. There were families in Oyama, Moto Kariya, and Shigehara, of distinguished lineage, considerable wealth, and recognized power, which compared favorably with any in Kariya.

Two early mayors, Tanizawa Bunjirō and Fujii Seihichi, were drawn from such families in the settlement of Oyama. Tanizawa's service as mayor of Oyama in the 1890s, and his membership on the county assembly between 1903 and 1906, affirm that he came from a family of some social and economic status.[41] Fujii, mayor of Kariya from 1919 to 1921 and a county assemblyman for three years, was also a member of a prominent Oyama family.[42] In 1924 the Fujii family was one of only two in Kariya which owned over 50 *chō* of land (125 acres). (The other was the Ōta merchant house.)[43] The family lands covered 66 *chō*, and employed well over 200 tenants. Fujii devoted his lifetime to management of the

[40] Kcs, p. 402; Kss, pp. 624–626; and Kumai, p. 626.
[41] Kcs, p. 411; Kss, pp. 624–626; and Tanaka, p. 91–92.
[42] Kss, pp. 624–626; Sangyō kenkyūjo, *Watakushi no ayanda michi* (Tokyo, 1965), pp. 97–125; and Kumai, p. 44.
[43] Nōgyō hattatsu shi chōsa kai, ed., *Nihon nōgyō hattatsu shi*, 7 vols. (Tokyo, 1955), 7:257.

family's holdings, to development projects in the county, and to the directorship of two banks. He was related by marriage to the Okamoto family, another Oyama house which produced a village mayor and later a member of the Diet. So strong was the economic base of the Fujii house that it persisted through the Occupation's land reform to sustain another political career, that of Seihichi's son in the prefectural assembly.

In virtually every case, the men who held political office during these years were descendants of families which had exercised authority in local affairs since the late Tokugawa Period. Murai had himself been an overseer for rural matters in the Kariya domain. Masaki, Katō, and Okamoto were all heads of families which had been *shōya* in the castletown. Finally Tanizawa and Fujii came from families of the sort which had provided *shōya* in the villages of the domain. For a full half-century after the Meiji Restoration, the leading political figures in town were drawn from virtually the same families which had governed the area in the preceding period. While there are many gaps in the data, evidence which survives for Nishio, Koromo, and Handa affirms a similar trend in those communities.[44] There, as in Kariya, status and wealth guaranteed political position, just as the Meiji leaders intended.

Diet representatives during this period came from social backgrounds similar to those of local officials. From the first election in 1890 until his retirement in 1924, one man consistently dominated Diet politics in the district in which Kariya was located. He was Hayakawa Ryūsuke. Hayakawa's father was a retainer (*hatamoto*) to the Tokugawa family; he ruled over lands in southern Hekikai County with an allotment equal to about one-tenth that of the Kariya domain. Young Ryūsuke studied both Chinese classics and English in his youth, while he trained as a steward to succeed his father. The Restoration cut short those plans, but it did not impair his ability to continue as a political personage in the area of his birth. During his lifetime, he was mayor of his village, a representative to both the county and the prefectural assemblies, and a member of the Diet. He stood for election to the Diet on thirteen occasions, won election on ten, and served for all but seven years between 1889 and 1924. It was immaterial that he belonged to a particular party. In fact, he belonged to five during his career, including at different times after 1900 both of the major parties. Party affiliations meant very little to local voters. They returned him, first, because Hayakawa enjoyed the wealth and status to be eligible, and second, because acting on the basis of customary practice, they wanted to affirm his tenure in a virtually hereditary position, from which his family had long exercised the mantle of political authority in this part of Aichi.

[44] The case of Handa is discussed more fully in the following chapter. Since Anjō emerged as a community only after 1889, it is a unique case which does not really apply here.

The Meiji leaders created a system of government which by its very nature encouraged continuity in local leadership. Such continuity had significant implications for stability in local politics. The castletown and village *shōya* who served as civil officials during the Tokugawa Period carried out relatively few tasks. They collected taxes, enumerated the population, adjudicated disputes, and oversaw construction projects. They functioned under the close eye of samurai superiors at the behest of laws laid down by the domain lord.

The laws of local government enacted in 1889 changed the structure of those relationships, but they preserved the organizational mode. Even under the new laws, local officials were still responsible for essentially the same tasks as before: tax collection, population counts, resolving disputes (to a small extent), and local construction, plus the new duty of overseeing a system of public education. Moreover, town and village mayors still functioned under the eye of governing superiors. They were now officials of the prefectural and central government, but the relationship between them and local officials was essentially similar to the one existing three decades earlier between samurai administrators and castletown *shōya*. Local officials still operated at the behest of laws made above, now by the nation-state rather than the domain lord. Thus, even under the laws of local self-government, the mode and patterns of authority continued essentially unchanged.

Moreover, the men who held office after 1889 were themselves former local officials. Having conditioned themselves once to such modes of authority, these men—such as Murai and Takano, to cite only two examples from Kariya—conformed easily and loyally to the new structure of government. They were not rebellious instruments of local authority at all. On the contrary, they became willing servants of the state. They viewed government as a system of hierarchic relations in which they carried out the will of higher bodies at the local level. They hardly imagined that local government could function as an instrument for resolving and implementing the conflicting demands of a local constituency.

Nor did the populace itself. The status of the people as subjects was clear. They functioned politically to pay taxes and to staff public works projects. For most of them, government meant an activity conducted by men who were born to rule. Although the suffrage expanded during the early decades of this century to permit modification of such a view, most voters preserved a traditional perspective on politics. They used their ballots to sanction the choice of prominent figures in the community, men whose families had been influential in local affairs for as long as they could remember. This helped to preserve the consensual and stable quality of local politics in Japan. It also undercut the possibility of making party ties or issues criteria for voter choice; they preferred to support a man for his prestige value.

In many respects Kariya lived out these years in an atmosphere of responsive dependence. The responsiveness of local business leaders had assured a station on the Tōkaidō, construction of the Mikawa Railway, and establishment of the brick and tile factories. But the town was dependent on outside men and capital for these key facilities and enterprises. In politics, too, the town was dependent on an outside agency—the state. Due to legal frameworks, administrative guidance, and long-standing practices, local government depended heavily on the prefectural and central governments for funds and resources. In this context, political struggle was not so much a resolution of conflict *within* communities, but more a contest for scarce resources waged *among* communities, as we shall see in the next chapter. The populace acquiesced to this situation, for they too were characterized in their behavior by a responsive dependence, usually on the social superiors who led them.

By the end of this period, Kariya had assuredly moved toward integration with the nation-state. It enjoyed excellent ties to the growing national rail system, thanks to the efforts of local leaders. But this communication link had only marginally improved Kariya's economic position. Through the 1910s it remained out of the mainstream of industrial expansion, watching nearby communities reap the economic benefits of the textile industry. There were some contacts with the national market, through the brick and tile firms, the paper bag enterprise, and local commercial houses, as well as through the emigrating youth who were joining the national labor force. But 1920 found Kariya still an essentially commercial settlement embedded in the surrounding agrarian economy.

Kariya had made no dramatic mark for itself politically either. If anything, it had regressed on this count. Having once been the county's political center, it watched Anjō assume that distinction during the 1910s, as that new market town attracted more schools and, in 1914, the offices of the county government. Kariya was, however, accumulating electoral experience and building a firm basis for political solidarity, which it would put to excellent use in the next decade. If the community had not been dramatically successful in linking itself with the center on all counts, it had witnessed some progress since 1889. By 1922 it was poised to exploit an opportunity that would thoroughly transform it in coming decades.[45]

[45] This chapter has analyzed the problem of national integration from the perspective of one small community looking toward the center. An insightful explanation of the same problem, viewed from the center, is Kenneth B. Pyle's essay, "The Technology of Japanese Nationalism: The Local Improvement Movement, 1900–1918," *Journal of Asian Studies* 33:1 (November 1973), pp. 51–66.

4

THE ADVENT OF INDUSTRIALISM, 1922–1931

The economic boom which accompanied World War I stimulated rapid expansion and strong earnings at the Toyota enterprise, a textile maker in Nagoya. Eager to expand its operations further after the war, Toyota managers began looking for a new factory site outside the city. The company first sought land in Taketoyo, a small town with a fine harbor located twenty miles south of Nagoya. For two years company officials carried on negotiations with local citizens. Landlords living in the textile center of Handa owned most of the prospective sites in Taketoyo, however, and fearing recession in their own community if the plant were built in Taketoyo, they joined together to prevent sale to the Toyota firm. Frustrated by this opposition, Toyota gave up and began looking elsewhere. Gamagōri, a port town and textile center in eastern Aichi, was the second choice. But while surveying Gamagōri, Toyota discovered the possibilities of a site in Kariya.

People in Kariya first learned about the prospects for a Toyota factory in late June of 1922, when the manager of a local transport firm brought word of Toyota's interest to the Enterprise Council. The Council held two meetings in quick succession to discuss what they should do. Within a week, they invited Toyota Risaburō, the manager of the Toyota firm, to visit Kariya and to view the sites they felt were most appropriate. The firm needed thirty-three *chō* (about eighty-three acres) of land. The Council recommended three sites which met that requirement. Two lay north of the Tōkaidō Line away from town; the other lay between the tracks and town. After some discussion, both parties agreed on the latter site. Immediately, the members of the Enterprise Council began to drum up popular support for the factory and to undertake negotiations to purchase the land for it.

Two groups conducted these activities. One, called the Toyota Support Club, was made up of the directors of the Enterprise Council. A physician and heir to an ex-samurai family named Shishido Shunji presided over the group, assisted by Ōno Ichizō, the vice-president. The second group, called the Welcome Committee, was really the mayor and town council acting in the role of promoter. Both groups encountered opposition from farmers who feared damage to croplands from the proposed factory. Eventually, proponents of the factory overcame the opposition, and the Support Club was able to purchase all the land it needed by December. Construction began on a building to house 500 experimental looms one month later. By mid-1923 several hundred workers were employed at the new factory on the eastern edge of town. Industrialism had arrived in Kariya.[1]

In the following decade, Toyota interests established two more factories in Kariya. In 1926 they built a factory to produce textile equipment, and in 1929, another to spin and weave cotton. In the decade after 1922, therefore, Kariya developed a close association with the organization which has shaped its industrial economy ever since. The first part of this chapter provides a sketch of that organization, in order to illustrate the origins and the character of the Toyota enterprise. The second part of the chapter presents a discussion of local politics during the 1920s. The discussion introduces several prominent politicians who played an important role in local affairs until the 1950s. It also describes electoral behavior in the 1920s and illuminates the decision-making process in local politics by examining the resolution of a school funding crisis in Kariya in the early 1920s. The discussions of the Toyota enterprise and of local politics contribute to the ultimate purpose of the chapter, which is to illustrate how its first decade of industrialization changed Kariya socially and politically.

In 1922 the Toyota enterprise was a textile maker which owed its existence to the creative ingenuity and the dogged persistence of Toyota Sakichi. Born in 1867, Sakichi was the son of a farmer and part-time carpenter from Shizuoka Prefecture. As a youth, he helped his father at the building trade, but he found the experience an unhappy one. Although he possessed only an elementary education, he decided to leave home at age eighteen to become an inventor. In time he discovered that his destiny would be to help his nation achieve its place in the eyes of the world, by inventing a loom that surpassed any made in the West.[2]

Sakichi pursued his life's goal with unwavering determination. While he was a young man, he worked wherever he could find space and materials, usually in dark, crowded rooms above tiny factories. As his work attracted favorable attention, he was able to improve his surroundings. His major achievements came during the 1920s, when he designed in the splendor of a spacious Shanghai mansion. By 1930 he had succeeded so well that one of Britain's leading textile equipment makers, the firm of Platt Brothers,

---

[1] Kcs, pp. 208–209; and Shashi henshū iinkai, ed., *Toyota jidō shokki seisakusho 40-nen shi* (Kariya, 1967), pp. 103–105 (hereafter referred to as *40-nen shi*).

[2] For Sakichi's life see Kajinishi Mitsuhaya, *Toyota Sakichi* (Tokyo, 1962) and Toyota Sakichi ō seiden hensanjo, *Toyota Sakichi den* (Nagoya, 1933).

was willing to pay him ¥1 million for the use of his patents, an event which brought Sakichi's achievements to the front pages of Japan's newspapers. Sakichi's primary contribution was the perfection of an automatic loom which permitted production of a higher quality weave with a mere quarter of the manpower previously required. While perfecting his loom, Sakichi achieved a large number of technical advances. When he died at sixty-three in 1930, he held 100 domestic and more than 50 international patents. His looms were recognized at home and abroad as a distinctive contribution to the weaving industry.[3]

Toyota Sakichi left the stamp of his own strong personality on the enterprise he founded. He was a diligent, competitive man, the sort of individual who carried a struggle to the very doorstep of his opponent, as his comments on the world textile market reveal:

> We must progress in the conviction that we Japanese are the masters of the China market. . . . We must strive to gain our advantages on the basis of the quality of Japanese products and the integrity of our commerce. When the China market becomes the basic market for Japanese textile goods, this will naturally become the first step towards an international position. Then Japanese products can even penetrate the very foundation of the textile industry, London. We can conduct commercial battles with France, Germany, Belgium, Italy, and even America. India and the Southeast Asian region we take for granted. Already Japan is supplying cotton goods to the markets of the world; we must push forward with the conviction that we can do a great service to all the peoples of the world.[4]

This blustery self-confidence characterized Toyota Sakichi in virtually all his undertakings. It deserves mention here, not only to demonstrate his personal qualities, but to convey a sense of the moral atmosphere in which the enterprise itself came of age. Sakichi's bold vision and assertive confidence have been living qualities among Toyota executives, many of whom knew Sakichi in their early days. The unwavering determination of this simple inventor still drives the enterprise he founded, nearly a half-century after his death.

Sakichi seldom wavered when confidence was called for, but he encountered numerous difficulties in establishing an organizational base for the Toyota enterprise. His first venture, a small weaving shed and loom assembly shop in Tokyo, folded after one year. His next venture was the Toyota Commercial House, established in Nagoya in 1895 to sell weaving

[3] Sakichi's achievements meant that technological advances by a native Japanese played an important role in boosting production in the leading industry in prewar Japan. This contradicts the thesis of a recent study by Henry Rosovsky and Kazushi Ohkawa, entitled *Japanese Economic Growth* (Stanford, 1973), and it illustrates the serious need for empirical studies of the role of technology in Japan's economic development.

[4] Kajinishi, p. 114.

equipment which he made. It survived for only four years. In 1899 he became chief technician in the Iketa Commercial House, a manufacturing firm established with Mitsui assistance. Sakichi joined the firm at the urging of a close friend, Fujino Kamenosuke, an executive in the Mitsui Trading Company. He thought he would be given funds to experiment with his loom, but the directors soon became more interested in expansion than experiments. He left Iketa after three years to try his own hand at business again, establishing the Toyota Commercial Company in 1902. This firm did very well, sometimes earning ¥6,000 a month, a large sum for those years. In 1906 he built a second factory in Nagoya to produce his looms.[5]

By this time, domestic demand for weaving equipment was brisk. The Russo-Japanese War had stimulated a sharp expansion in the number of small weaving sheds which were attracted to Sakichi's looms. Anxious to satisfy this market, the Mitsui organization pressed Sakichi again to join a firm which would make looms under his patents. In 1907 Osaka and Nagoya financiers invested funds to establish the Toyota Weaving Equipment Corporation. Sakichi became an executive director, expecting to use company profits to underwrite his research. The owners felt differently; they preferred to pour profits back into expansion. A collapse in demand occurred about this time which only exacerbated the differences between Sakichi and the owners, and in 1910, the other directors forced him to resign. His departure led to repeated litigation which continued through the 1920s. Sakichi maintained nominal relations with the firm until 1924, but he never played an active part in its management again. To clear the air of this unhappy experience, he departed for a seven-month tour of Europe and America. He was modestly wealthy, but in fifteen years he had engaged in five different undertakings. Two of them had left him permanently suspicious of outside investors. Already in his early forties, he still had no stable firm behind him to support his inventive activities.

During his American tour, Sakichi developed a sharper appreciation for sound business practices. Returning to Japan in 1911, he put this new-found business sense to work. Using funds which remained from his previous venture, he established a small factory with 100 looms in Nagoya to weave and sell cloth. He used most of the looms for productive purposes but reserved 8 for experimental use. Profits went to support his research. When he won a patent settlement from his former associates in 1913, he used the funds to double the number of looms. In the same year he took out a loan from the Japan Industrial Bank. Adding this to an advance

[5] For the early history of the Toyota enterprise see: Okamoto Tōjirō, ed., *Toyota bōshoku kabushiki kaisha shi* (Nagoya, 1953); Nozaki Seiichi, ed., *Toyota shiki bōshoku kabushiki kaisha sōritsu 30-nen shi* (Nagoya, 1936); and *40-nen shi*, pp. 1–113.

from his friend Fujino at Mitsui, Sakichi purchased 6,000 cotton spindles, in order to provide a source of dependable yarn for his looms. This investment coincided with the economic boom caused by the First World War. Within a matter of months his firm expanded five-fold and Sakichi had to set aside his research to devote full time to managing his profitable textile firm. For the first time, but not the last, the Toyota enterprise became a *senso narikin,* or wartime *nouveau riche.* Finally, after nearly fifty years of precarious financial existence, Toyota Sakichi found himself with a sound business organization behind him.

He deserved only partial credit for this achievement. His compulsive attachment to experimental work had been the bane of his existence. What business success he enjoyed was due in large measure to the skills of relatives and friends who managed his enterprises. Among them his second wife, Asako, played an instrumental role.[6] To her fell the responsibility for managing the Toyota Commercial House, then for overseeing the Toyota Commercial Company, and finally for guiding the weaving factory built in 1911. Sakichi's younger brother, Sasuke, assisted her in all these endeavors. Together they were able to sustain viable operations while Sakichi devoted his attention to experiments.

Two persons outside the Toyota family played a key role in Sakichi's business life during those years. They were Kodama Ichizō and Fujino Kamenosuke. Both Kodama and Fujino were executives in the Mitsui Trading Company, one of the most important cotton importers and textile dealers in Japan. Both had close ties with Nagoya and Osaka financial circles, and both helped Sakichi with his undertakings by providing managerial advice and personal funds. Kodama made a further contribution to the Toyota concern; he arranged the marriage of his younger brother, Risaburō, to Sakichi's only daughter.

The Kodama family, which would have so much to do with the managerial fortunes of Toyota, was a former samurai household from Hikone (a small city northeast of Kyoto). Ichizō was the eldest of three brothers. Trained at the Shiga Commercial School, he joined the Mitsui trading firm in 1900. After several years in China and England, he returned to Japan in 1911 to become head of the Mitsui office in Nagoya. In this capacity he met Toyota Sakichi and established close ties with him. In later years, Ichizō sat on the board of several Toyota firms. By that time, however, he was a member of the family, in a literal sense. His

---

[6] Toyota Sakichi was married twice and had two children of his own. He married his first wife in 1893 and divorced her two years later. She bore him his only son, Kiichirō, in 1894. In 1897 Sakichi married Hayashi Asako. She bore him one daughter, Aiko, in 1899. This daughter married Kodama Risaburō, who then became an adopted son bearing the family name Toyota.

younger brother, Risaburō, was also the product of a commercial education, at more prestigious schools in Kobe and Tokyo. Risaburō took his first job with the Osaka trading house of Itō Chū in 1912. After service in Kobe and Manila, he resigned and returned to Japan. In 1915 he married Sakichi's sixteen-year-old daughter and adopted her family name of Toyota. There would be a third relation from the Kodama household who would play an important role in Toyota's fortunes. In 1913 he was still a young man named Sawada Taizō. But for the time being, it was Risaburō who stepped into a strategic post at his father-in-law's firm. For the next three decades, Toyota Risaburō would preside over the destiny of the Toyota enterprise.

The firm which Risaburō joined in 1915 was a substantial industrial enterprise. It had grown from Sakichi's small weaving shed to employ 1,000 workers at 34,000 spindles and 1,000 looms. Three years later this firm recapitalized and incorporated to become known as the Toyota Spinning and Weaving Corporation. Having undergone two unsatisfactory experiences with private investors before, Sakichi determined this time to confine ownership and control to people whom he could trust. Therefore, shares in the new corporation were divided among only four family groups, bearing the names Toyota, Fujino, Kodama, Sonoda (related by marriage to the Kodama house), and Suzuki (a business associate). Sakichi owned the largest portion of stock, 48 percent. Fujino Kamenosuke came next with 29 percent, followed by Toyota Risaburō with 10 percent and Kodama Ichizō with 9 percent. All others owned less than 1 percent each. Control was divided among the largest shareholders: Sakichi was president; Risaburō, chief operating officer; Fujino, a director; and Kodama, auditor (*kansayaku*). Toyota was now a modern corporation, but it was still a tightly controlled family concern.

For the next decade, this corporation was the center of the Toyota concern. Even in the uncertain 1920s, its net profits never sank below 6 percent, and in good years they far exceeded that rate. These earnings generated funds for two purposes: to underwrite new firms and to support Sakichi's work on his automatic loom. Between 1918 and 1932 Toyota Spinning and Weaving participated in the establishment of six other corporations engaged in textile making. Sakichi himself organized one of these, the Toyota Spinning and Weaving Factory. Established in 1920 in Shanghai, this firm incorporated in the following year and operated until the end of the Second World War. Toyota sources are silent about this company. But it must have returned the profits which Sakichi had hoped for in order to support his experiments, because his work progressed rapidly during the early 1920s. By 1924 final improvements made the loom ready for full-scale use. When he encountered problems in finding a firm to produce the 1,000 looms he needed for his final, practical experiments, he decided to build his own firm. In 1926 the Toyota Spinning and Weaving Corporation gave birth to still another corporate offspring which in a few years would replace it as the center of the Toyota concern.

Sakichi and his associates organized this firm, the Toyota Automatic Loom Corporation, to manufacture and sell his weaving equipment.[7] He also expected it to support still more of his research, now on a cylindrical loom. Like its predecessor, the loom firm was tightly owned and controlled by the Toyota family and its immediate relations and friends. Among individual shareholders, Sakichi, his two brothers, and his two sons owned the largest portion, 20 percent. Kodama Ichizō owned another 5 percent and eight company executives divided 11 percent of the shares among them. The remaining shares were owned by two corporations: the Fujino Company with 2.5 percent and Toyota Spinning and Weaving Corporation with 61.5 percent. Toyota Risaburō assumed the presidency while Sakichi's own son Kiichirō, a thirty-two-year-old engineer trained at Tokyo University, became chief operating officer. Sakichi served only as a consultant, refraining from active management in order to pursue his research. The pattern of close control by members of the Toyota family and their loyal subordinates was now firmly established.

There were two reasons for this manner of operation. One had to do with Sakichi's mistrust of outside investors. This account has illustrated how his experiences with the Iketa firm and the weaving-equipment maker soured him to working under the authority of others. Too often they preferred business as usual, while Sakichi was insistent on research. He decided that he could best achieve his own aims by working through firms which he and trusted relatives and friends controlled.

The second reason for Toyota's financial practices was due to the business climate in Nagoya, where the firm was still headquartered. Nagoya was notorious for its treatment of "outsiders," whether they were humble farmers' sons from Shizuoka, such as Sakichi, or prominent urban firms, such as Mitsui. Local business leaders were, for the most part, descendants of Tokugawa Period merchants who were both suspicious and jealous of men from outside the city. They were also reluctant to extend financial assistance to anyone outside their circle and were slow to draw newcomers into it. They withheld recognition from Toyota, for example, until 1933, when they elected Risaburō vice-president of the Chamber of Commerce (but they would never make him president). Toyota's closed

[7] The official English name of the loom factory in Kariya is Toyoda Automatic Loom Works, Limited. The firm still uses that name and spelling on its products. For the sake of consistency, however, I have used the spelling which is currently most familiar in the United States, i.e. Toyota, rather than Toyoda.

financial operations, therefore, were also a response to—and perhaps caused by—the exclusiveness of Nagoya business circles.[8]

Sakichi's convictions and Nagoya's business customs thus fostered an atmosphere of isolated independence at Toyota, which the firm's own business operations reinforced. In the 1920s Toyota spun and wove mainly for the export market. Its largest customers were India, Korea, China, and Manchuria. Most of its raw materials were imported. It had to rely on the domestic economy only for labor. Even that need could be obviated, as the Shanghai factory demonstrated, if it proved more advantageous to locate plants elsewhere. Tied as it was to international currents of economic activity, Toyota assumed a posture which was both distant and aloof. It had only shallow roots in the communities where it located, and it had few branches reaching out into the business and financial world.

Toyota did maintain external ties with one prominent enterprise, the Mitsui organization. In fact, it is often alleged that Toyota is a corporate offspring (*kogaisha*) of Mitsui. The allegation is not exactly true. As earlier pages revealed, Toyota's ties with Mitsui were not necessarily close and cordial. It was Mitsui, after all, which pressured Sakichi into his unhappy experiences with Iketa and the Toyota Weaving Equipment Corporation. Henceforth, he was wary of outside investors, and some of his suspicion must have directed itself at Mitsui as an organization.

If Toyota had ties with Mitsui, they were not those which linked a corporate center to a branch firm. They were rather personal bonds between trusted individuals. Two key figures at Toyota, Sakichi and Risaburō, had close, personal ties with three men at Mitsui: Kodama Ichizō, Fujino Kamenosuke, and Yada Isao. Kodama, as noted earlier, was close to both Toyotas. Fujino first befriended Sakichi at the turn of the century, when he was manager of the Osaka branch of the Mitsui Trading Company. They remained close thereafter, and Fujino served on several occasions as an investor in Sakichi's firms. Yada Isao arrived in Nagoya in 1902 to become manager of the local branch of the Mitsui Bank.[9] He and Risaburō were neighbors; they often sought each other's advice on business matters. All of these men thus enjoyed friendships which were rooted in the rich social ambience of the family and the neighborhood. More than corporate relations, it was these informal bonds between individuals which tied the Toyota firm to the Mitsui organization in the 1920s.

Despite these ties, Mitsui—as an organization—did not invest in the early Toyota corporations. In all cases, individual investors, or corporate groups owned by them, owned and controlled all the stock in the major Toyota firms. Financially, Toyota operated in a very isolated context. It

---

[8] For a discussion of the Nagoya business community, see Hayashi Tōichi, *Nagoya shōnin shi* (Nagoya, 1966).

[9] Ibid., p. 406.

would pay a price for its isolation when it needed funds to build the auto company in the 1930s.

When the Toyota enterprise decided in 1926 to build a new factory to make its looms, its plants were located in Nagoya, Shanghai, and Kariya. Since the plant in Kariya was an experimental site, where Sakichi was observing the operation of his loom, it was sensible to locate the factory there. To see if there were land available for another factory in Kariya, Toyota Risaburō called on a local politician named Ōno Ichizō for assistance.

The idea of a loom factory enthused Ōno greatly. He returned to Kariya, button-holed a member of the council, and explained the Toyota request. His friend was less than enthusiastic. Toyota wantd another 33 *chō* of land, which he felt would be very hard to acquire after a similar purchase just two years before. Momentarily stumped, Ōno struck on a shrewd solution. He recommended that Toyota use vacant land on the previous site for the new factory. That land was designated for company housing, but housing sites could easily be found in the town's several wards. This would not only make it easy to buy the land, it would also generate popular support for Toyota's expansion. His idea was so attractive that it took only a month to make the necessary purchases. By 1927 Toyota Automatic Loom was in full operation, turning out 300 machines a month. When Toyota needed land for the new Central Spinning and Weaving Corporation two years later, Risaburō again called on Ōno to intercede. He did so willingly, and once again the town helped make land available for Toyota. By then there was a firm compact between the Toyota enterprise and its political agent on the local scene, Ōno Ichizō.

Ōno was the head of Kariya's most distinguished samurai lineage.[10] Having arrived with the Doi lord in the mid-eighteenth century, his family had lived in Kariya for eight generations. During the Tokugawa Period, its househeads had served the Doi lords as councillors. The last to do so was Ōno Sadame, who, as noted in the second chapter, fell out of favor in the 1860s but regained his position in 1868. Following the Restoration, Sadame stepped forward to assume leadership of the Kariya samurai. He guided the commercial enterprise and organized the brick factory. He also held important political offices; he was a representative to the prefectural assembly and a mayor of the castletown. Although he had two sons of his own, he passed headship of the Ōno house to his younger brother Kaizō when he died in 1884.

[10] Sources for the following discussion of the Ōno family are: Kcs, pp. 40–45, 404–406; Kss, pp. 624–626, 802–803; Ōno Ichizō, *Kariya ga shi ni naru made no hatten shi* (Kariya, 1955); and Ōno Ichizō, *Kiju ni mukaete watakushi no ashiato* (Kariya, 1961). Ōno Zenji, a younger brother of Ichizō, also provided information for this sketch of his family in an interview in Kariya on January 26, 1970.

Ōno Kaizō stepped easily into his role. He had served as a high-ranking domain official himself in its last days and was accustomed to wielding authority, something he had numerous opportunities to do. He was a member of the town council between 1907 and 1911, a delegate to the county assembly from 1899 to 1903, and a director of the Kariya Samurai Society from 1884 to 1917. Kaizō also inherited his brother's role in the brick firm, which he managed from the early 1880s until 1919. This prompted his interest in local business affairs, which he pursued through his membership on and presidency of the Enterprise Council. For thirty-five years he was an influential figure in the political and economic affairs of the community. Three years before he died in 1922 at age seventy-five, he passed the mantle of family authority to his eldest son Ichizō.

Young Ichizō grew up in an environment much different from the contentious political atmosphere in which his uncle Sadame and his father Kaizō had matured. Born in 1885, he came of age during Japan's imperialist era. News of his country's dramatic victory over the Chinese in 1895 reached him when he was still a youngster in the local grade school. When Japan defeated Russia in 1905, he had already completed middle school training in Kobe and was studying ceramics manufacture at Tokyo's best technical institute. Degree in hand, he spent one year working and another year in the army before setting out to make his mark in the colonies. In 1910 he accepted a job with the South Manchuria Railway. He progressed through a series of minor posts to become head of an experimental laboratory in 1916, although to read his accounts one might think that he was personally responsible for the materials that built the Japanese Empire. Visions of greatness pursued him to his end, but his father's ill health intervened to cut short his career in Manchuria. In 1917 he returned to Kariya to assume headship of the Ōno house.

For more than a decade after his return, Ichizō continued to use his technical training for business purposes. In 1917 the founders of the Tōyō Taika Renga firm retained him to help with the planning for their new factory. He stayed on to become chief technician and plant manager, but an attack of pleurisy forced him to retire in 1921. Shortly before that he had assumed direction of the family brick firm, which was still producing at its site on the old castle grounds. He stayed in the position through the mid-1930s, when the firm finally had to close because of his other activities.

Ichizō's first career was politics. Almost from the moment he returned from Manchuria, he was—to have him tell it—literally herded into office. It is common for local politicians in Kariya to deny personal ambitions. They prefer people to think that they undertake the hallowed duties of public office only out of a sincere, self-abnegating response to popular pressure. Ichizō writes constantly in this vein, always eager to foster his image as a selfless public servant. It is patent nonsense, of course. There may have been some pressure, but it was not elicited by his honest, retiring and altruistic qualities. Public pressure imposed on him to enter politics because he was the heir to one of Kariya's leading political families. He was bred to rule by the experience of his father and uncle, and by the very personality of the Ōno house. The Ōnos were hereditary political figures and they conducted themselves accordingly. They were stiff, confident, and appropriately condescending. Ichizō fit nicely into this mold. Moreover, he accepted office eagerly, despite his disavowals.

Ōno Ichizō stood at the center of Kariya politics from 1922 until his death in 1967. By then he had filled virtually every political position the community could offer: ward chairman, council member, mayor, prefectural assemblyman, and Diet representative, in addition to the nominal leadership of numerous social organizations. While his long career is interwoven with the rest of this book, what concerns us here is its beginning. That occurred in 1922, shortly after his recovery from pleurisy, when the town council appointed him chairman of the old castletown ward. His father had long held the post, so it must have seemed natural that it continue in Ōno hands. Moreover, the Toyota firm had already expressed its interest in a factory site, and the council felt a man of Ōno's stature would assist them in their dealings. In May of the following year he joined the town council. At the age of thirty-eight, he had already taken two steps up the political ladder.

He took his third step upward in September 1923. For several years community leaders in Kariya had felt the need for a representative in the prefectural assembly. They wished to raise an issue before the assembly and needed a strong spokesman for their cause. Ōno, with his political pedigree, his brusque self-confidence and his colonial experience, would be a fitting candidate. With a little arm-twisting, they persuaded him to run. The vice-mayor resigned from office for several months to devote full time to Ōno's campaign. He was a good administrator who also had political contacts in Koromo, with which Kariya hoped to ally to capture a seat. With virtually unanimous support and ¥16,000 in campaign funds, Ōno took office with a large plurality.[11]

Knowing how Ōno won office in 1923 would contribute greatly to an understanding of local politics in the 1920s. Unfortunately, there are no surviving records which describe his campaign organization or the contest for office. It is impossible, therefore, to fully understand electoral politics at the prefectural level, but it *is* possible to examine the electoral process at the Diet level. The following discussion of Diet politics in the Kariya area

[11] Ōno, *Kiju*, pp. 82-83.

in the 1920s serves as an introduction to a closer analysis of local politics which is presented later.[12]

Taketomi Sai was the Diet representative from the Kariya area during the 1920s. Local voters were as loyal to him as they had been to his predecessor, Hayakawa Ryūsuke. Taketomi was a native son, born in Kuma in 1879 and educated through the eighth grade in Kariya. Following adoption by a government official from Hokkaido, he finished his education in Tokyo, completing the law course at Tokyo University in 1907. After a brief career in the Justice Ministry, he entered private legal practice in the capital.[13] Taketomi made his first unsuccessful attempt at the Diet in 1917, when he ran alongside Hayakawa as a candidate for the Kenseikai. He sat out the following election in 1920, enabling Hayakawa to capture a seat in the newly formed small district.[14] When Hayakawa retired at the end of that term, Taketomi stood again and was successful. He won reelection in the following four campaigns, serving in the Diet until his death in 1936. Taketomi's victories in 1928 and 1930 reveal the central features of electoral politics in this decade.

To capture a seat in one of Japan's multi-member districts, a candidate needed a large, secure electoral base (*jiban*). This base was a source of support tied personally to the candidate. A *jiban* assumed two spatial forms; it was either focused or diffused. Taketomi's was a focused *jiban*, which operated as follows. There were approximately 94,000 voters in the Fourth District at the end of the 1920s. To win a seat, some 15,000 to 17,000 votes were necessary. Taketomi concentrated on Hekikai County, where more than 70 percent of his supporters lived. The focus of his base was his former hometown of Kariya. He could count on it for about 2,000 votes. Other points of strength lay in the towns of Takahama, Shingawa, Ōhama, and Chiryū, and in the city of Okazaki. From these he was able to build a base which numbered about 20,000. This easily sustained him in office for five terms. It was more dangerous, and therefore less common, for a candidate to establish a spatially diffuse base of support, but some did. They relied on small pockets of strength in each of the counties in the district. Sometimes this strategy was successful; more often it failed. A

[12] The following analysis relies primarily on Shūgiin jimu kyoku, *Shūgiin giin sōsenkyo ichiran*, 30 vols. (Tokyo, 1904–1973). I consulted volumes reporting returns from the seventh through the twenty-first general elections for this analysis.

[13] Kumai, *Mikawa chimei jinshi roku*, pp. 554–555.

[14] With each electoral reform after 1890, the size of the Diet district in which Kariya was located changed. Between 1890 and 1899 Kariya was in a rural district embracing the counties of Hekikai and Hazu. From 1900 through 1919 Kariya was in the single rural district in Aichi which embraced all of the prefecture except the city of Nagoya. From 1919 through 1925 the county of Hekikai made up a single district. After 1925 Kariya was located in the Aichi Fourth District. Made up of the cities, towns, and villages in the counties of Hekikai, Hazu, Nukata, and Nishi and Higashi Kamo, this district returned three members from 1928 through 1945. Since 1947 it has returned four. In such a multi-member district, voters cast a single ballot and candidates with the largest number of votes are returned.

focused base, rooted in a hometown, was the most stable, because it formed a solid core of supporters whose own influence a candidate could multiply many times over.

Identifying one's target area was only one step in establishing a *jiban*. Equally important was the need to stabilize the personal ties on which the base was built. There were many ways to do this. The candidate usually began with his family and kin groups and moved outward from them to encompass their relatives and friends. He also called on associates from organizations to which he belonged and occupational groups with whom he had contact. Such ties lay at the core of a *jiban*, but they did not suffice to establish a large, stable base. Two other inducements were essential. One was material; the use of cash gifts to voters was common. The second was social; candidates appealed to voters on the basis of their personal prestige. The criteria for prestige changed during this period, from an emphasis on hereditary status to meritorious achievement. Hayakawa had appealed to constituents by parading his status as a *hatamoto* descendant. Taketomi gained supporters by flashing his professional achievements: graduate of the Tokyo University Law School, former central government bureaucrat, knowledgeable Tokyo lawyer, etc. To the humble farmers and townsmen of Hekikai, these were impressive accomplishments. He made them seem more enticing with the added claims that he was a local boy who had made good, and a man familiar with the politics of the center in Tokyo.

Candidates sometimes manipulated status appeal to ridiculous extremes. Ōno Ichizō recounts his experiences as campaign manager in 1924 when Taketomi handily defeated Okada Kikujirō, an Anjō politician. One of the men Okada called on to promote his candidacy was Yamazaki Nobuyoshi, the superintendent of an agricultural school in Anjō famous throughout the country. As a teacher (*sensei*, in the Japanese context), Yamazaki was a patron to all his former students; in life as in school, his word carried authority. For Okada, his endorsement insured votes. Ōno set out to subvert Yamazaki's appeal by sending his henchmen to plaster Yamazaki's speaking locations with posters booming Taketomi. After his talks, as Yamazaki got into his car to leave, Ōno would have his men drive up in theirs, to escort him off between their cars flying the Taketomi banner. Local farmers were never sure if Yamazaki was supporting Okada or Taketomi! [15]

Ties of family, kinship, friendship, membership, and occupation, coupled with money and status, were the key elements in building a personal electoral base, but on occasion, other vehicles were employed. This was the case in Anjō with Okada Kikujirō, a local boss who was often

---

[15] Ōno, *Kiju*, pp. 83–85.

a thorn in the side of Kariya politicians.[16] Although he came from humble stock, Okada's father was a prominent figure in the community. He made a comfortable living as a mill operator and fertilizer dealer, having been among the first settlers of Anjō when it was just a small village near the new station on the Tōkaidō Line. In a sense, then, Okada was from a founding family. Through his father, he met many prominent local politicians when still a youth. They sparked his interest in politics, and by the time he was twenty-one, he was well on the way toward a political career. He went on to become mayor of Anjō, serving for a total of thirty-one years, and a prefectural assemblyman, where he sat for thirty-nine years. But the foundation of his political power was rooted in his membership on the governing committee of the Meiji canal.

Thanks to this post, he enjoyed personal relationships with many Hekikai farmers which he exploited for political purposes. As a committee member he was important to virtually everyone in southern Hekikai. He helped to determine who got water, when, in what quantity, and for how much money. These decisions were of paramount concern to owners and tenants alike. Water was essential, and the fees they paid to get it were an important part of their investment capital. It made good sense to curry committee favor.

In later years Okada was the leading official in the canal district. In this capacity he resolved water disputes. This formal position alone made him a local power. Combined with his guaranteed visibility and his informal prerogatives, Okada exercised wide influence among thousands of farm households. He wielded his influence aggressively—contemporaries claimed he would cut off water to his political antagonists—to build a bloc of loyal supporters who made him a major force in local politics. Moreover, he exercised his power for the benefit of Anjō, much to the distress of Kariya's citizens, as they discovered when a school funding crisis arose in the early 1920s.

Kariya's educational system had long been a source of local pride. Already in the mid-nineteenth century, samurai and selected *chōnin* sons pursued a rudimentary formal education in the Bunreikan, a private school staffed by retainers who stressed Confucian learning. Following the Restoration, the Bunreikan became the foundation for Kijō School, Kariya's oldest elementary institution. Several persons mentioned in previous chapters were among the one hundred students who pursued the four-year course at Kijō in its first decade of operation. When six years of education became compulsory in 1886, Kariya moved to keep abreast of change by establishing a higher elementary school next door to Kijō, the first in the county. By 1894 over six hundred students attended Kariya's

[16] For Okada see Kichiji Shōichi, *Okada Kikujirō den* (Anjō, 1954), pp. 1-40.

schools. They included two in every three of the community's school-age children, a rate well above the national average.[17]

Kariya maintained its interest in education into the twentieth century. Getting wind of plans in 1917 for a new middle school in Aichi, several local citizens began to promote Kariya's location. Handa and Nishio were the first choices, but Kariya would not be outdone. Local leaders pressured politicians, imposed on prefectural officials, and finally visited the Minister of Education himself. In 1918 he gave them permission to establish a new middle school, providing advanced education for 600 boys from the town and its vicinity. This school was barely completed when the mayor formed a committee to study the establishment of a girls' school. Having just raised a large sum of money to build the boys' school, local officials hesitated to undertake another construction program so quickly. They won approval from the Ministry of Education, however, and in 1921 a general higher school for 400 girls set up temporary quarters at Kijō. Having nearly exhausted the town treasury to build the boys' school, the community soon found itself short of funds for this one. There emerged a financial crisis which took four years to resolve.[18]

Such a crisis was not unusual, for financial problems were endemic to small Japanese communities. The obvious tax sources—property, income, enterprises, brewing—were tapped by the central government, whose subsidies for industries, armies and navies required immense revenues. Towns were restricted by law to one modest source of revenue—a house tax—with which to execute the limited but costly tasks they had to undertake. Among these education was the most important. National laws required that each local entity provide an elementary education for all of its school-age children; that it finance construction, maintenance, and operation of all facilities; and that it pay all teachers' salaries.[19] By the turn of the century such expenses absorbed over half the budget in many Japanese towns and villages. Without increased financial support, there was a threat of deterioration in educational quality. Perceiving this, the Ministry of Education sought and won funds with which to subsidize teachers' salaries, and other funds with which to provide assistance to schools in dire need of money. The latter were allocated by the Ministry to prefectural governors and were disbursable only with the Ministry's approval. Some of these funds were frequently distributed, through county governments, to local communities for support of higher girls' schools. By 1921 county governments were underwriting 55 percent of the expenses in

[17] *Kariya chō shi* (Kariya, 1894), Education Section.
[18] The following account is based on: Kss, pp. 718–721; Aichi ken gikai jimu kyoku, ed., *Aichi ken gikai shi*, 7 vols. (Nagoya, 1953–1973), 5:317–324, 739–758; and Takekasa Keisuke, *Aichi kenritsu Kariya kōtō jogakkō jisshūnen kinen* (Nagoya, 1931).
[19] Mombushō, *Gakusei nanajūnen shi* (Tokyo, 1942), pp. 136–137.

such schools.[20] When the counties were abolished as administrative entities with budgets in that year, many towns had to find new funds for their girls' schools.

Kariya's financial crisis stemmed from this loss of county revenues. Originally, the county had provided about 50 percent of the costs of construction for the new school. Community contributions had provided another 10 percent, but a large deficit remained, equal in size to the total town budget in 1920. A first solution was tried. House taxes, about ¥7 annually in 1920, were suddenly hiked to ¥40 per year. At that time artisans and factory laborers in Nagoya earned on the average about ¥1.5 per day; Kariya's new house tax might thus have absorbed one month's salary for a normal worker.[21] The burdens created by this tax were too onerous, and town leaders looked to the prefecture for financing, as a means of reducing the school's cost to the community.

When the counties were abolished, prefectural governments assumed many of their duties, among them financial assistance to local education. In Aichi Prefecture, the governor (a Seiyūkai member) recommended in 1921 that thirteen higher schools (seven former county schools and six community schools) be transferred to prefectural jurisdiction. The Kariya school was one of these thirteen. The governor's recommendations were reviewed by an assembly committee, composed of eleven Seiyūkai and four Kenseikai members. This committee excluded the Kariya school, substituting instead a girls' school in neighboring Anjō which had been founded in the same year as the Kariya school. In October 1922, the committee's report was approved and Kariya was left without prefectural assistance.

It was obvious that the community needed an effective spokesman in the prefectural assembly. In September 1923, local residents united around the candidacy of Ōno Ichizō. Following in his father's footsteps as a Seiyūkai party member, Ōno took office with a popular mandate to win prefectural jurisdiction for the girls' school. Given the large Seiyūkai majority in the assembly at the time, success seemed probable. After all, Seiyūkai members numbered twenty-nine in a body of forty-nine, and party votes were decisive in settling school issues. Unfortunately, Okada Kikujirō, also a Seiyūkai member but a more powerful one, obstructed this solution. He wanted only one girls' school in Hekikai, the one in Anjō.

Difficulties with Okada were compounded by party politics—local and national—in 1924. In January of that year, the national Seiyūkai (at that time the ruling party) split, leading to the creation six months later of a new ruling coalition and a Kenseikai government. Okada entered the successor of the Seiyūkai, but Ōno Ichizō did not. He joined the Kenseikai instead, due to Kariya's support of Taketomi Sai. Shortly after the

[20] Mombushō, *Nihon teikoku mombushō daiyonjūkyū nempō* (Tokyo, 1921), p. 347.
[21] Aichi ken, *Aichi ken shi*, 4:728.

Seiyūkai split, Taketomi Sai declared his Diet candidacy on the Kenseikai ticket. Aided by a unanimous local consensus based on community pride and built with the money and skills of party organizers, Taketomi won his Diet seat in the May election. Kariya's voters had thus—within an eight-month period—returned a Seiyūkai candidate to the prefectural assembly but a Kenseikai candidate to the Diet. This suggests the extent of popular indifference to party affiliations, and bespeaks the importance of personal, group, and community considerations for the voter. Politicians themselves, however, were differently affected by party labels. Ōno had to change his party as a result of Taketomi's victory, out of deference to his seniority and his higher office, and because Taketomi had now made Kariya a political base for the Kenseikai.

Given the Kenseikai association, Ōno and Taketomi were in a new position to bargain over the school issue. Party government meant party appointees, and Aichi soon had a Kenseikai governor. In December 1924, he presented a bill recommending transfer of the Kariya girls' school to prefectural jurisdiction. The assembly (still controlled by the Seiyūkai adherents) rejected the proposal in a vote that followed party lines, now drawn tightly against Ōno in retaliation for his switch. The governor ordered a re-vote, but that also failed; the prefectural budget was passed without appropriation of funds for the Kariya school. Undaunted, the governor—at Taketomi's instigation—petitioned the Home and Finance Ministries for additional funds for its support. An official of the Ministry of Education, who was a personal friend of Taketomi and a Kenseikai Diet member from Aichi, assisted the governor in negotiations with the other ministries. As a result, the Home Ministry ordered that funds be granted for the operation of the Kariya school, which on March 6, 1925, became a prefectural institution. Assembly opponents threatened further political action in the assembly, but abandoned their plans when the governor made ¥3,000 available to them for an "observational trip" to China.

As a representative case, this issue reveals significant aspects of the political process in prewar Kariya. Notable is the relative passivity of public involvement. The public played no role in promoting the school, in determining its operation, or in solving the problems it created. Residents were probably lukewarm to the original proposal, sensing that it might lead to higher taxes and realizing that only the wealthiest families could send their daughters there.[22] Once established, the school operated under national laws with county funds, its personnel, curriculum, textbooks, and expenses beyond local control. Even when the costs of the school burdened many local citizens greatly, they did not take political action. Only once, when they deferentially supported the leaders' candidate for the prefectu-

---

[22] In fact, during its first decade of operation, only 20 percent of the student body was from Kariya *machi* and a mere 8 percent from the villages.

ral assembly, did the public play a role in this issue. After the problem was moved to the prefectural assembly, the public was incapable of influencing its outcome.

Public disinterest was attributable in large part to the weak powers of local government. The community was the least powerful unit in a hierarchy culminating with the central government, where ultimate decision-making powers usually rested. Kariya itself had little say in the founding or the operation of the school. The Ministry of Education granted permission for its creation, appointed its teachers, defined its curriculum, and authorized its textbooks. The community was obliged by law to provide operating expenses, but its inability to expand revenues forced it to rely first on county and later prefectural funds for assistance. In the end, even these funds came from the central government, through a ministry which was subject to manipulation by knowledgeable and well-placed politicians, but virtually free from the interference of public pressure or demands.

Such politicians, occupying executive positions, played the major role in the school issue. The town mayor appointed the deliberative body which proposed that the school be constructed. He initiated talks with county officials, who granted subsidies under executive authority. The prefectural governor tried to resolve the Kariya problem on several occasions by introducing favorable bills in the assembly. Rebuffed, he circumvented assembly opposition by appealing to national ministries. There, bureaucrats issued a final decision, exempt from public scrutiny but open to party influence. At all levels, this issue reveals how final decision-making power inhered in executive—rather than popular, representative—organs of the Japanese polity during the prewar years.

Kariya's school crisis casts light on another aspect of local politics in prewar Japan. The incident reveals clearly how the system of government laid down in the Meiji constitution shaped the contours of local political action. Limited resources and scant taxing authority obliged communities to turn to the state when they encountered financial problems, or when they undertook a major public project. At such times, a community found itself in competition with others for the scarce resources which the state distributed. Such competition occurred on two occasions in Kariya during this period. The first instance involved the boys' school, when Kariya competed successfully against Nishio and Handa. The second instance concerned the girls' school, when Kariya struggled against Anjō to win external funding for its school. This kind of competition characterizes politics of the pork barrel in many societies. But in prewar Japan it was especially pronounced. Legal codes and financial dependence kept communities subservient to the state. Under such conditions, political struggle was not a contest conducted among groups within a town for resources allocated by the local government; political struggle was a competition among communities for the scarce resources distributed by the state.

Victory in such a contest required access to executive decision makers. A community acquired such access by relying on politicians whose contacts, influence, and knowledge made them effective negotiators. Their contacts may have stemmed from college days, when they attended university with men who later moved into important bureaucratic posts. Their influence depended on their patrons and their patrons' power. Their knowledge was a product of experience, often acquired in the bureaucracy itself. A man like Taketomi provided all of these capabilities: he was a graduate of Tokyo University, which trained most government officials; he had influential patrons in the party to which he belonged; and his own years at the Justice Ministry gave him experience in the bureaucracy. It was advantageous for a community to have a man such as Taketomi represent it in the Diet.

Some communities attached themselves to such men with ease; others did not. During the 1920s, for example, Nishio consistently split its vote among many contestants, never delivering more than a quarter or a third of its votes to one man. Other communities were able to marshall virtually unanimous support behind a single candidate. Kariya and Anjō always gave one candidate more than 80 percent of their votes. This made them more effective in inter-community competitions. By nurturing the loyalties between a candidate and his *jiban* and by insuring long tenure in office, Kariya and Anjō attracted representatives adept at bargaining for their advantage.

The requirements of electoral politics thus made community solidarity imperative. In elections at the prefectural and national level, voters tried to unite behind a solid front to elect the candidate of their community. This maximized their political effectiveness. A community could simply not harbor divisions which would be reflected in electoral politics. That would weaken its appeal for strong candidates and erode its ability to support effective representatives. Community solidarity was a must. This in turn had two significant implications for political behavior.

First, loyalty to a community superceded loyalty to a political party. Earlier pages have described the social bonds which tied a *jiban* together: family, kinship, friendship, membership, and occupational relations; money and status. None of those, with the exception of money, hinged on an identity or association with a political party. Rather, those bonds gravitated out of social relationships based on mutual obligation and dependency. For example, a tenant depended economically on his landlord and was obliged to follow his advice, or a shop clerk was deferential to his manager and out of a sense of obligation obeyed his wishes. Those relationships were non-political, but during elections, they were exploited for political purposes. By a process of downward diffusion, men in the highest social positions passed word of their political wishes through the entire hierarchy of local society. Thus, the mayor told his friend the landlord that it was essential to back candidate X in this election; the landlord in turn passed this information to his tenant, who received it as a kind of obligatory advice. As long as the leading influentials shared agreement concerning a candidacy, they could mobilize an entire community behind a single candidate. Kariya did this effectively throughout the 1920s.

It is critical to bear in mind that mobilization occurred through social channels controlled by local influentials. There were no purely political networks, no bases of support rooted in an identity with a party. On the contrary, the parties themselves worked through the local influentials who—for social and economic reasons—controlled political supporters. Parties had no offices and no activists on the local scene, nor did they establish at the local level new structures of political influence. Rather, they accommodated themselves to existing circles of influence. Thus, during the alleged heyday of the parties in the 1920s, they were actually taking no root at all in the social foundations of the Japanese polity. Voters thought first of solid community support for their candidate. Once he was elected, then they could use the parties for what they were: agencies facilitating contact with the political center.

Second, it goes without saying that voters placed a low premium on issues in any campaign. Issues simply disappeared in a misty vapor of pleas and promises. What mattered was one's candidate, his experience, his contacts, and his tenure in office. Contacts and experience were a function of his status, so status assumed paramount importance in any political contest. This helps to explain why during the 1920s, when liberalism and democracy were alleged to have been at their height, so many communities elected men to office who represented historical ruling circles. It was simply good political sense to send someone like Ōno Ichizō to deal with prefectural or national officials. His pedigree, his training, and his experience conformed to the social traits of the men in the bureaucracy with whom he would deal. A fishmonger from Sakana-machi would not have fared nearly so well. Thus, at a time when the rhetoric of politics was moving in a more "democratic" direction, the realities of politics kept local communities enmeshed in the past.

The backgrounds of political figures in Aichi communities during the 1920s illustrate the hold which the past was exercising over political life. In Kariya, Ōno Ichizō's growing dominance in local affairs attests to the appreciation of status as a requirement for political office. This was also true at lower levels. Both of Kariya's mayors in the 1920s fit the mold of

historical leadership. Katō Itsuhei, mayor between 1923 and 1928, was the
head of a landowning family in Oyama which had long exercised political
influence in that village. Ino Naoji, mayor after 1928, was the scion of a
landowning merchant house in the old castletown. Like their predecessors,
they assumed office by virtue of status, age and experience, after a long
apprenticeship on the town council. During this period, the town council
also continued to draw its members from the same families who had been
sitting on it since the 1890s. Even in 1928, in the first election held after
the grant of universal manhood suffrage, a larger proportion of incumbents returned to office than ever before.[23] Democracy of the type
proclaimed by liberals in Tokyo during the 1920s did not take root as a
result of universal manhood suffrage. Broadening the vote merely extended the support for ruling political groups ever deeper into the body
politic.

In this regard, Kariya did not differ greatly from the communities
around it. In Koromo, Anjō, and Handa, the 1920s witnessed a
comparable continuity in the social attributes of political leaders. In
Koromo, the mayor for nearly half the period between 1908 and 1929 was
a man named Usami. He was the third son of a former councillor (karō) in
the Koromo domain and he served as the local postmaster, a fitting office
for a samurai descendant. In Anjō, Okada Kikujirō was mayor for all but
four years during the 1920s. The member of a founding family in a town
which had only emerged after 1890, he enjoyed in Anjō the kind of
privileged social status which accrued to landlords or samurai descendants
in towns such as Kariya and Koromo.[24]

But continuity in leadership ranks was most striking in Handa. As a
port town, handicraft center, and farming settlement, Handa's leading
families for some generations had been merchants and landlords. Two of
the town's most prominent families were the Nakano house, of which there
were six branches, and the Oguri house, related by marriage and descent
to the Nakano lineage. In the four decades before 1930, five of the ten
mayors in Handa were members of the Nakano house and another two
were members of the Oguri house. Together, they governed Handa politics
for thirty-four of the forty-one years between 1889 and 1931.

The two families based their claim to political office on a profound
economic domination of the community. They owned large amounts of
land, warehouses, and a local railroad; they operated a large vinegar
distillery and a number of banks; and they controlled a major interest in a
beer brewery and the town's largest spinning factory. Both the Nakano

[23] Kcs, pp. 41–44.
[24] Materials are simply too poor to permit an assessment of local political leaders in Nishio
in the first decades of this century. For Usami see Chōjō Tomichika, ed., *Aichi ken shichōson
jinshi roku* (Nagoya, 1929), p. 37.

and the Oguri families had been prominent brewers, traders, and shippers in Handa since the early nineteenth century. Handa thus represented a case in which industrialization focused political control directly in the hands of industrial magnates. This was a fairly rare occurrence in Japan. It only arose in Handa because of the long-standing prominence of, and the nature of investments by, the Nakano and Oguri families. The point to be made here, however, is that Handa witnessed the same continuity of local leadership which other nearby communities did in the 1920s.[25]

This chapter has now related the early history of the industrial organization which dominated Kariya's economy after 1922, tracing its origins under Sakichi's direction, its development during the 1910s, and its subsequent expansion into Kariya. The chapter has also presented a discussion of local politics, which focused on important leaders at the local and Diet levels, on the methods of electoral politics, and on the process of decision making and political competition in local communities. It is now possible to carry out the final task of the chapter, which is to examine the specific influence of industry on social and political life in Kariya.

The industrialism which Toyota ushered in had by 1930 wrought significant changes in local society. Together, the loom factory, the spinning mill, and the spinning and weaving establishment employed 2,346 workers.[26] Their arrival radically altered the make-up of the local work force. The number of manufacturing jobs in town tripled during the 1920s; the number of jobs in commerce and the services doubled. By 1930 farmers comprised only three in every ten workers, while clerks, shopkeepers, teachers, officials, dentists, lawyers and others added another three. The remaining four in ten workers were industrial laborers. In one important way, the *machi* had assumed the mark of an industrial town.

Rapid industrial expansion stimulated a visible increase in population mobility.[27] Mobile populations had long characterized cities undergoing swift economic change, as Nagoya had been at the end of the nineteenth century. (See chapter 2.) Mobility became even more pronounced in the twentieth century. This was especially the case in textile towns such as Handa, where in 1920 two in three workers were mill hands or factory operatives. In that year only 32 percent of the town's population was native-born. By 1930, when the textile industry was in retreat in Handa, the rate of native-born residents had risen above 40 percent, a proportion common in industrial centers. In 1930 Kariya was approaching that mark,

[25] Handa shi, *Handa shi shi*, 3:881 and 395–570.
[26] Kcs, pp. 207–225.
[27] The following discussion of demographic and occupational changes in Aichi is based on an analysis of: Naikaku tōkei kyoku, *Kokusei chōsa hōkoku: 1920;* Naikaku tōkei kyoku, *Kokusei chōsa hōkoku: 1930, Aichi ken* (Tokyo, 1933).

for less than half the people in town were native-born, by contrast with more than two-thirds only a decade earlier. Thus, as Kariya industrialized, more outsiders arrived in town. Some found secure jobs and settled permanently. Others, however, lived in Kariya for only a few months, or a few years, then moved on. As a result, people began to flow both in and out of this once very stable community in greater numbers than ever before.

Mobility fed rapid population growth. For the preceding half-century, Kariya had been a dormant rural town which experienced virtually no population growth. In the 1920s that changed suddenly. While the national population expanded by 15 percent, the Kariya (city area) population grew more than 30 percent to exceed 31,000. Even more dramatic was the sharp growth within the town proper, where population shot up 71 percent, from 8,648 to 14,779. In one short decade, Kariya became one of the fastest growing settlements in Japan. Only Kawasaki among Japan's 114 cities (in 1930) grew faster in the 1920s. In Aichi Prefecture, Kariya's rate of growth outstripped Nagoya's, which itself expanded nearly 50 percent; it outpaced growth in Anjō, Nishio, and Koromo by three to seven times; and it offered a dramatic contrast to Handa, where population dropped 5 percent in the 1920s. Kariya *machi* was still smaller than these communities, but it was moving briskly to catch up.

Toyota's arrival was helping Kariya catch up industrially, too. By 1930 it had nearly the same percentage of industrial workers as Nagoya and Handa. For a decade or more, some 40 percent of the workers in those towns had been industrial laborers; now Kariya had reached that level. Moreover, Kariya had developed a structure of business and industry which was equal or superior to those in nearby communities. Koromo could boast of only one large factory in 1930, a silk filature capitalized at ¥500,000 which employed about two hundred local girls. Nishio had a few more factories, but the largest was a weaving shed employing less than one hundred workers with a capital of only ¥200,000. Handa's industrial fortunes rested with its modern brewery, its food processors (vinegar, soy sauce), and a single, giant spinning firm. The latter fell on bad times in the 1920s, and with it fell the town. Anjō, too, its three major factories' silk reelers, suffered badly by 1931. By contrast, Kariya now had three major factories. Each was capitalized at ¥1 million or more and together they employed over two thousand workers. Kariya also had the Mikawa Railway headquarters, which employed another six hundred workers. The older brick and tile makers as well as the sake breweries still remained in business. And there was finally the Ōta family. It presided over a group of companies, with a combined capital nearing ¥1 million, engaged in commerce, real estate, paper making, and money lending. In the 1920s Kariya took a firm step toward its industrial future.[28]

Kariya's industrial progress ran contrary to general economic trends, because the 1920s were years of recession. For the most part, growth rates declined, expansion ceased and stagnation ensued.[29] Toyota countered those trends for two reasons. First, despite a general decline in the value of all foreign trade in the 1920s, the Toyota enterprise was able to find an overseas market for its products. The new loom factory produced about seventeen thousand looms between 1926 and 1931; one-fourth of them were exported. Second, even though industrial expansion slowed, a program of rationalization in the textile industry created a demand for the advanced Toyota looms. They were more expensive than those of their competitors, ¥600 in contrast to ¥200, but they were far more efficient in the use of labor. One industry publication estimated that a factory operating 1,000 automatic looms could get by with less than 200 workers, while one employing conventional looms would require 850 workers.[30] Given the consistently higher quality of the finished product, it is little wonder that Toyota was able to sell its looms regularly, even in the 1920s. Thus, as Toyota's sales rose, so did the economic fortunes of this Mikawa town.

It must have been an awkward looking little place in 1931. The first thing to catch the eye as the train pulled into town was a series of factories laid out along the tracks. The Toyota works was a low-lying mass of long, wooden barracks, slung along the horizon beyond the eastern edge of town. Nearby were the Tōyō brick firm and the tile factory, their smokestacks piercing the flat skyline. The town itself still clustered densely some distance away. With the construction of new buildings it was creeping ever closer to the factory area, but it had yet to close the gap. Within the town, the road system was a maze; not even one straight road ran north through town to Nagoya. This was annoying for only a few, however, since there were only eight cars in town during the entire decade. One of those was unfortunately eliminated when a curious traveler came upon it in the dark, mired in a rice paddy, and lit a match to see what the matter was![31]

Parochialism was a standard feature of the community. A teacher recalled how depressed he had been at his first sight of Kariya when he arrived to take up his job in the new middle school.[32] He was appalled by

[28] Sakano Kenjirō, ed., *Aichi ken kaisha sōran* (Nagoya, 1935).

[29] See Hugh Patrick, "The Economic Muddle of the 1920s," in James W. Morley, ed., *Dilemmas of Growth in Prewar Japan* (Princeton, 1971).

[30] *40-nen shi*, pp. 118–120.

[31] Katō Bunzaburō, *Aru shōgai* (Kariya, 1968), p. 84.

[32] Adachi Muneharu, *Aichi ken Kariya chūgakkō kaikō jisshūnen kinen* (Kariya, 1928).

the health standards at the local bath, but he was pleasantly surprised by
the school itself, which sat in solitary splendor amidst rice paddies well
away from town. A student of his remembered that he had never had
Western-style shoes before entering the new middle school, and even then
he preferred carrying them in his hands to wearing them on his feet. Most
of his friends still wore clogs and Japanese-style clothes, as did most of the
townspeople. Ōno Ichizō was one of the few men who made it a practice to
wear a Western suit during the 1920s. On the whole, Kariya must have
put forward a rather rustic appearance in that decade, especially by
contrast with the nation's cities.

In keeping with its rustic appearance, other aspects of social behavior in
Kariya persisted. Most notably, a small group of families continued to
dominate social leadership in the community. Inherited family status was
perhaps the most important factor behind their position. People in the
town continued to look with great favor on old-line families which had
long played a leading role in local affairs. Thus, descendants of the Ōno
and Odani families (whose ancestors had been councillors in the domain)
and the Shishido family (whose ancestors had been the lord's personal
physicians) were able to assume positions of leadership during the 1920s in
political life, on the Enterprise Council, and in the Kariya Samurai
Society. The only group which they did not dominate was the Imperial
Reservists' Association, which in Kariya clearly attracted a lower social
following. Increasingly, talent was becoming an ingredient of leadership.
But the old-line families had the resources and leisure to see to it that their
descendants measured up on this count, too. Ōno Ichizō studied at Tokyo's
best technical institute; Shishido Shunji, at the medical school at Tokyo
University. Obviously, wealth was also a factor which determined a
family's prestige, but at this point it was a facilitating agent, not the
primary measure.

Status, talent, and wealth were the criteria for leadership in Kariya, but
they could not have guaranteed continuity without the practice of two
important social customs among the leading social groups: adoption and
intermarriage. Adoption was a social device used to ameliorate biological
fate. Many leading families did not have their own sons, but they acquired
them by marrying their daughters to talented young men who were
adopted as heirs. This is precisely what the Shishido family did. They
adopted a young man from the village of Yosami named Utsunomiya
Shunji. He was bright enough to win entry to the best preparatory school
and university in the country. He returned home eventually to open a
medical practice and brought continued fame to the Shishido house as an
officer of the Samurai Society, a member of the town council, a
vice-president of the prefectural medical society, and president of the
Kariya Enterprise Council. Adoption thus enabled a family to continue its

role in local affairs without threat of biological interruption. It was also a promising avenue of upward social mobility for young men of talent, as well as a device for lifting the sagging fortunes of a once-prominent family.

Adoption was actually one aspect of intermarriage, a social custom employed to keep the circle of status tightly controlled. Intermarriage took place among prominent families within the community. For example, Okamoto Hirotarō (townsman, sake brewer, twon mayor) married his daughter to Asai Kinji (samurai, physician, President of the Kariya Samurai Society). Intermarriage also tied families of high status in Kariya to those of similar status in outside communities. Thus, Odani Jōya (samurai, physician) married the daughter of the mayor of a town across the bay from Kariya. Leading families in the community relied heavily on adoption and intermarriage to regulate access to the circle of prominence in Kariya. This enabled them to perpetuate their social and political leadership over local society. The first decade of industrialization did nothing to shake their position.

The first decade of industrialization also did little to alter local political behavior. Men from old-line families continued to occupy leadership positions in local politics, while the mores of electoral behavior persisted. In contrast with the town of Handa, industrial magnates did not assume political leadership in the community. In fact, the Toyota enterprise remained quite aloof from local political affairs. Although the firm was actively engaged in the local economy by the time the funding crisis reached a peak, there is no evidence that the company or its workers played a role in the problem. Nor, during this period, did the company designate candidates for political office or overtly support candidates who worked for the company. It appears from the scant data which survive that Toyota took virtually no interest in local politics during the 1920s.[33]

There are several reasons for Toyota's lack of involvement in the school issue. It was at worst hostile to, at best, indifferent to, the creation of a higher girls' school. Advanced training for women clashed with management's view of textile workers. They preferred young girls who were politically docile. They did not want more, and possibly brighter, girls who were postponing their entry into the labor market. With such a view in mind, Toyota might have worked behind the scenes with its sympathizers to scuttle plans for the school, but there is no evidence that it did. Even if it had wished to do so, the company could not have spoken out publicly in opposition. That would have risked the opposition of the whole community, which was obviously dedicated to better schools. Toyota had no intention of doing that, at a time when it needed community support in order to purchase more cheap land.

[33] The Toyota enterprise played no direct role in the government of Koromo either during the prewar period, according to the findings in Nihon jimbun kagaku kai, *Gijutsu kakushin no shakaiteki eikyō* (Tokyo, 1963), pp. 252-253.

The company's newness and its absentee character played a part in its political position, too. In 1924 the Kariya factory employed a few middle-level managers, some technicians, and several hundred female operatives. The girls were of course outside the political process, so would not have participated under any circumstances. The managers and technicians were too new to have been absorbed into local political networks. The aloofness of the firm, which closed out local investors, and its primary location in Nagoya also worked to keep it out of local affairs. It is not surprising, therefore, that Toyota did not play a role in the school issue.

While these factors explain why the Toyota enterprise did not participate in a specific political incident in the 1920s, they provide no explanation for its general political posture. For this there are three explanations, having to do with Sakichi's ideas, the local tax structure, and the goals of the enterprise. As a practical policy, Toyota eschewed political involvement. Toyota Sakichi himself instilled this approach. He was an inventor, pure and simple, and he felt that politics and economics should be separate endeavors. His injunction worked to keep the company out of local politics. The tax structure of local communities in prewar Japan also worked to dissuade firms from political involvement. There were no heavy taxes on fixed capital assets, so Toyota did not face anxieties about local projects which might raise taxes and cut profits. Finally, Toyota was intent on maintaining a low posture to preserve what it valued most highly in the community: cheap land and abundant labor. It was probably not eager to see the town undertake efforts to lure in other firms, because a prospering community meant higher prices and costlier land when plant expansion was undertaken. As long as it could attract workers and produce at a low overhead, the Toyota enterprise was content with the local situation. For all these reasons, the Toyota concern maintained a low political profile in Kariya. During its first decade, good will and the status quo were its most valuable properties.

One decade of industrialization left only a small imprint on the community of Kariya. The greatest changes were a rise in the number of new jobs, an expansion in business activity, a sharp increase in movement in and out of town, and a dramatic growth in population. While all this was taking place, however, old-line families preserved a comfortable continuity in their dominance over local affairs. This was especially true in the political arena, where the head of the Ōno house assumed a major role during the 1920s. He also served as Kariya's agent in dealing with Toyota and its managers. Working closely with Risaburō, Ōno Ichizō created a pattern of association in which Toyota dealt at the top with leading influentials who mediated for it on the local scene. This insured its respectability and made its presence in town welcome. Staying aloof from both community and political affairs, Toyota concerned itself with business matters. In 1931 it was—as the raw appearance of its factories beyond the eastern edge of town symbolized—an appendage to the community, distant in a physical, political, and psychological sense. This would change entirely in the next thirteen years, however, as the following chapter reveals.

5

A DESIGN ON THE FUTURE,
1932–1945

Far more than historians have yet demonstrated, key aspects of postwar Japanese society took shape during the 1930s. Perhaps the most fundamental change to emerge out of that period was a strong emphasis on rational, comprehensive planning at the national level. The central government had played the major role in determining national policies since the Meiji Restoration, of course, but in the war period central planning assumed a new level of intensity. After 1937 officials formalized central planning by establishing agencies which systematically controlled and distributed the nation's resources. Postwar bodies, such as the Economic Planning Agency and the Ministry of International Trade and Industry, carry on the practices implemented during the war years. They symbolize a legacy of planning which stems directly from the 1930s. In the absence of that legacy, Japan's postwar economic history would certainly have followed a different path.

There are other ways in which the 1930s set the stage for this postwar era. During that decade Japan developed an industrial structure which differed markedly from the preceding one. Japan ceased being a nation of textile mills and weaving sheds and became in a short period a land of shipyards, munitions factories, vehicle makers, and chemical plants. This change in its industrial structure anticipated the path of postwar economic growth. In the new firms and factories which grew during the 1930s, young executives managing new plants or new divisions earned invaluable experience. They put this experience to work after 1945, when they rose to the top of the managerial hierarchy in command of entire enterprises. In their activities during the 1930s they developed habits and relationships which would also follow them into the postwar world. They learned how to deal with administrative guidance from the central government; they learned how to develop and utilize new technology in new organizations; and they learned how to use cartels to engage in the delicate task of export marketing. Out of the 1930s came economic institutions and practices which have been at the center of the postwar economy.

Economics was not the only sphere in which prominent postwar figures developed their abilities. Many postwar political leaders established themselves in important positions during the war years. Sometimes they began as elected politicians, creating a base in their local district or inheriting a mature *jiban* from an elder politician. Miki Takeo, a leading figure in the postwar Liberal-Democratic Party, was just one who followed this path. In other cases, ambitious young men laid a foundation for a later political career with their work in central ministries. Kishi Nobusuke began as an official in the Ministry of Commerce and Agriculture. He quickly worked his way to the top of the new Ministry of Commerce, then into a cabinet seat under the Tōjō government. Within eight years of his release from prison, where he served as a Class A War Criminal, he became president of a united conservative party and ascended to the post of Prime Minister. Many of Kishi's friends and colleagues were men who rose to political prominence through similar channels. By virtue of their careers, practices, and personalities, they formed a strong link of continuity between prewar and postwar Japan.

The 1930s set the stage for the postwar era at the local level, as well as the national. After 1937 the Toyota enterprise underwent vast changes which produced the industrial empire that dominated the postwar economy of Kariya and western Mikawa. Wartime expansion also drew together the social forces which would determine the shape of postwar political action. During the 1930s the leading politicians in the community and the region built bases of electoral support which endured into the postwar era. At the same time, a group of managers at Toyota acquired valuable executive experience which enhanced their social standing in Kariya and propelled them to the forefront of community affairs after the war.

This chapter presents an analysis of the political and economic history of Kariya and its region during the years between 1932 and 1945. It illustrates how people earned a living, how they behaved politically, and how war affected them. But the primary purpose of this chapter is to interpret the war years as a prelude to the postwar world. For this reason, attention focuses on three subjects: the rapid development of heavy industry, the pattern of labor-management relations, and the alignment of local political forces. During the war years a dramatic alteration occurred in the structure of Aichi's industrial economy and of the Toyota enterprise. There also developed a pattern of relations between workers and managers which established a strong claim on the allegiance of Japanese laborers. That pattern of relations declined momentarily after the war, but it revived to exert significant influence later. Finally, during the war years subtle changes occurred in the social foundations of local politics which would have an important bearing on postwar political life. This chapter treats these three subjects in some detail, in order to illuminate how wartime alterations shaped postwar society.[1]

In comparison with other countries, Japan industrialized very quickly. She telescoped into less than a century economic developments which Britain required a century or more to carry out. Nonetheless, industry was slow to dominate the Japanese economy in the prewar era. In 1930 fully one-half of the labor force still found employment in agriculture. Manufacturing had expanded dramatically since the late 1890s, and especially during the First World War, but there were still less than 6 million industrial laborers in a work force of 30 million, barely one in five. Moreover, a little less than half of the manufacturing workers were located in just seven of the nation's forty-seven prefectures. Vast areas of the country still had no modern factories at all. They relied on farming and fishing to sustain their economies. Although Aichi Prefecture had long since shed its economic reliance on agriculture, a large portion of its residents still farmed and fished in 1930. They numbered about four in every ten workers and formed the largest segment of the labor force. But against that agrarian background, the prefecture's industrial economy had become one of the largest in the country.

Aichi enjoyed a secure position among the seven prefectures which dominated Japanese industry in the early 1930s. It ranked third after Tokyo and Osaka in the number of manufacturing workers. The prefecture was especially active in the handicraft and light industrial sectors. It had more persons engaged in pottery and tile manufacture and more operatives in the textile industry than any other prefecture. Its workers in the food processing and lumber industries ranked third behind only Tokyo and Osaka. It had been slow to develop a heavy industrial capacity, but by 1930 its workers in precision metals ranked fourth in the nation; its machine and vehicle workers, fifth. Having been among the country's major industrial areas as early as the Restoration, Aichi maintained that position largely unchanged for six decades thereafter.[2]

Industry within the prefecture was heavily concentrated in old Owari. Nearly half (44 percent) of Aichi's manufacturing workers were located in Nagoya. Another 16 percent found work in four cities of Toyohashi,

[1] As this chapter is written (in 1973), no social history of Japan in the 1930s exists in English yet and woefully few exist in Japanese. Proper materials for the period are distressingly scant. When found, they are unduly fragmented or overly general. This chapter is thus only a tentative analysis based largely on materials from Aichi Prefecture. I hope, however, that it casts the 1930s in a new light. The time has come to stop viewing events between 1932 and 1945 as irrational aberrations which came to a sudden halt with Japan's surrender. Instead, we should begin viewing those years as an integral and enduring part of Japan's historical experience.

[2] Naikaku tōkei kyoku, *Kokusei chōsa hōkoku: 1930* (Tokyo, 1933), 1:152–153.

Okazaki, Ichinomiya, and Seto. The remaining 40 percent were scattered throughout the rest of the prefecture, clustered for the most part in textile towns such as Handa or pottery towns such as Takahama. About eighteen thousand industrial workers resided in Hekikai County. They comprised only two out of every ten laborers, six of whom in the county were still farmers. These industrial workers were, moreover, heavily concentrated in a few towns; nearly half of them resided in Takahama, Kariya and Anjō. They engaged mainly in the pottery trades, textile production, and machine manufacture. At the beginning of the period covered in this chapter, therefore, Aichi was still a heavily agrarian prefecture which ranked among the most industrialized areas in the country. There were pockets of industry scattered among rural towns, but most factories were in Nagoya and the other cities. Finally, the textile trades continued to dominate the industrial economy of the prefecture, as they had for decades.[3]

During the 1930s Aichi's industrial economy experienced a radical alteration. The number of factories in the prefecture nearly doubled, many of the new ones rising in small towns well away from Nagoya rather than in the city or its suburbs. The number of factory workers more than doubled, bringing industrial jobs abreast of farming as the mainstay of employment. And, finally, the nominal value of industrial production almost quadrupled. In rate and magnitude, these changes outpaced any which had occurred in the prefecture's industrial economy before.[4]

There also took place over that decade a thoroughgoing alteration in the structure of Aichi industry. Tables 1 and 2 illustrate this graphically. From the perspective of labor, the traditional employments lost their importance. Textile workers found virtually no new jobs after 1937. Stagnant demand, coupled with the scuttling of textile equipment for the war effort, put a ceiling on expansion in that industry. The pottery trades added a second fifteen thousand workers during the war, but they declined in relative importance. Beside these once active industries, there arose a massive structure for the production of machines and vehicles. Between 1933 and 1941 the number of workers in that industry expanded from a mere 25,784 to a remarkable 186,880. At the beginning of the period they had produced only a tenth of the prefecture's industrial output, but by 1941 (a year or two before their effort peaked), they accounted for 41 percent of the prefecture's factory output by value. Having surpassed the textile trades in importance, machine and vehicle manufacture rose to the position of dominance in the Aichi economy during the war period.

Between 1932 and 1945 the Aichi economy therefore moved decisively into a third phase of industrial development, assuming the form it would

[3] Naikaku tōkei kyoku, *Kokusei chōsa hōkoku: 1930, Aichi ken*, pp. 48–62.
[4] Ats: 1933, 4:28–29; and Ats: 1941, 3:1–6.

TABLE 1

FACTORY WORKERS IN AICHI PREFECTURE, 1933–1941
(PERCENTAGE, BY INDUSTRY)

Industry	1933	1937	1941
Textiles	59	47	28
Machines and metals	17	27	47
Pottery trades	12	14	10
Food processing	4	3	5
All others	8	9	10
Total	100	100	100

SOURCES: Ats:1933, 4:28–29; Ats:1937, 4:181; and Ats: 1941, 3:1–6.

TABLE 2

FACTORY OUTPUT IN AICHI PREFECTURE, 1933–1941
(PERCENTAGE OF TOTAL VALUE, BY INDUSTRY)

Industry	1933	1937	1941
Textiles	65	54	26
Machines and metals	12	19	44
Pottery trades	7	10	11
Food processing	9	7	9
All others	7	10	10
Total	100	100	100

SOURCES: Ats:1933, 4:30; Ats:1937, 4:3; and Ats:1941, 3:1–6.

take following the postwar depression. Many firms contributed to the change in Aichi's industrial structure but few played as central a role as the Toyota enterprise. An examination of developments at Toyota between 1932 and 1945 helps to illustrate the wartime processes of heavy industrialization out of which emerged the postwar economic structure of western Mikawa.[5]

At the beginning of this period, the pillars of the Toyota enterprise were two spinning and weaving concerns—in Nagoya and Shanghai—and the automatic loom factory in Kariya. Both of the spinning and weaving concerns did well financially during the sluggish interwar period. The Nagoya organization, for example, earned a substantial profit every year

[5] The following account of developments at Toyota between 1932 and 1945 relies on: 40-nen shi, pp. 114–308; and Shashi henshū iinkai, ed., *Toyota jidōsha 30-nen shi* (Toyota, 1967), pp. 1–232 (hereafter cited as *30-nen shi*).

from its founding in 1918 until its dissolution by merger in 1941. Even during the precarious depression years from 1929 to 1931, it managed to pay a dividend of 5 percent. Once the Takahashi reflation stimulated economic resurgence after 1932, profits rose, and with them dividend rates, which stood at 8 percent in 1940. Despite the vicissitudes of the industry as a whole, the Toyota textile concerns were consistently profitable operations during the 1920s and 1930s.[6]

Toyota Automatic Loom was also a profitable operation, which became even more profitable as the 1930s progressed. This firm, too, experienced difficulties in the years between 1929 and 1931, but they were never severe. Buyers at home and abroad created a steady demand for Sakichi's looms. In the decade after 1932, the firm sold nearly fifty thousand looms, 57 percent of them to domestic firms and the remaining 43 percent to foreign firms, most of them in China and India.[7] Between 1930 and 1943 the loom firm also produced spinning equipment which sold well on the domestic market. As a result, the firm never failed to turn a profit or to pay dividends. Profits at first were modest, running at ¥100,000 on annual sales of more than ¥1 million. But after the reflationary program took effect in 1933, profits moved rapidly upward. They doubled in 1933 and quadrupled in 1934. By the time the firm celebrated its tenth anniversary in 1937, gross profits for the first decade amounted to almost 16 percent of total income. In a period when the Japanese economy as a whole was sluggish, the Toyota loom firm reaped handsome profits from steady sales.[8]

The rising financial stature of the loom firm bespoke the profitability of the Toyota enterprise as a whole. When that firm was established in 1926, it was capitalized at ¥1 million, all of which was raised internally. In the following decade, Toyota Automatic Loom re-capitalized three times. In 1934 it raised its capital to ¥3 million; in 1935, to ¥6 million; and in 1936, to ¥9 million. All of this additional capital was raised internally too, primarily from the textile concerns. In 1936 the Nagoya spinning and weaving concern owned 52 percent of the stock in the loom firm and the Shanghai concern owned another 33 percent. The remaining 15 percent was divided among the original investors (mainly the Toyota and Kodama families) and one newcomer, Nishikawa Shūji, who managed the Shanghai factory.[9] Profits from its own operations plus those from the older textile concerns made Toyota Automatic Loom the core of the Toyota enterprise in 1936. But it was about to give birth to an offspring that would soon dominate the enterprise.

The offspring was of course Toyota Motors, which was born officially in

---

[6] Okamoto, *Toyota bōshoku kabushiki kaisha shi*, p. 2.
[7] *40-nen shi*, p. 701.
[8] Ibid., p. 688.
[9] Ibid., p. 693.

August of 1937.[10] Legend has it that Sakichi first broached the idea of a Toyota auto to his son Kiichirō in 1927, after an audience with the empress, as the Toyota men sat in their shirtsleeves at home and Sakichi revelled in his cups.[11] Whatever the authenticity of the legend, it is clear that Sakichi, ever since his travels to America and England in 1910, had been entranced with the automobile and its potential. He felt the time would come when Japan would have to make her own, and he thought Kiichirō should lead the way. Just as Sakichi had replaced imported textile machinery with his inventions, so his son should replace imported automobiles with his.

However romantic the notion may seem, Kiichirō's personal determination to mass produce an inexpensive automobile was one of two essential elements in the early history of Toyota Motors. Like his father, Kiichirō was a compulsive tinkerer. His training was more sophisticated than his father's—Kiichirō graduated from the College of Engineering at Tokyo University—but the impulse to invent was the same. Anything was fair game, from better spinning equipment during the precarious depression years to salt-making survival kits during the grim days of war. But he devoted his primary attention to perfecting a Japanese automobile.

Critics chided his efforts from the beginning. After all, major industrial firms such as Mitsubishi had not succeeded in making a go of auto production; how was a country enterprise like Toyota to do it? There was even opposition from within the enterprise. Oldtimers at Toyota who were dedicated to the textile industry resented the risks which Kiichirō took. They feared his expensive gamble would bring the entire organization to ruin. Nonetheless, Kiichirō persisted. He displayed the same kind of dedication which his father did, living above the shop so it would be easier to put in twenty hours a day at his work. By force of example and personality, he created a number of loyal followers who carried on for him when he resigned from the company after the war. Kiichirō never lived to see his dream achieved, but his legacy—both organizational and spiritual—to the Toyota enterprise made fulfillment of his goal possible.

There was a second, indispensable consideration which helped bring Toyota Motors to life: government policy. Government interest in automobiles dated from the turn of the century, when the armed services first recognized the value of trucks for military use. Little came of that interest until the late 1920s. By then, both Ford and General Motors had plants in Japan, and their output dominated the Japanese market. As the international situation worsened in the 1930s, the Japanese government grew anxious to replace foreign producers with a domestic auto industry.

[10] The official English name of this firm is Toyota Motor Co., Ltd. For convenience, I refer to it as Toyota Motors.

[11] Mainichi shimbun sha, ed., *Ikiru Toyota Sakichi* (Tokyo, 1971), p. 82.

This desire won political expression in the Automobile Manufacturers Enterprise Law, passed in May 1936.[12] The law slapped a ceiling on the production of cars at Ford and General Motors. With subsequent changes in import laws and tariff duties, those firms closed in 1939. The law moreover created a climate in which Japanese auto firms could grow. It stipulated that more than half the shares, capital, and rights in auto firms had to be controlled by Japanese or Japanese corporations, and that more than half the officers had to be Japanese.[13] This discouraged foreign firms from undertaking joint ventures. To prohibit such ventures entirely, however, the law decreed that only "approved" firms could produce automobiles. In September of that year the two approved firms were announced: Nissan and Toyota. As a final incentive, the government granted the two firms a five-year holiday on income and enterprise taxes and allowed them to import materials duty-free, with government approval. While Kiichirō's determination had put Toyota in this position in the first place, these regulations insured that it would flourish, at least until the end of the war.

Despite its very obvious benefits, some people at Toyota considered government protection a mixed blessing. They realized the government would interfere in purchasing, production, and marketing, and it quickly did. As the war progressed, the government assumed a larger and larger role in the decisions of the firm. This galled Kiichirō especially, because he saw the chance to pursue his dream slowly drift away from him. He was first and foremost dedicated to the completion of a mass-produced automobile sold at a low price. He preferred to pursue his goal in a capitalist system that was fiercely Darwinian in his conception. In this respect, he was much like his father, the diligent worker of humble origin overcoming all obstacles to make a personal fortune and benefit the country. There was always a tension in Sakichi between achieving personal ends and aiding his nation, and he passed the ambivalence to his son. Kiichirō knew the nation was in crisis during the 1930s and felt a genuine desire to support it as well as he could. But he never foreswore his personal goal, or the advantages of private enterprise in achieving it. Those who inherited Kiichirō's ambition shared his view in many respects.[14] Thus, even though Toyota benefitted from government control of auto production, some Toyota officials were always chary—if not openly resentful—of government interference in their affairs, even before war broke out in 1937. This suggests that the relationship between business and

[12] 30-nen shi, pp. 69–82.

[13] Toyota would establish similar restrictions on its own in the 1960s, in order to prevent loss of control due to foreign ownership of its stock.

[14] Kiichirō's ideas appear in a pamphlet, parts of which are reprinted in 40-nen shi, pp. 194–207.

government in Japan has probably never been as cozy or consenting as some would have us believe.

Toyota's involvement with auto making actually dated from 1931. Using a corner of the Toyota Automatic Loom plant, Kiichirō began by building small engines, then moved on to examine the structure of whole automobiles. One technique was to purchase imported models and disassemble them on the floor of the loom factory, learning as much as possible about their construction. His efforts moved slowly at first. They were carried out in the utmost secrecy and involved only a few trusted members of the staff. By 1933, however, the loom firm decided to establish an Automobile Department. In following years this part of the company absorbed much of the new capital which the loom firm raised. There were hardly any payoffs until 1936, when, to commemorate the tenth anniversary of the firm, Toyota displayed five of its new trucks at an auto show in Tokyo. Hundreds of viewers attended and Toyota won sudden acclaim as an auto maker. To cap this achievement, the government designated it an approved company just a week later.

In 1936 Kiichirō was still producing his trucks and cars at several sites in Kariya, under the auspices of the loom firm. He decided a new factory was necessary, one where he could integrate production on a single site. He approached Kariya influentials to see if land were available there. It was not. Ōno Ichizō and others tried to create an adequate site by negotiating with Fujimatsu and neighboring Chiryū, but to no avail. By then, however, Kiichirō had found a location in Koromo that met his needs. His first requirement was cheap land. Since the site he had in mind at Ronjigahara was hilly and arid, he thought it would be easy to acquire. Moreover, since Koromo was suffering from the depression in the sericulture industry, he thought landlords would be eager to sell. A second requirement was a location where "simple farmboys" (to use his phrase) were readily available as laborers. Koromo also met that need. Located deep in the country, Koromo was a fatiguing hour's ride from Nagoya by train, a little less by car. In 1937 it was essentially a rural village virtually untainted by urban ways and city costs. Anxious to lure factories to town because of the depression, Koromo responded eagerly to Toyota's inquiries.

The conditions under which Toyota acquired its land illustrate that the trait of responsive dependence (discussed in chapter 3) persisted in Aichi's small towns well into the 1930s. Toyota approached Koromo through the town mayor, who carried word of a possible factory site to the town council. Just as in Kariya a decade before, the council formed a Factory Invitation Committee and began to foster support for the factory. In July 1934, the town of Koromo concluded an agreement with Toyota, the terms

of which expressed its dependence on the economic prospects this new firm
held out for the community. In summary form, Koromo agreed to:

1. buy all the land Toyota needed and to deed it over by September 1934;
2. sell all the land at a cost not to exceed ¥60 per *tan* (about one-fourth of an
   acre);
3. vacate all roads in the area and sell that space to Toyota at the stipulated
   rate;
4. repair no roads in the area without consulting Toyota and following its
   wishes;
5. buy the land which Toyota designated when it was ready to build a spur
   from the Mikawa Railway to the factory;
6. cooperate in surveys and settling accounts; and,
7. allow Toyota to use the land when and how it wished.[15]

Landowners were hesitant to sell and delayed purchase of necessary land
until December 1935. They also drove prices up, to ¥90 per *tan*.
Nevertheless, Toyota held the community to the agreement, so Koromo
was forced to cover ¥77,000 of the purchase price with funds from the
town budget. It now had the factory it wanted, plus a large debt which it
had not anticipated.

Factory site acquired, production under control, and government
approval won, Toyota moved to establish the auto firm. At ten in the
morning on August 28, 1937, twenty-three men met in the office of the
Toyota Spinning and Weaving Corporation in Nagoya to approve the
articles of incorporation and form the Toyota Motor Company, Limited.
Immediately thereafter, the shareholders elected directors. The pattern
was now a familiar one. Toyota Risaburō became president, and Kiichirō,
vice-president. Two men became managing directors, Ōshima Risaburō
and Takeuchi Kenkichi; they were incumbent directors of the loom firm
who had been associated with Kiichirō's venture from the beginning. The
other six directors were either executives in the loom firm or men brought
into the firm because of their previous experience in auto production and
marketing. Many of the founding fathers were only in their thirties or
forties. They were all attaching their stars to the unknown fortunes of a
still rigorously controlled family enterprise.

Following the now standard practice, Toyota Motors raised all of its
original capital from within. Its "approval" by the government had not
brought any financial support; that remained Toyota's problem. Original
plans called for capitalization at ¥32 million, but that proved too
ambitious. The war which had broken out in China just eight weeks before
scared off many investors. The Toyota reputation for closed dealings kept
others away. In time the company had to cut back on its designs. It finally
capitalized at ¥12 million, of which ¥9 million was immediately

[15] Ibid., pp. 215–217.

subscribed. The Toyota loom firm was the biggest investor; it controlled 75 percent of the shares. The spinning and weaving concern in Nagoya controlled another 4 percent. The remaining 21 percent of the shares went to two corporations and twenty-four individuals, all of whom were either members of the Toyota, Fujino, or Kodama families, or directors and employees of the new firm. For the second time in its short history, the Toyota enterprise had established a new firm well suited to take advantage of the economic opportunities of an impending war.

In one respect the auto firm was not very successful during the war. It was never able to achieve hoped-for production levels. At their first meeting, directors set an annual production target of eighteen thousand vehicles, to be reached by the fifth month of operation. In the best year of the war, Toyota Motors was able to produce only sixteen thousand vehicles. Most of its output was in the form of large trucks for military use. Kiichirō pursued his ambition to build a small car, but faced by extreme supply difficulties, he was able to make only 539 in the best year (1938). Soon after, the firm ceased all auto production and devoted full efforts to military output. In the eight years between 1937 and 1945, Toyota Motors produced a total of ninety thousand vehicles, a humble achievement by contrast with 1967, when it produced that number in just one month.[16]

In other respects the Toyota enterprise did extremely well during the war. One important achievement was to train a new generation of managers. Working under the trying conditions of war, a number of middle- and high-ranking officers learned valuable lessons which they would put to work at Toyota in the 1950s and 1960s. One of them was Kamiya Shōtarō, brought to Toyota in 1937 from Japan General Motors by Kiichirō to become the firm's marketing director. He remained in that position thereafter and still presided over the Toyota Auto Sales Company in 1972. Another was Ishida Taizō. Joining Toyota Automatic Loom Corporation in 1941 as a director, Ishida took charge of military production at the loom factory during the war. After the war he guided the destiny of Toyota Motors as president and later chairman of the board. There were others as well. Toyota Eiji, Sakichi's nephew, joined the firm in 1937 at twenty-five. He was responsible for supervising production and long-range planning during the war. In 1967 he became president of Toyota Motors. Iwaoka Jirō oversaw machine tool production and Tatematsu Iwao superintended the chassis factory in Kariya during the war. They both later became presidents of corporate affiliates, the Aishin Seiki Company and the Toyota Chassis Company, respectively. The war years, therefore, were a crucible in which central figures in Toyota's postwar expansion first proved their mettle.[17]

[16] *30-nen shi*, pp. 766–767.

[17] Too much can be made of the hiatus between prewar and postwar managers in Japanese industry. At Toyota, most of the important postwar managers already had positions of major

The Toyota enterprise made notable financial gains also during World War II, just as it had during World War I. As noted earlir, Toyota Spinning and Weaving never had a losing year between 1918 and 1941. Despite production problems and the cost of continued experiments, Toyota Motors also did well between 1937 and 1945. After registering a loss in its first year of operations, it tallied a profit in every fiscal period through the end of the war. For the eight years between 1937 and 1945, it earned profits of 7 percent (before taxes) on all sales.[18] But the most profitable firm in the enterprise was Toyota Automatic Loom. More diversified than the others, it began the war period producing looms and spinning equipment, but after 1941 shifted to the production of vehicle parts and military materiel. By the end of the war, military products dominated output, accounting for 60 to 80 percent of sales in 1943 to 1945. For the eight-year war period as a whole, they accounted for more than a third of total sales. Military production was a rewarding endeavor, because cumulative profits (before taxes) for the years 1938 to 1945 amounted to almost 20 percent of sales.[19] For the second time in its history, Toyota profited immensely from war.

Toyota used its wartime earnings to expand existing plants and to give birth to several related companies. Between 1940 and 1945 Toyota Motors and Toyota Automatic Loom fathered four corporate offspring. The new firms arose out of necessity, for internal and external reasons. Internally, Toyota was anxious to create a vertically integrated auto concern. There were bottlenecks at critical points (steel and machine tools, for instance), and Toyota sought to resolve them by adding new firms to the enterprise. Externally, wartime conditions made Toyota more self-reliant. The curbs on imported goods and the policies of the government forced industrial organizations to find substitutes for imports. Like many other firms, Toyota was obliged to produce for itself goods which had once been available from abroad. As a result of these requirements, the Toyota enterprise—and the town of Kariya—witnessed a major expansion during the war years.

The new firms which incorporated between 1940 and 1945 all located in Kariya. The first was the Toyota Steel Corporation. It formed in 1940, giving separate corporate identity to a steel works which had been on the site since the early 1930s. It was followed in 1941 by the Toyota Machine Works, established to make precision tools for the auto and loom firms. Two years later another firm emerged. Originally called the Tōkai Aircraft Corporation, Kiichirō founded and presided over this organiza-

responsibility by the early 1940s. See M. Y. Yoshino, *Japan's Managerial System* (Cambridge, Mass., 1967), pp. 85–117.

[18] *40-nen shi*, p. 707.

[19] Ibid., pp. 688–689.

tion because he saw a future for travel by helicopter and small aircraft. It quickly turned to production of war materiel, however, and later reorganized to become Aishin Seiki. Finally, a fourth firm incorporated in 1945. Called the Toyota Chassis Company, it was actually the Kariya factory of Toyota Motors in a new guise. It continued to make truck and auto bodies, as it had before.

Toyota did more than create new firms within its own organization. Its expansion also spawned a number of small enterprises which served the parent firms as subcontractors. A number of such enterprises rose around the loom firm in Kariya as early as the 1920s, engaged in such tasks as collecting scrap metal, preparing subcomponents, and supplying parts. The number of such firms expanded rapidly during the war, especially after the formation of the auto firm. That firm needed an immense variety of parts, not all of which it found economical to produce itself. As a result, literally hundreds of small shops and factories appeared in Kariya and Koromo which did such things as drill cylinder heads, make body springs, produce electrical components, and press metal. Some of them were merely backyard efforts, employing a mother, father, and their children during off hours. Others were substantial operations (for the time) employing several hundred persons. The Tsūda Steel Works was one such firm. Established in a small plant near Kariya Station by a former employee at Toyota Automatic Loom, this firm became a subcontractor for both the auto and the loom firm. It employed only a hundred or so workers at the end of the war, but its protective relationship with Toyota Motors led to rapid expansion later. By 1972 Tsūda employed over one thousand workers in its several factories.

By the end of the Second World War, Kariya's industrial structure was characterized by a clear duality. There were, on the one hand, six large factories all of which were a direct part of the Toyota organization. Toyota Automatic Loom was the oldest and largest with about 2,500 workers. It was followed by Toyota Chassis with 1,100 workers; Toyota Machine Works, with 1,000; Aichi Industries (successor to the aircraft plant), with 600; and Toyota Steel, with about 400 workers in Kariya. In addition, there were 1,400 workers employed at a Toyota Motors branch factory which made electrical components. These six factories employed some 7,000 laborers who made up nearly 80 percent of Kariya's industrial labor force.[20] On the other hand, there were numerous small firms. Some were in the metals and machine industry, working as subcontractors to Toyota. Others were older industrial establishments: the brick factory, the tile firm, the sake breweries. And some were very small shops processing food or making household products. The remaining 20 percent of Kariya's

[20] *40-nen shi*, pp. 706–719.

manufacturing workers found jobs in this sector of the industrial economy. Kariya's postwar industrial structure had taken shape.

Its wartime industrialization left Kariya a markedly different community, especially by contrast with the other towns nearby. War changed them, too, but not as thoroughly as it did Kariya. After 1937 Handa diversified industrially and shook loose from its dependence on the textile industry. In the 1940s an aircraft factory, a glass manufacturer, and two steel mills located in Handa. With almost half of its work force in manufacturing and another third in commerce and the services, Handa was becoming a mature urban area. Koromo assumed after 1937 the striking dual character which it retained into the 1970s. At the end of the war it had a large industrial sector, an equally large agrarian population, and a tiny commercial establishment. Despite the giant Toyota factory south of town, Koromo still gave the appearance of a rural village. Anjō benefitted economically from the war by attracting several textile firms and machine makers to the community. At their peak of operation in 1944, they employed forty-two hundred workers. The town remained primarily an agricultural market center, however, as did Nishio, which underwent virtually no industrial change due to the war. By 1945 the demands of the wartime economy had pointed these communities irrevocably in the direction they would take during the next two decades.

The impact of war revealed itself in population changes, also. Largely untouched by wartime industry, Nishio grew only 16 percent between 1930 and 1941 (the last year for which war period figures are available). Anjō grew a bit faster, but expanded only 25 percent. Handa, which absorbed two other towns to become a city in 1937, expanded by nearly 30 percent during the period. But the most rapid growth occurred in Koromo and Kariya. For the eleven-year period, Koromo ranked second to Kariya in its growth, most of which occurred after Toyota Motors opened its factory there in 1937. Between 1937 and 1945 Koromo's population leaped from about 15,000 to over 30,000. Almost overnight it became the boom town in Aichi Prefecture. Between 1930 and 1941 Kariya *machi* continued to lead all of these towns in its rate of growth. By 1941 it surpassed Nishio, Koromo, and the Handa *machi* section of Handa City, and, at almost 25,000 was only 2,400 shy of Anjō. The villages of Fujimatsu and Yosami also grew during the 1930s, so that the city area reached the 50,000 mark sometime before 1945. The war had laid the demographic foundation for the postwar city.[21]

It had also defined the social character of the postwar city. The villages remained outside the swiftest channels of social change. They were in 1945 essentially agrarian, with three of every four workers still farmers. But the

[21] Figures for 1930 come from *Kokusei chōsa hōkoku: 1930, Aichi ken*, pp. 2-8; for 1941, from Ats: 1941, 1:17-34.

forces of industry and the lure of town employment were drawing villagers into the town's more urban web. By the end of the war, nearly two thousand persons living in Yosami and Fujimatsu found work in factories nearby. That was a substantial number for the villages, but it paled in contrast with the town. At war's end some eight thousand industrial laborers lived in Kariya. They comprised two in every three of the town's workers. For the first time in its history, an industrial working class dominated Kariya's population. Since this group would play a prominent part in Kariya's postwar history, its character and behavior between 1932 and 1945 deserve attention here.

The industrial labor force embraced two groups, which—for purposes of convenience—could be characterized as white-collar and blue-collar workers. Technicians, managers, and directors at Toyota Automatic Loom were characteristic of the first group. Most of them were young men in their twenties and thirties when they arrived at the firm after 1927. They came from Aichi and nearby prefectures, such as Shizuoka, Gifu, and Mie. Most of them had grown up in cities or towns, rather than villages, and they had pursued an education well beyond elementary school. After 1927 the majority of new, high-ranking personnel at Toyota possessed degrees from higher technical schools (roughly equivalent to a Bachelor of Science Degree) or from major universities. They joined Toyota for a probationary period of two years, during which time they earned about ¥500 per year (in 1935), plus bonuses, which sometimes doubled their base salary.[22] Directors earned about ¥200 per month, plus bonuses. Those were low wages for the time, in some cases half the basic salary of older, more reputable firms. These ambitious young men entered Toyota, nevertheless, because it offered the prospect of immediate responsibility and rapid promotion.

There were clear social distinctions between the managerial staff and the production workers. The latter were usually younger. Most of them joined the firm at age thirteen or fourteen. At the most, their education consisted of a higher elementary degree, signifying eight years of formal training. Usually, six years was as much education as these workers acquired before they took a job. They came predominantly from rural families engaged in agriculture, rather than from urban families like the managers. They were also more local than the managers, most of them having grown up in a village in Hekikai, Hazu, or Kamo Counties. In 1935 they earned on average ¥640 per year; more if they were older than the norm, less if they were younger.[23]

Despite obvious social differences, owners at Toyota liked to view these groups—generally speaking the white- and blue-collar workers—as equal

[22] *Ikiru Toyota Sakichi*, p. 119.
[23] *40-nen shi*, p. 669.

members in a joint undertaking. As the history of the firm states, it had inherited from Toyota Spinning and Weaving Corporation "a beautiful air of a familial spirit of warmth and love, of research and invention, and of integrity and health." [24] Sakichi had helped to foster such feelings. In the early days of his enterprise, he would often come down from his second-story office to eat with the workers in the company mess hall, where his wife often joined him. He felt such responsibility and kinship toward his employees that as early as the 1910s he established a profit-sharing program in a Nagoya subsidiary in which production workers as well as managers could participate. The company most certainly did have a past in which employees and employers alike worked in kindred spirits in a family-like atmosphere.

Sakichi's successors tried diligently to perpetuate the vision of the firm as family. As Marxist ideas gained popularity in the 1920s, one found Toyota Risaburō (and the enterprise as a whole) trying to minimize the differences between workers and capitalist. His aspiration was to make workers capitalists and the capitalists workers. As he put it in a memo written in 1927:

> I don't believe that a capitalist purchases the labor of his workers, or that workers sell their labor to capitalists. Both work together under the manager's hand to administer the enterprise. In this situation, you can imagine the worker—who invests himself in the company—as a kind of stockholder. My father often told me that the administration of any enterprise must be undertaken for the good of the country. Even if a few wealthy men appear, as long as the people are poor you can't speak of national glory. [25]

In other words, management at Toyota viewed workers as members in a joint partnership which worked at management's direction to achieve the goals of the firm and to improve the welfare of the nation.

Risaburō's lofty idealism could not hide, however, the ambiguities of his conception. There obviously was a difference between workers and management. Management clearly enjoyed an upper hand. It established the goals of the firm and it directed the firm's operations. Workers might benefit from this, and indeed they should, as should the nation, but—by implication—profits were an overriding concern. To achieve them, workers were expected to subordinate themselves to the aims of the company.

Toyota demonstrated its real conception of workers in its personnel policies. We have already noted that Kiichirō, when seeking a factory site for Toyota Motors, made a rural setting amidst an abundant supply of "simple farmboys" a first requirement. Risaburō also spoke frequently

[24] Ibid., p. 171.
[25] Ibid., pp. 171–172.

about the virtues of a labor force made up of young rustics. They wanted workers who were pliant and trainable—in a real sense, still children. Once they recruited them, they left nothing to chance. The firm put new workers through a rigorous socialization program which left no doubts about how they should behave. A few lines from the work code established shortly after 1927 illustrate the encompassing nature of Toyota's concern:

> Work uprightly to build a prosperous paradise.
> First, compose yourself; then go to work.
> Don't lose your spirit for work.
> Don't look around when working.
> Don't think about anything else when working.
> Don't let your hands wander when working.
> Don't leave your station when working.
> Talking to someone who is working is prohibited in the factory.[26]

Just to print such a code revealed the severely paternal expectations of childlike conformity which Toyota demanded from its workers.

The firm did not stop with mere exhortation. It established other means of securing compliance from its workers. One of the most effective was its pay system. Until the end of the war, Toyota Automatic Loom paid its workers on a complicated piece-work, incentive basis. Wages depended on one's ability to meet a standard quota established by the firm. Those who exceeded the quota did well; those who did not, suffered. At first, Toyota established quotas on an individual basis, so that a worker could strive to achieve his quota independent of others. Later, it established collective quotas. Under that system, one's wages were calculated on the basis of a ratio between the group's quotas and the group's actual output. This obviously enforced diligence through the use of peer pressure to conform and produce. With its piece-rate pay system and its mode of socialization, Toyota revealed its actual view of workers. They were clearly subordinates operating under the tight managerial control of the owners.[27]

Toyota succeeded to a remarkable degree in eliciting the kind of behavior expected of its workers. It is difficult to measure their loyalty, but profits attest to their compliance with the firm's goals. They were also more than docile politically. There is no evidence of labor disputes, work stoppages, or unionization movements at any of the Toyota factories in the prewar period. In explanation of this compliance and docility, a number of reasons deserve mention.[28]

[26] Ibid., p. 177.
[27] Ibid., pp. 665–669.
[28] The following interpretation of labor relations applies to regular workers (jōyōkō), and somewhat less to the impermanent workers whom Toyota referred to as contract laborers (ukeoukō) in the prewar period. No breakdowns of the work force at Toyota Automatic Loom are available, but at Toyota Motors regular workers comprised approximately a quarter of

Management was not the only group which believed workers were members of a joint enterprise. The workers also shared that conception. Having come from farm villages, most of Toyota's young workers were accustomed to very diffuse labor relationships. They grew up in areas where nearly everyone participated in frequent, voluntary exchange of labor during the planting and harvesting seasons, all of which took place in an atmosphere of mutual reliance. Although people valued labor and calculated its worth, they also knew, for example, that in time of trouble a neighbor would be willing to help—without computing his costs by the hour. The same aura of mutual reliance prevailed in the factory. In return for the worker's loyalty, the firm provided him not only with a specific wage but with other compensation as well. At Toyota these included company-sponsored lectures and training programs, athletic facilities, dining rooms and meals, dormitories or company housing, and a company-subsidized journalism club. In return, the firm expected the worker to accept overtime at peak periods of production or to forego a holiday if the company so desired. There *was* a contractual relationship between employer and employee, but the specific character of the contract was clouded by an aura of extra-contractual obligations. This enabled workers to believe, as management wanted them to, that they were part of a joint undertaking.

The formal education of young workers disposed them to easy acceptance of existing custom. In fact, increasingly during the 1930s, education was a medium for inculcating acceptance of the status quo. Students were taught respect for superior authority, beginning at the top with the emperor and moving down the social hierarchy to the closest older friend. They learned that one achieved self-fulfillment by helping achieve the goals of the nation. They also learned that dissent was anathema. Conformity and consensus were the sanctioned social goals. Those sanctions derived from the closed nature of prewar Japanese society. Most of the populace still grew up in tight little social systems where they had to spend their entire lives dealing on a face-to-face basis with the same small group of individuals. The social imperatives of such a system would foster conformity and muffle outward dissent in any cultural setting. Workers socialized in the closed atmosphere of the village thus shrank from dissent as a matter of course.

The organization of the modern factory replicated essential aspects of the social system. The piece-rate system at Toyota, for example, imposed

the work force between 1939 and 1943. They would ordinarily have been a higher percentage, but wartime conscription limited the labor supply and reduced the normal number of permanent workers. The regular workers are the subject of this discussion because they were the men who formed the core of the organized labor force at the Toyota firms after the war, and it was their previous work experiences which played a major role in dictating the behavior of organized labor in the postwar period.

severe pressures for conformity and performance on all members of a group. There was already a strong inclination to work together collectively, but a system of that sort compelled collective effort. Failure to produce meant loss of income and social respect.

There was another aspect of factory life which cushioned the novelty of the factory and embraced the new worker in a familiar social ethos. This was the pattern of *sempai-kōhai* relations. A *sempai* is one with the good fortune to have preceded another, sometimes in birth, other times in entry into a school or firm. He is a superior, a leader, a benefactor, and an alter ego all in one. The *kōhai* is his follower. Young men entering the loom factory were attached to *sempai* from the beginning. In some cases *sempai* were older men who had been with Toyota since its inception. Imbued with the values of the firm, they cultivated those same values in their followers. In other cases a *sempai* might have been an older boy from the same village, perhaps the local swimming champion whom village youngsters had always admired. A young worker just entering the factory would be more than pleased to emulate such a predecessor. By mitigating the impersonality of the factory experience, and by embracing the newcomer immediately into a tight social relationship with an already loyal employee, the *sempai-kōhai* system insured a high measure of compliance from new workers.

Reinforcing the effectiveness of the *sempai-kōhai* relationship was the essentially deferential status of the newcomer. He was a subordinate who realized he must act accordingly. Age accentuated his low status. Entering a factory at thirteen or fourteen, he came into immediate contact with older men of long experience on the factory floor. In the rather alien environment of the factory, it must have been a source of reassurance to adopt their ways. The young factory worker also recognized the vast difference in education between him and the company's managers and directors. As men with college degrees, they deserved awe and obedience in the eyes of the newcomer. He was also conscious of social distinctions. Most of the production workers came from humble farm families. The Toyota family, on the other hand, now enjoyed such social recognition that its sons could marry into the nation's leading families. The immense gap between the social rank of the owners and the humble status of the newcomer's own family surely elicited a submissive response.

The sheer novelty of the factory experience also made conformity natural. Thankful to have jobs and eager to learn, the impulse was to soak up what one was taught and to obey one's superiors. Having come from farms, Toyota's recruits did not enter the factory steeped in a legacy of griping. They carried no chronicles of complaint recorded by fathers beaten down by industrial life. These young men were not the products of a historical proletariat at all. The factory system was new to them. They were not familiar with its long hours (ten daily, six days a week in 1942); its demanding schedules; and its unremitting monotony. Novelty probably made factory work acceptable, if not attractive—at first.

Finally, it would be remiss to ignore the air of crisis which hung over this period. The nation was in an emergency. By the early 1940s it was struggling for its very survival, and Toyota was playing a key role in the effort to fend off enemies. The firm and its employees worked under a cloud of fear. For some time the sense of crisis was adequate incentive to produce and conform, but eventually it lost its efficacy, leaving the labor force psychologically shattered by war's end. That trauma produced a radically different pattern of worker behavior after 1945, but through the war years, conformity and docility prevailed. There were no strikes, no work stoppages, no rancorous confrontations between management and labor. Both groups accepted the view that they were joint participants in the familial undertaking of the Toyota enterprise, working for the benefit of the firm and the nation.

We have seen how the national crisis of the 1930s and early 1940s wrought significant changes in the economic structure of Aichi Prefecture, the Toyota enterprise, and the community of Kariya. The prefecture shifted from its historic emphasis on textiles to a more diversified form of heavy industrial output. The Toyota enterprise was one of the driving forces behind the change, as it grew to become a vertically integrated manufacturer of steel, machines, vehicles, and military materiel. Toyota's expansion, much of it carried out in Kariya, transformed that country town into a center of heavy industry, its population dominated by a large group of industrial workers recently arrived from outside the community.

Despite these thoroughgoing economic and social changes, the political life of Kariya and western Mikawa remained strangely unaffected. With the exception of one subtle change, which would have important implications for postwar politics, a strong measure of continuity characterized political behavior in this area between 1932 and 1945, as the next and final portion of this chapter illustrates.

As the sense of crisis deepened during the 1930s, people in the communities of Aichi Prefecture acted as if they were seized. They lost all appearance of flexibility in their political behavior. They might have been responding to an intrusive atmosphere of nationalism, fostered deligently by the Japanese military. They might also have sacrificed their right of political choice until the period of uncertainty was at an end. Or they may have felt sincerely that the men leading them were the right ones, and that they should continue to hold office. Whatever their motives may have been, the voters in Kariya and nearby towns behaved with profound conservatism in making their political choices.

Theirs was conservatism of a literal sort, opposing change and preserving the status quo. The selection of mayors at the local level offers compelling proof of this. Without exception, mayors elected in the early or middle 1930s remained in office until the end of the war. In Kariya, the duty of presiding over the town during the years of crisis fell to Ōno Ichizō. By the early 1930s, he was the political leader of the community. He was a central figure on the town council, a presiding officer in the prefectural assembly, and a campaign manager for the local Diet representative, Taketomi. When Ino Naoji retired as mayor after his second term in 1936, Ōno succeeded him. He held the office without interruption until he was purged in 1946.

It is very difficult to evaluate the significance of Ōno's long incumbency for local politics in the 1930s. Written materials are virtually non-existent, and men with personal knowledge of those years have passed away. One thing is certain. The partnership Ōno struck up in the 1920s with Toyota continued and flourished. Each time Toyota needed land for expansion during the 1940s, Ōno acted as intermediary again, approving the choices and persuading the council and the community to go along. Ōno may have been acting out of pure self-interest, cooperating with Toyota in return for campaign contributions at election time. It is impossible to prove whether this was the case or not.[29] More likely, Ōno assisted Toyota because he was convinced of the merits of Kariya's industrialization. He and other influentials worked gratefully for the enterprise, because they recognized that the town's fortunes depended on those of Toyota.

Budget data for the years 1936 and 1937 support the assertion that political leaders in Kariya and Koromo valued industry highly. Kariya's anticipated expenditures in several important budget categories appear in table 3, along with those for Koromo, Handa, and Anjō. The comparatively high outlay set aside for construction in Kariya and Koromo was due to Toyota, which began construction of the auto plant in Koromo in 1936 and continued building in Kariya in 1936 and 1937. Each time a new plant went up, new roads and drainage systems were necessary. The community, not the firm, footed the bill for those expenses. But Kariya and Koromo supported Toyota's expansion eagerly, as the data affirm.

The alacrity with which local leaders in Kariya and Koromo served the interests of the Toyota enterprise made unnecessary its direct participation in the political process. In this period, as in the preceding decade, Toyota firms in Kariya and Koromo did not intervene in the electoral process to

[29] It will probably be impossible to prove conclusively whether or not Ōno received financial assistance from Toyota in his political career, because the principals and their associates have died leaving very few personal documents. When I asked Ōno's surviving brother if Ōno had ever accepted campaign contributions from Toyota, he found the question absurd. There were other forms of indirect compensation for Ōno, however. His son got a job at the auto company on graduation from college and eventually rose to become a director.

place their candidates in power. In neither community, in fact, did an employee of a Toyota firm hold an elective office in the prewar period.[30] Rather the firms in the Toyota enterprise were able to achieve their political ends by dealing informally with community leaders. Those men recognized the importance of the enterprise to their communities and the benefits which it would return in the form of jobs, income, community growth, and expanded business activity. They were consequently more than willing to heed its wishes, even if that meant neglect in other areas.

TABLE 3

BUDGET EXPENDITURES FOR FOUR AICHI TOWNS,
AVERAGE OUTLAY FOR 1936 AND 1937
(BY PERCENTAGE)

	Kariya	Koromo	Handa	Anjō
Administration	11	12	6	11
Construction	23	22	13	4
Education	32	42	40	53
Debt retirement	4	4	13	9
Other outlays	30	20	28	23
Total	100	100	100	100

SOURCE: Aichi ken, sōmu bu, *Shichōson tōkei ichiran* (Nagoya, 1938).
NOTE: These are proposed, not final, figures. They reveal what the communities expected to spend, not what they actually spent.

Support for industry occurred at some social expense to the community. Although the people of Kariya probably did not realize it, their taxes subsidized industrial expansion at the cost of their children's education.[31] By the mid-1930s Kariya was spending less money to educate its elementary students than any nearby town, about ¥17 per pupil. Nishio, a larger community with a poorer tax base, managed to spend ¥20 per pupil, and Anjō and Koromo almost ¥30 per pupil. Kariya's scrimping on education resulted in one of the highest teacher-pupil ratios in the area, one teacher to fifty-six students, by contrast with Koromo and Anjō where the ratio was one to fifty.[32] Thus, in order to lend support to industry,

[30] Proof for this assertion rests on the fact that none of the mayors or councilmen in Kariya and Koromo between 1922 and 1945 were Toyota employees.

[31] This discussion is based on Aichi ken, sōmu bu, *Shichōson tōkei ichiran* (Nagoya, 1938), pp. 42–45.

[32] These figures suggest a further reason (in addition to the general emphasis on authoritarianism and their own training in a military-like atmosphere) why teachers in prewar Japan cultivated obedience among their wards. With fifty to sixty students in every class, regimentation was probably the only way to get any teaching done.

Kariya's town fathers were willing to cut corners on the quality of education they provided for the children of the community. This choice was significant, because it anticipated a willingness—long before the economically expansive postwar period—to forego social investment for the sake of industrial development.

The pattern of conservative political behavior which Kariya displayed in returning Ōno Ichizō to the mayoralty between 1935 and 1946 repeated itself in Koromo, Anjō and Handa. In 1929 Koromo elected Nakamura Jūichi to the mayoralty. Born in a village near Toyohashi, Nakamura arrived in Koromo in 1924 to become the chief of police, an appointive office controlled by the central government. Selection of an outsider for mayor was unusual in these communities, but Koromo citizens may have felt that a man of Nakamura's experience would be able to get their sluggish town moving. He did (as we have seen); for that reason he remained in office until 1946. Anjō citizens relied yet again on their political war horse, Okada Kikujirō. He was a vigorous sixty-six when he took office as mayor for the sixth time in 1933, and a recalcitrant seventy-nine when the purge forced him to step down in 1946. Citizens in Handa turned predictably to their leading political house during the war. In 1937 the town of Handa consolidated with two others nearby to become the sixth city in Aichi Prefecture. Citizens of the new city elected as mayor Nakano Hanzaemon. Scion of one of the six branches of that important family, he was a major investor in the beer brewery and the spinning factory. His election marked the eighth time since 1891 that a Nakano had assumed the office of mayor in Handa. Thus, in many nearby communities as well, voters clutched with desperate fidelity to their political leaders during the years of war.[33]

In Diet elections, too, local voters stuck with their candidates. One might have expected something different. After all, political parties suffered an apparent loss of power after the early 1930s. That loss of power might have been associated with an influx of new, weaker Diet members. Moreover, many politicians themselves became disenchanted with the party system and even called for its reform or abandonment in some cases.[34] That might have reduced the meaning and vitality of electoral politics. Finally, given a high level of corruption, the parties allegedly suffered from lack of popular support. One might therefore have expected an effort at the local level to throw some rascals out. But none of these things occurred, at least in Aichi Prefecture. In fact, there was an

[33] Once again lack of materials prevents discussion of political affairs in Nishio. For Nakamura, see Chōjō, *Aichi ken shichōson jinshi roku*, p. 308. For Nakano, see Handa shi, *Handa shi shi*, 3:395–571.

[34] Gordon M. Berger treats this subject in some detail in his "The Search for a New Political Order: Konoe Fumimaro, the Political Parties, and Politics in the Early Shōwa Era" (Ph.D. diss., Yale University, 1972), especially chapters 2 and 3.

impressive continuity of Diet candidacies and memberships during the war years, the origins of which stemmed from the 1920s, as table 4 reveals.

The Diet members listed in this table were of two different types: national professionals and local influentials. The national professionals were Taketomi, Okamoto, Kobayashi and Ogasawara. Ōno and Honda were the local influentials. Four attributes defined the national profession-

TABLE 4

AICHI FOURTH DISTRICT DIET MEMBERS, 1924–1946

Election Year	Members Elected		
1924	Taketomi	Okamoto	Urano
1928	Taketomi	Okamoto	Yamazaki
1930	Taketomi	Okamoto	Kobayashi
1932	Taketomi	Ogasawara	Kobayashi
1936	Taketomi	Okamoto	Kobayashi
1937	Ōno	Okamoto	Ogasawara
1942	Ōno	Honda	Ogasawara

SOURCE: Kōmei senkyo renmei, ed., *Shūgiin giin senkyo no jisseki* (Tokyo, 1968), pp. 340–429.

als. First, they were talented men who left their homes early for study elsewhere. Second, they possessed degrees from good colleges or the best universities in the country. Third, they pursued careers in the central government, in universities, in law, or in business and banking. Finally, when their work did not carry them elsewhere, they resided in the capital, Tokyo. By contrast, local influentials may have acquired some higher education elsewhere, but they usually remained in their home towns and pursued their adult careers there. Their political training ground was the prefectural assembly. A closer look at these Diet members brings their qualities to light.[35]

The first national professional to appear as a Diet candidate in this area was Taketomi Sai, in 1917. As noted earlier, Taketomi left Kariya after completing eight years at Kijō School. After graduation from Tokyo University, he worked for several years in the Justice Ministry before establishing a private legal practice in Tokyo, where he lived until his death in 1936. He was followed shortly after by Okamoto Jitsutarō. Born

[35] In addition to the regular biographical sources, I have drawn materials for discussion of Diet politicians from the following sources. Ogasawara: Tokiwa Yoshiharu, *Ogasawara Sankurō den* (Tokyo, 1957); Kimura Hitoshi, *Ogasawara Sankurō sensei kaisō roku* (Nishio, 1967); and Ogasawara Sankurō, *Jiden: Jinsei wa mijikai*, 2 vols. (Tokyo, 1967). Kobayashi: Takayama Fukuyoshi, ed., *Kobayashi Kanae sensei* (Toyota, 1963). Okamoto and Honda: Sanage chō shi hensan iinkai, ed., *Sanage chō shi* (Toyota, 1968).

in the hamlet of Kamekubi near Koromo, Okamoto left his home area at nineteen to study law in Tokyo at what became Meiji University. From 1904 through 1920 he was an official in the Monopoly Office of the Ministry of Finance, a job which took him to several of the country's major cities. After two years as a business executive, he established a law practice in Nagoya in 1922, which he maintained until he moved his office to Tokyo in 1932. Ogasawara Sankurō left his home village near Nishio in 1901 at sixteen to study in Tokyo. After taking a degree from Tokyo University, he joined the Bank of Taiwan. When he was not stationed overseas, he resided in a new white-collar suburb in Tokyo. Kobayashi Kanae left his home village of Takahashi at fifteen to study law in Tokyo. He finished his education with a Doctor of Laws degree from Berlin University in 1926, and returned to Tokyo to practice law and teach at Nihon University. The pattern is clear: an early departure from home for training in Tokyo, followed by work and residence in the capital.

The local influentials led somewhat less cosmopolitan lives. Ōno Ichizō had managed to spend several years in Manchuria as a young man, but he passed the rest of his adult life in Kariya. The other local influential, Honda Kōji, came from a hamlet just north of Koromo. He possessed a middle school education and worked as a farmer, while serving as director of several business firms and officer of local agricultural societies. From 1923 until his election to the Diet in 1942, he sat in the Aichi Prefectural Assembly, where he was presiding officer during his last term. Ōno and Honda were, therefore, men whose political experiences were rooted in the more parochial atmosphere of the prefecture.

That absentees like the national professionals could represent local areas in the Diet was not unusual. There were no residential requirements for candidacy. Their ability to win election after election deserves a bit of explanation, however. Earlier pages laid some stress on the role of status as a means of voter appeal. With the rise of the national professional, status assumed increased importance. Here were local boys—"from the sticks"— who had gone to Tokyo and done just as well as the sons of the old samurai or the offspring of the new business classes. They had demonstrated their talent and ability, and now they wanted to put them to use for the people back home—or so they wished it to seem. Recognizing them as prestigious achievers, the local citizenry responded eagerly to endorse their status by sending them to the national Diet. The career of Ogasawara Sankurō illustrates how this political system operated.

Ogasawara grew up in a rustic village called Muroba, today a part of Nishio. His father "was a farmer who did not put his hand to the sickle or the hoe; he spent most of his days working as village headman." [36] His

[36] Ogasawara, *Jiden*, p. 8.

eldest brother, who inherited the family property in 1897 when the father died, followed in his footsteps; he was mayor of Muroba on three occasions. A second brother also served as mayor in a village to which he moved after his marriage by adoption. As village notables, the Ogasawaras were able to provide a sound education for young Sankurō. He completed eight years of instruction in local schools, where teachers inculcated the virtues of Tokugawa Ieyasu, patience and persistence. He put those values to work in the next decade as he sought an education in Tokyo. He struggled for six years to win a middle school degree. Finally, in 1911, he received perhaps the most valuable passport to success in Taishō Japan, a law degree from Tokyo University.

That degree gave him entry to both a new social realm and an expansive business world. Through the good offices of a professor, Sankurō married the daughter of an official in the Justice Ministry. His mother had already given him freedom to find his own wife, something young men did infrequently at that time (usually parents arranged a marriage). She felt that a local girl would not do for someone of his position. With his marriage he gravitated out of local society into the lower reaches of a growing class of bureaucrats and other professionals who were assuming a significant position in Japanese society. Again with the help of his professors, he found a job with the Bank of Taiwan. Starting in Tokyo, he accepted appointments in Canton and Singapore before returning to the capital in 1921. He stayed with the bank until 1926, when he resigned at age forty-one in anticipation of a political career.

Ogasawara formed three important friendships during his years with the Bank of Taiwan which set the course of that career. The first was with Yamamoto Teijirō. Yamamoto was a director of the Taiwan Sugar Company and a member of the Diet when Ogasawara first met him. An influential Seiyūkai adherent, he served on two occasions as Minister of Agriculture. At one of their early meetings, Yamamoto proffered some advice to Ogasawara, which nicely encapsulates the tone of social conduct at the time:

> It is no good for people to hurry. Nor is it good for people to be *rikutsu* (a mildly derogatory term used of people who are argumentative, theoretical, or pushy). When you silently tag along after your superiors, you'll find that you're progressing in no time. Tonight you're sitting in the last seat, but if you don't hurry and you don't get pushy, in a few years there will be a lot of people gradually filling in the seats behind you.[37]

Ogasawara took this advice to heart, and in return for his deference, Yamamoto was there with money and contacts when Ogasawara entered politics in 1928.

[37] Tokiwa, p. 195.

Ogasawara established ties with a second patron in 1923, while he was in charge of cleaning up some of the bank's rather loosely managed affairs. As part of his duties, he was asked to collect a debt of ¥21 million from Kuhara Fusanosuke. Kuhara was an ambitious entrepreneur who played a role in the creation of the Hitachi electrical enterprise. When Ogasawara met him he was about to become a prominent national politician. The bank solved its problem with Kuhara by collecting ¥9 million and writing off another ¥12 million, a settlement which Kuhara might well have found pleasing. When Ogasawara later entered the Seiyūkai, he did so as a member of the Kuhara faction.

His third and most important friendship was with Nakagawa Kojūrō, president of the Bank of Taiwan from 1920 to 1925. Nakagawa was one of the select men of Meiji: a graduate of Tokyo University; an official in the Ministry of Education; and a private secretary on two occasions to Prince Saionji Kimmochi. He pursued a dual career in business and education. In addition to his position with the Bank of Taiwan, he presided over Ritsumeikan University after 1913. He capped his career with an appointment to the House of Peers in 1923. Nakagawa was the motive force behind Ogasawara's political career, the groundwork for which was laid in a conversation between them in the late 1920s. Nakagawa put it this way:

> If you're interested, I'll take care of the financial worries as much as possible. You find an election district for yourself. If you feel your home area of Mikawa is alright, get in touch with prefectural assembly members, town and village mayors, and local influentials in the area; you've got to start these preparations. If there are people whom it would be good for me to meet, I'll be glad to see them; just introduce them or bring them with you—because I have the intention of working for you.[38]

This was an enticing offer, and Ogasawara seized it.

It took Ogasawara some time to act successfully on Nakagawa's advice, but once he did, he built a lasting *jiban*. Ogasawara first stood for election in 1928, finishing last in a field of five. His only support came from voters around his home village. When the next election took place in 1930, he struck a bargain with a local influential which set him on his path to victory. His cohort was the old nemesis of Kariya politicians, Okada Kikujirō. The two of them agreed that Okada would run in the 1930 election, and that Ogasawara would not stand. Regardless of the outcome, Okada would thereafter support Ogasawara. Okada did poorly. His supporters were confined to his own sphere of influence in southern Hekikai. Having made too many enemies in the prefectural assembly, he received virtually no support elsewhere. Once the two of them worked

[38] Ibid., pp. 150–151.

together, however, they were able to establish a *jiban* so secure that it endured into the postwar period.

Ogasawara and the other Diet members from the Fourth District who won re-election with such regularity during the 1930s based their success on a shrewd division of the electorate. Their district encompassed about one hundred thousand voters spread throughout five counties. Two counties, Nishi and Higashi Kamo, were mountainous and sparsely populated; voters there comprised about 20 percent of the total. Nukata County and Okazaki City formed a second section of the district, which was hilly and also sparsely populated. Its voters made up another 25 percent of the total. The third and final section of the district lay in the southwestern quadrant. That was an area of densely populated paddy land, dotted with ports, market centers, and industrial towns. The remaining 55 percent of the voters lived there, 20 percent in Hazu and 35 percent in Hekikai. In a four-man race, a winning candidate required a constituency of some twenty thousand voters. Obviously, the richest base to cultivate lay in Hekikai and Hazu. If a man could capture half the votes in Hekikai, in fact, he was virtually assured election. That is precisely what Taketomi, and after him Ōno, did. By taking slightly over half the votes from Hekikai and adding a few from elsewhere, they handily won election seven times running. Once Ogasawara and Okada struck their bargain, they were able to attract the rest of the voters in the populous southwestern tier to build a second, secure *jiban* there. These were both focused *jiban,* which relied heavily on the status appeal of a successful hometown boy.[39]

The other candidates in the district relied on diffuse *jiban* for their support. Okamoto's constituency, for example, was spread throughout the remaining three, sparsely populated counties and Okazaki. He also had a small group of supporters in Hazu, with whom he had established ties when he taught school there for a brief time at the turn of the century. When Ogasawara stood for election, however, Okamoto's backing in Hazu dissolved. Support for a prominent local son superceded that for a former teacher. Kobayashi competed with Okamoto for votes in virtually the same area. Since the number of votes in that area was insufficient to support two candidates, one of them always went down to defeat. When Okamoto decided to retire from politics in 1942, he passed his *jiban* to a younger politician from his own village, Honda Kōji. Two decades in the prefectural assembly gave Honda widespread contacts in Nishi Kamo County, and he easily bested Kobayashi in the contest for office in 1942.

That election is alleged to have been exceptional for several reasons. It

---

[39] This analysis of Fourth District *jiban* and voting patterns during the years 1932 to 1942 is based on Shūgiin jimu kyoku, *Shūgiin giin sōsenkyo ichiran,* for general elections eighteen through twenty-one.

was the only one held during the war with the United States. It was the
first held after dissolution of the Japanese political parties. And it was
carried out under the sponsorship of the Imperial Rule Assistance
Association (*Taisei yokusan kai*). For this last reason, it is believed that the
1942 election largely returned men sponsored by the Association who
would simply rubber stamp the policies of the military government. As is
so often the case when examining Japanese politics, the rhetoric of the
center has obscured the reality of local politics, at least in Aichi Prefecture.
In 1942 thirteen incumbents ran for the Diet from the prefecture; ten (77
percent) won re-election. That compared almost exactly with the average
rate of success for the three preceding elections, which was 75 percent.[40]
The Association promoted sixteen candidates, of whom fourteen won. Half
of them, including Ogasawara and Ōno in the Fourth District, were
incumbents with secure *jiban*. The other half were newcomers, such as
Honda (with Okamoto's old *jiban* secure in his control) and Nakano
Hanzaemon (mayor of Handa and head of its leading political family). It
appears that in this area the Association simply endorsed the candidacies
of incumbents and newcomers who had the best chance of winning, and let
it go at that. Beneath the surface, the election of 1942 carried forward the
pattern of continuity characteristic of local politics in the 1930s.[41]

It did so for the last time, however, because 1942 witnessed some subtle
changes in support patterns which would assume considerable importance
in the postwar era. These changes were not due to national policies or
party programs. Rather, they were a product of the social transformation
which the district itself was undergoing. Earlier pages have mentioned the
rapid growth in population in Kariya between 1925 and 1937, and in
Koromo after 1937. That growth disrupted the spatial setting of former
jiban, by sending loyal voters out of their home districts into others. Even
though a man moved from his home village to another town nearby, he
usually retained his allegiance to the candidate from his old *jiban*. The web
of social relations on which a *jiban* was based guaranteed this continuing
support. Thus, as more outsiders settled permanently in a town, they set in
motion a process which eventually undermined the social basis of
community political solidarity.

Kariya is one case in point. In the 1937 Diet election, Ōno Ichizō
captured 2,970 out of 3,147 votes in Kariya, or 94 percent of the total.
Ogasawara Sankurō won 83 votes and Kobayashi Kanae, 39. Between

[40] The figures were as follows. In 1932, fifteen incumbents ran; ten won election (67
percent). In 1936, thirteen incumbents ran again; eleven won election (85 percent). Finally,
in 1937, fifteen incumbents ran and eleven won election (73 percent). It was very difficult by
the 1930s to unseat an incumbent. The presence or absence of an endorsement by the IRAA
in 1942 thus had rather little to do with the outcome of a contest.

[41] Berger comes to the same conclusion in his examination of IRAA successes at the
national level. See pages 491–492 in his dissertation.

1937 and the next election in 1942, some six hundred new voters were added to the rolls in Kariya. Most of them were men in their late twenties and early thirties who had arrived in Kariya after 1927 to work in the loom factory or elsewhere. Their previous homes were in nearby areas, such as the western portion of Nishi Kamo County or the northern portion of Hazu County. When the 1942 election took place, Kariya voters divided their support as follows: Ono, 2,714; Ogasawara, 408; Kobayashi, 406; and Honda, 216. These results are explained by patterns of migration. Newcomers to Kariya from villages northeast of town voted for Kobayashi and Honda, because their home areas were located where those men had their *jiban*. Newcomers from villages to the south voted for Ogasawara, because their families were a part of the Okada *jiban* in southern Hekikai County or of the Ogasawara *jiban* in Hazu County. These differences were not dramatic, nor were they strong enough to unseat an incumbent. But they accelerated during the war, and once it ended, they had produced lasting effects.[42]

Migration shattered Kariya's political solidarity for several reasons. As more newcomers arrived in the community, long-term residents found it increasingly difficult to absorb them in the web of associations that ordered local life. Due to the dispersed location of their housing, the newcomers often lived well away from old residential areas. This complicated their joining into neighborhood activities. Furthermore, the newcomers did not always have family or kinship ties in the community. This impeded their acceptance and made it difficult for them to penetrate existing social organizations. Finally, the new migrants to Kariya had their own social focus which differed from that of many persons in the community. Their work place occupied them, not only during the day, but in evenings and on off-days as well. Indeed, by virtue of the leisure time activities undertaken at the factories in Kariya, workers were as likely to concentrate their social energies on their place of work as on their neighborhoods. For all these reasons, old-line politicians and their agents found it difficult to embrace newcomers effectively in their networks of political support; Ōno Ichizō's declining share of the vote attested to this. At the same time, Ōno's losses signified newly emerging patterns of political affiliation which would bear importantly on Kariya's postwar politics.

This discussion of Diet politics in the Aichi Fourth District encourages some speculative comments on the nature of Japanese political life during the war period.[43] One's attention is drawn first to the political parties.

[42] This argument is based on an analysis of three different sources: (1) *40-nen shi*, p. 672; (2) Naikaku tōkei kyoku, *Kokusei chōsa hōkoku, Aichi ken*, for the years 1920, 1930, and 1935; and (3) *Shūgiin giin sōsenkyo ichiran* for the twentieth and twenty-first general elections, pages 203–206 and 298–304, respectively.

[43] The following discussion is based on a very limited sample of evidence, so I do not present it as a definitive analysis of Japanese politics in the 1930s. We need many detailed,

From all appearances, the parties were strongly biased toward the center. Their leading figures were men educated in Tokyo who pursued careers there. Many of their recruits, as we have seen in this chapter, also studied and worked in the political center. The parties co-opted promising individuals who had proven themselves in the universities, banks, and businesses of the capital, then had those men find a constituency which would sanction their choice. Thus, for many party politicians, Tokyo *was* the political arena. It defined the personal associations—university ties, marriage relations, business contacts, and bureaucratic bonds—with which the parties bound themselves together. But, to the misfortune of the Japanese people, Tokyo was an island attuned to its own concerns, and they did not always mesh with the realities of economic and political life in rural Japan during the 1930s.

The parties, furthermore, were not purely political groupings. They were social constructs based on a diffuse set of relationships extending well beyond the political realm. Ogasawara established ties with a particular Seiyūkai faction because he had business dealings with its leader in the 1920s, and because his banking duties had brought him into contact with another Seiyūkai politician. Because parties were social constructs, their members behaved according to the conventions of Japanese social behavior. Yamamoto's fatherly advice to Ogasawara illustrated one of the salient conventions: deference to one's superior. Any young man absorbed into a party in the way Ogasawara had been thus acted under severe restraints. He was virtually unable to adopt a mode of autonomous behavior. Rather, he was obliged to follow the advice of his elders. Needless to say, this prevented the parties from becoming any better than the skill and intelligence of their ablest elders could make them. When party leaders adopted fruitless programs, the parties themselves withered.

This material also casts significant light on the candidates themselves, especially the national professionals. Those men were not well known in their districts. All of the national professionals were absent from the district from the time they were adolescents onward. In fact, they all left at or before the turn of the century, and thus failed to experience the changes which took place locally between 1900 and 1930. Many people were conscious of this. A schoolmate of Kobayashi who later organized supporters for him once wrote, "After the *sensei* (leader) graduated from grade school, he studied in Tokyo and Germany. He seldom returned home, and he was not very familiar with the local people." [44] Another local observer was critical of Kobayashi's candidacy, citing the fact that he

---

full-scale studies, based on local and national sources, before we make sense of the 1930s. My purpose is merely to suggest hypotheses which might provoke controversy and lead to new ways of viewing the politics of that era.

[44] Takayama, pp. 136–137.

had been in Tokyo all the time and was unfamiliar with the district.[45] His unfamiliarity with the Fourth District was one reason why Kobayashi found it so difficult to establish a secure *jiban*. The same local observer criticized Ogasawara Sankurō in a similar vein by noting that "he had been overseas and is a leader of the business world, but he is not well known at home." [46]

The corollary to being unknown at home was knowing little about home. The national professionals who represented the Fourth District during the 1930s were divorced from the reality of local affairs. Ogasawara, for example, was preoccupied with international economic problems; Kobayashi, with an abstract interest in criminal law. They were not well prepared to formulate ideas which would resolve the pressing social and economic dilemmas of that era because they knew dangerously little about their constituencies.

This observation helps explain the political history of the 1930s. It suggests that the Diet and political parties had become essentially central organs, badly out of touch with conditions in local Japan. They were not capable of formulating programs to alleviate the larger social and economic problems at home. Instead, they diverted their attention to matters overseas and drifted according to the mood at the center. Dominated as it was by military thinking, the center carried them to war.

That this system endured with so little change may seem surprising, but it is not difficult to explain. Simply put, it survived because it served the immediate interests of all its participants: voters, candidates, and parties alike. The prestigious men whom voters returned were responsive to short-term interests, such as getting a new school, repairing a dike, or building a bridge. Most voters believed that the broad problems of farm prices and unemployment were national dilemmas, fostered by a harsh international atmosphere. In the eyes of the populace, they were not subject to easy solution through representative institutions. That being the case, the electorate was content to pursue immediate political goals in the manner to which it had grown accustomed.

Candidates found satisfaction with the system because in all too many cases their purpose was to seek status and influence. They sought office for the prestige it brought, and only incidentally for the purpose of rectifying the nation's ills. The parties also benefited from the system. It returned to office men of different socio-economic coalitions, for whom the Diet served as just one of many channels of influence. In all fairness, there were many politicians whose motives were informed by high political purposes. But, in all accuracy, there were many others whose motives were more personal and material. Nakajima Chikuhei, who used his influence in the Diet to

[45] Suzuki Kiyosetsu, ed., *Mikawa kensei shiryō* (Nagoya, 1941), p. 428.
[46] Ibid., p. 452.

build his industrial enterprise, is just one case in point. There were immediate benefits for everyone in the system: roads and schools for the voters; status for the candidates; and influence for the parties. What it failed to provide were the vision and conviction necessary to parry the political challenges laid down by the military.

For this failure, the Japanese people paid dearly. The most overwhelming cost of the war was registered in terms of human deaths. It is estimated that over 1.5 million military personnel and nearly 3 million civilians died during the war. Everyone lost friends and relatives in the army and navy, and many were touched by the destruction of cities at home. Kariya avoided destruction because it was so small, but had the war lasted another week, it too would have been a target for bombing.[47] That it escaped the bombing did not relieve the suffering of human loss. At the Toyota loom firm alone, 362 former employees gave their lives for the war effort. The number of war dead in Anjō reached nearly fourteen hundred; Kariya would have sacrificed a similar number.[48]

Loss of life was only one part of the suffering. There were constant disruptions to a normal way of life after 1937. Full scale mobilization of national resources drew virtually everyone into the war effort by the end. Young men had to leave their jobs to serve abroad. Wives and mothers had to leave home to work in shops and factories. And children had to forego schooling for the sake of the war. As early as 1941, the country began using school-age children to work in factories. Toyota Looms began employing students from the nearby girls' high school to work on the assembly of machine guns in that year. Two years later the company moved its tools directly into the classrooms, so the girls could provide labor service as an integral part of their school experience. Eventually the net widened to embrace higher elementary school students, and by the end even grade schoolers. In the all-consuming effort to produce for war, education was just one aspect of a normal way of life sacrificed for the sake of the nation.

Material sacrifices were also severe. After rising somewhat during the early 1930s, nationwide expenditures for personal consumption plummeted by 40 percent between 1937 and 1944.[49] Rationing and short supplies forced this drop. Luxuries were cut first. By the early 1940s tobacco, for example, became a rarity, and those who wanted to smoke had to satisfy themselves by rolling dried grass in old newspaper and smoking that. By 1943 food and other essentials were so scarce that a family of four was allowed only three bars of soap, six eggs, and one bundle

[47] U.S. Strategic Bombing Survey, *The Effects of Air Attack on Japanese Urban Economy: Summary Report* (Washington, D.C., 1947), p. 66.

[48] Anjō shi shi hensan iinkai, ed., *Anjō shi shi* (Anjō, 1971), p. 1055.

[49] Nakamura Takafusa, *Senzenki Nihon keizai seichō no bunseki* (Tokyo, 1971), p. 258.

of firewood per month.[50] Bread was limited to one loaf per person per month, and *tōfu* (bean curd, an essential protein source in the Japanese diet) to one cake a person each month. The government urged the citizenry to cut down on rice consumption, by mixing it with barley or by substituting bread. It also ballyhooed the virtues of the *hi no maru bentō*, a lunch box which substituted a small, salty plum for what in better days might have been a vegetable or piece of fish. The crimson circle of the plum called forth the image of the national flag, for which the lunch box was named. Other essentials fell into short supply, also. In Kariya, people who could find neither fish nor pork went to the mountains in search of wild boar. Others made do with horsemeat, dogmeat, or snake meat. As a result of rationing and shortages, many people in Japan were consuming less than fifteen hundred calories a day by the end of the war.

There were still other sacrifices made during the war which were lost forever or would take years to replace. The lack of steel and iron ore imports required that temple bells, memorial tablets, and statues be collected and melted down for war use. Innumerable historical treasures were lost because of this. Trees were cut wherever they could be found. Kariya was virtually de-nuded by the war, as the remaining woodlands around the castle area at Kijō School disappeared in the name of national survival. Food production required that most land be used for cereal grains. Consequently, nearly two thousand acres of fruit orchards were dug up in Hekikai County. The barren appearance of the countryside around Kariya in 1972 was in large measure a legacy of the war years.

And there were the invisible costs, needs ignored during the crisis of war. School buildings fell into decay. Roads went unrepaired or unbuilt. People failed to remodel homes or build new ones. Towns let harbors silt over. They built no offices, no public auditoriums, no libraries. In 1972, after two decades of prosperity, those invisible costs still remained glaring and conspicuous, but the Japanese people were beginning to acknowledge them at last, as they were forced to send their children to dilapidated schools, drive on dangerous roads, and live in outmoded housing.

By early 1945 it was obvious the end was near. The nation was very short of essential materials. Factories could not find workers. Devastated by air attacks, Japanese industry was nearing a standstill. Sixty-six cities had fallen victim to the air war and almost one-half their settled areas lay in ruins. More than 8 million people were homeless.[51] The final acts of destruction occurred in Hiroshima on August 6, 1945, and in Nagasaki three days later. The bombs dropped on those two cities symbolized the dawn of a new historical epoch, as they brought an end to the long night of war.

[50] *handa shi shi*, 3:642–643.
[51] This material is drawn from the Strategic Bombing Survey mentioned in footnote 47.

Kariya emerged from the war vastly different from the community it had been in 1932. Most conspicuous was its change from a rustic country town to an industrial city. Expansion in the Toyota enterprise propelled that change. As the loom firm and the auto company grew after 1937, they spun off new factories which attracted rising numbers of workers. By 1945 an industrial working class dominated the labor force in Kariya. Made up in large part of outsiders, this group had helped to undermine the social basis of political solidarity in the community. At the same time, it fostered new patterns of social relationships in which the factory and the work group became primary points of reference. This helped to loosen the bonds of social conformity and would provide a volatile social underpinning for the impending postwar era. In step with its industrial growth, the political role of the Toyota enterprise also increased; by virtue of numbers, Toyota workers would be a dominant force in postwar electoral politics. So also did the status and power of Toyota's managers increase. During the war they worked hand in hand with prestigious old-line family heads, such as Ōno Ichizō, to assist the national cause. Having played a loyal, critical role in Kariya's everyday affairs for over a decade, industrial managers had become indispensable, high-standing members of the community by 1945. As peace dawned, Kariya entered a period which would severely test the cohesion of this tenuous new social order.

6

A RADICAL INTERLUDE,
1945–1955

Defeat in war and occupation by a foreign power were unprecedented experiences for the Japanese people. They were the more difficult to bear psychologically because they occurred under such dismal material conditions. When General MacArthur landed in Japan in August 1945, nearly half the nation's industrial capacity lay in ruins. Transport systems were outmoded and ill-functioning. Resources of all kinds were in short supply and food was especially scarce. Japan waited uncertainly as its American occupiers embarked on their tasks. Determined to prevent Japan's ever becoming a military power again, Occupation authorities quickly bent their energies to reform. A foreign power wielding ultimate authority over the nation was an experience radical enough for Japan. The American dedication to thoroughgoing change made it only more so.

In their earnest desire to remake Japan in the American image, Occupation authorities left few stones unturned. They transformed the political structure of Japan. They abandoned the Meiji Constitution in favor of a newly written document which went into effect in May 1947. It retained the emperor as a figurehead and placed ultimate power in the hands of the people. They elected representatives to a parliament which in turn established the cabinet that would carry out the executive tasks of government. The scope of political participation widened to include both men and women above the age of twenty. A rash of supplementary laws established a new system of local government. By divorcing prefectural and municipal governments from the intrusive control of the central government, the new laws extended greater autonomy to local bodies than they had enjoyed before. Voters could now choose their prefectural governors and mayors in popular elections, and recall them if they wished. The Home Ministry lost its power over local affairs as it was broken into a number of parts. Other laws established a new tax structure for local communities, giving them financial authority to make political autonomy meaningful. As a result of the new laws, Occupation authorities wrought fundamental changes in at least the appearance of the Japanese polity.[1]

[1] The best discussion of these changes at the local level is Kurt Steiner, *Local Government in*

The Occupation focused its attention on key social institutions also. The educational system was a major target for reform. Convinced that Japan's military problem lay in some part with the content of the elementary schools, Occupation authorities revised curricula, censored textbooks, purged former teachers, and instituted a new regime. They abandoned the shrewdly diversified structure of Japan's prewar system in favor of a homogeneous American system: six years of elementary school, three of junior high, and three of senior high, followed by four years of college, and graduate school beyond that. The reform placed an undue burden on the existing physical plant and resulted in numerous anomalies: old high schools became universities overnight and suffered the onus of their nickname, *ekiben daigaku*.[2] In other cases, middle schools were pressed into use as high schools. Kariya, for example, converted the middle school of which it was so proud into a new community high school. More important than the structural reforms, however, were changes in the substantive content of classroom instruction. Under the guidance of young teachers, many of whom supported thorough reform, the classroom came alive with a new atmosphere. Teachers and students alike shunted aside prewar values and morality in an almost fervid anxiety to become more "democratic."

Occupation authorities treated Japan's large industrial conglomerates (*zaibatsu*) as another of the evils of the prewar era. Within a month of their arrival, American officials set out to abolish the *zaibatsu*. They removed former managers from their posts, seized the holdings of the largest firms and families, and broke down the conglomerates into smaller, presumably less odious parts. To protect the new business environment, American officials established a Monopoly Board, whose duty it was to police reconsolidation. The *zaibatsu* dissolution program achieved its initial aims among the largest firms. But as the political situation in China and Korea changed, Occupation officials lost their reformist zeal toward big business. By June 1949, they had begun to wink at reversions of one kind or another; it was only a matter of time before support for this reform evaporated entirely.

To guarantee the political viability of the new constitution, Occupation officials felt the need to create new social groups to support it. One purpose of the agrarian reform, carried out between 1947 and 1950, was to establish a yeoman farmer—an independent proprietor in the American

---

Japan (Stanford, 1965), pp. 64–113. I draw heavily on Steiner's conclusions throughout this book.

[2] *Daigaku* means university in Japanese. An *ekiben* is an inexpensive, Japanese-style lunchbox purchased at a train station. Each station is recognized for its own specialty—or used to be until the age of standardization. An *ekiben daigaku* thus implies a kind of educational potpourri, with a derogatory overtone concerning the cheapness and ready availability of the fare a school offers.

image—whose self-interest would make him a bulwark of democracy. The Occupation succeeded handsomely in establishing a yeoman peasantry. Within three years pure tenants almost disappeared from the Japanese countryside. In their place arose a vast number of small farmers who owned all or most of the land they tilled. The political significance of these changes has been complex and is subject to no easy generalization. At the very least, the yeoman farmer became—if not the bulwark for democracy —the indispensable electoral base for conservative party rule.[3]

Occupation authorities were also eager to establish urban groups to safeguard democracy. Under the influence of New Deal thought, they felt labor unions were the obvious instruments to inhibit authoritarianism in the city. On December 22, 1945, they promulgated a law which made legal the right to organize and to bargain collectively. It went into effect in March 1946. Almost overnight thousands of unions sprouted to enroll millions of members. Within three years over half the eligible work force had organized itself into unions to bargain collectively and to act politically. Much to the Occupation's dismay, the unions became far more active than officials had anticipated. They quickly regretted the day they had created them, and they acted to thwart union power. Beginning in January 1947, when General MacArthur prohibited a general strike, Occupation authorities worked to bring the powers of the union movement under control. They were successful in large measure, but they could never quell the powerful force which they themselves had created. Indeed, Occupation policies drove the union movement into the arms of the Socialist parties, which have functioned to restrain the powers of conservative governments ever since. To the extent that they provide an alternative and a brake on untrammeled conservative power, the union movement and the Socialist parties have been the main forces of opposition in postwar Japanese politics.

Due largely to the political influence of organized labor, Kariya witnessed an unusual period of political behavior in the decade after 1945. As the local economy languished, workers became more anxious about their political and economic well-being. They abandoned the docile ways which had characterized the work force during preceding decades and confronted management in harsh assemblies, demanding wage increases and job security. They turned their attention to the political arena as well. By the end of the decade, in early 1955, they had proved themselves powerful political opponents. The local mayor owed his position to union support. The city's representative in the prefectural assembly was a member of the Japan Socialist Party. And unions had, with the support of

[3] The most reliable discussion of this subject presently available is R. P. Dore, *Land Reform in Japan* (London, 1959).

workers in Toyota,[4] elected a representative to the national Diet from the
Japan Socialist Party. The torpid atmosphere of consensual politics and
community solidarity disappeared, and for a brief interlude, Kariya
underwent a radical political experience.

This chapter explores Kariya's radical interlude from two perspectives,
one economic and one political. The first part of the chapter details the
changes which occurred in Kariya as an organized labor force exerted its
economic influence for the first time. It deals in turn with the following
subjects: the evolution of the major form of union organization in Kariya,
the enterprise union; the manner in which prewar restraints on labor
activism broke down after 1945; the strike activities of workers in the
locale; and the reasons for the outcome of worker activism. The second
part of the chapter examines the political thrust of organized labor in
Kariya and western Mikawa between 1945 and 1955. It illustrates how
different rates of economic recovery affected political change in the cities
of the region, and closes with an analysis of the achievements of
progressive political groups in the first decade after the war.

Worker Activism

Japanese workers responded enthusiastically to the right to organize and
bargain collectively.[5] Although relatively few workers had organized in
Japan before 1945, within seven months of the Occupation order nearly 5
million workers joined together in over seventeen thousand unions to
bargain collectively. The union tide which swept the country moved
swiftly through Kariya. Workers at the Toyota loom factory were the first
to organize. They formed a union in December 1945, even before the
Occupation law was enacted. Workers at Toyota Motors organized at
almost the same time. At the end of 1946, two other large unions formed in
Kariya, one at the machine tool plant and the other at the steel factory. In
addition, employees at a large number of small firms in the community
organized. Within a year after the legalization of unions, nearly two of
every three employed persons in the town of Kariya belonged to a labor
union.[6]

With virtually no previous union experience, workers adopted the only
organization with which they had any familiarity, the enterprise union.
Numerous Japanese labor historians attribute the selection of this union
form to the wartime influences of Sampō, the League for Industrial

---

[4] In 1959 the old city of Koromo changed its name to Toyota, in honor of the auto
company headquartered there. Although it is not entirely accurate to do so, I refer to that
city hereafter as Toyota—for the sake of consistency.

[5] See for example Ōkōchi Kazuo, *Sengo Nihon no rōdō undō*, rev. ed., (Tokyo, 1961), pp.
35–102.

[6] Aichi ken, rōdō bu, rōsei ka, *Rōdō kumiai meibo* (Nagoya, 1954), pp. 67–71.

Patriotism. Sampō originated in 1938 with a call from the Aichi Prefectural Police Department for labor-management unity and industrial cooperation. This idea appealed to national leaders, and in 1940 the Sampō organization emerged formally as a part of Prince Konoe's new panoply of government. During the war virtually every factory in the country had a Sampō unit whose primary duty was to support the national cause through increased production. Since the Sampō units were organized at the factory or enterprise level, it is argued that they provided workers in the postwar period with a logical precedent for an organizational form, the enterprise union.[7]

To adopt this view is to accept a position which is historically shortsighted, because Sampō was merely a formal apparatus superimposed on already existing organizations. The Toyota loom factory illustrates this point.[8] When Toyota built its factory in Kariya, it set out immediately to create an atmosphere of familial solidarity in the factory, as the previous chapter explained. One vehicle for achieving solidarity was a group known as the Hōyūkai, or Friends of Toyota Society. All workers joined and participated in its activities. These included sports contests and publication of an in-company newspaper, among other things. Workers may have suggested some of the groups' activities, but the personnel department supervised what they did. When the Sampō movement gained popularity in 1938, Toyota officials quickly jumped on the bandwagon. In November of that year, they organized a Sampō branch. It is significant that the company history explains the function of this group by saying, "Henceforth, the personnel management in the company was carried out under the name of Sampō." [9] In other words, Sampō was simply a formal title superimposed on a structure and set of practices which had existed since the establishment of the firm in 1927. Certainly, Sampō injected into the factory atmosphere its own air of patriotism, to which workers were probably quite responsive. But Sampō activities were only conventional personnel policies cast in a somewhat different light. Sampō did not condition workers to organize at the enterprise level; it merely reinforced that tendency, which had existed before Sampō appeared.

Workers thus organized in enterprise unions because they were accustomed to undertaking their activities on an intra-company basis. Another reason for adopting the enterprise union had to do with employment practices. Since the 1910s Japanese managers had implemented personnel policies designed to attract a loyal and stable work

---

[7] See, for example, Taira, *Economic Development and the Labor Market in Japan*, pp. 187–190; and Solomon Levine, "Postwar Trade Unionism, Collective Bargaining, and Japanese Social Structure," in R. P. Dore, ed., *Aspects of Social Change in Modern Japan* (Princeton, 1967), p. 257.

[8] *40-nen shi*, pp. 178–183.

[9] Ibid., p. 292.

force. Their key inducements were salary increases based primarily on seniority and the promise of a substantial retirement bonus. They sought with such policies to retain workers in a firm until their retirement. As long as a firm's wages were good and its condition sound, workers usually did remain until retirement. This was certainly the case at Toyota Automatic Loom, where a retirement bonus equivalent to seven years' pay must have been an enticing lure for many workers.[10] Under such a system, workers did not seek promotion and salary increases by moving from one firm to another, so they became occupationally quite immobile, especially as they became older.

The relatively stable work force, which emerged in the large firms where the above policies applied, had important implications for the pattern of union organization. [Workers recognized that their economic fortunes lay with the company where they worked, not with a better job in another firm.] Consequently, their economic future rested with their firm and its well-being, not with the economic conditions of an industry. Therefore, workers at Toyota Motors concerned themselves primarily with the condition of that company alone, rather than with the welfare of the auto industry and auto workers as a group. They had a weak perception of their interests as part of a major industry, and this impeded organization along industrial lines.

Work practices adopted by companies which favored lifetime employment impeded organization along craft lines. Under the lifetime employment system, companies hired workers in their teens and retained them until they were fifty or fifty-five. Rather than hire an employee in a specific capacity, companies hired their employees with no job classification in mind. This left the company free to retrain and reassign workers as necessity demanded. For this reason, factory workers were slow to develop a consciousness of their roles as craftsmen. Even if a man became a skilled machinist, he did not think of using his skills to capture a better job elsewhere. This certainly reduced his interest in establishing uniform hiring and pay practices for all workers in a certain trade, and it inhibited organization along craft lines, while it affirmed the worker in his choice of the enterprise union.

Past practice and the nature of the labor market disposed Japan's workers in the postwar period to organize along enterprise lines, and that is just what they did in Kariya. Men employed by Toyota Automatic Loom formed two unions, one for the factory in Kariya, another for a second factory in Ōbu. Each union remained autonomous and collected its own dues, handled its own negotiations, possessed its own contracts, and managed its own grievances. Across the tracks, workers at the Toyota

[10] Ibid., p. 340.

Machine Tool Company established a separate union. They were skilled machinists like the workers at the loom factory and might have found an identity of interest because of their occupation. In fact, both groups later affiliated with the same national body of metal workers. Nonetheless, they preserved their enterprise form, and remained wholly independent of each other in regard to wage scales, contracts, and benefits. The other large firms in Kariya also established separate unions, organized along factory and/or enterprise lines. Thus, even though two-thirds of the community's workers were organized, each union operated in virtual isolation from every other, its fate tied to the destiny of its firm. This organizational pattern dictated the course of union activism in the postwar period.

Enterprise, or company, unions are subject to well-known weaknesses, from the worker's point of view.[11] They are too small to marshal ample financial or human resources. They identify with the interests of the firm of which they are a part. They consequently devote little attention to universal concerns, such as the goal to win equal pay for equal work. Lacking concerns shared by all industrial laborers, enterprise unions struggle alone in contests with management. They operate without the advantage of outside pressure brought to bear by the union movement as a whole. Due to these shortcomings, the workers in Kariya found themselves in a relatively weak position as they bargained with management in the early postwar years.

Workers in Kariya, however, refused to allow weaknesses inherent in the enterprise union to inhibit their activities. On the contrary, they overlooked the weaknesses as they undertook actions unprecedented in their assertiveness. The quickness and completeness with which workers in Kariya organized and their use of collective strength to confront management were both surprising events. After all, as the previous chapter illustrated, there were many impediments to labor activism in the community. But defeat, occupation, and depression reduced those impediments. At the same time, they also created a historically distinctive environment which gave rise to radically altered relations between workers and managers. The following pages explain why this new worker activism arose in Kariya.

To understand the causes of labor dissidence in the postwar period, it is helpful to re-examine the reasons for docility mentioned earlier. In addition to the general atmosphere of national crisis which hung over the 1930s and fostered harmony between management and labor, there were five other reasons for labor docility in the decades before 1945. These included (1) the shared conception of workers and managers that they were members in a joint undertaking, (2) the effects of an educational

[11] They are explained in Shirai Taishirō, *Kigyō betsu kumiai* (Tokyo, 1968), pp. 39-50.

system which inculcated the traits of obedience and conformity, (3) the social organization of the factory, especially its pay system and the *sempai-kōhai* pattern of relationships, (4) the ingrained deference of the young men entering the factory, and (5) the novelty of industrial work, both for the workers and for their families. Before the war, these considerations muffled labor conflict or prevented it entirely, so that workers carried out their tasks docilely under management's unquestioned authority.

The passage of time, defeat in war, and the policies of the Occupation undermined these causes of docility, negating some of them entirely and converting others to different uses. The Occupation ushered in a new vocabulary of political discourse which challenged the old conception of labor-management relations. The ideas of Marxism, unionism, and democracy constituted a three-pronged attack on the old view that laborers and managers were simply members of a single, happy family. Marxism encouraged the worker to see his interests in conflict with those of management. Unionism, legalized for the first time by the Occupation, provided a social instrument to carry out that idea. And democracy, of the enthusiastic sort which Occupation authorities fostered for a brief time, insured a political climate in which both the new ideas and their social instruments could be put to active use. There were enough adherents of the ideas in Kariya that many laborers abandoned the old view of labor-management relations in favor of a new, more contentious one.

The same influences which undermined the old view of factory relations also mitigated the effects of the prewar educational system on many workers. Many Japanese struggled in a morass of moral anomie during the early postwar years. They had seen their nation and the value system on which it was built nearly destroyed, then condemned by international opinion. It was difficult to follow with any assurance older ways that were being constantly discredited. For several years after 1945, such uncertainty diluted unquestioned obedience and conformity among workers and freed them somewhat from social constraints that would otherwise have retarded labor activism.

Changes occurred in the social organization of local factories which liberated workers from their stifling embrace. In late 1946 Toyota Automatic Loom instituted a new pay system.[12] It retained incentive pay, which comprised on the average about a fourth of a man's salary. But it also granted a base pay, determined by one's age and experience, as well as other compensation, in the form of dependent's pay, a commuting subsidy, overtime, and vacation pay. Although he was still expected to perform at full capacity in order to earn at full potential, the worker now

[12] *40-nen shi*, pp. 667–668.

received a guaranteed salary, irrespective of his performance. This freed him from the repressive constraints of the group-based, piece-rate system.

The social climate of the postwar world converted the *sempai-kōhai* relationship to different uses. As long as a firm could count on the unquestioned loyalty of its older employees, the *sempai-kōhai* relationship worked effectively to translate that loyalty down the line. But if older workers lost their fidelity to management's goals and adopted a new set of goals and action, they threatened to socialize everyone with their new principles. In this way, *sempai-kōhai* relations became a vehicle to spread dissent within the factory. New workers were attaching themselves, not only to management loyalists, but also to middle-aged men imbued with the ideas of Marxism, unionism, and democracy. Under such conditions, the grounds of labor-management solidarity were eroded.

In many cases it was not necessary for a *sempai* to socialize his *kōhai* to the new values. The schools and the general atmosphere of ideas would already have done so. By 1950 young men entering firms in the Kariya area had been exposed to three or four years of instruction in schools where "democracy" was the keynote. They understood the basic idea of egalitarianism, which called into question the customary deference to superiors. It was unimportant to them that the Toyota family was successful and famous, because allegedly they could be too, in time. New recruits in the late 1940s were thus less cowed by the authority of owners, managers, and superintendents than their predecessors had been a decade or two earlier.

Finally, by the late 1940s the novelty of factory life had lost its value as a repressing agent. Families in the Kariya area had experienced and witnessed the nature of industrial life for two decades. There were now many fathers, uncles, and brothers in the community who formed the first generation of an industrial proletariat. It was more difficult to enter the factory ignorant of its ways and awed by its novelty. Moreover, many workers in the factories were now older. They were more sophisticated than they had been as raw, farm youth a decade or more before. They understood the operations of the factory, the implications of the pay system, the value of retirement pay, and the meaning of a cutback. They were, quite simply, less manipulable than before.

Workers organized and struck against management in the postwar period because the old constraints on labor weakened considerably after 1945, as the preceding comments illustrate. Nonetheless, these causes were not sufficient to provoke the enthusiasm which workers displayed. They merely facilitated the acceptance of activity which was fostered by another cause.

The force behind the union movement and labor activism was the lurching Japanese economy. Problems of inflation, deflation, depression, and unemployment plagued the country from late 1945 until the early 1950s. In the immediate postwar years, prices rose at precipitous rates, negating the value of wage increases again and again. Deflation followed inflation, leading to a sharp drop in the demand for manufactured products. Depression persisted as reconstruction proceeded slowly and foreign trade stagnated. Unemployment was endemic. It drove millions— as a last resort—to leave urban areas and return to the farm, where they were at least able to eat, if not to find profitable work. These conditions affected the entire country, but they struck some locales with particular severity.

Kariya had the bad fortune, during the first postwar decade, to be allied with one of the most depressed industrial sectors in the economy. Vehicle making, machine manufacture, and the metals trades recovered more slowly than other industrial sectors. Between 1948 and 1953 employment in vehicle and machine making actually declined nationwide.[13] Employment conditions in Kariya were especially dire. Between 1945 and 1955 Toyota Machine Tools Company cut its labor force from 1,480 to 893, a loss of 587 jobs. Toyota Chassis Company cut its work force from 1,090 in 1951 to 689 in 1955, for an additional loss of 401 jobs. Nippon Densō, which employed 1,526 workers when it incorporated at the end of 1949, cut over 350 workers from its payroll before it began rehiring again in 1955. Only Toyota Automatic Loom managed to weather the storm of the postwar economy well. But in 1955 it employed only 62 more workers than it had in 1945.[14] During the very worst year of 1950 nearly three thousand persons sought assistance from the local unemployment office.[15] Although conditions improved after 1951, Kariya's industrial labor force was still 8 percent *smaller* in 1955 than it had been in 1947.

To appreciate the economic dilemmas which Kariya faced between 1945 and 1955, it is necessary to understand conditions at the Toyota enterprise.[16] As the previous chapter illustrated, Toyota was a highly diversified concern by 1945. It included separate companies engaged in the manufacture of textiles, textile machinery, vehicles, aircraft, machine tools, and steel. Several of its firms were located in China, and Toyota lost them at the end of the war. Most of the firms, however, were located in Kariya, Nagoya, and Toyota. The original Toyota Spinning and Weaving

[13] Asahi shimbun sha, ed., *Shiryō Meiji hyakunen* (Tokyo, 1966), p. 622.
[14] *40-nen shi*, pp. 706–723.
[15] Kss, p. 251.
[16] The following account is based on: *40-nen shi*, pp. 309–374; *30-nen shi*, pp. 233–323; Shashi henshū iinkai, ed., *Aichi seikō sanjūnen shi* (Tōkai, 1970); Toyota Kōki nijūnen shi hensan iinkai, ed., *Toyota kōki nijūnen shi* (Kariya, 1961), pp. 160–186; Shashi hensan iinkai, ed., *Toyota shatai nijūnen shi* (Kariya, 1965), pp. 80–137; and T. M. Hout and W. V. Rapp, "Competitive Development of the Japanese Automobile Industry," in J. Cohen, ed., *Pacific Partnership* (Lexington, Mass. 1972), pp. 221–240.

Company, located in Nagoya, was destroyed by bombing, and did not resume production until the early 1950s. The other factories in Kariya and Toyota all escaped destruction, however, and were able to resume production of civilian goods soon after the war ended.[17]

There were marked differences in the rate of recovery among firms within the enterprise. The first firms to resume profitable operations were those which manufactured textile equipment, Toyota Automatic Loom and Toyota Machine Tool. The loom factory produced almost as many looms between 1945 and 1955 as it had between 1932 and 1945, plus a far larger quantity of spinning equipment. Even in the depressed postwar years, Toyota Automatic Loom earned profits without interruption. They were lower than they were before the war (only 5 percent before taxes), but such steady profits were unusual for the Toyota enterprise during the first postwar decade.[18]

All of the remaining Toyota firms recovered more slowly than the loom company. The steel firm had the greatest difficulties. Although it increased output and sales dramatically, it also suffered losses in three of the years between 1945 and 1955. These forced it to reduce its labor force by one-third. The machine tool factory recovered in 1947 by manufacturing textile equipment for which there was considerable demand. But when it converted to machine tool production again in 1952, it experienced a drop in sales and financial deficits, which resulted in the layoff of 400 workers. The old aircraft plant changed its name to Aichi Industries in 1945 and began producing household goods, such as sewing and knitting machines. It was able to make modest gains, and after 1951 began hiring in small numbers. The other two large Toyota firms in Kariya escaped losses during this period, but they hardly flourished. These firms were Toyota Chassis and Nippon Densō, the former Electrical Components Department of Toyota Motors which incorporated as a separate organization in December 1949. The fate of these two firms hinged directly on the fortunes of Toyota Motors, whose own condition during this period set the tone for the enterprise as a whole.

Toyota Motors languished economically for the first decade after the war. In ten years it produced 129,305 vehicles. Only 19,249 of them were automobiles; the rest were trucks and buses. That was only a modest gain over production during its first troubled decade after 1935, when it turned out 90,018 vehicles. Production problems were not the only ones which the company experienced. It also failed to earn the profits it had grown

[17] The main auto assembly plant in Toyota (then the town of Koromo) suffered slight damage when it was struck on August 14, 1945. Other plants in Kariya and Toyota suffered no damage due to the fact that the Japanese motor vehicle industry was never a primary target for air attack. U.S. Strategic Bombing Survey, *The Japanese Motor Vehicle Industry* (Washington, D.C., 1946), p. 2.

[18] *40-nen shi*, p. 689.

accustomed to. In 1949 and again in 1950 it suffered substantial losses. It was very near bankruptcy when the 1950 strike occurred.[19] Only after 1951 did it regain its momentum and its profitability.

The economic difficulties at Toyota Motors derived largely from government economic policies. These were of two types: reconstruction policy and Occupation policy. Appreciating the need for rapid recovery in essential industries, the Japanese government decided to postpone reconstruction of the auto industry in order to rebuild other industrial sectors. Until 1951, therefore, when the government altered its policy, the auto industry found it difficult to acquire financial assistance as well as essential materials. The reconstruction policies of the Japanese government thus retarded the rate of recovery of Toyota Motors.

Occupation policy had a mixed effect on Toyota. When Occupation authorities set out to destroy the old *zaibatsu*, they had four objectives. They wanted to (1) remove former managers from positions of influence, (2) disperse the corporate holdings of *zaibatsu* families, (3) destroy the *zaibatsu* holding companies, and (4) break up the conglomerates into a number of smaller, independent companies. The first two efforts did not affect Toyota. Although eighteen of its managers were investigated on two occasions, none of them was forced to step down. Nor did the Toyota family have its holdings seized. Since corporations within the enterprise, rather than members of the family, owned most of the shares in the Toyota combine, the Toyota family did not suffer financially under the Occupation as the Mitsui and Iwazaki families did. The enterprise thus preserved its family-like character as well as its prewar managerial personnel, despite Occupation policies.

The other two aspects of Occupation policy did affect Toyota. The government forced the dissolution of the family holding company, a firm known after 1942 as Toyota Industries. This firm originated as the Toyota Finance Corporation in 1936. Kiichirō established it to finance auto sales. Six years later it changed its name and undertook management of the stock holdings of Toyota firms. It was never as important as the holding companies at Mitsui and Mitsubishi, however, so its dissolution had a relatively minor impact on the enterprise.

Occupation authorities never required firms in the Toyota enterprise to break up into smaller companies, but they did require some divestment of shares and transfer of authority. Toyota Loom had to dispose of two-thirds of its holdings in Toyota Motors. The auto firm had to cede its rights in some forty firms in which it held stock to a government agency between 1947 and 1952, but it retained ownership of the stock and re-acquired its

[19] Hout and Rapp, "Competitive Development of the Japanese Automobile Industry," p. 224.

authority after the treaty settlement in 1952.[20] Its loss of rights over
affiliates inhibited the ability of Toyota Motors to integrate production
vertically. This threw firms within the enterprise on their own devices, and
forced them to survive as best they could. Few of them flourished as a
result. Only after the Occupation ended and the government revised its
policies was the enterprise able to overcome the sluggishness which
characterized it between 1945 and 1951.

The dilemmas of the Japanese economy and the specific problem of
recovery in the Toyota enterprise were the general causes of labor
dissidence in Kariya between 1945 and 1955. All of the major strikes
occurred at a time of rapid inflation or falling profits. Workers struck
when their wage increases did not keep pace with increases in the real cost
of living.[21] They struck out of necessity, just to win a living wage. They
also struck in opposition to layoffs, cuts in retirement benefits, and wage
reductions.

These were the deeper causes of labor unrest, but the immediate and
precipitating cause was nearly always management policy. Virtually every
major strike in Kariya began when Toyota managers declared a reduction
in retirement benefits, usually without consulting the workers. By so doing,
management reneged on the important customary understanding that it
would not roll back the benefits which workers had secured for themselves.
Management broke another customary agreement when it laid off
workers. By dismissing regular members of the work force, management
challenged the principle of lifetime tenure which lay at the very
foundation of the employment system in firms such as those in the Toyota
enterprise. Finally, on some occasions management actually failed to live
up to a written agreement promising no dismissals. When companies failed
to honor their promises, whether they were written and explicit or
unwritten and customary, workers no longer felt the necessity to honor
their part of the understanding. This strained relations and often led to
strikes.

It is useful at this point to examine the forms which worker activism
took in Kariya. Between 1947 and 1955 Kariya experienced over 100

---

[20] The reason why Toyota Motors was designated a *zaibatsu* warrants brief mention,
because it may be a source of misunderstanding concerning Toyota's relationship with
Mitsui. At the end of the war, the Mitsui enterprise owned some 210,000 shares of Toyota
stock which it had inherited from an affiliate, Tōyō Menka, in 1943, when the Central
Spinning Corporation was absorbed by Toyota Motors. Central Spinning originated as a
joint venture between Tōyō Menka and the Toyota Spinning and Weaving Corporation, at a
time when Kodama Ichizō headed the former and his brother Toyota Risaburō managed the
latter. This was yet another case in which personal relationships led to a corporate venture.
The peculiarities of wartime consolidation made it seem that Mitsui actively invested in the
Toyota auto firm, but as the company history states quite explicitly, "Our company was not
an affiliate of Mitsui's enterprise headquarters." [*30-nen shi*, p. 259].

[21] *Toyota shatai nijūnen shi*, app., p. 30; *40-nen shi*, p. 668.

incidents of labor conflict, 37 of them in 1950 alone.[22] Six major strikes at the large Toyota firms in Kariya resulted in 153 days of lost work. As a result of these strikes, labor and management engaged with each other in a mood of anxiety and distrust, which came to characterize the social and political climate in Kariya in the immediate postwar years.

The major strikes in Kariya repeated a similar pattern. Strikes nearly always arose against a background of slow sales and falling profits. Slow sales were sometimes caused by a simple lack of demand in a depressed economy; at other times, by deflationary policies of the central government. Whatever the cause, the result was the same: sinking profits. In an enterprise whose firms had seldom if every suffered a bad year, management reacted to falling profits with strict measures to cut overhead. Labor costs were always a favorite target. With predictable regularity, management signaled its intention to reduce labor outlays—through a reduction in the labor force itself—by revising retirement-pay schedules downward. Having acted unilaterally to reduce retirement benefits, management would then invite workers to retire or it would resort to blanket dismissals. At this point, workers banded together in a brief moment of unity to oppose management and to strike. In the course of the work stoppage, the union membership generally split, enabling management to play off passive loyalists against active unionists. With few exceptions between 1947 and 1955, strikes ended with a settlement clearly beneficial to management's position. There were nuances of difference between disputes, but this pattern duplicated itself with monotonous regularity, as the following sketches of three major disputes illustrate.[23]

The first major strike in Kariya occurred at the Toyota Automatic Loom plant in June 1947, and lasted twenty-five days.[24] Resentment over a retirement-pay settlement precipitated the strike. In December 1946, workers at the factory had struggled to revise retirement-pay schedules. According to the existing agreement, the firm paid workers with thirty years of service a retirement allotment equivalent to 82 months' salary at their highest rate of pay. In the highly inflationary year of 1946, rising prices cut the real value of that allotment by 75 percent, and there was certain prospect of further reduction in the future. Workers demanded a bonus equivalent to 120 months' salary. After more than a month of negotiation, labor agreed to accept a figure well below its demands and

[22] See Aichi ken, rōdō bu, rōsei ka, *Aichi ken rōdō undō nempyō (kō): 1945–1950* (Nagoya, 1963); and, by the same author, *Aichi ken rōdō undō nempyō: 1951–1960* (Nagoya, 1964).

[23] This account is based on *Rōdō jōsei*, an unpaginated and unindexed collection of looseleaf reports originally compiled by the Kariya Labor Affairs Office. They are now bound and retained in their original form in the library of the Aichi Kinrō Kaikan in Nagoya. I base my analysis of labor disputes in this chapter primarily on these documents, because they have an objectivity lacking in both management and labor accounts.

[24] For a discussion of the Toyota Loom strike, see *40-nen shi*, pp. 335–348.

even below the existing figure. Retiring workers would receive 60 months' salary at their last rate of pay. When the union voted on this figure, it split almost evenly, with 1,075 voting in favor and 956 against. This unfavorable settlement left a reservoir of resentment among a large group of the union's membership.

Five months later, under the direction of a new leader, the union pressed management for a wage increase to boost their salaries to ¥1,900 per month, plus taxes. Management countered with an offer of ¥1,800 including taxes. The union members refused the offer, and on June 3, 1947, began an unlimited strike. They entered the factory, barricaded the gate, raised the red flag, and demonstrated on the factory grounds. This was such a seminal event that the Secretary General of the Japan Communist Party, Tokuda Kyūichi, himself came to support the strikers. For almost three weeks they stopped work at the loom plant. But by June 23, a non-strike faction emerged within the work force, and on June 28, they marched into the factory. Almost immediately, the union agreed to halt the strike and submit its demands to arbitration. Department heads, who had declared themselves neutral at the moment the strike began, served as arbiters. In the resolution which won approval in mid-July, the union agreed to a complicated scheme for a wage increase. It exceeded management's original offer, but fell well short of the union's demand. It was also agreed that strikers would receive no pay for the days they had struck, and that the union would henceforth work to increase production at the firm.

Following the strike at the loom factory, and another which occurred at the same time at the steel factory, there were no major strikes until 1950. Then a dispute took place at Toyota Motors which had a telling effect on the fate of the union movement in this area.[25] In late 1949 Toyota Motors suffered its first deficit since it began operations in 1937. It was plagued by overproduction in the face of strong sales resistance. In order to secure financing just to finish the fiscal year, the auto firm sought a loan with a banking consortium. After overcoming the opposition of the Bank of Japan, a group of twenty-four banks agreed to provide Toyota with almost ¥200 million to enable it to pay salaries and purchase materials. Before approving the loan, Bank of Japan officials pointedly urged auto union representatives, who were making preparations for a strike, to call off the strike *and* to accept a 10 percent wage reduction as a condition of the loan. Workers had already suffered a 10 percent cut in pay in August 1949, but in return for a written promise from the company vice-president that Toyota Motors would not lay off workers if the union accepted the wage cut, union leaders acquiesced to the bank's demands. On Christmas Eve,

[25] This account of the strike at Toyota Motors relies on *Rōdō jōsei: 1954; Ikiru Toyota Sakichi*, pp. 175–186; and *30-nen shi*, pp. 290–305.

1949, it appeared that Toyota's financial problems were solved and that all workers had managed to retain their jobs.

Persistent difficulties at the auto firm shattered that illusion. Sales continued to lag and profits continued to fall. The company fell behind in its wage payments. By April discontent among the workers came to a head. On April 11, the union called a one-day strike. Eleven days later, management declared its intention to lay off 1,600 workers and to cut the pay of remaining workers by yet another 10 percent. With this announcement, management openly disavowed the written promise made earlier and ignited the opposition of the union. Workers conducted additional one-day strikes on April 24, May 8 and 15, and June 3. They slowed production to only a third of what it had been before. Management itself conducted a lock-out between April 29 and May 1. For a month, the company nearly ground to a halt.

As the impasse continued, managers in the firm began a concerted effort to persuade many workers that they would not lose their jobs, if only they would return to work. Managers hoped to create a basis of support for their position within the union. If they succeeded, they could split the union and facilitate a rapid settlement. They adopted a twofold strategy to achieve their objective. The first part of the strategy was to identify and draw to management's side potential company loyalists. One tactic intended to secure this end was a letter writing campaign, begun the second week of May, in which the potential loyalists were told:

> As the company faces this crisis, we hope for your cooperation in a mood of abundant faith and enthusiasm and for your loyal actions in the future. The company will guarantee your status and your compensation to the hilt.
>
> Toyota Motor Company, Ltd. (Seal) [26]

This tactic proved very effective. Within a short time, all but 1,700 of the firm's 8,000 workers agreed to comply with a new program of rationalization.

Complementing this action was a second letter campaign directed at less compliant workers in the firm, a group which the management referred to politely as "those seeking dismissal." Their letters were more blunt. They contained explicit directions to send resignation papers to the appropriate officials in return for which the company would grant them a retirement benefit, one month's base pay, a small dependent's allowance, and wages for the months of April and May. The letters closed with the statement that those who dallied in submitting their resignations would suffer a considerable cut in severance pay. Eventually, many workers availed themselves of the opportunity to "retire."

Management's designation of retirees was a tactic used in several other

[26] Nihon jimbun kagaku kai, *Gijutsu kakushin no shakaiteki eikyō*, p. 106.

Toyota factories later, so it deserves a moment's attention. Toyota Motors designated the following types of persons for dismissal:

1. Persons who are not good about getting to work,
2. Persons who do not accept the orders of superiors and who cause trouble in the factory,
3. Those injured and unable to work at full capacity,
4. People who lack the quality of cooperativeness,
5. Persons whom it would be difficult to transfer to another task,
6. Recent recruits and those about to retire,
7. Those with other jobs,
8. Persons who are of little value to the firm.[27]

Such criteria were obviously so nebulous and vague that management could fire virtually anyone it wished to.

The split in union ranks enabled management to do just that. By June 10, the dispute at Toyota Motors was resolved. The company fired 102 workers outright and designated another 1,566 "retirees." There were no further work stoppages; nor did the unions undertake any court action against the firm. Those fired and dismissed were no longer a force in the union (since employment at Toyota Motors was one requirement for membership). The workers who remained accepted obedience to management policies as the price for job security, even at lower pay.

With this strike, and another which took place at the same time at the Nippon Densō factory, in Kariya, the local union movement suffered a severe setback. From a purely economic position, it had clearly lost ground. It also suffered major organizational losses. Among the many persons fired at Toyota Motors and Nippon Densō in 1950 were most of the activists in the union movement.[28] Management used its very nebulous criteria for dismissal to rid itself of what it considered to be the dire influence of "outside Communist agitators."

New Occupation policies provided a climate of support for these actions. Fearing the power of a growing Japan Communist Party, the government began removing "anti-democratic elements" from public life in 1949. As a result of this program, which came to be known as the "red purge," more than twenty thousand alleged Communists were dismissed from government posts and from positions of influence in publishing, broadcasting, and the union movement.[29] The government removed many persons under explicit orders from Occupation authorities. Private concerns removed many others, acting with the support of Occupation officials. In Kariya

---

[27] Rōdō jōsei: 1954.

[28] Nijūnen shi henshū iinkai, ed., Nijūnen no ayumi (Toyota, 1966), 155; and Aichi ken chihō rōdō iinkai, ed., Aichi ken rōdō nempō (Nagoya, 1959), p. 83.

[29] Hans H. Baerwald, The Purge of Japanese Leaders under the Occupation (Berkeley, 1959), p. 78.

and Toyota, managers in the Toyota enterprise availed themselves of the "red purge" to eliminate many key union leaders. In the process, they dampened severely the mood of dissidence among remaining union members.

The final major labor dispute occurred in Kariya in 1955, when workers at the Toyota Chassis factory conducted a twelve-day strike.[30] The chassis firm was about to convert from the output of wooden truck boxes to the assembly-line production of steel truck bodies. Experiencing a mild drop in sales, managers sought to resolve their problems by reducing the labor force. They began by announcing a one-third to one-half cut in previously agreed upon rates of retirement pay. Without consulting the union, the firm implemented the new program on August 1. Shortly after, it distributed a list of 128 persons who would be dismissed, citing virtually the same criteria used by Toyota Motors in 1950. On August 1, the union began an unlimited strike. Within a week, however, sixty-nine voluntary "retirees" had appeared and the strike mood began to diminish. By August 13, the union voted to stop the strike, and on August 25, strikers returned to work. The union had sought discussion of hours, work conditions, and new pay schedules, but all of their issues were tabled. The company dismissed all but 20 of the 128 workers, retaining 4 as regular employees and 16 as temporary. A remark in the company history serves as a fitting conclusion to this discussion: "At this juncture the red flag—which had flown within the company for some time—disappeared, and the workers one by one pledged not to repeat this regrettable memory again." [31] Once again, the management position prevailed.

In the light of foregoing evidence, one must conclude that management, by disavowing customary promises concerning work security and retirement benefits, lit the powder which ignited the keg of labor dissent in postwar Kariya. Waning constraints exercised by prewar values prepared the way for an explosion, but in the end, management's reaction to the problems posed by an uncertain economy actually set off the charge.

The preceding pages have traced the evolution of the enterprise union as the dominant form of labor organization in postwar Kariya; they have shown how an unprecedented level of worker activism manifested itself in the early postwar years; and they have described some of the major strikes which occurred in the late 1940s and the early 1950s. The cause of worker activism was a lurching economy and particularly management policies adopted as a result of economic uncertainties. Finally, the sketches of the major strikes illustrated clearly that management was always able to achieve its desires at the expense of the work force and union movement,

[30] "Toyota shatai rōsō sōgi keika," in *Rōdō jōsei: 1955*; also, Shashi hensan iinkai, ed., *Toyota shatai nijūnen shi*, pp. 133–134; and, *Nijūnen no ayumi*, p. 69.

[31] *Toyota shatai nijūnen shi*, p. 134.

whether that meant laying off workers, reducing retirement benefits, or cutting wages. It remains only to explain why workers did so poorly in their competition with management in order to conclude this analysis of labor's economic role in Kariya during the Occupation period.

In view of the preceding analysis, it is not difficult to understand why unions in Kariya enjoyed so little success in their confrontations with management. They had three sources of weakness. First, they suffered the disadvantage of being company unions. Had they been members of a nationwide industrial union, they might have been able to conduct their struggle simultaneously against all major producers and to win their demands. But workers in Toyota Motors, for example, were bound primarily to that firm and had only weak ties to the outside. If they struck for a prolonged period, they might damage their firm to such a degree that competitors would forever surpass it. Workers in other firms confronted the same dilemma. They concluded that a prolonged strike threatened the very existence of their employer and therefore everyone's job. This constrained union opposition drastically.

The second source of union weakness was the presence of a considerable reservoir of support for the old manner of labor-management relations. Only a portion of the work force freed itself from the constraints which inhibited labor activism before the war. A large portion of the workers retained an allegiance to the concept of partnership between labor and management. They preferred to remain deferential to their superiors and to seek harmonious relations with management. There was always a tension within the union, therefore, between those willing to fight to establish the authority of the union and those disposed to accepting management's directives without question.

The third source of weakness was the ominous threat of unemployment. Men laid off their jobs at the loom factory or the auto company in the early 1950s would have had considerable difficulty finding work. The most expansive sectors of the economy at that time were not employing men with their skills. The specter of prolonged unemployment, in the event of layoffs or even in the event of a drawn-out strike, restrained many union members from excessive acts and dimmed their enthusiasm for contentious strikes.

These sources of weakness were the cause of splits within union ranks which management could play on very successfully in the course of a strike. There were many in the unions who valued the enterprise. They believed that their fortunes depended on the ability of the company to produce efficiently. They also favored the use of the union as an instrument to unite workers behind production goals. Men who felt this way were, for the most part, members of an old guard which remained unaffected by new perceptions of the role of labor. They comprised, therefore, a body of company loyalists which management tried to split off from the more contentious segments of a union.

As a strike dragged out, management worked to persuade men with these sentiments that they would not lose their jobs. They were already suffering economically, either due to late pay or payless strike days. They also faced the prospect of unemployment, as long as the company's "retirees" remained undesignated. Management's tack was therefore to identify those loyal to the company and assure them that they would retain their jobs, if only they would accept an early settlement. With this tactic, management was usually able to isolate a majority of company loyalists from those whom it portrayed as "extremists." When the company released, fired, and purged the "extremists," the loyalists did not resist. They accepted short-term economic losses and the dismissal of many fellow workers. But they retained their own jobs by doing so, and were pleased to join together in the wake of a strike to get the company moving again.

Thus, from an economic perspective, Kariya's decade of radicalism produced relatively few gains for members of the organized work force. Despite the rapidity with which workers organized, despite their strength in numbers, and despite their new-found activism, they achieved relatively little for their efforts when measured against their demands. They did succeed in establishing themselves as a potent force with an undeniable claim to legitimacy as a bargaining unit. This was a significant achievement, in view of the position of workers before the war, but it was one which workers in the Occupation years might justly have assumed was a guaranteed right. Having seen how workers behaved in their role as economic actors, it is now possible to turn to an analysis of their behavior in the political arena. The second part of this chapter deals with that subject.

Political Activism

The economic struggles in which workers engaged were just one aspect of their role as organized laborers. They also undertook concerted political action. Operating through national affiliates, organized workers gave electoral support and financial assistance to the Socialist and Communist parties. Within two years of war's end, the Socialists had gathered enough strength in the national Diet to establish a Socialist-led cabinet, in coalition with a conservative party. The cabinet was based on a precarious balance of factions and survived only seven months. Although it was never able to establish another government, the progressive opposition—relying heavily on organized labor—managed to secure a constitutionally significant one-third of the seats in the Diet.

While organized laborers were active on the national level, they were even more active politically on the local level. This was especially true in Kariya. Using the experience gained in bargaining with management on economic issues, unions in Kariya began to exert forceful pressure on the local political system which produced a new air of political competition in the community.

The purpose of this part of the chapter is to describe how a more competitive form of political behavior emerged in Kariya and western Mikawa in the first decade after the war. To understand changes in Kariya properly, it is necessary to portray its political history against the background of conditions in neighboring cities, because differences in the pace of economic recovery helped to determine political alignments and preferences. After describing the tone of political life in Kariya and elsewhere, this section closes with an analysis of progressive party achievements in the Fourth District between 1945 and 1955. Relying on case studies of one mayoralty contest in Kariya and two Diet *jiban* in the Fourth District, this analysis describes the evolving complexity of political behavior in the Kariya area after 1945.

Kariya had become so dependent on Toyota by 1945 that conditions at the enterprise dictated the fortunes of the town. As Toyota languished during the early postwar years, so did Kariya. After leading the prefecture for two decades with its rapid rate of growth, Kariya skidded to the bottom of the ladder during this period.[32] Between 1947 and 1955 the city-area population expanded by only 5 percent, from 50,022 to 52,470. Most of that growth occurred in the villages rather than the town. Beginning in 1943, when Japan's cities came under American bombing attacks, people returned in ever larger numbers to the relative safety of rural Japan. By the late 1940s, those returnees had swollen the population in rural areas to levels they had not witnessed since the turn of the century. Kariya would actually have lost population in this period, had the villages not proved a haven for those fleeing the bombed out cities and others returning from the colonies.

The four cities around Kariya all experienced more rapid growth during this period, as table 5 illustrates.[33] Handa was the fastest growing

[32] The following discussion of demographic and occupational changes in the five cities relies on two sources: Ats:1947, pp. 24–29, 38–49; and Sōrifu tōkei kyoku, *Kokusei chōsa hōkoku: 1955, Aichi ken* (Tokyo, 1958), pp. 26–32, 142–154.

[33] In chapters 6 through 8, I take some liberties in the way I treat the five communities in this study. After the war all of them (except Handa) consolidated with other towns and villages on one or more occasions. As a result, they all became cities (*shi*), and they all increased in size and area. Kariya became a city in 1950; Toyota (then still Koromo) in 1951; Anjō in 1952; and Nishio in 1953. In the remaining chapters, my comments on each community apply to the area which lay within each city's boundaries in 1972, unless the comments are otherwise qualified.

city. It added some ten thousand persons to expand 18 percent. Even isolated Nishio grew more rapidly than Kariya, expanding by 12 percent between 1947 and 1955. Anjō and Toyota also outpaced Kariya, but only modestly—Anjō expanded by 9 percent and Toyota by 6. In every case, these cities grew more slowly than the prefecture as a whole, whose population expanded 21 percent between 1947 and 1955.

Population growth in these five cities depended on the pace of recovery of their primary industry. Previous comments noted that some industrial sectors recovered more rapidly after the war than others. Table 6 illustrates this explicitly. Immediately after the war, the largest number of factories still operating in Aichi Prefecture produced metals and machines.[34] They employed over half the industrial labor force and turned out almost half of the industrial product by value. Textile factories employed only 18 percent of the labor force and accounted for only 14 percent of industrial output by value. In the following decade, textile output and employment boomed, employment alone increasing more than 500 percent. Employment in food processing and the pottery trades also increased substantially. Only the machine and metals industries stagnated. Those industries increased employment hardly at all while they witnessed a sharp decline in the relative value of their output, from 47 percent of all industrial production in 1946 to only 26 percent in 1954. In the first postwar decade, Aichi's industrial structure reverted briefly to the form it had assumed before the economic boom of the 1930s, when the textile industry had been king.

Between 1946 and 1955 the textile industry again became king in Aichi,

TABLE 5

POPULATION GROWTH IN FIVE AICHI CITIES, 1947–1955

City	1947	1955	% Increase
Kariya	50,022	52,470	5
Toyota	92,538	97,751	6
Anjō	57,423	62,853	9
Nishio	58,866	66,143	12
Handa	57,347	67,827	18

SOURCES: Ats: 1947, pp. 24–29 and 38–49; Sōrifu tōkei kyoku, *Kokusei chōsa hōkoku: 1955, Aichi ken* (Tokyo, 1958), p. 28.

NOTE: These figures have been adjusted for boundary changes. They cite the population of all areas lying with the 1972 boundaries of the five cities.

[34] The following analysis is based on Ats: 1946, pp. 156–166; and Aichi ken, *Aichi ken tōkei nenkan: 1956* (Nagoya, 1957), pp. 220–238 (hereafter referred to as Atn).

and cities which were textile centers boomed as a result. In 1955 over half of all industrial workers in Handa, Nishio and Anjō were textile workers. The growth of those cities was a function of expansion in the textile industry. In Kariya and Toyota, on the other hand, men employed in the auto and machine industries made up nearly two-thirds of the industrial labor force. Tied to an essentially stagnant industrial sector, Kariya and Toyota experienced slow rates of growth during the first postwar decade, well below the rates of growth in the textile centers.

The rate of industrial recovery had a conspicuous impact on employment opportunities. Table 7 illustrates this dramatically. Handa created 7,676 new jobs between 1946 and 1954; 4,359 of them were in manufacturing. Nishio created 4,211 jobs, two-thirds of them in manufacturing. And

TABLE 6

FACTORY WORKERS IN AICHI PREFECTURE, 1946 AND 1954

Industry	1946 No.	(%)	1954 No.	(%)
Textiles	33,818	(18)	172,749	(41)
Machines and metals	101,834	(53)	115,157	(27)
Pottery trades	18,402	(10)	38,838	(9)
Food processing	7,173	(4)	33,057	(8)
All others	31,657	(15)	64,637	(15)
Totals	192,884	(100)	424,438	(100)

SOURCES: Ats: 1946, pp. 156–166; and Atn: 1954, pp. 220–238.
NOTE: The figures for 1946 enumerate all workers in factories employing five or more laborers; for 1954, in factories employing four or more.

TABLE 7

FACTORY WORKERS AND THE LABOR FORCE
IN FIVE AICHI CITIES, 1946 AND 1954

City	All Employed Workers 1946	1954	% Change	Factory Workers 1946	1954	% Change
Kariya	24,387	23,134	−5	10,000	9,187	−8
Toyota	45,713	45,450	−1	10,450	11,241	+8
Anjō	29,027	32,245	+11	9,025	10,921	+21
Nishio	28,208	32,419	+15	7,479	10,115	+35
Handa	22,024	29,700	+35	9,646	14,005	+45

SOURCES: Same as table 6, above.
NOTE: These figures have been adjusted for boundary changes. They enumerate workers resident in all areas lying within the 1972 boundaries of the five cities.

Anjō added 2,218 jobs, most in manufacturing. In sharp contrast to the expansive developments in these cities, Kariya and the town area of Toyota lost jobs during this period. Due to cutbacks at Toyota Motors, there were 600 fewer industrial workers living in the former area of Koromo *machi* in 1955 than in 1946. The city as a whole witnessed an increase in industrial jobs only because people living in the villages surrounding the town commuted to industrial jobs elsewhere, usually in Okazaki. Cutbacks in Kariya were even more pronounced than in Toyota. It lost 813 manufacturing jobs in the eight-year period. The first part of this chapter illustrated what those reductions meant for union activity in Kariya. Job reductions and a stagnant economy also had direct political repercussions. These were reflected clearly in the electoral behavior of the five communities in the first postwar decade.

Relying on the voting strength provided by their members, labor unions emerged after the war as one of the most important agents for mobilizing voters in the industrial cities of western Mikawa. The scope of union participation differed. In some instances, unions at the factory level promoted their own candidates independently. In other cases, several unions in a town or in an industry supported a candidate jointly. And in still other cases, a large group of unions joined together under the direction of a national organization to promote a candidacy. Whatever the scope of their activity, the unions always supported candidates of the political left, that is, of the Socialist and Communist parties in contrast to the successors of the prewar conservative parties. As a result of the political activities of labor unions, a new tone of competition injected itself into local politics. Previously, communities had witnessed only the mildest contests between men espousing essentially the same conservative political goals. Now they were exposed to a sharp struggle for votes among adherents of two radically different political programs, conservatives on one hand and progressives on the other. The Aichi Fourth District provides a good illustration of the growth of a progressive opposition in an area renowned for its conservatism.

Labor unions and their progressive supporters did not find it easy to establish themselves in the Aichi Fourth District. In the Diet election held in 1947, after promulgation of the new Constitution, candidates affiliated with progressive parties captured about fifty thousand votes in the district, a bare 18 percent of the total. In the next election, in 1949, their share of the total rose to 22 percent, giving them nearly sixty-three thousand votes. Maintaining the same percentage in 1952, 1953, and 1955, they were able to collect a steady sixty-six thousand votes. Moreover, they succeeded in establishing one *jiban* secure enough to return a member of the Japan Socialist Party to the Diet.[35]

[35] Aichi ken senkyo kanri iinkai, ed., *Aichi no senkyo 20-nen*, 2 vols. (Nagoya, 1965–1966) is

While progressives found it difficult to secure a *jiban* for their candidates, they found it almost impossible to win support in some areas. A comparison of cities in the Fourth District—Kariya, Toyota, Anjō, and Nishio—illustrates this clearly. As table 8 shows, there was a marked difference in the level of support for progressive Diet candidates among these four cities. The two industrial centers in the northern part of the district, Kariya and Toyota, were the most supportive. The two agricultural and textile centers, Anjō and Nishio, were least supportive of progressive candidates. Throughout the district, farming villages lying in rural areas provided only a small measure of support for progressives. The old town areas, the first parts of the district to industrialize, were the centers of progressive voting strength.

At first glance, it appears that a city's level of industrialization

TABLE 8

PROGRESSIVE VOTE IN DIET ELECTIONS IN
FOUR AICHI CITIES, 1947 AND 1953
(PERCENTAGE OF TOTAL VOTE)

City	1947	1953
Kariya		
Town area	36	44
Village area	10	24
City area total	22	35
Toyota		
Town area	52	51
Village area	19	22
City area total	29	32
Anjō		
Town area	18	22
Village area	10	13
City area total	15	19
Nishio		
Town area	18	22
Village area	12	12
City area total	14	16

SOURCE: Aichi ken senkyo kanri iinkai, ed., *Aichi no senkyo 20-nen: Shūgiin giin senkyo hen* (Nagoya, 1965), pp. 99, 106–107, 115, 122–123.

NOTE: Town area-old *machi* area; village area-former *mura* area; and city area total-overall vote in consolidated, contemporary city, defined by 1972 boundaries.

the source from which I draw election results and on which I base my analysis of Diet and local elections in this chapter.

determined the nature of its political support. But it is important to recognize that industrialization *per se* was not a sufficient cause of progressive voting strength. The four cities all had an industrial labor force in 1955 which comprised 25 to 40 percent of the occupied population. In the least progressive communities, Anjō and Nishio, industrial workers comprised one in three members of the work force. In the most progressive communities, industrial workers comprised both the highest rate among the four cities (40 percent in Kariya), and the lowest rate (25 percent in Toyota). Obviously it was not the rate of industrialization which mattered; it was something else.

The structure of local industry determined the nature of local politics because of the type of work force factories attracted. In Anjō and Nishio, women employed as textile operatives comprised a full half of the labor force. About half of those operatives were under twenty years of age, and thus too young to vote. In other words, in Anjō and Nishio, one in every four or five industrial workers was still unable to participate formally in the political process. In addition, many of the women were transients who spent just a few years in a factory before returning home for marriage. They did not invest their energy in local politics. Finally, union organizations in the textile industry were less pervasive than in other sectors. This was especially true in Nishio, which was a weaving center where textile production occurred in numerous, small, dispersed enterprises. The structure of the textile industry thus impeded opposition politics in many ways. Its workers were too young to vote, too mobile to take a deep interest in political affairs, and too dispersed occupationally to provide a unified organization.

The work force in the auto and machine industries in Kariya differed greatly on many counts. Workers were overwhelmingly males over twenty years of age who were also married householders. As many as two-thirds of them were permanent residents of the community who had already lived there for many years. They enjoyed the right to vote, and they took an interest in political affairs, because such issues as schools, taxes and local leadership influenced them directly. Moreover, the vast majority of those men worked in the city's six large factories, each of which had a well-organized union. Acting collectively through their unions, those men developed a new sense of conviction concerning their rights and status in the community. Although they often faltered when they sought economic benefits from management, they would not be deterred from engagement in opposition politics. In the course of the first postwar decade, they made themselves a considerable political force.

In fact, Kariya came under greater progressive influence than any city in the district. Table 8 illustrated that a larger portion of the voters in

Kariya supported progressive Diet candidates in 1955 than in any of the other three cities. But they did not confine their support to Diet candidates only. In contrast with the other communities in the district, Kariya's voters also supported progressive candidates in local elections. It was the only community in the entire district, with the exception of Okazaki, which returned a Socialist to the prefectural assembly. All of the other cities, as well as the rural areas, consistently elected conservatives. Kariya was also the only community in the district, and one of the very few in the entire prefecture, in which a mayor won election with the open assistance of progressive forces. Even in Toyota, where progressive voters were in the majority, the community returned conservative candidates espousing avowedly conservative programs. Of the cities examined in this study, Kariya was the only one which witnessed the success of progressive forces at all levels of government.

In comparison with its neighbors, therefore, Kariya became an unusually progressive political community. Forces opposed to the ruling conservative governments assumed far more strength in this city than in the others nearby. The final portion of this chapter examines how this change occurred and what it meant for the city's political participants.

In the course of the decade, progressive influence on local politics went through three phases: from growth, to maturity, to inertia. The phase of growth began in 1945 and lasted through mid-1948. During that period, progressive forces organized for the first time and began a concerted effort in local politics. The second phase, of maturity, spanned the years from 1948 to late 1952. In those years, the progressive forces achieved their greatest electoral successes. Beginning in 1953, a state of inertia overcame progressive forces in Kariya, one which continued to afflict them thereafter. The results of elections at the local, prefectural, and national level illustrate these phases of change clearly.

Any discussion of electoral politics in the years between 1945 and 1952 must begin with an account, however brief, of the purge conducted by Occupation officials.[36] Originating with orders from the American military in November 1945, the purge was an effort to remove from positions of influence all those men who had contributed to Japan's war effort. In time, the objectives of the purge expanded to such a degree that its directives were used to justify removal of alleged Communists from positions of influence in 1949 and 1950. As a result of the purge, over 200,000 persons lost the right to hold office and participate in political affairs. Among them were nearly 35,000 men designated as "political figures." They included virtually all prewar Diet members and most men

[36] The standard account in English is Baerwald; see note 29 above.

of influence in local politics, including prefectural governors and assembly-men, and city, town, and village mayors. Without political rights, those men could not participate in local politics—at least overtly—during the Occupation. For approximately five years between 1947 and 1951, therefore, many key local politicians had to give up their positions and allow new men to stand for office.

The purge by no means guaranteed, however, that new social groups would sweep into power. In the years from 1945 to 1948, while the progressives marshalled their forces, former ruling groups maintained their hold on the mayoralty in Kariya. Ōno Ichizō, who had been mayor since 1936, had to step down in 1946 when he was purged. Immediately, local influentials from the town council, the wards, and the block associations (chōnaikai) met and nominated his successor, Takenaka Hichirō.[37] In April 1947, Takenaka won election to the mayoralty in his own right, when Kariya's citizens voted in their first truly popular election for mayor. At the same time, Takenaka also won election to the Upper House of the Diet, having run simultaneously for two offices. He had to resign one, and chose to enter the Upper House. One month after the first mayoralty election, Kariya's citizens selected their second postwar mayor, Ishihara Heiichirō. Both Takenaka and Ishihara were members in good standing of the prewar ruling group in Kariya, as their personal backgrounds indicate.

Takenaka Hichirō was a prefectural assemblyman from Kariya be-tween 1936 and 1946. He was the eldest son of a dye shop owner from Sakana-machi. Following an elementary education at Kijō School, he attended higher schools in Okazaki and Nagoya, completing his education with a degree in medicine. After three years of specialization, he returned to Kariya in 1921 and opened a private practice. As his practice flourished, he turned his attention to politics. By the early 1930s he was a town assemblyman and an assistant to the Diet representative, Taketomi. This connection brought him into close contact with Ōno Ichizō. When Ōno resigned his assembly seat to enter the Diet in 1936, Takenaka succeeded him. Ishihara never held high elective office, but he was a member of the old ruling circle. Born in 1882, he was the son of a wealthy Kariya merchant. He pursued a formal education as far as Waseda University in Tokyo, but left school before completing a degree to become postmaster in Kariya at age twenty-five, in 1907. He held the post for over thirty years. Ishihara served on the town council between 1911 and 1920, and again from 1924 until the end of the war. He was a leader in the Enterprise Council and an active supporter of local educational projects. Both Takenaka and Ishihara, therefore, represented a continuation of the influence of the prewar ruling group on Kariya's postwar politics.[38]

[37] Kss, p. 248.

Prewar influentials continued to dominate Kariya's political life despite two major reforms initiated by the Occupation, the purge and the land reform. The purge had forced Ōno Ichizō to step aside, but it left Takenaka, who was in a sense his political heir, untouched. The purge also left untouched other local influentials who had not held leadership positions in the Imperial Rule Assistance Association and the Imperial Reservists' Association. Consequently, former councilmen and town leaders were available to fill what was really only a partial vacuum left by Ōno's departure.

Land reform had a negligible political impact in Kariya. In many communities, land reform reduced the political influence of the landlord class, essentially by undermining its status in the community.[39] It might have done the same in Kariya had it not been for the very small number of landlords affected by the reform. There were only three landlords in Kariya holding more than 5 chō (about 13 acres) when the reform began.[40] Two of them, the Ōta group and the Fujii family, had resources so diversified that the loss of their land did not damage them financially, or, as we will see, politically. Moreover, there was always a large group of influentials from the town area, men engaged in commerce and industry, who could continue the old pattern of governance. Therefore, neither the purge nor the land reform in and of themselves inhibited the old ruling group from exercising its political authority in Kariya into the postwar period.

In elections for the prefectural assembly and the Diet, conservative candidates dominated during the 1945 to 1948 period. Voters remained loyal to the patterns of support to which prewar politics had accustomed them. They returned men sponsored by the local influentials, remaining deferential to their social superiors. Progressives made some inroads in the electorate. In the 1947 Diet election, progressive votes amounted to about one-third of the vote in town. But a conservative candidate easily outpolled the Socialist candidate to capture first place among local voters. Progressive strength was growing, but it had yet to make a mark.

Between 1948 and 1952 the progressives in Kariya did make their mark on local politics. Labor unions were the source of progressive strength and a local labor council was the guiding force. Formed in February 1946, the labor council was a coordinating body to which belonged all of the large unions in the Toyota plants as well as several other unions made up of transportation workers and public officials. In its early days, the leader of the labor council was Ishihara Tenryū, a man in his thirties who headed

---

[38] For Takenaka see: Kss, pp. 626, 791–792; and Kumai, *Mikawa chimei jinshi roku*, p. 619. For Ishihara, see Kumai, p. 374.

[39] Steiner, pp. 99–102.

[40] Kss, pp. 245–248.

the union at the machine tool company. Ishihara, and the other young men around him in the leadership group, believed that unions should be used not only to achieve economic benefits, but also to engage in political action at all levels of government. They inspired local unionists to join together to give workers a tangible voice in local politics.[41]

Stimulating the political interests of local unions during this period were their ties with national unions. Japanese labor unions color their political activities in accord with the attitudes and policies of national centers, union federations working out of the capital. The national centers all support progressive parties, but they embrace a range of alternatives on the left of the political spectrum. In the postwar period, these have ranged from a fidelity to revolutionary Marxian ideology on the one hand to the mildest form of democratic socialism on the other. During the years from 1948 to 1952, the principal unions in Kariya aligned themselves with the most politically active national centers, Zenrōren and Sōhyō. Zenrōren was a union alliance formed in the wake of the abortive general strike in 1947 and abolished by the Occupation authorities in 1950. After its formation in 1950, Sōhyō became the largest national center in Japan. In 1951 and 1952 Sōhyō was especially active on the political front, demonstrating against resurgent militarism and what it considered to be the repressive policies of the ruling parties. The political activism of Sōhyō rubbed off on the principal unions in Kariya, and added to the political impetus already initiated by conditions in local society.

Prodded to action by their ties with national centers and economic conditions in local society, progressive forces won the first of five consecutive electoral victories in Kariya, when, in October 1948, they supported the winning candidate for mayor. In January 1949, progressives succeeded in raising the Socialist Diet candidate to the top of the list in Kariya, giving him 42 percent of the votes in town. Three months later, they elected Ishihara Tenryū to the prefectural assembly. He became Kariya's first Socialist representative to the prefectural body. They continued their successes in the 1952 Diet election by increasing the Socialists' share of the vote to 45 percent. Finally, in October 1952, the progressives backed the incumbent mayor in a dramatic contest which established their political credentials with convincing authority.

The 1952 mayoralty contest was a significant one. It illustrated clearly that new political alignments were forming in Kariya. The solidarity which had long characterized local politics appeared to be breaking down in the face of a competitive challenge from social groups new to the political arena. Also, the 1952 election pitted one of the community's leading conservative politicians against these new social forces. It was thus

[41] Interview with Narukawa Toshio, Kariya city councilman and chairman of the labor union at Toyota Automatic Loom Corporation, in Kariya, on August 24, 1972.

of intrinsic interest as a critical event in Kariya's political history. That contest provides the first of three case studies which portray the emergence of new political alignments in the Kariya area after 1945.

The incumbent mayor in 1952 was a man named Okamoto Kimpei. Okamoto was the head of a family which had circulated at the periphery of Kariya's ruling circle for several decades. His father operated a small drugstore on the town's main street and served as a town assemblyman between 1909 and 1920. Okamoto grew up in Kariya and attended Kijō School, where one of his classmates was Ono Ichizō. After his years at Kijō, Okamoto completed his education with a degree in pharmacy at the medical college in Chiba Prefecture (near Tokyo). At twenty-five years of age, he returned to Kariya and followed his father as head of the family drugstore. He married a daughter of one of Kariya's mayors and leading families, Okamoto Hirotarō (the families were not related, even though their surnames were the same), and settled down to a responsible life. In the 1920s he presided over the Imperial Reservists' Association; in the 1930s, he was the head of his block association (chōnaikai); and in the early 1940s, he became ward chief (kuchō) in the old castletown area. These posts represented a conventional path to local leadership and they were significant positions in the context of community life, but they enjoyed none of the prestige associated with office in the prefectural assembly or the Diet. They did, however, provide Okamoto with a set of social bonds to political supporters who helped him to win the mayoralty in 1948. The true test of those bonds came in 1952, when Ono Ichizō returned to active political life and challenged Okamoto for leadership of the community.[42]

By 1952 the progressives, working through the local union council, were the dominant single force in local politics. However, they were still a minority. They could not marshal enough votes to put a man in office themselves, but they could hold the balance of power in a contest in which the conservative electorate was divided. This was the case in Kariya in 1952. Okamoto's decision to run in that election created a split among the town's conservatives. Some of them remained loyal to Okamoto as the incumbent. Others were ready to rebuild conservative strength around Ono Ichizō. Under those circumstances, both conservative groups wooed the progressives for their support.

Ono initiated a prospective courtship by visiting Ishihara Tenryū, leader of the local progressive forces. Ono describes his interview with Ishihara as follows:

> I said, "I find it difficult to announce my views on the general problem of Kariya's government, so why don't you just ask me any questions you have." I

---

[42] For Okamoto see: Kcs, pp. 42-43, 161; Kss, p. 650; and Ōmi Tetsuo, "Chihō toshi ni okeru sangyōka to chiiki shakai no henka," Shakai kagaku tōkyū 11:1 (June 1965), p. 287.

answered his questions for over two hours. Then I said, "Have any more questions?" He answered that he did not. "Well, if there are any points where we differ we could go on talking," I said, and he replied there were not. So I figured that we had seen eye to eye.[43]

They obviously had not, because when Okamoto visited Ishihara later, he won the progressive endorsement. Ōno's inability to recognize his differences with the progressives betrayed the reasons for his losing the endorsement. Obviously, he entered the conversation with Ishihara prepared to lecture a younger man whom he considered a political upstart. Their meeting was a classical confrontation between the all-knowing *sensei* (teacher, leader) and a fortunate, prospective follower. Ōno spent most of those two hours lecturing Ishihara on the wisdom of harmony, obedience, and cooperation. If Ōno detected no note of difference between his views and Ishihara's, it was probably because Ishihara had not been able even to sound a note.

Ōno was a rather pathetic figure in the campaign of 1952. Having been deposed from office by a foreign power at the height of his political career, he was anxious to win the esteem and re-endorsement of his community. But he was not well equipped to understand the new political system. He had gained his position at a time when the voters bowed to the leading candidate because of his status and prestige in the community. In the 1952 contest, Ōno thought he enjoyed the upper hand on that count. As a result, he campaigned as he had before, which is to say that he announced his willingness to serve and let things go at that. Ōno did try to win the votes of new industrial workers in town with an issue-oriented appeal on a subject upsetting them. But he seems to have misunderstood that those workers were for the most part progressives, who were already committed to Okamoto by virtue of Ishihara's endorsement. When the vote was counted, Okamoto captured 7,493 ballots, and Ōno, 5,556. With one stroke, the progressives returned their man to office and turned back the town's leading conservative and political figure. Although Ōno's political influence in the community continued until his death in 1967, 1952 marked his last attempt at political office.

At approximately the same time progressive forces turned back Ōno Ichizō and established their candidate in the mayor's office, they also expanded their influence in national politics. They lent their support to a member of the left wing of the Japan Socialist Party named Itō Kōdō. Itō first ran for a seat in the district in 1947, but it was not until 1952 that he was victorious. By that time, he was the largest single vote-getter in the city of Kariya, drawing over 40 percent of the community's Diet vote. His success in the community and his victories in 1952 and 1953 were further

[43] Ōno, *Kiju ni mukaete watakushi no ashiato*, p. 92.

proof that the progressives in Kariya were a force to be reckoned with. The nature of his *jiban* provides a second case study in political change in Kariya during the first postwar decade.

It would be wrong to view Itō as a radical challenger to conservative power backed by ideologically committed, progressive supporters. Rather, Itō was a hybrid candidate. His success was based on two forms of support. He was supported by the new social groups—primarily industrial workers —who were flexing their political muscle in Kariya and nearby communities for the first time. But he could not have succeeded without votes from farmers, historically conservative, who supported him for reasons unrelated to his ideological position.

An analysis of Itō's *jiban* substantiates this claim. Itō ran as the endorsed candidate of the Japan Socialist Party in the Fourth District. It was expected that members in unions affiliated with that party would vote for him. They did so loyally in the areas where union strength was great: in the cities of Kariya, Toyota, and Okazaki, and in the villages nearby from which industrial workers commuted to work. However, such voters provided only half of Itō's electoral support. The rest came from villages and towns scattered throughout the prefecture, especially from mountain villages near Toyota. Tenant disputes had been infrequent in those villages before the war, and they had no history of participation in farmer-labor parties (which were often Socialist in prewar Japan). Voters in those areas were obviously swayed by credentials other than Itō's membership in the Japan Socialist Party.[44]

Voters supported Itō because he was a national professional, in the prewar mold outlined in chapter 5. Itō was born in Koromo *machi*. After attending local schools, he entered Tokyo University and graduated in 1923. In college he came in contact with a number of future leaders of the Socialist and labor movements. He himself participated in the Socialist movement until he was forced underground in the 1930s. After the war he rose quickly to a position of leadership in the Socialist party. He also became the editor of a prominent political journal and the author of a number of books on democracy. In the atmosphere of the early postwar years, Itō acquired status as a prominent national figure in the eyes of local voters. When he ran for the Diet, therefore, he appealed to voters using the very same attributes and techniques conservative politicians used. He, too, relied on his prestige, ties to a home place, kinship affiliations, friendship, and patronage. His primary base of support came from a new socio-economic group, organized laborers. But he was really a hybrid figure, combining the traits of a new politician with those of the old ones.

[44] *Aichi no senkyo 20-nen*, 1:106-107, 132-133, 160-161, and 188-189.

Itō's successful candidacies symbolize the texture of local politics in Kariya in the early years of the 1950s. On one hand, he represented the demands of industrial workers who were eager to exert a progressive influence on the political process at all levels. His victory bespoke the success which they enjoyed by 1952, when they could claim to have elected the city's most popular Diet candidate as well as its prefectural assemblyman and its mayor. On the other hand, Itō's victories proved that progressives were still too weak to seize power for themselves, without cooperation from conservative allies. Itō himself drew substantial support from farmers in rural areas whose political preferences were still conservative; they voted for him for essentially non-political reasons having to do with social obligations. Okamoto, sitting in the mayor's seat, was also a hybrid candidate, like Itō, reliant on a coalition of conservatives and progressives for his seat. As the period of maturity drew to a close, Kariya's progressives could claim a number of electoral victories, but they were still a long way from controlling a preponderance of power in the community.

By 1953 it became obvious that progressives would have to struggle mightily if they were ever to secure such power. A number of impediments stood in their way. There was first the intrusive presence of an entrenched conservative government which grew steadily more confident. There was also the long legacy of conservative, consensual behavior among the citizens of the region which inhibited a more competitive political environment. And, perhaps decisively, there was the amnesty of the former political figures who were purged by the Occupation authorities after the war. Just as the progressives were gaining a foothold in Kariya, a sturdy wind of reversion began blowing in the district and the period of inertia ensued.

The timing and objectives of the purge virtually guaranteed that prewar leaders would return to political life, once the Japanese regained sovereignty. Many of the men removed from office in 1946 and 1947 were in their late forties and their early fifties; they were just reaching the prime of their political careers. The purge disgraced them before the eyes of their supporters, calling into question the sincerity with which they had acted before. Most men who were purged in 1946, and who were still vigorous enough to return to political life in 1952, did so, to vindicate their own names if nothing else. Moreover, the nature of social bonds in Japanese politics guaranteed that oldtimers could come back, for two reasons. First, many voters—despite Occupation efforts at sweeping reform—retained their allegiance to customary voting habits. Second, political subordinates remained loyal to their former bosses. In some cases, they even held their seats for them as proxy representatives during the purge years.

Almost immediately after the purge was lifted, prewar politicians in the Fourth District sought restoration to office. In the Diet election that took place in October 1952, two familiar faces reappeared in the Aichi Fourth District. They were Ogasawara Sankurō and Kobayashi Kanae. At sixty-seven and sixty-four, respectively, they were both ready to resume their careers where the Occupation had cut them off five years earlier. In succeeding years, the reversion fairly swept through surrounding communities. In late 1954, voters in Nishio returned a prewar mayor to office. In early 1955, Nakamura Jūichi, mayor between 1929 and 1946, ran for re-election in Toyota and won. At the same time Anjō's erstwhile politician sought to make his comeback. In early 1955, Okada Kikujirō challenged the incumbent mayor in Anjō, at the age of eighty-eight! Even in conservative Anjō, however, voters finally recognized when enough was enough. They brought Okada's political life to a gentle close with a defeat by a margin of 9,921 to 9,253. New political alignments and old age prevented reversion in Kariya and Anjō, but elsewhere prewar politicians were frequently returned to office.

Ogasawara Sankurō's resumption of political power forms a third case study which illustrates how this process occurred.[45] As the previous chapter noted, Ogasawara became a Diet member because of his ties to influential politicians in Tokyo. As a result of those ties, he rose quickly during the 1930s and 1940s to a position of prominence in the Seiyūkai, the more conservative of the two prewar political parties. During the war he served on many policy-making committees and held the post of Administrative Undersecretary in the Ministry of Finance. When Prime Minister Shidehara formed his cabinet in 1945, Ogasawara accepted the post of Minister of Commerce and Industry. He was therefore one of the first targets of the purge when it struck in September 1946. For the next six years, Ogasawara played no overt role in politics. He became a director in a number of business enterprises, including a whaling company and a shipping concern, and spent those years in Tokyo.

Despite his absence, Ogasawara's old *jiban* did not wither. In fact, a young associate of his, Nakagaki Kunio, cultivated his old base as his stand-in. Running for the Diet in 1947 at the age of thirty-six, Nakagaki captured a seat in the Fourth District. His electoral base coincided exactly with Ogasawara's in 1942. Well over half his voters were located in the county of Hazu, and another large bloc of supporters were in the Anjō area. Nakagaki won re-election easily in 1949. Therefore, when the purge ended in mid-1951, enabling Ogasawara to run in the next Diet election, Nakagaki obediently stepped aside and allowed his political patron to regain his old seat.

Ogasawara won victory easily in 1952, simply by stepping before voters in a *jiban* which he had formed in the early 1930s. Although he needed

[45] For Ogasawara see Tokiwa, *Ogasawara Sankurō den*, pp. 331-343.

many more votes to win in 1952 than he had in 1942—eighty thousand
rather than twenty-six thousand—he accumulated them handily. He
simply called on his old supporters, along with their wives, relatives, and
children, and they cast their ballots for him unquestioningly. When he
won in 1942, Ogasawara attracted 53 percent of his votes from Hazu
County, 34 percent from Hekikai County (near Anjō), and another 4
percent from Nukata County.[46] When he won in 1952, he collected 48
percent of his votes from Hazu, 32 percent from Hekikai, and 9 percent
from Nukata.[47] Voters in the southern tier of the Fourth District thus
remained unequivocally loyal to a man whom they had first sent to the
Diet in 1932.

Other voters scattered about the district displayed a similar loyalty on
behalf of Kobayashi Kanae. By virtue of his age and his associations in the
capital, Kobayashi enjoyed favor within the Liberal Party. Winning the
endorsement of the party in 1952, he ran for re-election, also, after a
five-year absence from politics. He, too, captured a Diet seat. Despite
several years of intensive reform, the appearance of the Fourth District
Diet slate in 1952 conveyed a deep sense of *déjà vu,* as table 9 illustrates.

TABLE 9

AICHI FOURTH DISTRICT DIET MEMBERS, 1930–1958

Election Year	Members Elected			
1930	Kobayashi	Okamoto	Taketomi	
1932	Kobayashi	Taketomi	Ogasawara	
1936	Kobayashi	Okamoto	Taketomi	
1937	Ōno	Okamoto	Ogasawara	
1942	Ōno	Honda	Ogasawara	
1947[a]	Sakai	Senga	Nakagaki	Nakano
1949	Miyake	Senga	Nakagaki	Nakano
1952	Kobayashi	Itō	Ogasawara	Nakano
1953	Kobayashi	Itō	Ogasawara	Nakano
1955	Nakagaki	Itō	Ogasawara	Nagata

SOURCE: Kōmei senkyo renmei, ed., *Shūgiin giin senkyo no jisseki,* pp. 372–640.

NOTE: This table does not record the results of the 1946 Diet election. Due to the make-up
of the districts and the method of balloting in that election, it is not comparable with either
the prewar or the postwar elections.

a The Fourth District gained an additional, fourth seat in 1947.

The return of Ogasawara and Kobayashi to the Diet in 1952 attests to
the tenacity with which old voting habits still operated in this district.
Large sections of the electorate persisted in viewing the vote as a token of

[46] Shūgiin jimu kyoku, *Shūgiin giin sōsenkyo ichiran* (Tokyo, 1943), p. 299.
[47] *Aichi no senkyo 20-nen,* 1:160–161.

personal approval, rather than an opportunity for political choice. These habits were especially tenacious in the rural areas of the district, where population mobility was very low and where industrialization had not penetrated. Among the voters residing in those districts, reasoned political discourse was a taboo. The candidates accepted that stricture and promoted themselves with vague expressions of patriotic sentiment, eschewing rational discussion of issues. As they had before 1945, they relied on a political base formed by bonds of personal loyalty, ties to a home place, kinship affiliations, friendship, obligation, and patronage. In such a context, influential old-line families continued to play a role in forming networks of support, aided by prefectural assembly representatives, mayors, and local council members. In large parts of this district, the Occupation did very little to establish new modes of voter mobilization or to inculcate new patterns of political choice.

With the 1952 election the turnover of Diet candidates in this district subsided and several secure and enduring *jiban* either re-emerged for a second time or took form for the first time. They were geographically very similar to those which had existed in the district before. Ogasawara retained his focused *jiban* in the densely populated agrarian area around Nishio and Anjō. Kobayashi rebuilt his dispersed *jiban*, concentrated slightly in Higashi Kamo County, but otherwise spread throughout the district. Nakano Shirō, the district's third conservative Diet member, restored part of the conservative *jiban* originally formed by Taketomi and Ōno. And finally, Itō established an entirely new *jiban*, focused on the industrial cities of Kariya and Toyota, and the other large city of Okazaki.

Postwar *jiban* in the Fourth District bore strong geographic and organizational similarities to those of the prewar period. But that did not obscure the presence of a new phenomenon in local politics. There was now a political opposition in the district, returning a candidate who held sharply different views concerning the nature of the political process and the purposes of political action. The strength of that opposition was young and largely untested. But in the communities where it was based, the progressive opposition exercised substantial political power. With Itō's victory in 1952, and his subsequent re-elections in 1953 and 1955, Kariya's union members and their cohorts in Toyota injected a note of radical change in the political life of western Mikawa. American Occupation reforms greatly facilitated their ability to undertake political action and an uncertain economy stimulated their challenges to established power.

Progressives had been most successful in Kariya. By 1952 they had registered victories at all political levels. They had created an electoral base for the Socialist Itō Kōdō, giving them a representative in the national legislature. They had sent their own leader, Ishihara Tenryū, to the prefectural assembly. They were the indispensable electoral support of the local mayor, Okamoto Kimpei. And they even enjoyed some strength in the local council, where nine of thirty members in 1952 represented progressive interests. In contrast with the past, and with other nearby communities, Kariya had become a veritable hotbed of radical politics.

But before they could taste the fruits of their victories, the progressives in Kariya lost their momentum. In February 1955, the progressive vote suffered a decline in the Diet election. In the prefectural assembly election which followed in April, Ishihara lost to an influential conservative. And in a local election in July, another conservative re-captured the mayoralty. This resurgence of conservative power on the local scene was a product of two forces. The first was economic recovery at the Toyota enterprise, the origins of which could be traced to 1951. The second was the consolidation of conservative political power, symbolized by the formation of a united conservative party in 1955. As a result of these changes, a new political mood rooted in new economic conditions settled over Kariya and the Fourth District. In the following decade, progressive political power withered drastically on the local level in the face of an unprecedented economic boom, as the following chapter reveals.

7

INDUSTRIAL HEGEMONY,
1955–1967

The year 1955 marked the beginning of a new era in Japan's economic history. A full decade had passed since the war ended. By dint of persistent effort, the Japanese people had restored output to its prewar highs in most sectors of the economy. They were ready to move forward at a faster pace. Several events occurred in 1955 which symbolized the content and direction of their coming endeavor. In February of that year, government and business leaders established the Japan Productivity Center to promote awareness of the latest technology and managerial techniques, and to foster cooperation between labor and management. In July the Economic Planning Agency assumed its present form. Its purpose was to plan comprehensively for national economic growth. Two months later Japan entered the General Agreement on Trade and Tariffs. This signaled the nation's desire to become an active participant in international trade. Underlying these new institutions and arrangements was an emerging confidence in Japan's economic potential, which would soon realize itself with a vigor that the Japanese themselves found surprising.

A government program of "income doubling"—a Japanese version of the American aspiration to have "two cars in every garage"—set the tone for the ensuing period of rapid expansion. Proponents of the plan envisioned a program which would bring Japanese standards of living up to those of Europe in a decade. By 1970 they expected gross national product to nearly triple, exports to more than triple, and industrial output to rise over four times. As a result of these changes, they expected per capita incomes to more than double, thus the rubric "income doubling." If the economy grew at a rate of 7 percent annually, the plan would succeed.

In the event, "income doubling" occurred much earlier than anticipated. The economy actually exceeded projections, growing at a rate nearer 10 percent than 7. Within only five years the gross national product had already doubled. Exports also doubled in just five years. The output of such key industrial sectors as iron and steel increased nearly three times in the course of five years. The auto industry expanded its production by four times in the same period, far exceeding projected growth. As a result of such growth, the initial goal of doubled incomes was achieved in half the

time anticipated, and the cabinet of Prime Minister Satō abandoned the
program in favor of a new one in 1966.

The political credit for Japan's economic success fell to the Liberal
Democratic Party. That party formed in the critical year of 1955, which
was as significant politically as it was economically. In the Diet election
held in February of that year, candidates from progressive parties won
over one-third of the seats. This prohibited conservatives from revising the
Constitution according to their desires, since progressives could now
prevent such a move. To capitalize on their position, the two wings of the
Socialist movement reunited in October of that year to form a united
Japan Socialist Party. In part to meet this challenge and in part also to
create a stable political climate for economic growth, the two conservative
parties also united one month later, to form the Liberal Democratic Party.
Representing a coalition of big business, farmers, and small proprietors,
this party was an awkward political instrument holding together several
Diet factions. But it became a powerful vehicle for mobilizing political
support behind the nation's new economic policies. With its emergence,
the forces which shaped the political contests in the years after 1955 took
final form.

The political and economic changes which took place at the national
level in 1955 began almost immediately to reach into every corner of
Japanese society. The impact of economic growth and conservative rule
struck Kariya with penetrating force. Literally thousands of people flowed
into the city during this period to take a seemingly endless number of jobs
in the auto industry. The growth experienced when Toyota first entered
the community in the 1920s resumed, and Kariya became one of the
country's fastest growing industrial centers again. Output boomed, profits
rose, and incomes soared. These changes produced an economic environment entirely different from the one which had prevailed in the first
postwar decade, and they had a clear and decisive influence on local
politics. Gaining strength from the united conservative party at the
national level, local influentials moved vigorously to restore the political
position they had lost during the decade of radical change. Rather than
oppose this reversion, progressive forces largely acquiesced to it. Very soon,
they suffered a marked loss of power in Kariya, as the city and its
surrounding area came under the economic and political power of
Toyota's industrial hegemony.

This chapter traces the evolution of that hegemony, in two parts. Part
one treats Toyota's growth as an industrial power. It describes the recovery
of the auto firm, the appearance of new managers, the expansion of
affiliates in the auto industry, and the alteration in labor and management
relations. Part two of this chapter examines the consequences of Toyota's

expanding power for the political process in Kariya and the Fourth Diet District between 1955 and 1967.

Toyota's Economic Resurgence

During the era of "income doubling," the Tōkai Region became one of the most thriving areas in the country. Encompassing the prefectures of Aichi, Mie, Gifu, and Shizuoka, the region was blessed with fine ports, abundant water resources, expanding electrical power, and—perhaps most important—broad areas of land available for industrial development. New factories appeared throughout the Tōkai. Giant pulp and paper mills located in the eastern end of the region, at the foot of Mount Fuji in Shizuoka. At the western end, a huge petro-chemical complex took shape along the shores of Ise Bay near the city of Yokkaichi. In the central part of the region, machine and vehicle manufacturing plants sprouted like bamboo shoots after a spring rain. Within a decade, the once peaceful agrarian region of the Tōkai became a booming industrial zone.

Aichi Prefecture was the center of the Tōkai Region and its fastest growing industrial area. In 1955 the prefecture still had almost as many workers engaged in farming as it had employed in factories. Each group made up about a third of the labor force. In the next decade, Aichi witnessed the creation of nearly eight hundred thousand jobs, more than half of them in manufacturing. As a result, farm workers dropped to only 14 percent of the prefectural labor force while manufacturing workers rose to almost 40 percent. For the first time in the history of the prefecture, farmers became a small minority, in the face of a huge influx of workers employed in commerce and trade, the service industries, and manufacturing.

New factory workers found employment in virtually every sector of the industrial economy.[1] The traditional trades, such as pottery making and food production, nearly doubled job opportunities during the 1955 to 1965 decade. Textile plants continued to hire large numbers of workers, although the pace of demand slowed drastically by contrast with the preceding decade. And, as a result of diversification in the industrial structure of Aichi, there were new openings in fields which had not been important before, such as chemical manufacturing, the petroleum industry, and pulp and paper making. But the greatest increase in new industrial jobs came with the expansion in auto making. Almost half of the nearly four hundred thousand new factory workers found jobs in this industry, either in the thousands of small factories which made auto parts and components, or in the smaller number of steel mills, rubber and glass

[1] Atn: 1967, p. 181.

factories, and giant assembly plants. As a result of these changes, factory employment resumed the shape it had taken a quarter-century earlier, as table 10 indicates.

The industrial boom spread itself unevenly through the prefecture. A comparison of the five cities in this study reveals this in a striking way. (See tables 11, 12, and 13.) In the three cities of Anjō, Nishio, and Handa, new jobs increased at a rate lower than that for the prefecture as a whole. This was attributable to two reasons. First, they still relied heavily on the textile industry, and that industry created jobs at a slower rate through the late 1950s and early 1960s than most other industrial sectors. Second, Anjō, and Nishio especially, suffered from a disadvantageous location. They were still too far from the primary industrial centers to seem promising as sites for subsidiaries or new factories.

In contrast with these three cities, Toyota and Kariya created jobs at a rate that far exceeded that of the prefecture as a whole. Between 1955 and 1965, 31,733 new workers moved into the city of Toyota. Eight in every ten of them were in manufacturing, giving rise by the end of the decade to an increase of more than 200 percent in the number of factory workers residing there. Kariya also witnessed a dramatic expansion in its factory labor force, which accounted for nearly ten thousand new jobs between 1955 and 1965. In these two cities two in every three jobs opened because of growth in the Toyota enterprise. To understand the political economy of western Mikawa during this period, it is essential to know what took place at Toyota Motors after 1951.

TABLE 10

FACTORY WORKERS IN AICHI PREFECTURE, 1941 AND 1967
(PERCENTAGE, BY INDUSTRY)

Industry	1941	1967
Textiles	28	24
Machines and metals	47	40
Pottery trades	7	8
Food processing	5	6
All others	13	22
Totals	100	100

SOURCES: Ats: 1941, 3:1–6; and Atn: 1970, p. 132.

Toyota Motors suffered badly in the first years after the war. Although it was not damaged by bombing, the firm found it difficult to restore itself to normal operations. A depressed economy, government policy, Occupation reforms, and managerial problems all complicated its problems. After five years of severe difficulty, at which point it was near bankruptcy, the

TABLE 11

LABOR FORCE IN FIVE AICHI CITIES AND
AICHI PREFECTURE, 1955 AND 1965

Place	1955	1965	% Increase
Kariya	23,134	37,697	63
Toyota	45,450	77,183	70
Anjō	32,245	42,313	31
Nishio	32,419	37,972	17
Handa	29,700	38,378	29
Aichi Prefecture	1,737,431	2,493,860	44

SOURCES: Sōrifu tōkei kyoku, *Kokusei chōsa hōkoku, Aichi ken.* For 1955: (Tokyo, 1958), pp. 142–148. For 1965: (Tokyo, 1966), pp. 182–212.

NOTE: Figures in tables 11 and 12 enumerate workers who resided in areas encompassed by the 1972 boundaries of the cities.

TABLE 12

WORKERS IN MANUFACTURING IN FIVE AICHI CITIES
AND AICHI PREFECTURE, 1955 AND 1965

Place	1955	1965	% Increase
Kariya	9,187	19,627	113
Toyota	11,241	37,056	230
Anjō	10,912	16,329	50
Nishio	10,115	14,213	41
Handa	14,005	17,661	26
Aichi Prefecture	574,481	969,269	69

SOURCES: Same as table 11 preceding.

TABLE 13

POPULATION GROWTH IN FIVE AICHI CITIES AND
AICHI PREFECTURE, 1955–1965

Place	1955	1965	% Increase
Kariya	52,470	70,018	33
Toyota	97,751	136,728	40
Anjō	62,853	76,152	21
Nishio	66,143	70,432	6
Handa	67,827	76,027	12
Aichi Prefecture	3,769,209	4,798,653	27

SOURCES: Same as table 11 above. For 1955, pp. 27–28. For 1965, pp. 2–3.

NOTE: These figures enumerate persons resident in areas encompassed by the 1972 boundaries of the cities.

firm finally began to witness an improvement in its condition. Three changes were instrumental in reviving the fortunes of Toyota Motors: revised government policies, improved economic conditions, and new leadership in the firm.[2]

Toyota Motors came to life under salutary conditions created by government directives. When it originated in 1937, it was one of only two licensed auto producers in the country. That status guaranteed favorable treatment from the government, which regulated competitors in order to nourish the fledgling Japanese auto firms to life. After the war, the government decided to abandon protection of the Japanese auto industry because it felt that imported autos could meet domestic demand while the nation used its scarce resources to reconstruct more essential areas. By 1950, however, the government recognized that it could save foreign currency if Japan were to produce its own automobiles, so it changed its policy. It removed limits on prices and production established earlier, allowing auto firms to expand their output. In 1957 the government took a further step to insure the development of a domestic auto industry. It established a protective climate for Japanese producers by using tariffs, quotas, and taxes to discourage the importation of foreign autos. The government began lifting these restrictions as early as 1965, but even eight years of protection proved helpful. Government policy was not the sole cause of Toyota's resurgence, but it created an economic climate in which Japanese auto producers could establish themselves.

One critical problem during the difficult postwar years was a lack of demand for trucks and autos. Inability to sell the autos it produced was one of the reasons for Toyota's severe difficulties in 1949 and 1950. But just as the firm appeared to be going under, Toyota benefitted once again from war. In June 1950, amidst the worst strike in Toyota's history, the Korean War broke out. Demand for military materiel stimulated a boom in the Japanese economy from which Toyota Motors reaped substantial rewards. The American military needed trucks for its efforts in Korea and decided to buy them from Japanese makers. During the first year of the war, they ordered over three thousand trucks from Toyota Motors.[3] The number may seem small, but in 1951 it equalled over one-fourth of all of Toyota's production. The sales enabled the firm to exhaust its large inventories and to restore its factories to full operations. The large profits which the firm earned went to purchase new equipment. The Korean War thus aided Japan's economic recovery instrumentally at the same time it stimulated an essential spurt of expansion at Toyota Motors.

The Korean War boom gave the Japanese economy a much needed

[2] Events at Toyota Motors between 1955 and 1967 are covered in *30-nen shi*, pp. 323–704. Data on capitalization, output, sales, profits, and ownership appear on pages 766–803. I have also relied on relevant issues of Ōkura shō, *Yūka shōken hōkokusho sōran* for information on these subjects and on personnel changes.

[3] *30-nen shi*, p. 324.

boost. By the mid-1950s most important areas of the economy had recovered their highest prewar levels of output. They were ready for further advance. After 1955 the upsurge occurred quickly. It was not direct and uninterrupted. There was a recession in 1958 and later slowdowns on occasion. But in general, employment, output, sales and exports all rose at swift rates. After nearly a decade of depression, Japan began to experience an unprecedented boom, which only drew to a close in the early 1970s. These salutary economic conditions provided a business climate that was indispensable in fostering the expansion at Toyota Motors.

Government policy changes and general economic recovery were instrumental in reviving the fortunes of the Toyota enterprise after 1951. There were other causes as well, such as the widespread adoption of new technology, the quality of its labor force, and the increasing efficiency of its organization. There is one ingredient in Toyota's successful expansion, however, which deserves special attention: the nature of its leadership. The man who presided over Toyota's fortunes after 1950 was such a significant figure in Japan's postwar industrial history, and had such an unorthodox background, that his story is both relevant and interesting.

Members of the Toyota family itself had always held the highest offices in the auto firm. Toyota Risaburō became president of the firm when it was formed in 1937; Sakichi's own son, Kiichirō, became vice-president. Risaburō was largely a figurehead, however. Kiichirō acted as the driving force in the auto firm, assisted by able subordinates. In 1941 Risaburō accepted the new position of chairman of the board and Kiichirō assumed the presidency. A capable young executive named Akai Hisayoshi became vice-president at the same time, assuming virtually full responsibility for managing the firm. In 1945 Risaburō resigned as chairman and Akai was killed in an auto accident, leaving Kiichirō as both real and nominal head. He presided over Toyota Motors during the difficult postwar years, with the assistance of three executive directors. But Kiichirō's talents were those of the engineer, not the executive. His leadership only exacerbated an already difficult situation. He especially irritated other executives in the firm and its financial backers in 1950, when he insisted that no men be fired as a condition for the bank loans. He viewed workers as members of the family and invoked his father's maxim that everyone had to sink or swim together. Ultimately, the banks and other executives forced the dismissal of 1,600 workers. At that point, Toyota Kiichirō retired. With his departure, leadership of the Toyota enterprise passed into the hands of non-family members for the next seventeen years. The key figure during that period was Ishida Taizō.[4]

[4] This portrait of Ishida Taizō is based on the following: Okado Buhei, *Tōshi no ōkan: Ishida Taizō den* (Nagoya, 1965); Nihon keizai shimbun sha, ed., *Watakushi no rireki sho* (Tokyo, 1959), pp. 1–34; Ikeda Masaji, *Saigō no daibantō: Ishida Taizō no sekai* (Tokyo, 1971); Ishida

Ishida was the third figure from the Kodama family of Hikone to play a leading role in the Toyota enterprise. Born in 1888, his original name was Sawada Taizō. He was the fifth child of a farmer living in a small village on the western shores of the Chita Peninsula. Although the family owned just a small plot of land, Taizō's father was influential enough to be chosen the first mayor of the village in 1889. His mother traced her ancestry to samurai families, but her own father had been a sake brewer. The family thus enjoyed considerable status among the small farmers of their village. Young Taizō attended the village school and finished in 1902, with no plans in mind. But, as it would so often in later years, good fortune struck. Just as his parents began wondering what to do with their younger son, they received a visit from the mother's cousin, Kodama Ichizō. He had just joined the Mitsui Trading Company and was about to depart on his first foreign assignment. Convinced that young men would not be able to succeed in Japan without a formal education, Kodama persuaded the Sawada family to send Taizō to Hikone. There he would live with the Kodama family while he attended the middle school in town. Taizō spent five years in Hikone, where he came to know Toyota Risaburō as a brother. His marks at school were undistinguished, but he had managed to become coxswain of the rowing team when he graduated in 1907, with no very specific goal in mind.

For the next twenty years Taizō pursued a career which could not differ more from the stereotype of a Japanese manager's route to success. With no goals in mind and the draft hanging over him, Taizō spent his first year after middle school teaching in villages in central Japan. Once he failed the military's physical exam, he enjoyed some freedom. Deciding that he wanted to be a businessman, he set out for Kyoto. For the next five years, he worked as a clerk in a furniture shop. Always aggressive and attentive to the wishes of his superiors, he soon made a hit with the boss, who had him open a branch shop in Osaka. Taizō was growing bored with that job in 1913 when his foster mother in the Kodama family in Hikone called him to announce that she had the perfect bride for him. Marriage was not the first thing on Taizō's mind, but after some hesitation, he acceded to her wishes. His bride was the daughter of an allegedly wealthy Hikone merchant. He adopted her family name when he married in 1913; henceforth he was known as Ishida Taizō.

Expecting to settle down to a life of leisure, living off his wife's fortune, Ishida experienced a rude shock. There was no substance to the rumor that his wife's family was wealthy. Rather than wealth, he inherited a zany mother-in-law. Within a year she had driven him out of the house to find work with a relative in Tokyo. His job at the age of twenty-six

Taizō, *Jibun no shiro wa jibun de mamore* (Tokyo, 1968); *Ikiru Toyota Sakichi*, pp. 188–258; and Itō Jissei, *Toyota ke no shinwa* (Tokyo, 1972), pp. 147–176.

consisted of pushing a wheelbarrow stacked high with cotton goods into the outskirts of Tokyo and trying to sell his wares to farmers. He lasted less than a year. By this time, his patron Kodama Ichizō was back in Japan managing the Nagoya branch of the Mitsui trading firm. With his assistance, Ishida found a new job in the Hattori Commercial House, a cotton dealer whose owner was a friend and supporter of Toyota Sakichi. Ishida spent twelve years with the Hattori firm, learning the cotton business and developing a knowledge of the textile industry. When the firm closed in 1927, Kodama Ichizō persuaded his brother Risaburō to take Ishida on at the Toyota textile concern. After a desultory career in four different jobs, Ishida Taizō—at the mature age of thirty-nine—finally entered the firm he would eventually control.

For the next twenty-three years, Ishida worked at the parent firms in the Toyota enterprise. He was with Toyota Spinning and Weaving Company for fourteen years, where he became a director in 1939, at age fifty-one (the usual age for promotion in that firm). In 1941 he transferred to Toyota Automatic Loom in Kariya as an executive director (jōmu torishimariyaku). For the last three years of the war, he administered the production of military materiel at the loom factory.

From 1942 onward Ishida was the effective head of the loom concern. The Toyota brothers, Risaburō and Kiichirō, held the top positions but they devoted little personal attention to the firm. In time, Ishida won rank to accord with his position. He became managing director (semmu torishimariyaku) in 1945 and vice-president later in the same year. In 1948 he assumed the presidency of the firm. He kept that post until 1969, long after he had left the loom firm to direct the auto company.

It was during the early postwar years of his tenure at the loom firm that Ishida established his reputation as a manager. At the end of the war, Toyota Automatic Loom was manufacturing machine guns and small landing craft. It was in an awkward position when the time came to resume civilian production. But nothing daunted Ishida. He had workers in the factory make anything they could with the skills and materials at hand, including cooking utensils. Meanwhile, he bustled about among bankers and Occupation officials seeking financial support, materials, and permission to resume making textile equipment. He won permission quickly, and by early 1946, Toyota Loom sold its first postwar textile machines. There were some precarious times, but Ishida managed to turn a profit every year, even during the troubled year of 1947. He displayed further managerial skill in his handling of labor disputes. His tack was simple: be blunt. When workers sought him out for negotiations during the 1947 strike, he responded to the effect that if the workers did not give up their strike, they were not only going to lose wages they were also going to bring the company to ruin. He made grudging increases in wages, but somehow still retained the respect of workers. After 1947 there were no damaging disputes at the loom factory. When conditions at Toyota Motors in 1950 called for a man who could exercise a firm hand over administrative and personnel problems, everyone agreed that Ishida was the logical choice to assume the responsibility.

Ishida took a long time to get his career on the right track, but he did pick up some pointers along the way. One came from his forthright patron Kodama Ichizō in 1927, when Ishida approached him for a small loan to establish a business to sell cotton scrap:

> What kind of a stupid thing are you considering? Haven't you already lived off the good graces of small commercial companies for several years now? God, this is the age of big capital. Only by enlarging capital can you expect to grow; what are you thinking about with this dumb plan to make money with a puny little shop! You can't contribute to the world of Japanese finance with that view. I'm expecting to build several large companies. Basically, if I can't work my way into foreign markets with them, they just won't pan out. The kind of business you're thinking about will definitely fail. Give up the idea and go to work for Risaburō at Toyota.[5]

Ishida had just lost his position at the Hattori firm when he went to visit Kodama, so he was probably searching for something else in a mood of desperation. At any rate, Kodama's comments left a firm impression which survived for forty years. His remarks accomplished two things. They disabused Ishida of ever again thinking small when it came to business enterprises, and they taught him that investment in capital was a sound way to expand an enterprise. He put both lessons into practice once he had an opportunity to direct the Toyota auto firm.

Legends and rumors have grown to such a degree around Ishida Taizō that he enjoys a folklore all his own. Much of it embellishes the truth, of course, but it is worthwhile to mention some anecdotes about the man who has left such a mark on the Toyota enterprise as well as the political history of Kariya. Ishida liked to think of himself as a combination of the Ōmi merchant and the Mikawa samurai. Ōmi, the area around Hikone where Ishida went to middle school, was renowned during the Tokugawa Period for the commercial genius of its traveling merchants. They were diligent and frugal, and Ishida liked to think he embodied their traits. There is some agreement on the last point, because his critics in the Japanese business community liked to call him Ishida Kechizō, a play on his name which produced the derisive label of "Tightwad." The Mikawa samurai included such illustrious figures as Oda Nobunaga and Tokugawa Ieyasu, warriors noted for their ability to overcome great odds to rise to the top. Ishida fit that mold nicely himself.

[5] *Watakushi no rireki sho*, p. 21.

In addition to his frugality and perseverance Ishida had another trait which stood out: a strong self-confidence displayed in blunt aggressiveness. This was demonstrated in 1950 when Ishida met with three members of the Toyota family and another long-time family employee to consider the succession at Toyota Motors. After some discussion, they finally decided that Ishida was the only man for the job. Relieved to get it after having campaigned for it for several months, Ishida is alleged to have burst forth with the comment, "Okay, I'll take over, but I'm going to do it my way—and I hope there's no carping from the sidelines." [6] Rude, confident, and aggressive, Ishida was perhaps the decisive figure the company needed to lead it into the next era.

Ishida Taizō was the central figure at Toyota Motors after 1950, but he enjoyed the support of a group of able managers who assisted him in building Toyota's auto empire. Only one of them was a member of the Toyota family. The others were men whom Kiichirō had recruited at the beginning. Some of them had previous experience in other auto firms before they joined Toyota in the 1930s; others entered the auto company directly out of college. During the war they were section chiefs and department heads. By the early 1950s they were in their forties with nearly two decades of experience in the firm, and they rose to posts as directors. Their own careers were tied inextricably to the Toyota enterprise. Many of them, in fact, viewed themselves as Kiichirō's surrogates and worked to fulfill his dream. They made loyal and dedicated servants. For the most part, therefore, loyal employees who had been with the firm since its origin provided managerial direction during the expansion period.

During that period, only two members of the Toyota family were directors in the auto firm. They were Toyota Eiji and Toyota Shōichirō. Eiji was Sakichi's nephew and Shōichirō, his grandson. Twelve years older than Shōichirō, Eiji always assumed major positions before him. Eiji was appointed executive director in 1950, vice-president in 1960, and president in 1967. Shōichirō became a managing director in the same year Eiji assumed the presidency.

Although members of the family did not play major roles in the firm during the 1950s, they were obviously still favored. At the time of their promotion to a director's post, most men in Toyota Motors during the 1960s were in their late forties. By contrast, Eiji was thirty-two when he became a director, and Shōichirō was only twenty-seven. In other cases, also, members of the Toyota family became directors in their early thirties, while non-family members had to wait until their late thirties or their forties. Such favoritism was one mark of the family spirit which still pervaded the Toyota concern. Long-time employees, loyal to the memory

[6] Itō, p. 170.

of Sakichi, or of Kiichirō, treated members of the family with respect. Helping the boss's son was part of a social obligation they felt toward a firm which had provided well for them. That being the case, they were also cautious to see that even the boss's son did not go too far without demonstrating his talent. Eiji and Shōichirō got to the top more quickly than others because they belonged to the Toyota family, but they would not have been there if they were not also talented managers. Family loyalty was strong at Toyota, but it did not operate at the expense of merit.

The new team of managers which operated under the leadership of Ishida Taizō guided Toyota Motors through a period of remarkable achievement between 1955 and 1966. That eleven-year period witnessed the most rapid expansion in the firm's history. Combining labor and capital shrewdly, Toyota's managers increased production massively to reap handsome profits. Between 1955 and 1966 the value of paid-up capital at Toyota Motors increased twenty-three times, while the size of the labor force rose only five times. This potent combination of labor and capital produced immense gains in output. In all of 1955, the firm turned out only 23,000 vehicles, but in 1966, it produced that number in just two weeks! Doubling output at thirty-month intervals, Toyota Motors increased annual production of cars and trucks by twenty-six times over the eleven-year period. The value of annual sales increased seventeen times, rising from about ¥16 billion in 1955 to nearly ¥300 billion in 1966. Profits accrued at steady, lucrative rates. During this period annual before-tax profits ranged from 8.4 to 10.8 percent of total sales.[7] By the late 1960s, Toyota Motors was one of the largest, most profitable enterprises in the world.

The massive growth which Toyota experienced during the 1950s and 1960s substantially changed the once tightly controlled family organization. This was especially true of its financial structure. Occupation reforms forced some firms within the enterprise to divest shares they owned in others, thus releasing Toyota stock for public sale. More significantly, the insatiable need for capital after 1951 forced the firms to seek financial support outside. They listed their stock on exchanges in Nagoya, Osaka, and Tokyo. They also sought capital from banks, brokerage houses, and other corporations. As a result, ownership of Toyota firms became widely dispersed. Patterns differed from firm to firm, but as a general rule, financial institutions owned the greatest share of the equity capital in the large firms by the late 1960s. Firms within the enterprise retained ownership in others, but the rate varied from a low of only 5 percent to a high of 40 percent. In no case did one firm enjoy majority control over another, as they so often had during the prewar period. Nor did members

[7] *30-nen shi*, p. 796.

of the Toyota family itself play the dominant role financially which they once had. Sakichi's grandson, Shōichirō, was the largest Toyota shareholder in the auto firm in the late 1960s, but he controlled less than 1 percent of the firm's stock. Toyota was no longer a family-owned firm; it was a publicly-owned, private corporation managed by non-family executives.

In pace with the expansion of Toyota Motors, there arose a vast industrial complement made up of supporting firms and suppliers. This complement had three parts: direct affiliates in the Toyota enterprise, auxiliary firms, and small subcontractors. Direct affiliates included most of the firms which arose during the period between 1940 and 1949, such as the steel, machine tool, chassis, and electrical components firms. Auxiliary firms produced such essential materials as steel, rubber, and glass. The subcontracting firms provided components and parts for the larger firms and the assembly plants. Most of these firms sold the bulk of their output to a single enterprise in the auto industry, Toyota. In their entirety, these three groups formed Toyota's economic hegemony.

The major affiliates of Toyota Motors were all headquartered in Kariya. They were Toyota Chassis, Aishin Seiki, Nippon Densō, Toyota Machine Tools, and Toyota Automatic Loom. In the immediate postwar period, they had been quite separate firms trying to survive by producing on their own. In the early 1950s they all became an integral part of the Toyota auto enterprise. Toyota Chassis continued making trucks, and added a factory to assemble a compact auto as well. Aishin Seiki reduced its concentration on home products and turned to the manufacture of automobile parts, making everything from brake drums to door handles. Nippon Densō, founded in 1949 to produce electrical components for the entire Japanese auto industry, pursued its goal with vigor during the years under discussion. By the mid-1960s it was producing ignition switches, headlamps, sparkplugs, and car air conditioners as well. The machine tool firm continued to make industrial machinery, but also began to turn out auto parts, as did the loom factory. These were separate firms with their own directors and their own sources of capital, but they operated virtually as branch factories of Toyota Motors.

The physical proximity of these firms and the backgrounds of their directors both facilitated their close coordination with the parent firm. In most cases, one had only to walk across a street to be able to discuss business matters with the head of another company. What made this even easier was the long-standing personal relationships which many of the directors in the firms enjoyed with each other. Postwar monopoly laws curtailed the degree to which firms could interlock their directorships, but those laws could do nothing about informal contact based on long association. Within the five Toyota affiliates in Kariya, two in three of the directors had spent their entire career in the Toyota enterprise.[8] A large portion of all the directors (twenty-three of sixty-three) had worked previously at another firm in the enterprise. Only a third were newcomers from outside, and most of them were in Nippon Denso (a new firm requiring technical and marketing skills) and Aishin Seiki (product of a merger with two other firms). The makeup of the leadership in affiliates thus assured easy access and contact among managers in the enterprise as a whole. This facilitated coordination, and enhanced the ability of Toyota Motors to exercise tight control over its affiliates.

The five affiliates above comprised only a part of Toyota's auto empire. The complexity of auto making and its demand for a wide variety of components stimulated the growth of an extensive structure of auxiliary enterprises. Geographically widespread and organizationally varied, these enterprises complemented the Toyota companies at the center of the local auto industry. In 1967 there were 249 auxiliary companies.[9] Almost 200 of them supplied basic materials or auto components to Toyota Motors; 22 supplied machine tools; and 31 handled engineering and construction work. Only 100 of these firms were in Aichi, 38 in Nagoya and 11 in Kariya. The remainder were concentrated in the Tokyo and Osaka regions. Some of the 249 concerns were small ones employing fewer than one hundred workers; others employed several thousand. They provided goods, jobs, and incomes which greatly enhanced the economic importance of the core firms in the auto industry.

Beneath the auxiliary companies was a third group of small, subcontracting firms. They pressed, cut, drilled, and assembled parts which they sent to larger companies for further processing, after which they went to the assembly plants in Toyota or Kariya. Companies of this type were numerous in Kariya, numbering almost 300 in 1965. The majority were small concerns with fewer than 50 workers, but there were some firms with 100 to 200 workers and one steel plant with over 1,000 employees. Some of these firms originated in the 1920s and 1930s, but most dated from the postwar period and especially from the years after 1952. Their fate was tied directly to that of Toyota Motors, because most of them sold more than half of their output to a single higher affiliate within the Toyota organization. These small firms were among the most vulnerable elements in the economic hegemony which Toyota exercised over industrial efforts in western Mikawa. Unless they had diversified their outlets, they were the first to go under during a recession and the last to revive during a boom.[10]

[8] This analysis is based on data collected from a number of corporate reports published by the Ministry of Finance under the name *Yūka shōken hōkokusho sōran*.

[9] *30-nen shi*, pp. 692–694, 786–790.

[10] Aichi ken keizai kenkyūjo, "Tōkai chiku ni okeru jidōsha buhin kōgyō no kōzō henka to zaihensei" (Nagoya, 1966).

These small firms round out the list of auto enterprises in western Mikawa. Toyota Motors was the core of the auto industry. Its ability to sell what it made, and its consequent demand for parts and materials, dictated the pace of industrial expansion during the years after 1955. From the firms' headquarters in Toyota, managers exercised tight control over a large number of firms throughout the country. Its influence over firms in the immediate vicinity was especially pervasive. They had to produce at weekly, and sometimes daily, notice exactly what the assembly plants required. They produced under rigorous constraints, in close harmony with the parent firm. Operating according to the logic of the production process, Toyota Motors spawned, nurtured, and sustained a group of enterprises which were, in effect, the subjects of Toyota's economic domain.

This chapter has now illustrated some of the basic changes which took place in western Mikawa during the years after 1950. These changes included a sharp resurgence in the fortunes of Toyota Motors led by Ishida Taizō and the men under him, as well as a vast expansion in the industrial structure which complemented the auto firm itself. Due to these changes, large numbers of organizations and workers in the city of Kariya and the region of western Mikawa became subjects of Toyota's hegemony in the auto industry. Preceding pages have noted how organizations came under Toyota's control, but they have said little about how workers became subjects of the enterprise. In the same way Toyota brought affiliates and subcontractors under its wing, it also—through a concerted program of administration—produced a compliant work force in its factories. The results of its program had important implications for the political process in this area, so Toyota's new system of labor-management relations deserves attention before we turn to a discussion of political changes after 1955.

Executives at Toyota Motors systematically molded a new pattern of labor-management relations after the conflict-ridden days of the early 1950s.[11] Their purpose was to embrace workers firmly in the corporate fold, and simultaneously, to reduce the strength of the unions in the enterprise. They sought to create what they called the "Toyota Man," "a person who lives and works for the enterprise."[12] Such a person would display the "Toyota Spirit" in all his behavior, both inside and outside the company, because their purpose was "in addition to compliance with the company and the work place, to cultivate bright, warm human rela-

[11] The following account of Toyota's new labor policies is based on Nihon jimbun kagaku kai, *Gijutsu kakushin no shakaiteki eikyō*, pp. 88–133 and 160–178. Although this discussion applies primarily to the auto firm, other firms in the enterprise adopted similar labor relations practices at the same time.

[12] Ibid., p. 168.

tions." [13] The product of their new "worker construction" program would be an employee so well conditioned that he would intuitively serve the interests of the enterprise.

Inducements which managers used to achieve their ends were material, psychological, and organizational. Material or tangible inducements would remove the sources of dissatisfaction which had fueled worker unrest during the Occupation and give workers a greater feeling of financial reward. The first effort of this type occurred in 1950. Orders rose quickly in that year due to military demand, but Ishida Taizō directed that, rather than hire new workers, incumbent workers meet orders by working overtime. This, of course, boosted their paychecks dramatically, giving them incomes of a size they had not enjoyed for some time. The company also began to change its pay system. It de-emphasized the guaranteed base-wage and began to put more stress on merit pay based on productivity increases. Their union weakened by the events of 1950, workers had to accept the changes. It meant they would have to work harder to achieve pay raises, but that was precisely what the company intended. Finally, the firm expanded the leisure facilities it offered its employees. Even in the 1920s Toyota firms had provided their workers with athletic grounds for volleyball and softball. In the 1950s and 1960s they went well beyond those simple facilities. They built boat houses, tennis courts, and swimming pools. By the 1960s they were providing golf practice ranges, mountain lodges, and seaside villas for the use of both blue- and white-collar employees. All three of these changes—more overtime, increased incentive pay, and more leisure facilities—fostered a growing sense of affluence, which reflected itself in worker satisfaction and compliance with the goals of the firm.

Managers used psychological inducements, in a variety of guises, to draw the workers almost unwittingly into the ethos of the company. Beginning in the early 1950s, the company established a well-organized program of apprenticeship training. It identified capable middle-school graduates, put them through a three-year training program which was the equivalent of a high school course, and then assigned them to important jobs which usually called for technical skills. This program gave the prospective mainstays of the production force a solid technical education. But it also exposed them to a careful program of socialization, in which they learned to examine virtually all their actions with regard to their consequences for the company. Just one technique used to foster such awareness was a daily diary, in which apprentice workers were asked to record what shortcomings they had overcome that day, or what good things they had learned that day, or what things had left a strong

[13] Ibid.

impression on them. Staff officers from the Education Section read these diaries, made comments on them, and returned them to the apprentices. Such intrusive participation in the lives of their workers not only enabled company officials to keep close tabs on whatever they did, it also conditioned workers to accept close surveillance—willingly—from their superiors.

The company used other techniques of a social and psychological nature to draw workers into its firm embrace. To challenge the union, the company distributed its own publications. It began with a weekly in 1953 and added a glossy, monthly pictorial magazine in 1959. The company distributed the monthly pictorial magazine free of charge, while workers had to pay a nominal fee for their union paper. In 1959 a survey found that 82 percent of the workers "definitely" read each issue of the company's monthly publication. In the same survey, no one replied that he definitely read the union paper, and only 52 percent replied that they "sometimes" read it.[14] Consequently, the work force in the auto firm came to get most of its information from management, not the union. In the early 1950s the company also introduced "suggestion boxes." These served a specific, practical purpose. They gave workers employed on a rapidly changing assembly line an opportunity to point out ways in which new equipment and processes could be made more efficient. Suggestion boxes also served a less obvious psychological purpose. Giving workers a chance to participate—nominally and indirectly—in the decision-making process encouraged them to think of themselves as part of a unified corporation, rather than members of a large, hired work force. To further encourage workers in this direction, management made awards of as much as ¥50,000 to persons whose suggestions were especially valuable. Finally, the company relied on a vast array of extracurricular clubs, groups, and societies—which it supported with staff, facilities, and funds—as yet another psychological inducement with which to create an identity between the worker, his goals, and his company.

The company used many organizational inducements with which to draw workers away from the union. First, Toyota Motors began promoting former union officials into managerial positions. In the years between 1946 and 1951, many key union leaders were white-collar workers who held technical or clerical positions in the firm. They were as concerned as production workers about the issues of wages and promotions. Their leadership was instrumental in creating a union which included most workers in the firm. Such men, however, found the chance to "get on in the world" (*shusse*) attractive, so when the company gave them opportuni-

---

[14] Ibid., p. 101. Since a third party—the scholars who prepared the Toyota study in which this information is quoted—conducted the survey, it presumably reflected workers' actual reading habits with some accuracy.

ties for promotion after 1953, they accepted them. Absorbed by the management perspective, they lost their fervor for union activism. In the process, the unions suffered a loss of leadership while management enjoyed added loyalty from important employees.

Promoting former union leaders to managerial positions was one organizational technique which management used to undercut union power in the firm. A second major organizational change occurred in 1956 when Toyota Motors adopted the practice of hiring temporary workers (*rinjikō*). Temporary workers enjoyed no promise of lifetime security, as regular workers (*honkō* or *honshain*) did, and they received lower salaries than regular workers. They provided an economical way for the enterprise to meet labor needs at a low cost, without having to commit itself to a large increase in its permanent labor force. In the first year of the system, Toyota Motors hired about three hundred temporary workers. By 1960 temporary workers made up 42 percent of the labor force in the auto firm.[15] This proportion continued largely unchanged until 1967 when the system was finally abandoned in favor of a modified apprenticeship system. During its decade of operation, however, the temporary worker system had a depressing effect on union activism in the company. The presence of large numbers of *rinjikō* encouraged regular workers to think of themselves as an elite group, enjoying permanent employment, high wages, and the right to join a union. This undoubtedly nurtured loyalty to the company. The *rinjikō* themselves shrank from dissidence, because they knew it would mean summary dismissal, while docility and compliance might afford them a chance at a permanent position. The very make-up of the labor force which Toyota Motors organized after 1956 thus served as an important brake on union activism in the auto firm.

There were many other organizational changes on which Toyota relied to elicit compliance from its workers after 1950, but one final device warrants special attention. As part of its apprenticeship training program, the company established officers in the Educational Section whose responsibility it was to keep a worker's family informed of his behavior. These officers sent an annual report to parents, praising a worker if he had measured up to standards but criticizing him if he had not. Such criticism informed parents that their son was not performing adequately, and by implication, was bringing disgrace to the family name. Since most workers through the 1960s came from rural areas where the sense of family integrity remained strong, parents would obviously respond by pressuring their sons to do better. In this way, Toyota Motors relied on sanctions from one of the most powerful social organs in Japanese society—the family—to further induce compliance among its workers.

[15] This figure is based on the company's annual report to the Ministry of Finance and is quoted in ibid., p. 20.

Management's efforts to mold a new labor policy produced results quickly. As early as 1950 workers began reverting to the docile ways which had characterized them before the war. Public events were symbols of the change. In 1947, when the union movement was fresh, vigorous, and highly charged, eight thousand hungry demonstrators had gathered in Kariya to shout the slogans of revolution on the occasion of May Day celebrations. Less than a decade later, union members celebrated May Day with a perfunctory march down mainstreet with their families and picnic baskets. They were greeted by merchants who were flying the red flag before their shops and shouting the motto of the day: "Bright and happy!" Clearly, the mood had changed.

Within the company as well, workers were accepting changes which bespoke growing moderation in the union movement. Following the strike settlement in 1950, workers joined together under the banner of "restoring productivity." In 1952 and 1953 they conducted some work stoppages at the auto firm to force payment of higher wages. But following a damaging strike at Nissan Motors in 1953, and the creation of a new federation of auto workers, employees at Toyota Motors sought to restore an era of labor peace.[16] They began lobbying efforts to persuade the public to "love using a domestic auto." In 1956 the workers in the auto firm joined a Labor-Management Conference which served as a forum to plan for increases in efficiency and production. In the following year section chiefs, who had been among the most important union leaders up to then, voted to sever their ties with labor and to become a part of management for organizational purposes. All of these incidents revealed a growing mood of conciliation between labor and management.

The new mood of harmony culminated in an important agreement in 1962. By then managers in the auto company had worked to mold systematic labor policies for more than a decade, and their efforts were bearing fruit. With the intention of advancing product quality, lowering prices, and establishing a system of mass production, labor and management signed a joint declaration in 1962 dedicating themselves to:

1. Contribute to the development of the national economy through the prosperity of the automobile industry;
2. Base labor-management relations on mutual trust; and
3. Increase the company's prosperity and improve the workers' conditions through advances in productivity.[17]

Out of cooperation, personal wealth and national glory. The aim of this declaration is reminiscent of Risaburō's aspirations, set down some

[16] The strike and the new federation are discussed in the second half of this chapter.
[17] 30-nen shi, pp. 419-420.

thirty-five years before. With this agreement, the workers in the auto firm resurrected the prewar mood of harmony which was only momentarily buried by alien ideas during the Occupation period. They dedicated themselves anew to the economic objectives of the company, and they reaffirmed the belief that their interests coincided with those of the enterprise.

Labor-management harmony was well on its way to fruition when the Toyota enterprise began hiring workers in large numbers in the late 1950s. As firms expanded in Kariya to keep pace with the auto industry, they created new jobs in startling numbers.[18] Aishin Seiki hired 4,300 workers between 1955 and 1967; Nippon Densō, 5,800; Toyota Chassis, 2,500; and the loom and machine tool factories, another 1,200. In all, the number of manufacturing positions in these five Kariya firms rose from 6,400 in 1955 to more than 20,000 in 1966. In each year after 1955, three to five thousand new residents arrived in Kariya, most of them to take a position in one of the expanding Toyota firms.

New workers entering the city after the late 1950s were markedly different from the textile hands who had filled Kariya's first factories in the 1920s. Only half of the immigrants to Kariya in the early 1960s came from other settlements in Aichi Prefecture, or from neighboring prefectures. The remainder came from more distant places.[19] One in five of the new arrivals was a resident of Kyushu, Japan's southernmost island. Another one in six came from Japan's seven largest cities. For the first time in its history, Kariya lured workers from a labor market of truly national scope. Workers did not come from selected regions in northern Japan or western Japan. They came now from virtually all directions, informed about jobs and eager to find employment in a booming industry.

The vast majority of the new workers were men. In the large machine and auto factories in Kariya, they numbered eight or nine in every ten workers. Women, who comprised about one-tenth of the industrial work force, occupied primarily clerical jobs, although Nippon Densō had some female workers on its assembly lines. The men held virtually all production jobs, and all technical and managerial positions. They spanned a wide variety of ages. Most of the new recruits in the large factories were middle school graduates in their late teens. By the late 1960s young men under twenty-five comprised nearly half the industrial work force. Men over twenty-five, most of whom were married, made up the remainder.

Given employment practices in Kariya's large firms and the social attributes of the labor force, industrial workers in the 1960s were far more

---

[18] Changes at firms in the Toyota enterprise are treated in: Nippon Densō, *Nippon Densō jūgonen shi* (Kariya, 1964); *40-nen shi*, pp. 275–502; *Toyota shatai 20-nen shi*; and *Toyota kōki nijūnen shi.*

[19] *Kariya shisei yōran: 1966* (Kariya, 1967), pp. 26–27.

stable than their counterparts at the turn of the century. Managers and technicians were the most permanent members of the work force. As the comments on Toyota executives suggested, most of them settled in the city after finishing college, and if they moved at all, it was usually just from one firm in the enterprise to another. Production workers in the large factories were also quite permanent. They enjoyed a form of lifetime tenure in their firms and found it beneficial to remain until retirement, which a large portion of them did. At the loom factory, for example, there were 2,659 male workers between the ages of twenty and forty in 1953.[20] Twelve years later, the thirty-two to fifty-two age group numbered 2,498. Because the firm seldom recruited new production workers over the age of twenty, it is safe to assume that there were no additions to the first group after 1953. Therefore, well over 90 percent of those at the loom factory (in one age group, for one twelve-year period) became "permanent" workers. Managers and older production workers thus became quite stable residents in the community, if they found employment in one of the major firms.

Other segments of the labor force remained quite mobile, however, especially young men in large firms, employees in small- and medium-sized enterprises, and female workers. Despite the enticements of pay raises based on seniority and the security of job tenure, many young men remained with large firms for only three to five years; some quit after only six months. The system of temporary workers stimulated mobility, of course, but many workers with better prospects for advancement in the large firms were also mobile. The men between fifteen and thirty-five who worked in small enterprises were among the most mobile in the industrial work force. The firms in which they found work paid low wages, demanded long hours, and provided atrocious working conditions. Once they had gained some experience, young workers forced to enter a small firm at the beginning tried to improve their situation by acquiring a job at a better firm. This led to high rates of turnover in the small firms in town. As they had before, female workers continued to be short-term employees. Most of them joined a firm on graduation from middle or high school and remained for two to four years. By the late 1960s, when a labor shortage first began to appear locally, some firms offered dowries of household appliances if the eventual bride would remain six years in her place of work. The workers in these three groups were among the least permanent in the labor force. They contributed to a large and constant flow of persons in and out of Kariya, which witnessed the arrival and departure of fourteen thousand people in the year 1967 alone.

By the late 1960s the demand for labor, the influence of labor unions, and revisions in government laws all made conditions of work much better

[20] *40-nen shi*, p. 672.

than they had been thirty years before. A ten-hour day prevailed at Toyota Loom through the 1940s, but after the 1950s eight-hour days became common in the major Toyota firms.[21] Vacations increased, too. Few of the workers in large factories had to work on Sundays or national holidays, but through the 1960s, a six-day week was usual. Living accommodations provided by the companies improved visibly. There were numerous dormitories in the city, with heating and sanitary facilities that put the textile barracks of the 1920s to shame. Companies also provided loans and subsidies to workers able to build their own homes, a program which stimulated construction of many, new single-family dwellings in Kariya.[22] Finally, conditions in the factories themselves became far superior to what they once were. Safety standards in the large firms were high and well observed, keeping the frequency of industrial accidents low. By the mid-1960s factories were heated in the winter. They were better lit and cleaner than previously. Workers no longer risked life and limb to do their jobs amidst a jangle of ropes, pulleys, chains, and machines. The demand for efficiency in the new factories did not reduce the tedium of industrial work, but at least it improved conditions of employment.

The same situation did not prevail in Kariya's numerous small factories, however. Managers in those firms sometimes tried to emulate practices at the large firms, but they inevitably failed to meet the higher standards. They required longer work days, running nine to ten hours, and would have demanded seven days of work a week if they could have found employees to do it.[23] They had to provide dormitories and apartments for their workers, also, but they usually put up inexpensive buildings made from corrugated steel which were cold in winter and hot in summer. In the factories themselves, work conditions were visibly inferior. Safety standards were low, accidents numerous, lighting poor, ventilation inadequate, and heating in winter almost non-existent. From the standpoint of Kariya's industrial workers, these conditions were tolerable because only a minority—one in four—of all laborers had to put up with them.

Kariya's industrial work force actually divided into two separate groups. For purposes of description, they could be called the privileged workers and the industrial proletariat. The former group found work in the ten large firms in the city which employed over 500 workers. They enjoyed job security, good working conditions, and relatively high wages. The latter group worked in the small firms in the city with 500 employees or less. They enjoyed virtually no job security, they worked under comparatively inferior conditions, and they earned relatively low wages. In the nation as a whole, the group characterized here as the privileged workers comprised

[21] Ibid., p. 665.
[22] *Nippon Densō jūgonen shi*, p. 222.
[23] Kariya seinen kaigisho, *Rōdō jittai chōsa* (Kariya, 1965), p. 17.

only 33 percent of all industrial workers (in 1969), but in Kariya that group embraced a full 75 percent of the city's industrial work force. Moreover, while the proletariat worked in shops where there was seldom if ever a union group, the privileged all belonged to the large unions in the city. They were thus the only ones who enjoyed the organization to carry out concerted political action. As one might expect, the thrust of their political endeavors was colored by their status as workers, and especially by the benefits they enjoyed. This becomes clear in the second part of this chapter, which examines political change in Kariya after 1955.

Toyota's Political Dominance

The rapid industrialization which took place in western Mikawa after 1955 increased the electoral base of progressive parties dramatically. Since many of the new factory workers—perhaps 70 to 80 percent of them in cities such as Kariya and Toyota—entered large factories operating under closed shop rules, a very large portion of the work force joined labor unions. The growth in union strength led to a direct increase in electoral support for the united Japan Socialist Party after 1955.[24] The Japan Communist Party and, after the Socialist party split in 1960, the Democratic Socialist Party also benefitted from the influx of new workers. Diet returns illustrate the trend clearly. Whereas only 21 percent of the voters in the Fourth District cast ballots for progressive candidates in 1955, 41 percent did so in the 1967 Diet election. In the heavy industrial centers, the progressive vote rose to comprise a majority by 1967. In that year progressives cast 53 percent of the Diet ballots in Kariya and 51 percent in Toyota. In Anjō and Nishio the progressive share of the vote was smaller, 42 percent and 31 percent, respectively. Nonetheless, even in those cities the progressive share of the vote nearly tripled between 1955 and 1967.

Although the progressive electorate expanded dramatically, progressive parties had difficulty electing candidates at the Diet level. There were five Diet elections between 1955 and 1967. On only one occasion did two Socialist representatives win seats. That was between 1958 and 1960, when two members of the Japan Socialist Party held office from the Fourth District. In all other elections conservative candidates retained three of the four Diet seats in the district.

At the prefectural and municipal levels, progressive forces suffered a notable decline. There were three elections for prefectural governor in this period, in 1955, 1959, and 1963. The incumbent, a conservative named Kuwahara Mikine, won handily in each of them. In the Fourth District as

[24] The analysis of voting behavior in this chapter is based on Aichi ken senkyo kanri iin kai, ed., *Aichi no senkyo 20-nen,* 1:193–291; and Aichi ken senkyo kanri iinkai, ed., *Aichi ken senkyo kiroku: 1966–1967* (Nagoya, 1967), pp. 1–110.

a whole he ran up large majorities, receiving twice and three times the number of votes of his opponent. He also received a clear majority in every city in the district, despite the fact that progressives in cities such as Kariya and Toyota outnumbered conservatives. In the prefectural assembly elections held in the same three years, conservative candidates, running as Liberal Democrats or unaffiliated, captured virtually every seat. For the twelve-year period, only one Socialist candidate, from Okazaki, won election to the prefectural assembly. In all other communities, including Kariya and Toyota, conservative candidates captured every assembly seat.

Progressive forces suffered most dismally at the municipal level. In all four of the cities in this district, men who came from conservative backgrounds and who represented conservative interests monopolized the mayoralty. The two mayors in Kariya in this period were a former conservative politician and a former prefectural official. In Toyota, the two mayors were a former prefectural official and a former company executive. In Anjō, they were a businessman and a farmer. And in Nishio, the mayors were a farmer and a banker. Not one community elected a mayor who clearly represented workers as a socio-economic group, or who enjoyed the undivided support of progressive coalitions.

One explanation for the showing of progressive forces in the Fourth District between 1955 and 1967 rests with the nature of progressive parties at the national level. Ideological differences produced a number of groupings within the progressive movement. On some occasions these differences reflected themselves in separate parties, on other occasions, in the appearance of factions within parties. During the first five years of the period under discussion, there were two progressive parties: the Japan Socialist Party and the Japan Communist Party. After 1960, the Japan Socialist Party split, when moderate Socialists formed their own Democratic Socialist Party. Such ideological differences, manifested in separate party organizations, reduced the strength of progressive forces notably.

Lack of unity among progressives was most apparent during election campaigns, where its results proved most devastating. The Fourth District is an excellent case in point. In the 1958 Diet election, two Socialist candidates won seats in the Fourth District. They did so by dividing a constituency of one hundred twenty thousand voters evenly, allowing one of them to barely upset the third-ranking conservative. In the next Diet election in 1960, they had to work with essentially the same constituency. But by that time the Democratic Socialist Party had formed. It insisted on running its own candidate in the district. He won only twenty thousand votes, but in doing so, he attracted enough supporters from one of the Socialist candidates to unseat her. The same divisions, reflected in multiple-candidacies, afflicted the progressives in the 1963 election also.

Consequently, they were never able to return two progressives to the Diet. A proliferation of separate parties within the progressive movement thus inhibited the electoral success of progressive candidates in Diet elections in this district.

A second tendency which weakened progressive forces could be called cosmopolitanism. This term refers to the somewhat arrogant practice of the progressive parties to focus on national and international issues, to the exclusion of all others. The Japan Socialist Party was especially reluctant to direct its attention to local and prefectural elections. It preferred to concentrate its energies and resources on elections to the Diet. Consequently, progressive forces did not mobilize for local elections in the same way they did for national elections. This prevented them from exploiting the potent electoral support they enjoyed, support which could have produced progressive victories had the national party followed a different strategy.

Strategies of national parties provide, however, only one explanation for the electoral fortunes of progressives at the local level. A new set of conditions in local society also exerted a profound influence on local politics. Motivating the changes was the economic expansion which began in the mid-1950s. As business flourished and factories grew, industry began to impose specific demands on local governments. Dramatic changes in the labor market encouraged workers to assume different attitudes toward management and the political process. In pace with these developments, conservative forces restored themselves to power in the Fourth District and especially in Kariya. The radical interlude came to a swift conclusion. In its place there appeared a new political hegemony based in the Toyota enterprise. The remaining portion of this chapter illustrates the nature of Toyota's political hegemony in Kariya between 1955 and 1967.

The year 1955 marked a turning point in Kariya's history, as well as a turning point in the nation's economic and political life. That was the year in which Kariya consolidated with two nearby villages to become a much larger community. Local leaders had been discussing the possibility of consolidation for many years. They were eager to expand their small community to form a large city. In 1953 the central government passed a new law encouraging the consolidation of local bodies into larger units of self-government.[25] This law gave added impetus to local moves for consolidation. Vast numbers of towns and villages responded to the new law and a wave of consolidation occurred. In Kariya, local leaders conducted negotiations with several surrounding communities, some of them only villages and others already towns. Finally, Kariya merged with the villages of Fujimatsu (north of the city) and Yosami (south of the city).

[25] See Steiner, *Local Government in Japan*, pp. 186–194, for a discussion of this program.

On April 1, 1955, the enlarged city of Kariya was born. It covered an area three times its former size and had a population exceeding fifty thousand.

The enlarged city created an entirely new forum for local politics. Henceforth, Kariya residents would elect their mayors and their prefectural assemblymen from a district encompassing the heavily industrialized town area as well as two villages, still primarily agrarian. In 1955 the new constituency included 29,674 voters.[26] Of that number, 17,302 lived in the town area; the remaining 12,372 lived in the villages. There was a sharp difference in the political loyalties of the groups which appeared clearly in the Diet election in February 1955.[27] In that election, 58 percent of the voters in the town area supported conservative candidates, but another 42 percent supported progressive candidates. In the town area, progressives were approaching a majority. In the villages, by sharp contrast, conservatives won a full 80 percent of the vote, and progressives took a mere 20 percent. Despite their proximity to a highly industrial area, voters in the village areas of the new city remained inveterate conservatives.

However, one problem inherent in any consolidation stood in the way of united conservative action. There was a strong legacy of community solidarity in the towns and villages which joined new cities in the early 1950s. This impeded their integration into the larger communities formed by consolidation. It also created divisions between citizens living in the old rural areas and citizens living in the former town areas of a new city. These divisions often appeared in political contests, creating animosities which inhibited conservatives in rural areas from working smoothly with those in town areas.

Kariya was a city which exemplified the problem. The town was heavily industrial. Politically, it was split between a conservative group and a progressive group of comparable size. The villages, on the other hand, were overwhelmingly conservative. There were thus three political forces in the new community: urban conservatives, urban progressives, and rural conservatives. Under such circumstances, urban progressives could prevent conservative dominance by drawing together with a conservative faction. If such a coalition appeared, consolidation went for naught. But if the two conservative groups aligned, then they achieved the purpose of consolidation—to bury the progressives. Conservative local politicians were surely very enticed by the prospect of consolidation with two such villages.

Analyses of the consolidation programs undertaken in Japan between 1953 and 1956 attribute such programs to the desire of the central government to (1) expand its authority over local entities, and (2) to increase the efficiency of local government.[28] But there was a third motive

[26] *Aichi no senkyo 20-nen*, 1:208.
[27] Ibid., pp. 216–217.
[28] See Steiner, pp. 186–194.

which prompted support for mergers among conservative politicians. That was the opportunity to use consolidation as a means to restore conservatives to power in local communities.

Kariya is a good illustration of the third motive at work. Had the city continued as it was before 1955, economic expansion would have attracted more factory workers and enhanced the voting strength of the progressive parties. Already near a majority, they might have been able to elect a mayor themselves, and to seize full control of local government. The opportunity to consolidate with two heavily conservative villages made it possible to submerge the prospective progressive majority under a torrent of conservative voters. It was a matter of simple arithmetic. Conservatives preferred to have a larger community of 30,000 voters in which 20,000 were dependably conservative, rather than a small community of 17,000 voters of which only 10,000 or so could be relied upon. Consolidation promised to create an electoral base on which to restore conservative rule. Moreover, that electoral base would be large enough to block a progressive takeover for some years at least.

In the first election held after Kariya's consolidation, divisions between town and village did not appear. As a result, conservatives were able to exploit their support from the villages to defeat Ishihara Tenryū, Kariya's Socialist delegate to the prefectural assembly. On April 23, 1955, Kariya voters elected as their new assemblyman a conservative named Fujii Seihichi. Fujii was the son of a man of the same name.[29] His father had been mayor of Kariya between 1919 and 1921, its largest landlord, and a prominent figure in local financial circles. The younger Fujii assumed the headship of his family in 1929. During the prewar years, Fujii continued to oversee family lands as he undertook new business ventures. In the last years of the war, he presided over a merger of some fifty small transport firms which formed the Daikō Transport Corporation. At the end of the war, Daikō was a modest organization owning fifty old trucks and employing 150 drivers, but by 1965 it was the largest transport enterprise in western Mikawa. It owned 150 large trucks and 140 taxis and employed over 600 workers. Its primary business was to ship auto parts between factories in Kariya and Toyota. In addition to his presidency at Daikō, Fujii also presided over several other companies engaged in shipping, refrigeration, truck repair and commerce.

The election of Fujii Seihichi symbolized the direction which local politics would take during the next decade. Fujii was a man of impeccable conservative credentials. He was a direct descendant of the long-standing circle of influentials who dominated local politics in the years before 1945. His grandfather was a former village mayor, his mother was related to a

[29] For Fujii see Sangyō kenkyūjo, *Watakushi no ayanda michi*, pp. 97–125.

former Diet member, and his father was a former town mayor. Figuratively speaking, Fujii was also a bridge linking the old economic influentials in Kariya with the new. Since his father was a former landlord in the community, as well as a director of several banks, Fujii had ties to the agrarian and commercial groups prominent in Kariya. He himself had diversified the family fortunes by tying them to the expansive new industrial sector. This preserved the family's economic status in the postwar world. It also brought Fujii into direct association with the leaders of the Toyota enterprise. The fate of his firm now depended directly on Toyota, so Fujii had an immediate interest in creating a political and economic climate conducive to industrial expansion. Fujii won re-election in 1959 and 1963. For twelve years, therefore, Kariya's voters sent to the prefectural assembly a man representing the old ruling group who shared the expressed concern of Toyota managers for efficient local government in the service of industry.

For several years before 1955, conservative local politicians and leaders in the Toyota enterprise had rankled at the lack of efficiency in the Okamoto administration. They were also nervous about his ties to progressive supporters. The consolidation enabled them to remove the leader of the progressives from his post in the prefectural assembly. That victory encouraged them to unseat the incumbent mayor, as well. Conservatives began publicizing problems at city hall, particularly its budgetary deficits. Financial difficulties were endemic to Japanese cities at that time, and Okamoto's administration was not the sole cause of Kariya's problems by any means. Nonetheless, under conservative pressure, Okamoto Kimpei resigned from office in July 1955, a year before his term expired. He left under accusations of corruption. If that were not bad enough, he also bore the onus of imcompetence. Having enjoyed progressive backing, Okamoto thus stepped down under a cloud, leaving many voters with the impression that—as business leaders were quick to claim—progressives could not govern properly.

The mayoralty election which followed in July 1955 stirred up the town and village differences mentioned above and created some peculiar alignments. Conservative leaders in the town area nominated Takenaka Hichirō as their candidate. Takenaka enjoyed the backing of Ōno Ichizō and his local *jiban*, as well as the support of managers in the Toyota firms. In addition, he won endorsement from important economic figures, such as the president of the Chamber of Commerce, who was an executive with the Japan Tile Corporation.

Takenaka's opponent was Tomikawa Seiichi, mayor of Fujimatsu village when it consolidated in 1955. Tomikawa was ten years younger than Takenaka and brought much different credentials to office. He was a graduate of the Tokyo Agriculture School who had also studied briefly in the United States. His first job was with the prefectural government. Later he served in the office of the governor-general in Korea and as a section chief in the Manchurian Development Corporation. He returned to Kariya late in the war and took up farming. By the mid-1950s he was an influential figure among the farmers of Fujimatsu. Those essentially conservative voters made up the bulk of his constituency. Both candidates, therefore, represented conservative interests: Takenaka, the business and industrial community in town, and Tomikawa, the agricultural interests in the villages.

Having seen their electoral strength reduced to only a third of the total as a result of the consolidation, progressive leaders were unable to present their own candidate. They had to support either Takenaka or Tomikawa. They chose Tomikawa. They made the choice for two reasons. First, some progressive leaders had worked with Tomikawa while he was mayor of Fujimatsu. They recognized that he was a bit conservative, but they felt he shared some of their ideas and might be flexible. Second, the progressives were very eager to destroy Ōno Ichizō's influence on local politics. Takenaka was his protégé and they wanted Takenaka out. As the campaign neared its conclusion, a chance disclosure embarrassed the progressives badly. They discovered that Tomikawa was an ally of Ogasawara Sankurō. Ogasawara, as a prewar Diet member of considerable standing and a former businessman in the Japanese colonies, was every bit as odious in progressive eyes as Ōno Ichizō and his supporters. Nonetheless, progressives swallowed their ideological pride and continued to support Tomikawa.[30]

The contest was a close one. In the absence of tabulations for districts within the city, it is impossible to verify which areas voted for whom. One can make some hypotheses, however. Tomikawa's constituency was most likely made up of: (1) most of the voters in Fujimatsu, (2) a smattering of conservative voters in the town area, (3) a portion of the voters in Yosami, and (4) some portion—though hardly all—of the organized workers in the city. In the end, Tomikawa lost by 410 votes. He captured 11,009, but Takenaka won 11,419. Conservatives had retrieved city hall.

During the four years of the Takenaka administration, politics in Kariya underwent two substantial changes. The first change took place in city hall itself: it became a larger, more complex bureaucracy.[31] In four years the number of full-time employees rose from 135 to 240. A sharp rise in city revenues permitted this increase, and necessitated it at the same time. Between ·1955 and 1959 city revenues more than doubled, from ¥310 billion annually to ¥630 billion. Recognizing that city government was· no longer an avocational undertaking, Takenaka Hichirō recruited a

[30] I am indebted to Narukawa Toshio for this information.

[31] Data on budgets and the municipal bureaucracy in Kariya presented in this chapter are drawn from *Kariya shisei yōran*, an annual publication of the Kariya City Hall.

professional, administrative aide. On December 16, 1955, Takada Ichirō became the assistant mayor in Kariya. For twenty-five years Takada had been an official in the Aichi government. He was well-versed in the operations of bureaucracy. But more important, he was a friend and associate of men about to enter high-ranking positions in the prefectural government. Takenaka brought him to town for two purposes: (1) to take advantage of Takada's administrative skills in managing Kariya's affairs, and (2) to use his contacts to nurture closer ties with the prefecture. No longer a part-time undertaking, the Kariya mayoralty became during the late 1950s a full-time position demanding special administrative skills of its incumbent.

The second change which occurred after Takenaka took office involved the role of the Toyota enterprise in local politics. During the prewar years, as previous chapters noted, Toyota did not participate openly in Kariya's political life. There were three reasons why it did not. First, Sakichi had urged the company to keep out of politics and concentrate on business. Second, the enterprise did not have to involve itself in political affairs because the tax structure of local government imposed few levies on the enterprise. It was therefore not drawn into local politics as it might have been under the influence of a different form of taxation. Third, Toyota officials had a comfortable relationship with local influentials. These men acted as agents for the firm in the community, and this obviated the need for Toyota officials to engage in local politics themselves. By the late 1950s, changes in the enterprise, in the structure of local finances, and in political conditions in Kariya had all undermined the old pattern of relations. These changes weakened the constraints on Toyota's political participation. As a result, the company began to play a more overt role in local politics, the nature of which following pages examine in some detail.

The incident which first drew the Toyota enterprise into local politics arose in 1957.[32] In that year the Ministry of Education ordered the mayor of Kariya to consolidate two elementary schools located in the old Yosami village area. At the time of the order, there was one school in the hamlet of Noda with 320 students and another in the hamlet of Hadaka teaching 340 students. The residents of Hadaka were elated with the word of a new school. Their school was sixty years old and in bad repair. They wanted a new one. Noda residents, on the other hand, had just built a new elementary school. They did not oppose consolidation, but they wanted the new school in their building. City officials, however, insisted on a new school midway between the two hamlets. This inflamed Noda residents, who refused to send their children to school and who even staged a sit-in at

[32] For an account of the school issue see: Katsumura Shigeru, "Chiiki riidaa no kōsei to seisaku no kettei," *Shakai kagaku tōkyū* 11:1 (June 1965), pp. 407–414.

city hall. To resolve the impasse, the mayor called on Fujii Seihichi, union leaders, and Ōno Ichizō to serve as intermediaries, but all to no avail. Finally, in May 1959, Ishida Taizō entered the discussions between Noda residents and the city. By that time a compromise faction had emerged in Noda and the mood for settlement ran high. The city compensated Noda residents and the new school went up. Ishida was not instrumental in resolving the dispute, but that was less important than his presence. For the first time since Toyota had arrived in Kariya some forty years before, a Toyota official participated openly in local politics.

Two months after the school question was resolved, a second event occurred which drew the Toyota enterprise even more decisively into a public role in local politics. Takenaka's term as mayor would end in late July 1959, so an election was called for. The same groups which fought so earnestly for the mayoralty in 1955 came forth again, supporting the same candidates. But just as the second contest between Takenaka and Tomikawa heated up, Takenaka suddenly fell ill and died. His death threw the conservatives into confusion. They considered Ōno Ichizō as a stand-in, but at seventy-four he was too old to take the post. After Ōno, they tried to persuade Iwase Masami to accept the nomination. Iwase was an executive in the Japan Tile Company and the president of the Chamber of Commerce; he was an influential figure in the city's business community. Iwase refused the offer. Finally, almost in desperation, the conservatives turned to Takada Ichirō. There was resistance to Takada at first, but Ishida Taizō pushed his nomination through.

Takada's nomination was very unusual, because he was an outsider. Takada Ichirō was born in Ichinomiya, a textile center northwest of Nagoya. After graduation from Meiji University in Tokyo, he entered the government in his home prefecture and took jobs in a number of regional offices. He was not a long-time resident of Kariya. In fact, he had lived in the city for only three years. He had no hometown ties or family bonds in the community, and thus was not trusted by the people of Kariya. Nor did he have a knowledge of the political alignments within the community, a weakness that would make it difficult for him to govern with an even hand. Takada's candidacy marked the first time, since the office was established in 1889, that an outsider ran for mayor in Kariya.

An outsider suffered a number of disadvantages, but conservative groups in Kariya supported Takada because they suddenly faced a vacuum of leadership. Previously, local leaders had followed a well-trod path to the mayoralty, which led through ward offices, the town or city council, and sometimes a seat in the prefectural assembly. Only after proving himself during years of service could a man stand for mayor. Age and experience thus regulated recruitment. As they examined their list of potential candidates in 1959, conservative leaders in Kariya faced a difficult problem. The oldest and most experienced politician, Ōno Ichizō, was too old to run. Takenaka was dead. Two other logical candidates were Fujii Seihichi and Iwase Masami. They were both in their mid-fifties and properly experienced for the office. Neither of them was interested, however, because it was a full-time position that would interfere with their business careers. Slightly younger conservatives lacked experience. During the radical interlude in Kariya's politics, the progressives had effectively barred young conservatives from winning office. This prevented their acquiring experience that would have made them viable candidates in the late 1950s. The only other possibility was Takada Ichirō. An outsider with virtually no political roots in the community thus became the conservative candidate for mayor.

Takada stepped into the race with only seven days left before the election. He had virtually no popular base of support. But Ishida Taizō worked diligently to rectify that problem.[33] Ishida brought pressure on all of the unions in the Toyota firms to support Takada. The union at the loom factory refused to go along, but the others acquiesced. In addition, Ishida persuaded the prefectural governor to come to Kariya to campaign on Takada's behalf. Both men were over seventy years old, but Ishida Taizō and Kuwahara Mikine stood on Kariya street corners in suffocating mid-summer heat urging voters to cast their ballots for Takada. Ishida's efforts paid off. When the campaign ended, Takada captured 14,611 votes, defeating Tomikawa by a margin of 900 votes. Frustrated by two straight defeats, Takada's opposition did not even field a candidate when he ran for re-election in 1963. Thus, for eight years Takada Ichirō governed the city of Kariya.

Takada was an anomaly because he was an outsider, but in another respect he was a fitting candidate for the city. His experience as a bureaucrat coincided with the demands of city government and with a trend of the times. There was a strong tendency during the 1950s and 1960s for communities to select men with administrative experience as mayors. At one time, being mayor of a small city was a part-time job, undertaken as an avocation by men who had the wealth and leisure to do it. But by the mid-1950s many things had changed. Most local entities were much larger than before. With the industrial expansion of the "income-doubling" years, local government was also becoming more complex. Cities had to provide more services. This required planning and coordination with the prefectural and central governments. Communities now needed men with managerial skills who could treat the mayoralty as a full-time, specialized position. Increasingly, they turned to former government officials or corporate executives to find them. The city of Toyota, for

[33] Ibid., p. 415.

example, elected as mayor in 1956 and 1960 a man with three decades of experience in the prefectural government. In 1964 they elected as mayor a former department head from the city's largest corporation. These men represented a new type of elected official, the administrative mayor. Takada was a standard example of the type. He was a man whose administrative experience was as important to his supporters as his political skills.

Ishida Taizō was one of Takada's most ardent supporters, as the previous account illustrated. Despite Sakichi's old injunction against politics, Ishida had already served as a mediator in one political crisis. At the time of Takada's election, he assumed an even more openly political position by actually campaigning on street corners. These two incidents illustrate the degree to which the old constraints on Toyota's participation in local politics broke down during the 1950s. Yet another incident, involving the construction of a new technical school in Kariya, illustrates how pervasive the political influence of the Toyota enterprise—and especially Ishida—was becoming.

As in prewar Japan, postwar laws of the central government determined the form and content of political action involving local schools.[34] For a brief period after the war, local communities had school boards with the rights to make a budget, purchase textbooks, determine curricula, and hire and fire personnel. In 1956, however, the central government reduced local control over education dramatically. New laws created prefectural school boards, which assumed authority over personnel. Those boards also ruled on appointments of local superintendents of schools, who served as administrative aides to mayors and oversaw local educational affairs. The mayor prepared the school budget. The local board of education advised him in this task, but enjoyed few powers of initiative on its own. Control over textbooks and curricula was widely dispersed, but officials in the Ministry of Education provided constant "guidance, advice and assistance," which local schools usually heeded.[35] After 1956, as before the war, community authority was indisputably clear in only one area: financing. Prefectural and central governments paid teachers' salaries, but cities still had to pay for the construction and maintenance of educational facilities. As a result of these laws, community action on educational problems was confined to questions involving location of, improvements in, or additions to existing facilities.

The school issue under discussion arose when Kariya's leaders tried to attract a technical school to the city.[36] Plans for five technical schools in

[34] Steiner, pp. 252–255.
[35] Ibid., p. 253.
[36] This account is based on Kinenshi henshū iinkai, ed., *Aichi kenritsu Kariya Kōgyō kōtō gakkō sōritsu goshūnen kinen shi* (Kariya, 1967).

Aichi Prefecture dated from the early 1950s. The prefectural government had conceived the idea but had done nothing about it. In the late 1950s Ishida Taizō and Iwase Masami sought to revive interest in the plan by suggesting that one school be established in Kariya. They urged Mayor Takada to petition the prefectural governor, which he did, accompanied by Fujii Seihichi. At the same time, Fujii worked to persuade prefectural assemblymen from western Mikawa to sign a petition supporting Kariya's request. Ishida Taizō also lent his help by persuading politicians in the city of Toyota to support the Kariya request, in exchange for a promise of aid when they sought a technical college for their city. Meanwhile, city officials in Kariya re-zoned a large plot of land near the Nippon Densō and Toyota Loom factories. They also conducted negotiations with sixty landowners in the area to purchase space designated for the school. Members of the city council, of the Board of Education (of which Iwase was Chairman), of the Chamber of Commerce (of which Iwase was President), and Ishida Taizō all cooperated in the task of purchasing land.

In 1962 the prefectural government designated Kariya the site for one of three new schools. Construction began immediately. The prefectural government paid 60 percent of the costs of the land, and the city of Kariya assumed the remaining costs. The Toyota group helped generously. It contributed ¥5 million and offered the use of its machines for instructional purposes. After discussions with local officials and Toyota representatives, prefectural authorities organized the school into three units: a machine division, an electric division, and an automobile division. It was more than coincidental that the three divisions mirrored the structure of Kariya's major industries.

There are many striking parallels between this effort to lure a school to Kariya and the school funding crisis of the 1920s (mentioned in chapter 4). They deserve brief comment. In both cases, public concern for the new school was conspicuous by its absence. There were no popular appeals for the institution. Rather, influential economic and political figures in the community initiated the proposals. In the 1920s the Enterprise Council and men such as Ōno Ichizō managed the dealings to acquire a new school. In the 1960s economic leaders such as Ishida and Iwase were the prime movers. As before, executive organs of government played a major role in defining the issue and resolving it. In the 1960s it was the prefectural governor, rather than an official in a central ministry, whose support was crucial, but the essential point remains: executive authority dominated the resolution of local political issues. Finally, there were strong parallels between the supplicating position of Kariya in the 1920s and the 1960s. Even though the community raised substantial revenues on its own in the 1960s, it still needed prefectural funding for this major public project. This illustrates again the continuing financial dependence which local governments suffer in Japan. In summary, this issue illustrates that the shape of political action at the local level in the 1960s contained many features common to the prewar period. A low level of public initiative, a high degree of executive authority, and a considerable amount of financial dependence remained constant aspects of local politics in Japan.

The school issue just discussed provides a third illustration of the way in which the Toyota enterprise injected itself into local politics during the years after 1955. In the case of the technical school, Ishida Taizō suggested that Kariya have the school in the first place, he mediated with local politicians to win support, he aided negotiations to buy land, he expressed his preferences for a curriculum, and he helped finance and furnish the school. He could not have played a more instrumental role.

The preceding pages have illustrated how Toyota imposed its candidate for mayor on the city of Kariya and how it participated in two school issues in the community. Two other types of evidence lend final support to the claim that Toyota enjoyed a political hegemony in Kariya during the years after 1955. The first evidence comes from the allocation of community resources, in the distribution of which local officials betrayed their favoritism toward industrial interests. The second source of evidence appears in an extensive survey of local leadership undertaken in the mid-1960s.

It was obvious to anyone in Kariya during Takada's years in office that he was very responsive to the desires of the Toyota enterprise. Table 14

TABLE 14

BUDGET EXPENDITURES IN KARIYA AND
OTHER CITIES OF SIMILAR SIZE, 1965
(PERCENTAGE OF TOTAL, BY CATEGORY)

Category of Expenditure	Kariya	Other Cities
General affairs	27	19
Construction	23	14
Education	15	21
Sanitation	11	10
Welfare	8	11
Commerce and industry	2	4
Labor	1	4
All other categories	13	17
Total	100	100

SOURCE: Aichi ken, Kariya shi, *Kariya shi sōgō keikaku: 1968–1977* (Kariya, n.d.), p. 112.
NOTE: These are final outlays for funds actually spent. The source does not make clear with what other cities Kariya was compared.

offers proof of this claim. It illustrates that Kariya was willing to skimp on educational facilities in order to staff a large bureaucracy in city hall and to carry out the construction projects which appeared throughout the city. The city government built new roads, broad and hard-surfaced, past the factories at Nippon Densō and Toyota Chassis. It installed water lines and sewage ditches to the new factories, dormitories, and apartments for Toyota workers. And it financed construction of a new technical school, whose graduates provided a steady flow of recruits for Toyota firms. In many visible ways, the Takada administration ignored social needs in the community in order to devote more resources to meeting the demands of industrial expansion. Under Takada Ichirō, city government in Kariya came very close to being just another arm of corporate enterprise.

In fact, contemporaries saw it almost in that light. Thanks to the efforts of a research group from Waseda University, there exists a rare and valuable portrait of city politics in Kariya during the mid-1960s.[37] One goal of the Waseda group was to identify the city's most powerful figures. The group first selected a body of 108 persons who seemed to be among the most active and influential figures in the community. They made their choices on the basis of documents and interviews. Among the 108 were 7 city officials, 35 city council members, 41 prominent citizens, 13 corporation executives, and 12 union leaders. The Waseda researchers then asked the 108 persons who they thought wielded the greatest authority and influence over Kariya's government and other matters. Persons mentioned most frequently were assumed to be the most influential. The twenty-two leading figures appear in table 15.

Two aspects of this list draw one's attention. First, Kariya's leading citizens saw a close association between political office and political power. Five of the top ten choices were incumbent officials, either in the city government or the prefectural assembly. Moreover, seven of the remaining twelve choices were office holders, most of them city councilmen. Respondents agreed in large measure that the mayor and other office holders exercised real power in the community. Second, respondents also attributed great power to the community's economic figures. Eight of the twenty-two men on the list were heads of the city's most important industrial and commercial organizations. One of them, Ishida Taizō, ranked first in the eyes of Kariya's leading citizens as the most powerful man in the community.

The impression that Ishida was the city's leading power in 1964 was

[37] The Waseda study of Kariya appears in Waseda daigaku shakai kagaku kenkyūjo, ed., "Tokushū: Chihō sangyō toshi no kenryoku kōzō," *Shakai kagaku tōkyū* 11:1 (June 1965). A brief English-language summary of the views of one of the Waseda group, Akimoto Ritsuo, appears in Hiroshi Ito, ed., *Japanese Politics: An Inside View* (Ithaca, 1973), pp. 167–182.

reaffirmed by further surveys. The Waseda researchers designated the top ten members of the first list as the city's "key influentials," and then asked them to indicate their choices for the top decision makers in Kariya. The results appear in table 16. The "key influentials," allegedly the city's most powerful individuals and presumably the best informed politically, lent striking endorsement to Ishida's stature in the community. Even those who did not feel he was the most powerful placed him second. Most "key influentials" agreed that Fujii Seihichi and Ōno Ichizō ranked second and third after Ishida, followed by the two men from Japan Tile, Ida and Iwase. Clearly, there was strong agreement that the community's most powerful figures in 1965 were its industrial leaders and its native-born politicians.

Mayor Takada Ichirō found himself in a very peculiar position on the list of influentials. His own choices were rather unorthodox. Three other

TABLE 15

Top Influentials in Kariya in 1964

Name	Position
Ishida Taizō	President, Toyota Loom, Toyota Motors
Takada Ichirō	Mayor, City of Kariya
Fujii Seihichi	Prefectural assemblyman; Pres., Daikō Transport
Ōno Ichizō	Retired; former mayor of Kariya and Diet member
Iwase Masami	Managing Director, Japan Tile Company
Katō Kōmei	President, City Council; company official
Miyata Ichimatsu	Assistant mayor of Kariya; tile manufacturer
Hayashi Torao	President, Nippon Densō Company
Ida Yosaji	President, Japan Tile Company
Miura Keiji	Head, Department of General Affairs, Kariya
Sugiura Yoshio	City councilman; sake dealer
Tsūda Toyosuke	President, Tsūda Steel Company
Ogawa Kiichi	Farmer
Ebara Kametarō	City councilman; grocery store owner
Tatematsu Iwao	President, Toyota Chassis Company
Mori Gen'ichi	City councilman; pawnshop owner
Tomikawa Seiichi	Farmer; former mayor of Fujimatsu *mura*
Kamiya Shigeru	Kariya Superintendent of Schools
Katō Noboru.	City councilman; appliance dealer
Egawa Yukie	City councilman; farmer
Ōta Ichizō	President, Ōta Commercial Company
Fukaya Ritsutarō	City treasurer

SOURCE: Akimoto Ritsutarō, "Chiiki shakai ni okeru kenryoku bōtai to riidaa no kōsei," *Shakai kagaku tōkyū*, 11:1 (June 1965), p. 343.

men mentioned Ida Yosaji as a top decision maker, but none ranked him higher than third. Yet Takada placed him first. Provided his choice was not an intentional dodge on his part or a clerical error by the researchers, his choice bespoke his unfamiliarity with the community. He was not only unfamiliar with Kariya, however. He was obviously a weak figure. Only two men even mentioned him: Ishida, who had frequent dealings with him, and Miura, who was his subordinate. The alleged powerholders in Kariya certainly must have felt that Takada Ichirō was a minor figure. Indeed they demonstrated this assessment on the occasion of a roundtable discussion in 1960, when twelve distinguished members of the community gathered to discuss local affairs.[38] On such occasions the highest-ranking members speak first, followed by others according to a descending hierarchy of prestige. Takada Ichirō occupied the eighth position in the group, a fact which bespoke the low esteem in which influential city leaders held him. Ignorant of local affairs and abjectly dependent on the support of Ishida and the Toyota interests in Kariya, Takada functioned essentially as another executive carrying out the will of the Toyota enterprise. He symbolized the political thrust of Toyota's power.

The preceding pages have illustrated the nature of the Toyota hegemony over Kariya's political life, but they have not explained the reasons for it. Citing a breakdown of the old constraints on political participation suggests why Toyota's role changed, but it does not provide a

TABLE 16

KARIYA'S TOP DECISION MAKERS IN 1964, AS CHOSEN
BY THE CITY'S TEN "KEY INFLUENTIALS"

Key Influential	Top Decision Makers
Ishida Taizō	Takada Ichirō, Fujii Seihichi, Iwase Masami
Takada Ichirō	Ida Yosaji, Ishida Taizō, Fujii Seihichi
Fujii Seihichi	Ishida Taizō, Ōno Ichizō, Ida Yosaji
Ōno Ichizō	Ishida Taizō, Fujii Seihichi, Ida Yosaji
Iwase Masami	Ishida Taizō, Fujii Seihichi, Katō Kōmei
Katō Kōmei	Ishida Taizō, Fujii Seihichi, Ōno Ichizō
Miura Keiji	Ōno Ichizō, Ishida Taizō, Takada Ichirō
Ida Yosaji	Ishida Taizō, Ōno Ichizō, Tomikawa Seiichi
Miyata Ichimatsu	Ōno Ichizō, Ishida Taizō, Ida Yosaji
Hayashi Torao	Ishida Taizō, Fujii Seihichi, Iwase Masami

SOURCE: Same as table 15, pp. 350–351.

full explanation. To do so, it is necessary to analyze a variety of causes, all of which intertwined to bring Toyota to the forefront of local politics.

Any explanation must begin with Ishida Taizō. By virtue of his personality and status, he did more to bring Toyota into local politics than anyone else. His earlier sketch in this chapter portrayed him as an unpolished, aggressive figure. In Kariya, those qualities were advantageous because people in town were accustomed to such traits and valued them. Even the workers—whom he treated with companionable intransigence during strikes—respected his opinions. His personally aggressive nature convinced him that Toyota could not stand by and allow local political offices to fall into the hands of progressives, or others who would not be responsive to the demands of industry. He was not one to shrink from decisions, so he threw himself into local politics with the same vigor that he displayed in rising to the top at Toyota Motors.

In another way, Ishida's very status in the community drew him into local politics. His position as the real leader in the Toyota enterprise by now guaranteed him high status in the community. But he enjoyed another advantage as well. The old-line leaders, such as Ōno Ichizō, were somewhat discredited by the Occupation purge; Ishida was not. Consequently, his service to the nation during the war years was not called into public doubt. Moreover, in the trying years after the war, Ishida made the loom factory one of the few stable enterprises in town, and this enhanced respect for his managerial powers. By 1959 it was natural that the community should call on him as a prestigious figure to resolve a political dispute. He probably relished the task besides, because he was vain enough to think he was the only man for the job. As a result of Ishida Taizō's personality and status in Kariya, therefore, Toyota assumed a new role in local politics.

The vacuum of leadership caused by Takenaka's sudden death in 1959 was a second cause of Toyota's expanding role in local politics. Ishida Taizō supported Takada's candidacy in order to sustain Toyota's ties with local political leaders. Toyota had always worked in Kariya by relying on the good offices of its leading influentials, especially Ōno Ichizō. Ōno's power had now ebbed, however, and the power of his successor ended with Takenaka's death. In order to assure that city leaders would remain sympathetic to the goals of the enterprise, Ishida was determined to keep progressives from office. To do that, he had to encourage conservatives to rally around an acceptable candidate. In the prewar days of community solidarity, that would have occurred as a matter of course, and Toyota's ties to leading politicians would have continued. But in the more competitive environment of postwar politics, conservatives could not simply nominate their candidate—they had to work for him as well. This effort required that the Toyota enterprise engage more openly in local politics, so Ishida Taizō took to the streets to campaign for Takada.

Industrial leaders wanted a responsive, capable administrator in city hall; Takada Ichirō met their requirements. His availability and their needs coincided to provide a third reason for Toyota's overt participation in local politics. By 1959 Toyota Motors was undergoing the most rapid expansion in its history. In August of that year, the auto firm opened one of the largest assembly plants in the country in southern Toyota City. In the same year Nippon Densō broke ground for new factories in Kariya and Toyota Chassis began planning for expansion of its facilities. In addition, Nippon Densō was about to put up new dormitories near its main plant as well as a new housing development for married employees on the southern edge of Moto Kariya. Those projects could only be carried out with assistance from the city government. Officials in the enterprise expected the city to buy land for the Toyota firms, to build new roads into the undeveloped areas where the factories and apartments were located, to install water and sanitary facilities, and to build schools for the children of its workers. Toyota officials wanted Takada in office because he had the administrative ability to coordinate city projects with corporate expansion.

A fourth reason for the change in Toyota's role in local affairs had to do with postwar reforms of the local tax structure. In the prewar years, local taxes were collected largely in the form of surcharges on prefectural and central government taxes, which themselves were levied on property and households. During the Occupation Japanese officials heeded the proposals of American advisers and authorized several new sources of local revenue. The most important new tax was on fixed capital assets, a levy which struck corporations with great force. Previously, large corporations in small cities had paid very low taxes. Toyota Motors paid taxes in Koromo before the reform which amounted to barely 5 percent of the community's total revenues.[39] But following the reform, taxes paid by Toyota Motors comprised a full 50 percent of the community's revenues. The same was true in Kariya. By the 1960s the taxes on Toyota firms located there amounted to half of the city's revenues.

As by far the largest taxpayer in Kariya, the Toyota enterprise felt it deserved something in return. Ishida Taizō saw the problem this way:

> I'm darn dissatisfied. As a taxpayer, I think taxes are ill-distributed. The Toyota companies are paying huge taxes, but I think they are not being adequately returned. If they were using them appropriately for the development of the entire city, I'd like to work hard and pay as much as possible. But it just seems that city authorities and the city council have an inadequate understanding of industry's position and development.[40]

[39] *Gijutsu kakushin no shakaiteki eikyō*, p. 241.
[40] Katsumura, p. 403.

The Toyota enterprise thus felt itself drawn into local politics as a matter of necessity. It would not stand by and allow the citizenry and the local council to distribute local revenues, most of which came from the enterprise itself. Instead, enterprise leaders persuaded themselves that only participation in the political process would give their demands a fair response. Toyota officials thus went to some trouble to install a mayor in Kariya who was attentive to their wishes.

These four reasons for Toyota's increasingly active role in local politics all stem from a single, overriding concern: to create a political climate conducive to industrial expansion. The sheer magnitude of the auto industry required many changes never imagined during prewar periods of industrialization. In the 1920s, when Toyota first entered Kariya, a plot of land, a rail spur, and a labor supply were its only requirements. But now the auto industry made much greater demands on a community. Paved roads were needed everywhere to accept the heavy truck traffic that united scattered factories into the manufacturing process. Better roads were also needed for the automobile itself, if it was to be used—and sold. The rapid pace of expansion required constant additions to the water and sanitary facilities of a community, and to its educational resources. Advanced planning was needed to open undeveloped land for residential and industrial use. In most cases, city government had to meet those needs. Conservative industrial interests, personified by such men as Ishida Taizō and Fujii Seihichi, were determined that local government should fill their needs with alacrity and efficiency. This was the real motive behind Toyota's pervasive participation in Kariya politics during the years after 1955.

At first glance, Toyota's easy assertion of its political power in Kariya is somewhat surprising. After all, since 1948 progressive forces had exerted more and more influence on local politics. In 1951 they were able to elect a prefectural assemblyman and to lend decisive support to the mayor. The consolidation of 1955 set them back momentarily by diffusing their electoral strength. But rapid industrial growth soon began to restore their position. As more workers entered the city's factories, the ranks of the union—and of the progressive electorate—swelled. By 1963 progressives were a clear majority among the city's voters. In that year they cast 51 percent of the ballots in the Diet election. Four years later their share rose to 53 percent. Toyota's rise to power thus occurred at a time when progressive voting strength was nearly equal to or actually surpassed that of the conservatives.

To their disadvantage, progressives could not translate their voting strength into political power at the local level. They could not return either prefectural assemblymen or mayors after 1951. Even in 1963, when progressive voters were in the majority in the city, Fujii Seihichi captured

---

[40] Katsumura, p. 403.

58 percent of the assembly vote. In the same year, progressives proved unable to field a candidate to challenge Takada Ichirō for the mayoralty. Even though they enjoyed the strength to challenge conservatives successfully, they ignored the opportunity.

Political strategies adopted by progressive parties at the national level retarded the progressives locally. As earlier pages noted, the Japan Socialist Party devoted itself to national and international issues. It was, in effect, a metropolitan party. Most of its "card-carrying" membership lived in Tokyo, as did its leaders. The party had a very weak organization at the local level. It was little wonder that the progressives did poorly in prefectural and municipal elections; the party leadership wrote off such campaigns.

National party strategy was an important reason for the weak showing of Kariya's progressives. But it was not the only reason. Another impediment to progressive action was the lack of unity among local unions. The absence of a single labor leader from the list of Kariya's twenty-two top influentials attests to the weakness of the union movement in the city by 1964. Kariya's leading citizens felt the labor movement was not a force in local politics. Even labor leaders shared their opinion.[41] The impotence of the local union council symbolized the weakness of the labor movement. Less than twenty years old, the body which had united Kariya's workers so effectively during the early 1950s was now in a shambles. Some former officers remained, but they could no longer elicit the cooperation of the many enterprise unions in Kariya. The spirit of unity, so vibrant during the challenging days of the postwar decade, had long since dissolved.

One cause of the lack of unity among local unions was the pattern of affiliations between local unions and national centers, the federations with headquarters in Tokyo. During the years when labor activism reached its height in Kariya, the city's major unions were all members of one national center. At that time, the unions at the loom factory, the machine tool factory, the chassis factory, the steel factory, and the electrical components factory all belonged to federations which had ties with Sōhyō. Loose as those ties were, they provided a sense of common purpose among the workers in Kariya, a feeling that they were participating in a united political movement. In the mid-1950s, however, several local unions severed their ties with Sōhyō when the National Union of Auto Workers (*Zenkoku jidōsha sangyō rōdō kumiai*) dissolved. This had a critical impact on the unity of the local union movement, so the circumstances surrounding that dissolution deserve brief comment.

[41] See Katsumura, pp. 388–398.

The National Union of Auto Workers originated in 1947.[42] It was a federation whose membership included workers in the three major auto firms—Nissan, Toyota, and Isuzu—and workers in many smaller subcontracting firms. By 1953 workers in the three large auto firms comprised over half the membership of the national, and they were able to dictate its policy. But there were marked differences of opinion within the union. The head of the national union, who was also the leader of the Yokohama-based Nissan union, favored activism while the Toyota and Isuzu unions preferred accommodation. These differences came to a head in 1953, when the national union agreed to bargain for much higher wages than before, even if it meant striking. Workers at Toyota and Isuzu won early settlements, but those at Nissan did not. They struck, and management responded by locking its factories. This precipitated an extended strike during which Nissan workers accepted loans from the unions at Toyota and Isuzu to help them through. Within months a second union emerged at Nissan and the strike ended with a compromise favorable to management. In the meantime, however, Toyota and Isuzu had gone on producing briskly, to make obvious gains at the expense of the striking Nissan plants.

The 1953 strike at Nissan exacerbated relations within the national union so badly that it dissolved in December 1954. The public explanation for dissolution blamed it on the debts which Nissan incurred. Toyota and Isuzu unions claimed that the second union, which had taken control at Nissan and ended the strike, would not pay them back. They preferred to disband. The real reason for the breakup was rooted in the structure of the union movement. Workers at Toyota, Isuzu, and Nissan all belonged to enterprise unions. Each union had its own contracts, work conditions, and pay schedules. By 1954 workers in the Toyota unions were convinced that their best interests lay with increased productivity in their own firm, not in radical political action conducted through a national organization. They eschewed unity with all workers in the auto industry in favor of improving the position of their own firms. They had no interest in establishing industry-wide standards; they wanted the highest standards they could get at Toyota, regardless of what other unions wanted. Therefore, the goals of a national federation based on enterprise unions proved unattainable, and the National Union of Auto Workers dissolved.

Following dissolution, former members adopted new patterns of affiliation. Workers at Nissan quickly formed another national union and invited Toyota and Isuzu unions to join. They refused, however. Instead, the several unions in the Toyota enterprise established a new federation in

[42] The following account is based on: Rōdōshō, ed., *Shiryō rōdō undō shi: 1953* (Tokyo, 1955), pp. 137–167; and *Shiryō rōdō undō shi:1954* (Tokyo, 1955), pp. 866–889.

1955. This federation still existed in 1972. It was called the Association of National Auto Workers (*Zenkoku jidōsha sangyō rōdō kumiai rengōkai*). It was in effect an umbrella organization for enterprise unions in firms associated with Toyota Motors and most of its members were located in Aichi Prefecture. The Association was wholly unaffiliated and had no explicit ties to any of the national centers.

The independent stance of the Association complicated the achievement of labor unity in Kariya. After 1955 the major unions in the city enjoyed no common bonds to a single, higher federation. Instead, unions had affiliations which separated them, rather than bound them together. The unions at Nippon Densō, Toyota Chassis, and Aishin Seiki all belonged to the moderate Association of National Auto Workers. The workers at the steel factory belonged to a federation of steel workers that had ties to Sōhyō. The unions at Toyota Loom and Toyota Machine Tool had ties to Sōhyō's prefectural center, but only loose bonds to the national center. These diverse attachments impeded unity in the local union movement and drastically reduced the ability of the progressive forces to pursue common political goals.

The pattern of union affiliations in Kariya merely reflected a more deep-seated change which had taken place within the local union movement. It bespoke the mood of conciliation which characterized relations between management and workers in the Toyota enterprise after the early 1950s. The first part of this chapter illustrated how Toyota managers implemented a systematic program of labor-management relations in the enterprise after the 1950 strike. It also suggested the degree to which their efforts succeeded in creating a compliant work force by the late 1950s.

The new mood appeared just in time to create a harmonious atmosphere in which to socialize large numbers of new workers. Between 1955 and 1960 the three auto parts makers in Kariya (Densō, Chassis, and Aishin Seiki) added nearly four thousand workers to their labor force. The vast majority were elementary and middle school graduates still in their teens. Many of them came from remote areas in western Japan, southern Shikoku, and Kyushu where the political culture was deeply conservative. They were young, malleable, and deferent, and factory life was new to them. They were, in other words, exactly like the young recruits whom Toyota firms had first hired in Kariya in the 1920s and 1930s. Furthermore, they were entering local factories at a time when worker compliance with management goals ran high. Therefore, they were socialized to conform with company goals and to obey the dictates of their superiors. Toyota's managers were able to draw these workers into a warm embrace with the companies' aims. As the vast numbers of new workers hired after 1955 poured into the enterprise, they came into contact with superiors who valued conformity and sanctioned economic goals over political ones. In many respects, the industrial work force in this area resumed the docile manner which had characterized it before the war.

Only one aspect of their behavior conflicts with this portrait of docility: their continued support of Socialist and Communist candidates for the Diet. Between 1955 and 1967 the progressive vote in Kariya doubled to exceed seventeen thousand. Itō Kōdō and, following his death, his wife Yoshiko won a steadily increasing number of votes from the members of local unions. Not only the old workers but the new ones as well supported the candidates who had been the first to stand for the Japan Socialist Party in the city. Workers had begun to emphasize economic goals over political ones, and they seemed to have lost their will to challenge conservatives in local and prefectural elections. But they still turned out in large numbers to vote for Socialists in the Diet.

Their continued support must be explained by social, *not* ideological, causes. Workers in the Toyota and Kariya area first supported Itō Kōdō for office in the late 1940s. They forged a bond molded by a deep sense of personal loyalty and a strong commitment to common goals. Over the years, the strength of that bond was preserved among the union membership and especially among important leaders. As newcomers entered local unions, their predecessors—already tied to Itō by sentiment and personal loyalty—drew them into the social web which formed Itō's political constituency. Following her husband's death, Itō Yoshiko stepped forward to continue his work. Having been his personal secretary, she was as close to the workers as he was, and she naturally maintained their support. The company did not interfere with union choices, because a Socialist in the Diet was much less harmful than a progressive in the mayoralty. Workers in local unions thus continued to support a Socialist Diet candidate, out of personal and social loyalty to an individual and his wife.

The nature of the Itō *jiban* in Kariya and Toyota has important implications for our understanding of local politics. The progressive vote in Diet elections in Kariya between 1955 and 1967 probably exceeded the actual level of ideological and political support for progressive parties in the locality. Workers often supported the Socialist candidates out of a feeling of social obligation to peers and superiors, not out of a sense of political conviction. Many of them probably inclined naturally toward conservative candidates. Indeed, in elections where the obligation to vote Socialist did not operate, many of them voted for conservatives. Fujii Seihichi, for example, drew many votes from union members. Union members inclined to vote for conservatives made it possible for the Toyota enterprise to persuade workers to back Takada in 1959. They were not loyal adherents of a party and its programs. Rather, they acted out of

deference to superiors who made alignments for them and recommended
—if not dictated—their choices.

Union members supported candidates, as we have seen, for reasons of
personal sentiment and loyalty. In most cases, they voted for the candidate
designated by their superiors. Older union members, who had first
established ties with the Itō family in the 1940s, translated their
preferences downward through the union hierarchy. They relied on
sempai-kōhai bonds and the workers' strong impulse toward conformity to
create a solid base of support for the candidate they designated. A
structure of support of this type placed great emphasis on the decisions of
leaders. If they backed a particular candidate, the workers would, too.
When leaders chose another figure, the workers would naturally follow.
Under such circumstances leaders could shift their party ties and still
expect to carry their subordinates with them, since they were committed to
the choice of their leaders, *not* to the programs of a party. As the older
generation of union members passed from the scene in Kariya and Toyota,
the old affinity for Socialist candidates waned. Eventually other leaders
emerged who had moderate political goals. With the proddings of
management, they weaned workers away from the political left and
directed them toward the center, creating significant political changes in
the years after 1967 which will concern us in the next chapter.

In the decade after 1955 workers in Kariya persisted in their support of
progressive candidates. They continued to turn out heavily for Diet
elections and to vote for candidates of the Socialist and Communist
parties. But they did acquiesce to a conservative resurgence at the
prefectural and municipal level. They divided themselves in a number of
elections. Those allied with management accepted the direction of Ishida
Taizō and other company executives; they voted for conservatives such as
Fujii Seihichi and Takada Ichirō. Others persisted in a sincere effort to
promote the progressive cause, still convinced that the political goals of
labor and management were incompatible. They were a minority,
however. In the midst of their more acquiescent peers, they were incapable
of stemming the overwhelming influence which the Toyota enterprise,
through its managers, brought to bear on political life in Kariya during
the years after 1955.

Driven by economic opportunities, the determination of Ishida Taizō,
and the logic of industrial expansion, the Toyota enterprise established an
economic and political hegemony over the communities of western
Mikawa between 1955 and 1967. As the auto industry expanded, it
brought more and more factories and businesses under its managerial
wing. Managers, workers, subcontractors, suppliers, and service agents all
conformed to the demands of the enterprise, stimulated by the manifest

promise of material reward. The industrial behemoth also reached into the political arena. Its intention was to bring the political process under its managerial control, to instill efficiency in government for the benefit of industry. For more than a decade, Kariya experienced an unusual period of political and economic diffidence. It was hardly a partner any longer. It was more a subordinate on whom the Toyota enterprise worked its will. But twelve years was enough, and in the late 1960s, Kariya sought to restore its integrity and its sense of identity. It changed from an industrial boom town to an embryonic urban community, whose emergent qualities form the subject of the next chapter.[43]

[43] One political economist has remarked of Japan that "no nation of the modern world offers more striking testimony to the autonomy of politics from overriding economic determinism." [W. W. Lockwood, "Japan's 'New Capitalism,'" in W. W. Lockwood, ed., *State and Economic Enterprise in Japan* (Princeton, 1965), p. 511.] One community does not make a nation, but the evidence from Kariya presented here should demonstrate that it is incautious—if not wrong—to make such assertions.

8

ADAPTING TO AFFLUENCE, 1967–1972

Neither 1967 nor 1972 formed a perfectly neat dividing line which separated what went before from what came after. Together, however, they did bound a period which marked the end of one epoch and the beginning of another. It was a brief period characterized by flux and instability, caused largely by Japan's exceptionally high rates of economic growth during the 1960s. The pervasive influence of that growth affected everything from the nation's role in the international economy to the individual's role in local society. Forced to confront new problems due to its economic might, Japan's government had to readjust past policies in many ways. New economic policies had a particularly strong effect on communities such as Kariya which were heavily reliant on firms engaged in the export trade. As a result of the changes which occurred after 1967, Kariya and the surrounding region experienced what, by contrast with the immediate past, was a notable sense of drift. This chapter conveys an impression of this period of adjustment and what it meant for the city of Kariya.

The purpose of the chapter is to provide a final benchmark—a counterpart to the portrait of Kariya sketched in chapter 2—from which to draw conclusions in the final chapter. Consequently, the first portion of this chapter retraces our route through the community in 1872, this time from the perspective of 1972, in order to illustrate some of the physical features of the contemporary city. A discussion of social aspects of the city follows. It treats population growth, the consequences of demographic mobility, occupational change in western Mikawa, and the evolution of a new class of social leaders in Kariya. The final portion of the chapter examines the events of political life in Kariya between 1967 and 1972. It analyzes the selection of political leaders, the social and economic bases of their political support, and shifting patterns of party affiliation, illustrating how fragmentation and conservatism altered the political scene in Kariya after 1967.

Had we returned to Kariya in 1972 and retraced the steps which carried us through the old castletown a century before, we would have found a city dramatically different in physical appearance from the small country town of that early period. The differences strike us immediately as we glance around the area near the river, west of the city. Then, in 1872, a clear stream meandering casually between silty banks, the river is now in 1972 a black, oily flow shrunk to a tenth of its previous size. Fouled by industrial wastes, the river is no longer a fishing ground, or a swimming spot for the children of Kariya. Nor is it used for transportation purposes. After the railway came through Kariya in the 1890s, merchants relied on water transport less and less; by the 1920s they ceased using the river altogether. It runs now between concrete dikes, constructed to provide protection against the typhoons which have ravaged this area intermittently over the last century. For both good reasons and bad, men have destroyed the calm, natural setting of the river.

Turning to scan the horizon to the east, it is virtually impossible to distinguish what were once the villages of Kuma and Moto Kariya and the castletown of Kariya. They all blend together as a whole, because houses, shops, and factories have risen on the empty ground between them. Kuma has developed a reputation as a desirable residential area, because Toyota executives began settling there in the 1930s, probably attracted by Kuma's own history as a samurai section. Several small factories now string themselves along the narrow valley which once set Moto Kariya apart from the castletown. The Buddhist temples still perch on the high land above the valley, but they seem out of place now amidst stucco dormitories for workers and new homes with their bright blue tile roofs.

We encounter a vastly different scene now, in 1972, as we walk up the path from the river. As the Ōta family ceased using its warehouse at Ichibara, it turned the land to other uses. Adapting like everyone else to the age of the automobile, they have constructed an automatic car wash on the site where they once unloaded fertilizer from Hokkaido. It is complete with gas station and coffee house for waiting customers. The modern facility sits on the main east-west artery connecting Handa with Okazaki through Kariya, a road which flows with trucks, cars, and buses during the hours of the working day. The old path leading among the samurai dwellings is still here, and the same names which were posted in 1872 still appear on the name plates beside the entry gates. But descendants have subdivided the large, old estates, and modern homes are now squeezed into once open corners of land, beside simple dwellings whose foundations were laid centuries before.

Reaching the corner where the gate once stood dividing the castle from the *chōnin* quarter, we encounter the city's new public library. It rises in drab concrete splendor three stories above the street, and has a drive-in service window and central air conditioning. The library sits on the corner by Kijō School, which still provides an elementary education for thousands of the city's youngsters. The two-story wooden building put up near the turn of the century still remains, joined with an auditorium the city built when Toyota Risaburō donated funds to the city in the 1920s. The dilapidated school attests to the city's preference for industrial development at the expense of adequate social facilities. Despite a new library, the city still has some way to go in providing adequate social services for its citizens.

The land at the end of the road, where the center of the castle was located, has assumed much different uses. On the left is a brick dormitory for workers in the Tōshiba ceramics plant; to the right, a long, concrete dormitory for men who work at the Toyota loom factory. On the former equestrian grounds there is now a well-kept soccer field, ringed with seats for large audiences and fully lighted for night contests. It sits at the edge of a modest city park, which fits itself neatly around the moat and the foot of the knoll where the castle's watchtower stood a century ago. Beyond the park, to the north, an awesome mass of concrete squats against the horizon; it houses the city's indoor sports arena—a lavish facility built to keep pace with the civic accomplishments of neighboring cities.

On any day of the week we would encounter a flock of uniformed adolescents moving to and fro in this area, on their way to school, to the sports arena, or to a soccer match. These young men and women would be the great-grandchildren of the guide who led us through town in 1872, but they present a strikingly different appearance. Rather than aspiring to a height of five feet, most of these children have already passed that mark at twelve and are now on their way to six feet. They would tower over their ancestors, just as most of them reach head and shoulders above their parents. Their diet since the war accounts for the physical changes. They have eaten a varied fare, including meat, poultry, fruits, vegetables, milk and cheese, in contrast to the grains, vegetables, and occasional fish which their ancestors—and probably their parents—were raised on. In place of bare feet and cotton overshirts, these children wear leather shoes and black school uniforms, standard apparel for most between the ages of six and sixteen. All children attend school now, the childhood freedoms which their ancestors enjoyed having disappeared in the wake of compulsory mass education. They spend at least nine years in school; in a few years, it will be twelve. Many also go on to college, which they hope will become a ticket to professional success. In fact, not a few of them are so compulsive about reaching that goal—at the expense of any spontaneous, casual activity—that they have developed gray hairs at fifteen!

Moving eastward again through the old Sakana-machi and Hom-machi areas, the sharply new appearance of the city continues to strike us. Some things have endured. The streets are the same narrow lanes laid out centuries before and many shops still offer the same wares: vegetables, fish, rice, dry goods, and household utensils. But the dark, mat-floor interiors have given way to air-conditioned shops illuminated by fluorescent—or more recently, psychedelic—lamps behind tall glass windows. New shops of this sort stretch all along the street where coopers, *tōfu* makers, and herbalists once peddled their wares. There is a cooper left on the street, but he prefers to sell plastic bathtubs and shower stalls, not wooden tubs. To find *tōfu* today, one goes to the supermarket at the corner where it is just one commodity available among many far more exotic. There are herbalists in the city, but their shops hide along side streets. Choice locations on the main street are filled by modern pharmacies for whom medicine is just a sideline amidst the merchandising of expensive cosmetics. The list could go on and on: Western style shoes, television sets, home appliances, imported furniture, motorcycles, coffee, and the ubiquitous Coca-Cola. None of these items were here a century past; now they are standard fare, part of a universe of commerce which knows no national boundaries.

A skeptic once thought Suso-machi (Terminal Block) would mark the end of Kariya's commercial expansion. He could not have been more wrong. The area of shops and merchant dwellings which stretched only three blocks in 1872 now extends almost endlessly toward the eastern border of town. Modern stores with a prolific variety of wares continue through Sakae-machi (Prosperity Block) and Shinsakae-machi (New Prosperity Block), then out onto a broad avenue lined by small shops with apartments above, and finally, on toward the heart of the city's new commercial zone: the shopping center. First opened in the late 1960s, the shopping center fell on bad times and closed within a year. But two years of industrial expansion and wage increases created a climate for its revival. Complete with furniture emporium, department store, supermarket, and bowling lanes, the shopping center is the latest evidence of Kariya's progress toward the era of affluence and the auto.

Almost as a symbol of its dependence, the new shopping center is located beside the factory zone where sit the monuments to Kariya's industrial way of life. These have shattered the quiet serenity of the agrarian landscape which once lay between Kariya and the post town a few miles away. With insatiable appetites for land, the factories long ago swallowed the forest preserve in this area and they still absorb vast reaches of land. Their smokestacks punctuate a drab horizon of concrete and steel, spewing mists of biting soot. Huge trucks, on wide swaths of asphalt that have buried tree-lined paths, ply incessantly between factories and belch dark smoke into the once blue skies. Trains, too, their pathways having appropriated broad expanses of wooded highlands, fill the air with their rumbling.

The location of city hall is another symbol of industry's powers of attraction in this community. The old town offices once nestled amidst a grove in the center of the old *chōnin* quarter, where they were close to the community and the center of its activities. In the mid-1950s Kariya constructed a new city hall, another emblem of the race for status among cities. The site chosen was almost a mile from the center of the commercial district and at least a twenty-minute walk from the nearest residential area. It was, however, only a block from the entry gate at the spinning factory. In the Tokugawa Period a gatewatcher (*monban*) once stood at the entry to the castle. He was a servant to the lord and acted in his political interests. Without pressing the comparison too far, one can almost view Kariya's city hall—placed as it was in the 1950s at the entry to the industrial quarter—as a latter-day *monban*, the political servant of Kariya's industrial lords.

TABLE 17

LAND USE PATTERNS IN KARIYA, 1877–1971

| | | | Percentage of Taxable Land Used For: | |
| | | | Commerce, Residences, & Industry | Farmland, etc. |
Date	Area (in *chō*)			
1877	Kariya *mura*	(196)	5	95
1930	Kariya *machi*	(1,138)	13	87
1956	Kariya *shi*	(3,931)	12	88
1971	Kariya *shi*	(3,882)	23	77

SOURCES: For 1877, Murase Masayuki, *Bakumatsu-Ishin no Kariya* (Kariya, 1969), p. 59; for 1930, Kcs, pp. 50–51; and for 1956 and 1971, Aichi ken Kinugaura chiku tōkei kenkyū kai, ed., *Kinugaura no tōkei*, no. 4 (1972), p. 3.

NOTE: One *chō* equals approximately 2.5 acres.

The course we have just taken has covered two miles along the east-west axis of the city and brought us to the doorstep of city hall. Our walk has left an impression of only one small section of the community. It would be possible to continue this tour indefinitely. We could walk northward toward Fujimatsu, passing the modern Nippon Densō factory, the massive assembly plant of the Toyota Chassis firm, or the new teachers' college, set on grassy highlands overlooking a lilac pond which is a national treasure. We could also trek southward, into the industrial zone and the farmland of old Yosami village. With every step, we would encounter a society vastly changed from the one witnessed a century ago.

It is very difficult, however, to portray vividly in words the physical layout and appearance of Kariya. One can best understand it by visiting the city in person, but that opportunity is not available. In the absence of a visit, some impression of the whole of the city in the early 1970s can be derived from comparisons with the past, and with other cities nearby.

Table 17 illustrates patterns of land use in "Kariya" between 1877 and 1971. The warning "Kariya" is necessary, because figures for only two of the four years cover a comparable area. In 1877 the old castletown of Kariya was a dense residential settlement packed in amidst the surrounding farmland. Even in the area of the castletown, a kind of embryonic urban settlement, 90 percent of the land was used for agricultural purposes. By 1930 Kariya had become a *machi* embracing six different settlements, its area seven times larger than it had been before. Already in the town area a larger portion of land was used for residential and industrial purposes than had been in the castletown area earlier. Farmers continued to use the bulk of the town's land area for agricultural purposes, however. This remained the case even as late as 1971, long after the city became a highly industrialized settlement, and long after subdivisions began to spring up south of the city center, in the area north of Kuma, and in the vicinity of the new college. Even though Kariya was a populous industrial center in 1972, large parts of the city still served agricultural purposes and thus retained an agrarian appearance.

Despite such a pattern of land use, Kariya was not unusual, as a comparison with other cities illustrates. (See table 18.) Among the five cities discussed in this study, Kariya was actually one of the most urban in respect to its land use patterns. Only Handa devoted a greater share of its land to residential and industrial uses. In the other communities—Toyota,

TABLE 18

Land Use Patterns in Five Aichi Cities, 1971

| City | Area (in hectares) | Percentage of Taxable Land Used For: | |
		Commerce Residences, & Industry	Farmland, Forest, etc.
Kariya	3,850	23	77
Toyota	15,785	14	86
Anjō	7,013	16	84
Nishio	5,411	18	82
Handa	3,117	26	74

SOURCE: Atn: 1972, p. 9.

Anjō, and Nishio—a very high percentage of the city area remained under
cultivation, or, in the case of Toyota, under forestation. These cities all
shared the common but anomalous appearance of so many Japanese cities
which formed as a result of consolidations. They were essentially urban
nodes surrounded by agrarian landscapes, but by administrative design,
both the urban and the rural areas lay within city boundaries.

Census materials provide a second perspective on the tendency of
Japanese cities to be urban nodes surrounded by agrarian areas. Recognizing that the boundaries of cities extend beyond their natural demographic
centers, census takers in Japan have defined areas within cities called
Densely Inhabited Districts. These districts are made up of contiguous
census tracts, each having more than five thousand persons, all of which
have population densities exceeding ten thousand persons per square mile.
This level of density approximates that in American cities such as
Pittsburgh, Detroit, Cleveland, and St. Louis, and therefore measures an
area which is discernibly urban, in regard to numbers and proximity of
people. In the Japanese context, the Densely Inhabited Districts of a city
are its urban nodes. They are heavily settled by persons engaged in
commercial and industrial tasks, and they differ visibly from the less
densely populated, more agrarian districts which surround them.

The ratios which appear in table 19 provide an impression of the
demographic appearance of six Aichi cities in 1970. The ratios reveal
clearly the sharp differences between the oldest cities in the prefecture,
such as Nagoya, and the newer ones, whose greatest growth occurred after
1925. Nine-tenths of the population of Nagoya was settled on about 60
percent of its land area. Since roads, factories, parks, temples, and shrines
occupied much of the remaining 40 percent of its land, Nagoya was a city
largely blanketed by human settlement. In Handa, by comparison, human

TABLE 19

DENSELY INHABITED DISTRICTS IN SIX AICHI CITIES, 1970

City	DID Area as % of City Area	DID Population as % of City Population
Kariya	10	36
Toyota	3	23
Anjō	4	27
Nishio	5	33
Handa	29	69
Nagoya	59	91

SOURCE: Sōrifu tōkei kyoku, *Kokusei chōsa hōkoku: 1970, Aichi ken* (Tokyo, 1972), pp. 4–5.
NOTE: DID = Densely Inhabited District.

settlement covered only a third of the city's land area with dense habitation; the remaining two-thirds of the city's area remained sparsely inhabited farm, forest, or hill lands. The same was true of Toyota, Anjō and Nishio; to an even greater extent in those cities, vast areas of land remained thinly populated.

Toyota was perhaps the most anomalous case. A city of nearly two hundred thousand people, Toyota had two Densely Inhabited Districts in 1970. One was located in the old castletown area of Koromo; the other, around the headquarters and main plant of Toyota Motors. The two areas covered only 3 percent of the city's land area and they embraced only 23 percent of its total population. The rest of the population was scattered throughout the city area, in clusters of apartment dwellings, in hundreds of small rural hamlets, or in new subdivisions put down wherever developers could find an open plot of land. The city of Toyota was still such a raw, artificial creation that, when newsmen conducted a survey in the late 1960s, only a third of its residents felt it had a city center!

In comparison with its neighboring communities, Kariya ranked quite high on the urban scale defined by population densities. The share of city land in Kariya which was densely populated was at least twice as large as in Toyota, Anjō, and Nishio. Moreover, nearly four in ten of its inhabitants resided in the city's urban node. In 1970 that urban node embraced virtually all of the old town area, and it was already beginning to flow northward, stretched to greater distances by the people settling in the new subdivisions of Fujimatsu.

In trying to grasp a physical image of the city in the early 1970s, it was just such flows of population which left the most lasting impression. In 1972 Kariya's physical layout was characterized by fluidity, not fixity. Everywhere one traveled, there were old buildings being razed, new subdivisions going up, old roads being re-routed, new ones running through. The one visible trend was the persistent outward expansion of the city's center, which was forcing Kariya to shed its agrarian appearance in favor of an urban image.

Several factors accounted for the constantly changing physical appearance of the city. New plans carried out to make the city conform to the needs of the automobile were instrumental in revising the layout of the old castletown after the early 1960s. The very affluence of the populace also contributed, by enabling merchants to remodel old shops or build anew, and by enabling many families to build new homes away from the city center. But perhaps the most potent force for change was the constant growth and turnover of population in the city. As table 17 illustrated, land use patterns in Kariya had to change to accommodate the increasing numbers of people settling there. Population growth did more than reshape the city physically, however. It also fostered subtle changes in the social character of the local populace. To understand those changes, it will be useful to examine the nature of Kariya's demographic evolution and the alterations which stemmed from it.

After the 1920s Kariya was subjected to intense population movements of a long-term, middle-term, and short-term character. Long-term movements, combined with natural increases in population, produced a steady increase in the size of Kariya. Middle-term movements, in the form of annual arrivals in and departures from the city, regulated the long-range growth pattern of the city. Commuters who moved in and out of the city daily produced the short-term movements. All of these movements contributed to a level of social activity which may seem surprising in a community with such a rustic background.

In the half-century after 1920, Kariya's long-term population movements were characterized by a steady increase, as the figures in table 20 suggest. Between 1920 and 1970 the population of the prefecture as a whole rose from approximately 2.1 million to 5.4 million, an increase of 2.6 times. Three cities in this study—Anjō, Nishio, and Handa—experienced demographic growth which fell short of the prefecture's rate of expansion. In those three cities, populations barely doubled in the fifty-year period. In Kariya and Toyota, on the other hand, populations expanded by 3.7 times during the half-century. In those two cities, population growth surpassed that in a prefecture which was among the most expansive in the country. This made Kariya and Toyota two of Japan's fastest growing cities during the mid-twentieth century.

In the course of such growth, Kariya and the other cities witnessed the arrival of a wave of newcomers who grew to surpass native-born members

TABLE 20

POPULATIONS OF FIVE AICHI CITIES AND
AICHI PREFECTURE, 1920 AND 1970

City	1920	1970
Kariya	23,989	87,671
Toyota (Koromo in 1920)	53,998	197,193
Anjō	46,856	94,307
Nishio	40,100	75,193
Handa	42,942	80,663
Aichi Prefecture	2,089,762	5,386,163

SOURCES: Naikaku tōkei kyoku, *Kokusei chōsa hōkoku: 1920, Aichi ken* (Tokyo, 1925), pp. 2–5; and Sōrifu tōkei kyoku, *Kokusei chōsa hōkoku: 1970, Aichi ken* (Tokyo, 1972), pp. 2–3.

NOTE: Populations for 1920 include all persons living within the areas encompassed by the cities' boundaries in 1972.

of the community, as table 21 indicates. In the 1920s Kariya, Toyota, Anjō, and Nishio were essentially agrarian communities populated by persons born there who continued to live in their place of birth. They differed from the settlement of Handa, where a constant flow of textile operatives reduced the relative size of the native-born population. By 1970 native-born residents in all five cities comprised a minority of the population. There were some differences of degree. The still agrarian community of Nishio, for example, had populations more permanent and enduring than the expanding industrial cities. But in all cases, outsiders comprised a majority of the local populations.

TABLE 21

NATIVITY OF POPULATIONS IN FIVE AICHI CITIES
AND AICHI PREFECTURE, 1920 AND 1970
(BY PERCENTAGE NATIVE-BORN)

City	1920	1970
Kariya	74	28
Toyota	73	28
Anjō	73	34
Nishio	70	42
Handa	56	32
Aichi Prefecture	61	29

SOURCES: Same as table 20, above. For 1920, pages 46–47; for 1970, pages 178–196.
NOTE: The figures in this table actually refer to two different phenomena. Figures under 1920 indicate the percentage of persons residing in the city area who had been born there. Figures under 1970 indicate the percentage of persons living in the city area who had lived in their current place of residence since birth. The 1970 figures thus undercount the native-born populations, because they do not include all those who have lived in the community (as opposed to their current dwelling) since birth.

As more and more outsiders settled in Kariya, they reshaped the patterns of residence in the community. During the early years of Kariya's industrialization, new arrivals settled primarily in the old castletown section and in Kuma. The figures in table 22 illustrate the trend clearly. After the early 1950s, however, if not earlier, Kariya witnessed what in another context might be called the process of suburbanization. For two decades after 1951, the city center lost population to outlying districts. The old castletown section saw its population drop 30 percent, and Kuma also witnessed a small drop in its population. At the same time, areas north and east of the city center experienced a rapid inflow of new occupants. The populations of Oyama, Takatsunami, and Shigehara doubled, tripled, and

TABLE 22

DISTRIBUTION OF POPULATION IN
KARIYA TOWN AREA, 1876–1970

Settlement	1876		1951		1970	
	No.	(%)	No.	(%)	No.	(%)
Kariya	2,632	(35)	16,498	(52)	11,641	(24)
Moto Kariya	1,724	(23)	5,423	(17)	9,496	(20)
Kuma	1,020	(13)	4,244	(13)	3,994	(8)
Takatsunami	400	(5)	1,129	(4)	4,616	(10)
Oyama	1,114	(15)	2,881	(9)	8,512	(18)
Shigehara	722	(9)	1,514	(5)	9,724	(20)
Totals	7,612	(100)	31,689	(100)	47,983	(100)

SOURCES: For 1876, Kss, p. 319; for 1951, Kariya shiyakusho, *Kariya shisei yōran: 1952* (Kariya, 1953), p. 8; and for 1970, Aichi ken, Kariya shi, *Kariya no jinkō* (Kariya, 1970), pp. 12–14.

quintupled, respectively, in just two decades. This is the most compelling proof available of the manner in which population growth reshaped the physical layout of the city. Demographic increases would continue to reshape the city in the future as well, because the process of suburbanization, which had begun to work on the old town areas in the early 1950s, was continuing with vigor in the area north of town by the early 1970s.

One is tempted to think, given the steady upward trend in Kariya's population growth, that newcomers joined newborns to create an ever larger community, one which never regressed in its expansion and one which witnessed no loss of population from year to year. That was seldom the case. In addition to the steady flow of newcomers into Kariya, there was also a steady flow of people out of the community. Table 23 illustrates the magnitude of those population flows for just one year, 1970. The majority of persons moving away from the city in 1970 were males. Most of them were members of an urban proletariat which was highly mobile, moving from one job to another in small industrial, commercial, or service enterprises. Young girls terminating their short period at work in one of the city's factories or stores made up another portion of the outmigrants. Responding primarily to employment opportunities in the city, those migrants acted as individuals, but their collective middle-term movements regulated the scale and pace of Kariya's demographic expansion.

There was a third group of migrants, or transients, which contributed to the dynamic flow of population in and out of Kariya, in this case on a

TABLE 23

OUTMIGRANTS AND INMIGRANTS IN
SIX AICHI CITIES, 1970

City	Outmigrants	Inmigrants	% Mobile[a]
Kariya	7,402	8,240	18
Toyota	14,036	22,193	18
Anjō	5,026	7,703	14
Nishio	2,870	3,727	9
Handa	4,746	4,645	12
Nagoya	232,614	219,543	22

SOURCE: Atn: 1972, p. 54.

[a] This figure is a percentage arrived at by adding the number of outmigrants and inmigrants and dividing the total by the city's population in 1970. It expresses the number of people moving in and out of the cities in 1970 as a portion of the resident population.

daily basis. As early as the 1920s Kariya's location at the junction of the Mikawa Railway and the Tōkaidō Line and the presence there of large factories stimulated a gradual trickle of commuters into the city from outlying areas. The events of the 1930s and 1940s accelerated those movements sharply. By the 1970s Kariya was a veritable commuter mecca. Each day nearly thirty thousand persons came to Kariya from other cities to work in its factories, sell in its shops, or study in its schools. They comprised the largest proportion of inbound commuters in any city in Aichi Prefecture, as table 24 suggests. Arriving by foot, train, bike, and car, they swelled the daytime population of the city by 20 percent.

TABLE 24

COMMUTING POPULATIONS IN SIX AICHI CITIES, 1970

City	Outbound	Inbound	Index[a]
Kariya	12,425	29,012	119
Toyota	14,149	23,146	105
Anjō	15,763	12,851	97
Nishio	9,637	6,898	96
Handa	11,389	10,906	99
Nagoya	74,662	329,595	113

SOURCE: Atn: 1972, pp. 38-39.

[a] Index equals the city's daytime population divided by its nighttime population. Thus, cities with an index over 100 are ones which enjoyed a surplus of daytime commuters moving into the city.

Traveling long distances to and from work each day, they were perhaps
the most consistently mobile of the many persons who contributed to the
ebb and flow of population in Kariya after the 1920s.

Population mobility, in all its guises, had important implications for the
social and political life of the community. Mobility contributed first of all
to an air of transience which hung over Kariya, and particularly over its
leisure life. So many of the entertainment facilities in Kariya catered to
people on the move, short-term visitors who would be on their way in an
hour or two. *Pachinko* parlors were symbolic. A coin-operated machine in
which one tries to nurse steel balls into the proper wire pocket, a *pachinko*
machine exercised an almost diabolical lure over the young factory hands
in the city. Many of them wiled away an hour or two each night, or several
hours during their off-days, tripping switches and pushing levers—almost
as if they were back on the assembly line! The coffee house was another
institution which catered to the transient, the white-collar worker waiting
for the train home or the department store clerk meeting her friends before
supper. Motels which showed "pink films" and hotels which provided a
place for a brief tryst between lovers were other anonymous spots serving
the transient and the impermanent. Notably absent from the leisure world
in Kariya were facilities which symbolized the stability and refinement of
a more permanent world, such as a kabuki theater, a symphony, or an art
museum. The transience of the city's cultural life was just one reflection of
its impermanent populations.

Highly mobile populations weakened the bonds of social cohesiveness in
Kariya and undermined the sense of community. When everyone on a
block was born there, grew up there, and lived there for most of his life, he
knew his neighbors and engaged with them in a range of social activities,
both formal and informal. After the 1930s many neighborhoods were
inundated with a wave of newcomers. For some time native residents
greeted the newcomers and drew them into existing networks of social
activity, but eventually the numbers became so great that the effort was
abandoned. Consequently, there emerged in the city two distinct social
groups, characterized by their affiliations and patterns of activity:
long-term residents immersed in local mores, and newcomers poorly
integrated into the local community.

An example helps to illustrate this phenomenon. Each year in Kariya
neighborhood associations in the old ward areas conducted a celebration
at the time of the mid-year *obon* festival. Neighborhood leaders installed
lights, painted lanterns, and put up a drum tower on the grounds of a
nearby school, park, or Buddhist temple. For several nights, children and
adults gathered to chat, dance, and eat, presumably in celebration of
departed ancestors. The organizers and most of the participants in such
activities were people whose families had lived in Kariya for several

generations. Seldom did one encounter people from the company apartments which were just down the road, or young men and women who worked in the city's factories. They might have absented themselves out of a snobbish desire to be more "modern" (*obon* is a "traditional" festival). Or they may have had celebrations to attend at the firms where they were employed. More often, however, the newcomers employed in Kariya's factories did not participate in such festivals because they had no social bonds to the persons responsible for organizing them. Living in company dormitories, apartment buildings, or new subdivisions, they were socially isolated from Kariya's long-term residents. This produced a high level of social fragmentation in the community, leaving pockets of cohesiveness scattered in the old neighborhoods but an aura of anomie hanging over the rest of the city.

The isolation fostered by the decline of community in Kariya had important political repercussions. One result was a discernible drop in the rate of participation in elections. In the prewar years nine in ten of all eligible voters regularly turned out to cast ballots in elections.[1] In the late 1960s the rate fell to seven in ten for Diet elections.[2] For prefectural elections it was even lower, nearer five in ten. This drop in the level of participation was due in part to the weakening of social ties, or to their complete absence.

A second political result of social isolation and population mobility was the emergence of a large floating vote in each election. When fifteen thousand persons moved into and out of the city each year, politicians found it difficult to establish *jiban* secure enough to insure steady victories. This was especially true of Diet candidates. By the early 1970s the Fourth District embraced a population of more than six hundred thousand voters. To ignore the floating vote was to ignore a constituency large enough to guarantee a seat in the Diet. The presence of a large floating vote and the decline in rates of participation signaled the appearance of new imponderables in electoral politics. Between 1967 and 1972 they contributed to a new instability in local politics which the latter portion of this chapter treats in greater detail.

The long-term, middle-term, and short-term movements of people in and out of Kariya after 1920 had a thorough impact on the community. Those movements dictated the pace at which the community grew, a pace that exceeded that of most other cities in the prefecture. Population movements also contributed to a marked alteration in the pattern of residence in Kariya, leading after 1951 to an embryonic process of

[1] This comment is based on a detailed study of election returns for the prewar period. Tables illustrating the trends appear in Gary D. Allinson, "Kariya: A Japanese Community: Economy, Society, and Polity, 1870–1970," (Ph. D. diss., Stanford University, 1970), p. 159.
[2] Ibid., p. 177.

suburbanization. The movement of people had social and political implications as well, affecting the leisure life, the sense of community, and the manner of political behavior in Kariya. Industrialization was the force which motivated population mobility in Kariya. Just as it reshaped the demographic features of the community, industrialization also redefined the occupational character of the city.

Table 25 illustrates the occupational make-up of Kariya and four other cities in 1920 and 1970. The comparisons reveal the dramatic changes which took place in those communities under the impact of an ever-expanding industrial economy. In 1920 Handa was the only settlement among the five which was highly industrial. Having developed early as a textile center, Handa (and the two towns with which it later consolidated) saw its agricultural labor force shrink (in proportion) as textile workers flooded into the city to work in its mills. In 1920 all of the other settlements were still minor commercial outposts amidst a sea of farmers. The prefecture itself was still predominantly agrarian, so they were merely a small part of a larger rural landscape.

The prefecture and all five cities presented a radically different occupational appearance by 1970. In the prefecture as a whole, farming had shrunk to employ only one in twelve workers. Almost half the labor force worked in manufacturing with another half in commerce, trade, the services or the professions. The same general trend manifested itself in the five cities of the prefecture, although in different degree. Workers in the oldest industrial center, Handa, remained heavily engaged in manufacturing. They were joined by a comparable number of persons employed in other, nonfarm activities. Farming continued to employ large percentages of persons in Anjō and Nishio, but by contrast with earlier periods, they were quite heavily industrialized. The most industrial communities, however, were Toyota and Kariya. In both, the work force employed in manufacturing and construction made up almost two-thirds of the occupied population.

By the 1970s Kariya and Toyota were very much working-class cities. In both settlements, production workers in factories and general laborers made up more than half their employed populations, 57 percent in Kariya and 55 percent in Toyota. This contrasted with a ratio of 41 percent in the prefecture as a whole. As a result of their large working classes, both cities had small groups of persons engaged in white-collar occupations. In Kariya, managers, technicians, professionals, small proprietors, and clerical and sales personnel comprised only 29 percent of the work force; in Toyota, only 23 percent. The prefectural average was 37 percent, a comparison which illustrates the belated growth of service and commercial sectors in Kariya and Toyota. It is a comparison which also suggests the unimportance of a middle class in Kariya.

TABLE 25

OCCUPATIONAL CHANGE IN FIVE AICHI CITIES
AND AICHI PREFECTURE, 1920–1970
(PERCENTAGE OF WORK FORCE, BY SECTOR)

City	1920	1970
Kariya		
Primary	72	9
Secondary	12	62
Tertiary	16	29
Toyota		
Primary	76	12
Secondary	8	62
Tertiary	16	26
Anjō		
Primary	69	19
Secondary	16	50
Tertiary	15	31
Nishio		
Primary	58	21
Secondary	20	46
Tertiary	22	33
Handa		
Primary	26	6
Secondary	49	51
Tertiary	25	43
Aichi Prefecture		
Primary	46	8
Secondary	27	46
Tertiary	27	46

SOURCES: Same as table 20, above. For 1920, pages 24–43; for 1970, pages 224–254.
NOTE: Figures for both 1920 and 1970 include all persons employed and resident in the towns and villages encompassed by the cities' boundaries as of 1972.
Primary sector = agriculture, lumbering, and fishing.
Secondary sector = mining, construction, and manufacturing.
Tertiary sector = all other forms of employment.

It is difficult as well as dangerous to try to portray the class structure in a Japanese city. The lack of appropriate data on personal wealth, on perceptions of status, and on patterns of social intercourse all complicate the task. Making it perhaps fruitless is the penchant of most Japanese to consider themselves middle class. When asked in surveys to which class they feel they belong, virtually all respondents reply that they are, of course, members of the "middle" class. Obstacles of these types stand in the way of a comprehensive portrait of social class in Kariya at the beginning of the 1970s, but they do not prevent speculative comments about the city's leading social group.

There are social groups in any city to which its citizens attribute high status and prestige. Membership in such bodies is so prestigious that the people who belong are naturally perceived as social leaders. In Kariya after the 1950s the Rotary Club was the city's highest-ranking social body. There were other important social organizations, but they each had a special character. The Junior Chamber of Commerce, for example, drew its membership from men under forty who were active in business and industry. The Lions Club was made up of merchants or small manufacturers. The Chamber of Commerce was an open body with unrestricted entry. The Rotary Club, in contrast, reserved membership for the community's most respected and successful elder citizens. Members were invited to join after presentation by incumbents. They had to pass a careful screening, and they needed impeccable reputations. If there was a discernible social leadership in Kariya, it was sanctioned by membership in the Rotary Club.

The list of past Rotary Club presidents appearing in table 26 highlights the social attributes of the club's membership, and, by extension, the attributes of Kariya's postwar social leadership.[3] Seven of the past presidents were outsiders who had come to Kariya as adults to work in its industrial concerns and had risen to managerial positions. The leaders of the Toyota enterprise were well represented. Beginning with Ishida Taizō, head of the enterprise and the first president of the club, five men from Toyota firms held the office of Rotary president. Katō Shōhei, owner of a firm which had intimate dealings with the Aishin Seiki firm, was also, in a sense, a Toyota representative. The remaining six presidents were all men from old-line Kariya families engaged in sake brewing, commerce, or medical practice. Four of them—Inaba, Ichikawa, Takeuchi, and Nomura—were descendants of samurai families. Another, Ōta Ichizō, was the head of Kariya's oldest, most distinguished merchant house, founded in the late seventeenth century. The sixth, Hirose, was the director of Kariya's second oldest sake brewery, established in the 1890s. With only two exceptions, therefore, the Rotary presidents were the leaders of Kariya's most important business and industrial organizations.

Given the importance of industry in the community, one would naturally expect economic leaders to have enjoyed high status in the city. That had not always been the case, however. Through the war years,

[3] Three men on the list—Kuroda, Maejima, and Kamiya Hiroi—lived in communities without a Rotary Club and belonged to the Kariya club by courtesy, so I do not consider them in this discussion.

old-line families of merchant, samurai, and landlord background enjoyed a virtual monopoly on social status in Kariya. Their ability to preserve their position reflected a widespread prejudice against the social standing of industrialists, who found it especially difficult to win acceptance for their goals and their values.[4] During the 1930s and early 1940s, however, the old prejudice against industrialists waned, and with the end of the war it virtually disappeared. In Kariya, as previous chapters showed, industrialists had to step to the fore to provide political as well as economic

TABLE 26

PAST PRESIDENTS OF THE KARIYA ROTARY CLUB

Name	Age in Office	Position
Ishida Taizō	66	President, Toyota Motors; Toyota Loom
Iwase Masami	52	Managing Director, Japan Tile Company
Hayashi Torao	63	President, Nippon Densō Company
Tatematsu Iwao	54	President, Toyota Chassis Company
Inaba Etsuzaburō	54	President, Inatoku Sake Company
Kuroda Shin'ichi	63	President, Tōyō Tile Industries
Iwaoka Jirō	55	President, Aishin Seiki Company
Ōta Ichizō	45	President, Ōta Commercial Company
Hirose Sōhei	49	Director, Kikunoyo Hirose Sake Company
Ōjima Suzumatsu	56	Director, Toyota Loom
Ichikawa Kanji	58	President, Ichikawa Dry Goods Company
Takeuchi Masataka	57	Physician, Takeuchi Hospital
Nomura Kazuhiko	63	Physician, Nomura Hospital
Maejima Masami	53	President, Fuji Settō Industries
Kamiya Hiroi	50	President, Takahama Electrical Industries
Katō Shōhei	57	President, Kariya Wood Products, Inc.

SOURCE: Kariya Rotary Club, *Jūgonen no ayumi* (Kariya, 1969), pp. 8–9.

NOTE: Listed in order of succession so that Ishida served as first president in 1955 and Katō served as most recent.

leadership for the community. This was due in some part to their own desires, but it was also due to the inability of Kariya's historical ruling group to provide leadership at a time when it was needed. Consequently, people ceased to denigrate industrial leaders and began to accept them as prominent figures in the community's social life. The dominant role played by men of industry in Kariya's most prestigious social body after 1955 attested to their high degree of acceptance.

[4] A good account of this subject in the national arena is Byron Marshall, *Capitalism and Nationalism in Prewar Japan* (Stanford, 1967).

One's economic role was not the only criterion for social recognition, however. Past presidents of the Kariya Rotary Club shared two other attributes in common, education and wealth. All of the past presidents had at least thirteen years of formal education in the prewar school system and some had more. Several of the Toyota managers were graduates of prewar technical schools, the equivalent of engineering colleges in contemporary America. Others were graduates of postwar universities, and still others possessed advanced graduate degrees. By contrast with an earlier period, when formal education had not been an explicit criterion for entry into local leadership groups, a man's educational background had an important bearing on his social status.

In the same way, wealth had also become a far more explicit measure of a man's attainments. Income tax returns for 1966 illustrated that the four largest money earners in Kariya were Ishida Taizō, Tatematsu Iwao, Katō Shōhei, and Iwaoka Jirō. All were former presidents of the Rotary Club. Other former presidents who ranked among the city's fifty largest income earners were the physicians, Takeuchi and Nomura, and the merchant Ōta Ichizō. By 1967, of those still active, all but four past presidents were among the city's largest income earners. There were certainly other reasons why all of those men belonged to the Rotary Club, but their wealth was an important criterion for selection.[5]

In the course of two postwar decades, Kariya witnessed the emergence of a new class of social leaders. In a few cases, heads of old-line families which had enjoyed high status in the community for generations remained members of the city's leading social group. But outsiders who managed the city's largest industrial firms were both more numerous and more influential. Its membership determined by economic influence, educational background, and wealth, the new social leadership clearly personified the imposing power which industrial organizations wielded over the life of the community.

The power of the Toyota enterprise was a dominant force in Kariya's local life, penetrating all spheres of human action. During the late 1960s, however, the intrusive presence of the enterprise in local affairs began to recede somewhat. The list of Rotary presidents offers one signal that managers at Toyota were less free to participate in that social organization than before. Executives from the major Toyota firms in the city served as president before the early 1960s; after the early 1960s heads of old-line families who were merchants or physicians presided over the Rotary Club. This was just one indication of a more widespread retreat from the forefront of local affairs, a retreat necessitated by economic conditions in the auto industry.

[5] Kōjunsha, *Nihon shinshi roku* (Tokyo, 1967), pp. 340–341.

Three reasons accounted for Toyota's receding role in Kariya's community affairs in the late 1960s. The national program of economic "liberalization" was one reason. International pressure was forcing Japan to revise its economic policies and Toyota was affected by the outcome of the revisions. The geographic course of Toyota's expansion was a second reason for Toyota's diminishing presence in Kariya. The enterprise continued to expand, but it constructed new factories elsewhere, relieving the pressure on Kariya to conform with its demands. Finally, Ishida Taizō's gradual withdrawal from active leadership in the enterprise was a third reason for Toyota's receding role in Kariya. Thanks to his boundless energy, Ishida had become a prominent figure in all spheres of community life, but his successors, far more staid by comparison, adopted a retiring posture in their dealings with Kariya. These alterations all had a direct bearing on local political life, so each deserves brief comment before turning to a fuller discussion of political events in Kariya between 1967 and 1972.

Liberalization was a program imposed on Japan by foreign pressures, exerted primarily by the United States and the Organization for Economic Cooperation and Development (OECD).[6] The purpose of liberalization was to open Japanese enterprises to a greater measure of foreign investment and to reduce economic controls over foreign enterprises generally, in order to create a freer environment for trade. Fearing intervention, pressure, and competition from foreign auto makers, managers at Toyota faced the prospect of liberalization with considerable anxiety. As the movement toward liberalization got underway in the 1960s, Toyota managers developed an outlook which was simultaneously global and introverted. They became preoccupied with two problems: how to restructure the Japanese auto industry in order to compete internationally, and how to increase efficiency in their own firm in order to stay on top of the domestic market and to rise near the top of the international market. These problems turned their attention from community affairs to an intense concentration on matters internal to the firm and the auto industry. As they became more entrenched in internal affairs, and in political deliberations at the national level, Toyota managers lifted the political pressure which they had imposed on Kariya, and the city found it possible to regain some of its lost autonomy.

The direction of expansion within the Toyota enterprise also diverted pressure from Kariya. The same dramatic rates of growth which characterized the enterprise between 1955 and 1967 continued for the next five years. At the auto firm, an additional 8,500 workers joined the labor

[6] An excellent discussion of Japan's liberalization program appears in Chapter 7 of Dan F. Henderson, *Foreign Enterprise in Japan* (Chapel Hill, N.C., 1973).

force after 1967, raising the total to 41,000 in early 1972.[7] Production continued to rise at rapid rates, doubling again between 1967 and 1971. By 1972 Toyota Motors was turning out over 2 million vehicles a year. Other firms in the enterprise also expanded at rapid rates, most notably Nippon Densō. Between 1967 and 1971 it increased its labor force from less than eight thousand to more than fourteen thousand.[8] However, the impact of this expansion did not affect Kariya as it had during the 1960s, because both the auto firm and Nippon Densō were building new factories elsewhere. Toyota Motors put up two additional plants in areas north of Kariya, and Nippon Densō built factories in Anjō and Nishio after 1967. Consequently, the pressure once placed on Kariya to make it conform with enterprise goals lifted somewhat. This created a respite for the community after more than a decade of exuberant growth, and it gave people in Kariya an opportunity to survey the political future of their city.

The final explanation for Toyota's retreat from dominance in Kariya had to do with Ishida Taizō. Nearing the age of eighty, he began to withdraw from direct participation in Toyota firms during the 1960s. In 1961 he assumed the position of chairman at Toyota Motors and began delegating responsibility for operations in local factories to able subordinates. As pressures to liberalize grew, he devoted more of his energies to economic and political lobbying in Tokyo, assuming the role of elder statesman in the enterprise. He shed his responsibilities at Toyota Automatic Loom in 1969 when he became chairman of the board, a nominal position. Finally, in 1970, at age eighty-two, he resigned from all his offices in the enterprise and retired to a second home in Nagoya. Ishida's aggressive personality had left a clear imprint on both the Toyota enterprise and the political scene in Kariya. The individuals who followed him had little of his taste for political display. As a result, local politics lost a good deal of its color. But this, too, provided breathing space in which the community could begin to retrieve its political integrity.

The intrusive participation of the Toyota enterprise in Kariya's political affairs declined somewhat, but local citizens by no means turned their backs on the company's political wishes thereafter. Its importance was simply too pervasive to allow that to happen. Rather, a period of increasing political instability ensued, characterized by the electorate's drift into new alignments. By analyzing electoral behavior in the short but chaotic five years between 1967 and 1972, it is possible to appraise the outlines of a new balance of power in the community. Symbolic of the greatest change was the election of a new mayor in 1967, the topic which following pages discuss first. But the evolution toward a more complex balance of power appeared also in prefectural and national elections.

[7] Ōkura shō, *Yūka shōken hōkokusho sōran: Toyota jidōsha kōgyō K.K.* (Tokyo, 1971), p. 6.
[8] Ōkura shō, *Yūka shōken hōkokusho sōran: Nippon Densō K.K.* (Tokyo, 1971), p. 8.

These will be discussed in turn, in order to provide a closing portrait of socio-economic bases of political support and party alignments in Kariya and western Mikawa at the end of a century of industrialization.

The single, most dramatic effort by Kariya's citizens to regain control of local government occurred in 1967. For eight years an outsider named Takada Ichirō had administered the city as its mayor. As the preceding chapter illustrated, most people in Kariya regarded Takada as merely a subordinate of the Toyota enterprise, another manager carrying out its demands but, in this case, from his desk in city hall. Two terms of his administration had ired enough people in town that they began to hope for a restoration of government to the hands of a local man. This created a sense of dissatisfaction which a viable local candidate could easily exploit.

If the populace was generally dissatisfied with Takada's reign, two important conservative leaders had specific grievances. Ōno Ichizō was never pleased with Takada's selection. He felt that Takada made a fine administrative assistant, but that he was a poor politician. By the late 1960s Ōno was quite exasperated with Takada. The final break came when Takada appeared to dally in purchasing land for Aichi Teachers' College, which was to build a new, unified campus in Fujimatsu. Fearing that Takada's delays might lose the college, Ōno decided the time had come to place a local candidate in nomination. Iwase Masami, a director of the Japan Tile Corporation and a powerful figure in local affairs, concurred. They decided to throw their support behind a fifty-nine year old local businessman named Miyata Ichimatsu.[9]

Miyata differed from previous candidates for the mayoralty on two counts: he was of humble social origins and he had only a modest formal education.[10] Miyata's father was raised in a farm family in Moto Kariya during the early years of the Meiji Period. He often worked as a part-time laborer, especially in the clay diggings of the area. The family was quite poor and Miyata's father was never able to attend school, even though many children his age—even some older persons—were seeking education in the burgeoning public school system of the 1870s and 1880s. Possibly resentful, but in no way defeated by his own lack of training, the father decried the importance of schooling for his children. He was an apostle of hard work, and Miyata recalled a half-century later how his father often upbraided them with the order to work hard no matter what the task, because even a lowly job enabled one to eat.

The young Miyata, conceivably out of duty but perhaps out of impishness, took his father's example to heart. He often skipped class at

[9] Interviews with men of both progressive and conservative persuasion support this interpretation of Miyata's ascendancy.

[10] This sketch is based largely on material gathered in interviews with the mayor, conducted in December 1969 and August 1972.

Kijō School, even though his classmates pursued their education eagerly. Miyata was content merely to finish the required six grades. He was barely disturbed about not learning *kanji,* the Chinese script which constitutes an important part of the Japanese written language. Miyata felt that everything could be understood by using the pronunciation keys in Japanese script, and that the struggle to learn *kanji* was unnecessary. Equipped with such an education, and undoubtedly sharing his father's determination to get on in spite of things, Miyata left Kariya at the age of twelve to work in a textile mill in Toyohashi, an hour's train ride from home.

His brief factory experience left an indelible impression on him. Frequent mistakes and his obvious lack of education soon made him the butt of jokes and the laughing stock of the workers, mostly young farm girls with an elementary education. The embarrassment must have been doubly galling, coming as it did from women in a society devoted to the dominance of the male. He vowed to rectify his mistake and began a process of self-education which never really stopped.

He started a new life when he returned home to assist his father in a family venture. The economic prosperity and industrial expansion which followed World War I in Japan had created a great demand for building materials and the Miyata family decided to start its own small tile kiln. The children, now numbering eleven, were to serve as the labor force. Miyata's two older brothers quickly departed and at sixteen he became responsible for the commercial tasks of the concern. A sudden demand for tiles, fed by construction in Tokyo following the 1923 earthquake, brought economic prosperity to the new kiln. Through the 1920s and 1930s the firm was nursed to prosperity. It was incorporated in 1933. By 1970 it employed over one hundred workers on a fully mechanized assembly line that produced thirty thousand tiles a month, a far cry from the first small kiln with its handful of workers making a few hundred tiles monthly. It was among the most technically advanced firms in the western Mikawa region and was one of the area's largest producers, the more significant since Mikawa itself accounted for some 40 percent of the national output of roof tiles in 1969. Miyata's business acumen was eventually recognized, thanks to his unstinting effort at expansion and improvement. He was a director of two manufacturers' associations in the prefecture and was on the council of the national association of kiln operators.

In addition to his business interests, Miyata began early to participate in local political work. As a teenager he was active in the local *seinendan,* a youth organization given to quasi-military activities and self-improvement through education. He eventually rose to become president of his group. Later he served as a ward official for Moto Kariya. In the 1950s he became a member of the city council and was elected president two years later. He also took an interest in the educational and commercial affairs of the community, presiding over the local PTA organization during the mid-1950s and acting as an executive assistant in the Chamber of Commerce. In 1959, at the age of fifty-one, he became assistant mayor of Kariya. He occupied that post for six years, but resigned in 1965 over differences with Takada Ichirō.

Ōno Ichizō and Iwase Masami could not have found a more appropriate candidate with whom to challenge Takada Ichirō. Miyata Ichimatsu met the demands of virtually everyone who was against Takada. His deep roots in the community were his greatest asset for purposes of the campaign. His family had lived in Moto Kariya for generations, an area of the city where even in 1972 it seemed that every other house bore the family name Miyata. Miyata had also, much to the liking of his patrons, come properly up through the ranks. He had followed the time-tested path to political candidacy, beginning with low-ranking offices at the youth group and ward level, progressing upward through the PTA and the city council, and finally acquiring administrative experience in his six years as vice-mayor. He would furthermore prove an ardent campaigner. His resignation in 1965 left him bitter toward Takada and made him determined to get back to city hall. His long ties in the community, the size of his kinship group, and the backing of leading conservatives all gave him a solid base of electoral support.

The 1967 mayoralty election thus witnessed the first outright challenge to Toyota's hegemony in eight years. The enterprise, through its managers, continued to sanction Takada's candidacy. Ishida Taizō persuaded the prefectural governor, Kuwahara Mikine, to come to Kariya again to campaign. Ishida also brought pressure on unions within the enterprise to support Takada. With few exceptions, they did. Ranged against the candidate of the industrialists was a coalition of urban and rural conservatives and some progressives. Ōno Ichizō personified the support of the old-line conservative faction in the former town area. Iwase Masami exemplified the support of the indigenous business community, centered on the tile industry and small merchants. Pursuing an independent line, the autonomous unions in the Toyota enterprise threw their support behind Miyata. Finally, rural groups and those native to the community who felt a general need for change also supported Miyata. In a three-way race between Miyata, Takada, and a Communist candidate, Miyata Ichimatsu captured 52 percent of the vote and restored city hall to the control of the local community.[11] It was rumored that Toyota would support Takada again when Miyata's term expired, but they did not, and Miyata Ichimatsu won re-election to another four-year term in 1971.

[11] Aichi ken senkyo kanri iinkai, ed., *Aichi ken senkyo kiroku: 1966–1967* (Nagoya, 1967), p. 318.

The 1967 mayoralty election thus perpetuated a pattern of coalitions in
the community which dated back to 1955. The pattern was one in which
progressive and conservative constituencies split, sending a portion of their
support to different conservative candidates. The majority of the progressive constituency, organized industrial laborers, lent its support to Takada
Ichirō, the company candidate. A minority of the conservatives, perhaps a
fifth at most, also supported Takada. These two groups gave him 15,704
votes or 41 percent of the total. The winning candidate Miyata took office
with support from a progressive-conservative coalition which complemented Takada's. A minority of the organized workers in the city, those
belonging to the more independent unions within the Toyota enterprise
such as Toyota Loom, backed Miyata. So also did the vast majority of the
city's Liberal Democratic Party supporters. These two groups provided
Miyata with 19,724 votes, a slight majority of the total. His support came
from a curious alliance of independent Socialists and inveterate conservatives, many of whom had direct links with Ōno Ichizō's old *jiban* in Kariya.
Nonetheless, Miyata's victory was mildly symbolic of the community's
ability to assert some autonomy in the face of the Toyota enterprise.[12]

Miyata's successful challenge to Toyota's influence over local politics
did not, however, imply a crushing defeat for Toyota's political interests.
Miyata, like most other people in the community, was fully aware of
Toyota's significance to the city. Its major affiliates provided jobs for most
of Kariya's manufacturing workers, and its subcontracting firms created
jobs for a large share of the remainder. In addition, the general affluence
which Toyota had brought to Kariya stimulated prosperity in all other
sectors of the economy. Even Miyata's tile firm flourished as a result of the
demand for construction materials fostered by the growth which Toyota
led. Clearly, Miyata's administration would have to yield to the essential
demands of the enterprise. It made good sense to do so.

By virtue of his victory, however, Miyata could begin to reduce the
rather slavish adherence to Toyota's political demands which city hall had
demonstrated under Takada's regime. Miyata enjoyed some freedom—as
well as a political obligation—to address himself to more general
community needs. He could use the city's abundant tax resources for
purposes which benefitted the populace in its social activities, not just the
enterprise in its economic activities.

City budget expenditures provide one guide to the manner in which
Miyata's administration decided to allocate community resources. As the
figures in table 27 indicate, he chose to continue the city's long-standing
emphasis on construction. Kariya devoted an immense share of its annual
outlays to construction purposes, especially by comparison with nearby

[12] Ibid.

cities. As before, a smaller share than in other cities went for educational purposes. Unlike the past, however, scrimping on education did not occur at the expense of school children. Even though Kariya spent the smallest portion of its budget for educational purposes, it spent more money per pupil than any of the other cities, with the exception of Toyota.

TABLE 27

BUDGET EXPENDITURES FOR FOUR AICHI CITIES, 1970
(PERCENTAGES, BY CATEGORY)

Category of Expenditure	Kariya	Toyota	Anjō	Nishio
General administration	14	17	16	15
Health, labor, & welfare	15	19	17	24
Agriculture & fisheries	4	7	12	5
Construction	42	28	26	18
Education	17	18	19	21
Debt retirement	3	2	3	3
Other outlays	5	9	7	14
Totals	100	100	100	100

SOURCE: Atn: 1972, pp. 432–433.

NOTE: These are figures for "anticipated final expenditures," not final expenditures, so they could misrepresent actual outlays somewhat. What is important here, however, is the comparison of magnitudes, and for this purpose these figures are adequate.

Although the Miyata administration continued to spend large sums on construction in Kariya, there was a qualitative difference in the use of funds. In the past basic construction expenses had gone to finance roads, sewers, and water facilities near new factories or near dormitories and apartment developments put up by the Toyota enterprise. Under Miyata's administration construction continued apace, but the form and siting of new projects came to benefit the community at large, rather than the enterprise in particular. It was Miyata's administration, for instance, which built the city's new library. During his first term, the city also put up a new elementary school and established three new pre-school nurseries. In continued service to the automobile (and indirectly, to the Toyota enterprise), the Miyata administration pushed forward with redevelopment plans and road building. It created two large parking lots near the old downtown section. Although they facilitated auto travel, they also stimulated trade in the commercial area where Miyata derived important political support. City planners under Miyata also shifted their attention from development of the area north of town, where most of the Toyota factories were located, to development and subdivision of regions south of town near Moto Kariya, where Miyata's electoral constituency was rooted. On the whole, the tangible achievements of the Miyata administration appeared to benefit the community itself, and to restore a sense of attentiveness to the wishes of Kariya's citizenry—rather than its corporations. In a very mild sense, Miyata governed an administration with a populist character.

Miyata Ichimatsu's victory in 1967 and his easy re-election in 1971 signaled two important changes in local politics. First, his selection indicated that people in Kariya were prepared to return men to office who lacked the prestigious social backgrounds of previous local mayors, as long as the candidate enjoyed some administrative experience and as long as he had roots in the local community. Second, by sending Takada Ichirō down to defeat, the community of Kariya hinted that it would no longer brook unlimited interference in its political affairs from the Toyota enterprise. In the period under discussion, these two trends became more pronounced, because they came into play at the prefectural level as well as the municipal.

In the two prefectural elections held during this period, Kariya's voters returned two men who were farmers and natives in the community. In 1967 Egawa Yukie, a former city council president and a member of the Japan Socialist Party, won the prefectural assembly seat. He defeated one of the conservatives' weakest candidates in years, a pawnbroker named Mori. The election was so uneventful that almost half the voters failed to cast ballots. Egawa retired after one term in office. His successor as Socialist candidate was chairman of the union at the Toyota chassis factory. Conservatives put forward a stronger candidate this time, a farmer from the Fujimatsu area named Okamoto Tatsumi, at fifty a man with long experience on the city council and a two-year period as its president. In addition, the Japan Communist Party sponsored a candidate, who drew enough progressive votes to return the conservative. With a 2,000-vote plurality over his Socialist opponent, Okamoto Tatsumi won Kariya's prefectural assembly seat in 1971.[13]

These elections revealed a tendency for voters to choose candidates with backgrounds somewhat more egalitarian than before. Rather than emphasizing the pedigree of a man's family, those who nominated and elected candidates were more likely to emphasize his political service to the community and, in the case of the mayoralty, his experience as an administrator. The elections also implied that Toyota's influence in Kariya's politics was receding.

Results of mayoralty and prefectural elections in the neighboring city of Toyota highlight these tendencies in Kariya. In 1967 Toyota voters

[13] Aichi ken senkyo kanri iinkai, ed., *Aichi ken senkyo kiroku: 1970–1971* (Nagoya, 1972), pp. 224–225.

elected to a second term as mayor a man named Satō Tamotsu. Satō had worked for Toyota Motors for almost thirty years. When he resigned in 1963, he was head of the Department of General Affairs, an important administrative position which equipped him nicely to carry out the duties of mayor. Given his position in the firm and his long association with it, he was obviously going to be attentive to its wishes when administering the city's affairs. Like Takada Ichirō in Kariya between 1959 and 1967, Satō was the political manager for the Toyota enterprise, sitting behind his desk in city hall. Representatives of the enterprise also served prominently in the city's delegation to the prefectural assembly. Toyota had two delegates in 1967; with its growing population, that number rose to three in 1971. In both years, Nakano Takeshi, a former employee of Toyota Motors still associated with the firm, captured one seat. A farmer named Suzuki captured a second seat. The third seat in 1971 went to a man named Kurachi, who was related to a long-time assemblyman and worked in a firm with ties to the Toyota enterprise. After 1967 the city of Kariya was able to move out from under the political influence of the Toyota enterprise, but the headquarter city of Toyota remained under its vigorous political hegemony.[14]

Local election results revealed a third tendency which appeared in the region's politics between 1967 and 1972, a fluid, almost unstable, pattern of party support. In view of the support patterns in the Takada-Tomikawa race in 1959, the coalitions which appeared in the 1967 mayoralty election were not unusual. But in the prefectural elections, instability was more discernible. Egawa was the first Socialist candidate to win an assembly seat in Kariya since 1951, yet his party suffered defeat again only four years later. This somewhat quixotic behavior bespoke a more general sense of political drift which displayed itself most visibly in Diet elections.

Two signs of growing political fluidity appeared in the Diet elections held between 1967 and 1972. One was the increasing fragmentation of political parties, and the second was a shift in party affiliation by Kariya's largest constituency. Fragmentation was a product of political change at the national level. It began in 1960 when the united Socialist party split into two separate parties. Henceforth, both a quasi-Marxist Japan Socialist Party and a moderate Democratic Socialist Party would hoist the Socialist banner before voters on election day. Those two parties joined two others already in existence, the ruling Liberal Democrats and the Japan Communist Party. In November 1964, yet another party appeared

[14] Two reasons explain why the city of Toyota continued under the political domination of the auto firm. First, Satō himself was a longtime resident of the area, so he did not suffer the disadvantages or elicit the same type of opposition which Takada did in Kariya. Second, one union—the auto union—predominated in Toyota. This made it easier to achieve political unity among workers than was the case in Kariya, where many unions with different national affiliations fostered a divided union movement and a more disparate political culture.

with the formation of the Clean Government Party (Kōmeitō), the political arm of a Buddhist sect known as the Sōka Gakkai. In the 1969 Diet election, a Clean Government candidate ran for the first time in the Fourth District, giving voters five parties from which to select their candidates.

The 1969 Diet election also witnessed a significant shift in the party affiliation of Kariya's single largest constituency, organized industrial workers. In that election the major unions in Kariya and western Mikawa severed their ties with the candidate of the left wing of the Japan Socialist Party and lent their almost unanimous support to a candidate of the Democratic Socialist Party. The result of this shift was to dilute drastically the strength of the Japan Socialist and Japan Community Parties in the district, to undercut support for the Liberal Democratic Party, and to diffuse the vote across a broad array of parties. Table 28 depicts the result of those changes graphically.

TABLE 28

AICHI FOURTH DISTRICT DIET ELECTION RESULTS, 1969
(PERCENTAGE OF VOTES, BY PARTY)

	JCP	JSP	KMT [a]	DSP	LDP
Kariya	3	14	10	34	39
Toyota	2	9	11	41	37
Anjō	2	16	9	17	56
Nishio	3	11	9	9	69
Fourth District	2	13	10	21	54

SOURCE: *Chūnichi shimbun*, December 29, 1969, p. 11.
NOTE: Some columns do not add to 100 due to rounding.
[a] KMT = Kōmeitō, or Clean Government Party.

Comparison of the 1967 and 1969 elections illustrates the change clearly. In 1967 six candidates ran for the Diet in the district. Three conservative candidates captured nearly 60 percent of the total vote. Two Japan Socialist Party candidates and one candidate from the Japan Communist Party gathered the remaining 40 percent. In 1969 seven candidates ran, three from the Liberal Democratic Party and one each from the Clean Government Party, the Democratic Socialist Party, the Japan Socialist Party, and the Japan Communist Party. The combined vote of the last two candidates amounted to only 15 percent in the district, a drop of 25 percent for those two parties from the preceding election. The conservative vote for the LDP also dropped, from 60 to only 54 percent of the total. The Clean Government candidate, running for the first time, collected 10 percent of the vote. The Democratic Socialist Candidate, also running for the first time, won the remaining 21 percent of the total. There was no longer a simple two-way split between supporters of an entrenched conservative party and the backers of two challengers from the opposition. Beginning in 1969 there appeared a general fragmentation of the vote, leaving a bare majority in the hands of the Liberal Democratic Party and dividing the remainder among four minority, opposition parties.[15]

Voters in Kariya found themselves wholly fragmented by the choices placed before them in 1969. In the previous election they gave 53 percent of their vote to three progressive candidates, most (34 percent of the total) to Itō Yoshiko. Three conservative candidates captured the remaining 47 percent of the vote. In 1969 the conservative share of the vote fell to 39 percent, but their loss was mild in contrast to that suffered by the Japan Socialist and Japan Communist candidates. They were able to collect only 17 percent of the votes. The Clean Government candidate captured the same percentage of votes in Kariya as she did district-wide, 10 percent, and the remaining 34 percent—the city's largest single bloc—went to the Democratic Socialist candidate, Watanabe Takezō.

Watanabe was chairman of the central executive committee of the labor union at Toyota Motors in 1969. Born in a hamlet south of the Kariya city center, he attended school in Yosami for eight years before joining the Toyota auto firm at the age of sixteen in 1938. He remained with the firm thereafter, rising through the ranks to assume a position as union chairman in 1967. By virtue of his background, Watanabe personified the growing trend toward egalitarianism in the choice of candidates. He also exemplified two habits of mind which had been maturing among workers for over a decade and which finally took tangible political form with his election.

Watanabe's victory demonstrated first the success of management's effort to embrace workers and managers in a tight corporate web. His was not just a union candidacy. It was a company candidacy, supported by directors, managers, technicians, and production workers, as well as by subcontractors and their employees. The tendency toward labor-management conciliation, revived in the mid-1950s and nurtured to good health in the 1960s, assumed ultimate maturity with Watanabe's *jiban*. Both the union and the enterprise now saw eye to eye on political as well as economic issues. With Watanabe's election, the Toyota enterprise—workers and managers alike—hoped to use the country's most important political forum to lobby for the interests of their group.

Their group was a hierarchical organization which encompassed both

[15] Data on the 1969 Diet election appear in: Aichi ken senkyo kanri iinkai, ed., *Aichi ken senkyo kiroku: 1969* (Nagoya, 1970), pp. 1–128. For the 1967 election see *Aichi ken senkyo kiroku: 1966–1967*, pp. 50–51.

organized workers on the production line and white-collar technicians and managers. Eschewing ties with the labor movement as a whole, even with workers in other auto firms, the organized laborers in the Toyota organization identified their interests solely with the firm for which they worked. The identity of interests was especially strong on economic matters. In the 1950s, labor-management cooperation also began to impinge on political matters, as the victories of men such as Fujii Seihichi and Takada Ichirō indicated. Now, in the late 1960s, the political ties deepened, creating a tenacious bond between workers and managers within the firm. The Watanabe *jiban* provides compelling proof, if more were needed, that industrialization fosters an unpredictable political response. Under conditions of depression in the early 1950s, industrial workers adopted radical programs and backed left-wing Socialist candidates, but under the conditions of affluence in the late 1960s, they shunned radicalism and supported moderate Socialists.

The Watanabe constituency was secondly one in which political conservatism assumed a new level of importance. The signs were numerous. By his own character, Watanabe symbolized the emergence of political conservatism. In his campaign speeches he invoked the virtues of thrift, honesty, hard work, and obedience.[16] He articulated no program of political reform, as the university-educated Socialist Itō Kōdō might have. Instead, Watanabe made vague appeals to his supporters to seek stability and continued prosperity. Prosperity, indeed, was at the root of his candidacy. For more than a decade, workers in the Fourth District had watched their incomes rise steadily, especially those employed in the large plants at the Toyota enterprise. Between 1959 and 1969 alone, they enjoyed a doubling of their *real* wages.[17] Such material rewards were compelling proof that conciliation with the enterprise brought greater returns than confrontation, especially for those who remembered the precarious days of the early 1950s. Affluence made workers conform to the wishes of management, and it drastically restrained their inclination to dissent politically, or even to seek reform.

By affiliating with the Democratic Socialist Party, workers in the Toyota auto union did not desert the progressive cause, but they made a clear move toward a more moderate, if not conservative, position. The party with which they affiliated in 1969 was itself in a state of flux. Many of its leading members were about to die or retire. In the following election in 1972, the party suffered a crushing defeat at the polls, losing thirteen of its thirty-one seats in the Diet. Searching for policies which would create a

[16] *Aichi ken senkyo kiroku: 1969*, p. 90.
[17] Aichi ken Kinugaura chiku tōkei kenkyū kai, ed., *Kinugaura no tōkei*, no. 4 (n.p., 1972), p. 122.

viable identity for the party, the Democratic Socialists more often than not struck on a position which resembled that of the ruling conservatives. In fact, they found it comfortable to deal with the Liberal Democrats, especially in Aichi. In the 1971 gubernatorial election, the Democratic Socialists endorsed the candidacy of the long-time conservative incumbent, Kuwahara Mikine. Kuwahara obviously represented the interests of big business and industry, so the endorsement undercut the party's claim to lead the way to a new Socialist society.

In 1972 the Democratic Socialists began to change their policies and their alliances. They adopted some programs which ran avowedly counter to the policies of the ruling Liberal Democrats. They also began to join in coalitions with the other parties of the political left, in order to return fusion candidates in a number of local elections. These changes signaled a possible shift in the ideological leanings of the party. But they also bespoke its inability to define a stable course, one which was either clearly progressive or clearly conservative.

Despite the indecision of the party itself, the Toyota enterprise, its workers, and its managers continued to find the party's mildly conservative stance attractive. Watanabe ran for office again in the 1972 election. He won another clearcut victory. As a result, at the close of this century of Kariya's political history, the largest segment of the city's industrial working class was tied politically to a moderate Socialist party with programs of a conservative hue.

Indeed, by 1973 conservatism was the keynote of electoral politics in the region around Kariya and Toyota. Of the 515,188 votes cast in the 1972 Diet election, 280,740 went to three candidates for the Liberal Democratic Party. Another 101,229 went to Watanabe. Accepting the assertion that Watanabe represented a moderately conservative party in that year, a full 75 percent of the electorate in the Aichi Fourth District supported conservative candidates for the Diet. The make-up of the Diet delegation from the district reflected that fact. Three of the district's seats went to conservatives: Watanabe of the Democratic Socialists and Urano Sachio and Nakagaki Kunio of the Liberal Democrats. The remaining seat went to Ōta Kazuo, since 1958 a perennial candidate and intermittent victor from the left wing of the Japan Socialist Party.[18]

The four victors in 1972, along with a fifth losing candidate, all possessed their own distinct *jiban*. The make-up of those *jiban* provides a fitting subject with which to draw a concluding portrait of the social roots of politics in an area which had experienced over a half-century of vigorous industrialization. The location and the social composition of the five *jiban* provide evidence, first, of the striking continuities in the electoral

[18] *Nihon keizai shimbun*, December 12, 1972, pp. 5–8.

politics of this area and, second, of the manner in which socio-economic
changes reflected themselves in political life.[19]

The Liberal Democratic *jiban* bespoke the persistent continuities in the
behavior of voters in this district. Urano Sachio possessed one of the *jiban*.
Urano was a member of an extended kinship group which had been
politically powerful in the Toyota City area since the late nineteenth
century. Two of his ancestors had served in the Diet, one at the turn of the
century and another in the 1920s. Urano's own father had been a
campaign manager for Kobayashi Kanae.[20] The tie between Kobayashi
and the Urano family was so close that when Kobayashi died suddenly in
1960, Urano Sachio, who was then serving his third term as a prefectural
assemblyman from Toyota, filled out the unexpired Diet term. As
designated heir, Urano easily retained the loyalties of the voters in
Kobayashi's old *jiban* in the vicinity of Toyota and Okazaki. In 1972 he
won his fifth consecutive Diet victory, by relying on an electoral base
which traced its origins directly to 1930.

Nakagaki Kunio, another Liberal Democratic Diet member from the
district, also returned to office from a *jiban* formed in the prewar era.
Nakagaki was the temporary stand-in for Ogasawara Sankurō during the
years of the purge, as chapter 6 illustrated. When Ogasawara finally
retired from politics in 1958, his *jiban*—which dated from his first
candidacy in 1928—fell to Nakagaki, who cultivated it with uninterrupted
success through 1972. Thus, large groups of voters from the still most
agrarian parts of this district cast their ballots loyally for conservative
politicians or their direct successors for a period of more than four decades.

A third *jiban* also reflected the tenacity of conservative electoral support
in the less industrialized parts of the district. Between 1946 and 1972
Nakano Shirō won nine election victories from a postwar *jiban* based on
the cities of Hekinan and Nishio. His only losses came in 1955, 1958, and
1972. Farmers, fishermen, merchants, and small industrialists predominated in that area. In the prewar period they had backed men such as
Taketomi Sai and Okamoto Jitsutarō. In the postwar period they
continued their allegiance to the conservative persuasion by providing the
foundations for Nakano's Liberal Democratic *jiban*.

Men possessing the two final *jiban* in the district gave political expression
to the new socio-economic groups which emerged in such profusion after
the mid-1950s. Drawing his support mainly from the cities of Okazaki,
Toyota, Anjō, and Kariya, Ōta Kazuo represented the interests of

[19] The following analysis is based on a thorough review of voting patterns in the 1969 Diet
election in conjunction with the 1970 national census report for Aichi Prefecture. See *Aichi
ken senkyo kiroku: 1969* and Sōrifu tōkei kyoku, *Kokusei chōsa hōkoku: 1970, Aichi ken* (Tokyo,
1972).

[20] Takayama, *Kobayashi Kanae sensei*, pp. 121–122.

organized laborers who favored a progressive, or at least anti-Liberal
Democratic, political program. Ōta's constituency, however, embraced
only a small minority of the voters in the entire district (approximately 20
percent) and far less than half of its organized industrial laborers.

By far the largest group of industrial laborers gave their electoral
support to Watanabe Takezō. Voters in Kariya and Toyota, the major
industrial centers in the district, gave him 34 and 41 percent of their votes,
respectively. His support in those two cities alone sufficed to win a seat in
the 1969 election. Winning another large concentration of votes in
Okazaki (where Toyota subcontractors were numerous and from which
many people commuted to work in factories in the city of Toyota) and a
smattering of support from the district's villages, Watanabe was able to
build the largest *jiban* in the district in his very first campaign. This attests
to the vitality of the Toyota enterprise in its political role. It also
symbolizes the degree to which industrial laborers in the district paid their
allegiance to parties with programs which were centrist, rather than leftist
or progressive. The industrialization of Aichi's Fourth District had fostered
a complex political response from corporate executives and industrial
workers alike.

The preceding portrait of the years between 1967 and 1972 brings to an
end this study of Kariya's history. In 1972 the community was undergoing
a prodigious effort at reconstruction. Forced by the auto to change the
layout of a city designed four centuries earlier, and aided by the affluence
which industrial development brought, the government and the people of
Kariya were changing the face of the city daily. Socially, the city reflected
a comparable sense of flux and instability. Transients and commuters
produced a constant flow of people in and out of the community, affecting
the quality of its cultural, social, and political life.

These movements, amidst other changes, forced people to seek new
alignments and new policies appropriate to an era of affluence. In a
subdued way the people of Kariya seemed to be expressing in their
electoral behavior a desire for greater attention to their private goals, as
opposed to those of the industrial corporations on which the city's economy
was founded. But their expressions were far from singular. One substantial
group of the city's political actors viewed its interests in concert with those
of the Toyota enterprise and behaved accordingly. Another group tried to
challenge Toyota's political interests. Still another persisted in forms of
political behavior and party affiliations which dated back to the 1920s, by
supporting the candidates, policies, and methods of the Liberal Democratic Party. And a fourth, highly mobile group equivocated in its support,
affiliating unpredictably with minority parties advocating clean government, socialism, or communism.

Underlaying the shifting texture of local politics in the years between 1967 and 1972 were social and economic changes fostered by conditions in the Japanese economy in general and the auto industry in particular. Two decades of prosperous growth at the Toyota enterprise had promoted conformism and conservatism among the Fourth District's industrial workers. Enjoying real affluence as a result of their compliance with corporate goals, workers shrank from labor activism and adopted moderate, if not conservative, political affiliations. Their behavior contrasted diametrically with that of workers in the early 1950s, when depression, inflation, and recession undermined worker satisfaction and prompted both economic and political radicalism. In 1972 threat of eroding inflation and major slowdowns in economic activity began to appear again. Were such economic problems to persist into the 1970s, they might very well have undermined the bond between the workers and managers who drew so tightly together after 1969. But in 1972 it was too early to know what was to come. Fluidity characterized the community's social, political, and economic life in that year, and an ominous uncertainty was the keynote to Kariya's future.

9

CONCLUSION

The purpose of this conclusion is to summarize the major findings of this study and to examine them in the light of comparative evidence. Following a brief review of the social consequences of Kariya's industrialization, this chapter presents an extended analysis of changes in the structure of community power between 1872 and 1972. In order to illuminate the broader significance of Kariya's political experience, comparisons are drawn with community power structures in the United States and with the behavior of organized auto workers in the United States and Britain.

This study opened in 1872 on a rustic country town emerging reluctantly from the somnolence of its Tokugawa past. Some twenty thousand persons resided within the area which was to become the city of Kariya. Most of them, perhaps eight in ten, lived by farming. Many of the others were artisans or shopkeepers who made their living by trading or processing the output of nearby farms. The settlements which surrounded the old castletown in that year were small ones in which the populations were remarkably stable. They were governed by the same groups which had exercised political control during the preceding two centuries or more. Descendants of former samurai families continued in the 1870s to play a major role in the social and political affairs of the community; so also did leading townsmen and major landowners from nearby villages. In 1872 Kariya was a small, stable, agrarian community still infused with the habits and customs of the Tokugawa Period.

In the following century the population of that area grew to exceed ninety thousand. In place of the country town and rural hamlets, there arose a vigorous industrial city which sprawled across the once pastoral landscape. Farmers were only a tiny minority of its residents in 1972. More numerous were persons engaged in commerce, professions, and the service trades. But most numerous were those employed on production lines or in offices in the city's factories. By the early 1970s they comprised nearly 60 percent of the local labor force. They lent a work-oriented character to the social life of the city, and they stamped local politics with the imprint of their economic concerns. The men who represented Kariya's citizens in the mayoralty, the prefectural assembly, and the Diet after the 1950s reflected the influence which those laborers brought to bear on the city's political life. No longer small, stable, or agrarian, Kariya had become a dynamic industrial city whose residents in 1972 were adjusting to an unprecedented age of affluence.

The changes which Kariya witnessed between the 1870s and the 1970s were due primarily to the expansion of the Toyota enterprise. Development of that enterprise caused the city-area population to quadruple. It also contributed to the demographic mobility that undermined the stable community of the nineteenth century. And, of course, Toyota's industrial expansion fully altered the occupational structure of the community while giving rise to new social groups.

In the thirty-three years before 1925, when Kariya experienced virtually no industrial growth, the city-area population increased by about 35 percent. The nation's population grew by nearly 45 percent in that same period. The lag indicated that Kariya was losing many of its children and families to other, more thriving areas, a drain that was finally stopped when Toyota entered Kariya in the early 1920s. In the thirty-three years after its entry, the city-area population shot up by a dramatic 130 percent, a rate more than double the national average. Most of the increase was due to newcomers employed in Toyota firms or its affiliates and subsidiaries. Kariya's rapid growth in population after 1925 was thus one important social consequence of Toyota's expansion.

The growth of industry led to increased population mobility which had important political implications. In the late nineteenth century and well into the twentieth, persons born and raised in Kariya dominated the population. Their stability contributed to a persistent continuity of leadership in Kariya through the 1930s. With the advent of industrialism, however, large numbers of outsiders came to Kariya. By the 1940s they were more numerous than native-born residents in the town area. The newcomers, who had ties to other places and politicians, diluted the solidarity which had long characterized political activity in the community. Another wave of newcomers arrived in Kariya after 1955; they further undermined political solidarity. They also fostered a marked fragmentation of party ties and contributed to a sharp drop in voter participation.

Occupational change in Kariya between 1872 and 1972 was a third social consequence attesting to Toyota's influence on the community. When the first Toyota factory went up in Kariya in 1922, three in every four workers in the city area earned a living by farming. Only one in eight engaged in manufacturing or construction, usually in a small handicraft enterprise where manual production was dominant. The rest of the community's workers either sold goods in a small shop or provided services to the local residents. From the moment the new factory began operations, however, the occupational character of the community changed. As early as the 1930s the portion of manufacturing workers doubled, to 24 percent of the labor force. In the following quarter-century their portion doubled again, until in 1970 manufacturing workers made up 57 percent of the local labor force. Kariya's rapid, intensive industrialization had created a city in which factory workers dwarfed all other occupational groups. By virtue of their numbers, those workers determined the character of local politics.[1]

Finally, Toyota's expansion helped greatly to alter the structure of social prestige in Kariya. Leading members from three groups—samurai, chōnin, and rural landowners—had set the social and political tone in Kariya in the 1870s. For seven decades thereafter those men and their descendants exercised a virtual monopoly over the town's political, social, and economic organizations. By the 1940s, however, they began to share power with new claimants, the men whose decisions in the Toyota enterprise were exerting such a powerful impact on the community. A long war, followed by a foreign occupation, accelerated the dispersion of power, and in the postwar community industrial leaders such as Ishida Taizō rose to a position of dominance in local affairs. In the 1950s they assumed a paramount role in local politics, as chapter 7 described, and in the 1960s Ishida and his corporate colleagues came to dominate the social hierarchy in Kariya, also, as chapter 8 illustrated. Industrial managers did not entirely displace the old leaders. Rather, they overshadowed them, as the Toyota enterprise cast its influence over the life of the city. This was particularly so in the political realm, as the following analysis makes clear.

Two aspects of Kariya's political history warrant attention in this analysis of changes in the structure of community power between 1872 and 1972. They are the attributes of local leaders and the distribution of influence among political participants. In the course of this century of its history, the attributes of Kariya's political leaders—its mayors—changed considerably. From the mid-nineteenth century until 1946, heads of old-line families native to the community monopolized political leadership. With the beginning of the American Occupation in 1946, a thirteen-year transitional period ensued during which men on the margins of the old-line ruling group held office. A third period began in 1959, when Takada Ichirō took office. Although Takada's election was unusual in many respects, the characteristic of the period was the ascent of the administrative mayor.

[1] As long as there are many communities like Kariya in Japan, where industrial workers with their habits and values vastly overshadow all other occupational groups, it would be rash to label Japan a "post-industrial society."

The men who dominated local leadership until 1946 shared several attributes in common. First, they descended from families which had provided local leaders since at least the late Tokugawa Period. Their families were formerly members of the samurai, the *chōnin*, and the rural landowning classes. They had historically served either as bureaucratic administrators in the Kariya domain or as *shōya*, or headmen, in the town and the outlying villages. Second, by virtue of their long residence, heads of those families enjoyed considerable social prestige in the community. To some degree, therefore, they held office as a hereditary privilege which was granted deferentially by the town's other residents. Finally, those political leaders came from families which were among the community's wealthiest. Detailed evidence to prove this claim is lacking. Nonetheless, the presence among mayors of men like Fujii Seihichi (the area's largest landowner in the 1920s), Okamoto Hirotarō (owner of a major brewery), and Katō Shin'uemon (head of a leading merchant house) attests to their economic importance. Of these three attributes, wealth was probably least important. More significant were family pedigree and longevity in the community.

The transitional period in Kariya's leadership began with the purge of Ono Ichizō in 1946 and ended with the election of Takada Ichirō in 1959. In the interim two men served long terms as mayor. They were similar to the former leaders in many respects, but they were more from the periphery than the center of the old-line ruling group. The families of Takenaka Hichirō and Okamoto Kimpei had both lived in the community for several generations. They were merchant houses of modest means. Their members had not, however, served as *shōya* during the Tokugawa Period or with any frequency as councilmen after 1889. This bespeaks the relatively low standing of the Takenaka and Okamoto houses, especially by contrast with the Ono or Masaki families. As transitional mayors, Takenaka and Okamoto won office during a period in which the social obligation to elect men of high status diminished somewhat; their rise to power was facilitated by American Occupation reforms.

The third and final period of local leadership was the era of the administrative mayor. Takada Ichirō and Miyata Ichimatsu differed greatly from their predecessors, and from each other. Takada was a college graduate born outside the community who had been a life-long public servant. Miyata was a poorly-educated native of the community who had made a small fortune in the tile industry. Despite these differences, however, the two shared one attribute in common, their backgrounds as government officials. Takada had served in the prefectural government for twenty-five years before he came to Kariya as assistant mayor in 1955, a post in which he gained four more years of administrative experience. Miyata also had served as Kariya's assistant mayor, for six years between

1959 and 1965. Both men thus personified the political ascent of the administrative specialist.

The appearance of the administrative mayor in postwar Kariya confirmed changes which had been underway in the community and the nation for some time. Old-line family heads who had monopolized local politics through the 1940s held the mayoralty as an avocational calling. Assistants handled most of the routine work and the job was not demanding, enabling the holders to undertake a variety of other duties. As Kariya expanded during the 1950s, however, the mayoralty became a full-time position demanding special skills which previous office holders had possessed in only rudimentary form. Especially important was a knowledge of how to deal with government officials at the prefectural and national levels. Takada Ichirō was well-suited to provide such skills. His ascent to the mayoralty thus represented—in some, but not all, respects— the culmination of a long-term trend toward specialization. The trend was increasingly evident throughout Japanese society beginning as early as the 1920s, as positions in business, government, and politics became full-time roles demanding the undivided attention of their occupants. One consequence of the change was the need for local mayors to possess talent as administrators, perhaps more than aptitude as politicians.

Changes in the distribution of political power in Kariya over this century paralleled the changes in leadership. During most of the seven decades before 1946, local political power resided in the hands of a small minority of prominent families. The populace as a whole played only a small role in the political process. Its participation was sharply restricted by law through the mid-1920s, but regardless of legal restraints, the general population usually acted out of deference to its socially superior leaders. The result was a form of consensual politics characterized by community solidarity. In important cases, the community acted in concert to achieve political ends identified and shaped by its old-line leaders, as the discussions of the school issue (in chapter 4) and voting behavior (in chapters 4 and 5) illustrated. Observers who comment on the political solidarity of Japanese communities usually attribute it to social causes. As chapters 3 and 4 made clear, however, community solidarity was a logical political response to a structure of power which forced communities to compete among themselves for the scarce resources of the state.

Despite its potential for influence, the Toyota enterprise did little to alter this pattern of behavior during its first twenty years in Kariya. The enterprise and its managers played no direct role in local politics. Rather, as chapters 4 and 5 explained, Toyota preferred to work through local influentials to achieve its aims. Those influentials were willing to intervene on Toyota's behalf because they felt its presence would solve their most pressing need: local jobs. Toyota's presence also promised future growth and prosperity for the community. Consequently, local influentials shaped their political decisions to meet the expectations of the Toyota enterprise. Out of the arrangement developed Kariya's practice of placing local government at the service of industry.

This finding is an important one which deserves fuller comment. Given conventional views, it may seem surprising that Toyota did not simply "take over" local government in Kariya after 1922. Overnight it became the dominant economic force in the community, and it clearly enjoyed the cooperation of the town's native leaders. In the late 1950s it did not hesitate to subject local politics to its will. Yet it did not do so in the 1920s and 1930s in the same direct way. Chapter 4 provided some specific explanations for this which can be reaffirmed here in a broader light.

Herbert Gutman's study of nineteenth-century Paterson, New Jersey, a city experiencing the same type of industrialization which Kariya did in the twentieth century, suggests why Toyota managers may have adopted their approach in the 1920s.[2] Gutman notes that "the factory-owner symbolized innovation and a radical departure from an older way of life. His power was not yet legitimized and 'taken for granted.' . . . He . . . learned that the middle and professional classes did not automatically accept his leadership and idolize his achievements." Gutman notes further that industrialists inevitably encountered opposition in communities where they settled, from workers and their families, from old-line community leaders, or from small-scale manufacturers native to the community—or from combinations of the three. Such opposition often made it difficult for industrialists to settle quickly and comfortably into a new community.

Toyota might have encountered such opposition had it located in a community like Handa, which was dominated by powerful, local industrialists. (See chapter 4.) Rather than confront that opposition, Toyota managers struck up a beneficial partnership with local influentials in Kariya. Men of merchant and samurai backgrounds, they were interested in boosting their town's fortunes. In this way the Toyota enterprise circumvented the problem of legitimacy by exploiting the prestige of the town's leaders in the early 1920s. Those leaders sanctioned the claims of the enterprise to community resources and enabled it to carry out its economic functions smoothly. The bargain did not, however, guarantee immediate status and power to the industrial managers. As in nineteenth-century Paterson, Kariya's industrialists did not achieve high status and power until they had been in the community for several decades.

In 1946 the period of old-line family rule drew to a close and the transitional period in Kariya's leadership began. It coincided with the

[2] Herbert G. Gutman, "Class, Status, and Community Power in Nineteenth-century American Industrial Cities—Paterson, New Jersey: A Case Study," in F. C. Jaher, ed., *The Age of Industrialism in America* (New York, 1968), pp. 263–287. Quotations are from page 265.

"radical interlude" described in chapter 6. During that period Kariya split into a number of contending blocs, each vying for control of local office. The social divisions which underlay the new era were not solely a product of war's end or Occupation reforms. Rather, as chapter 5 illustrated, community solidarity began to break down in the late 1930s and early 1940s. Migration of large numbers of young men from towns and villages outside Kariya was responsible for the breakdown, which was then accelerated by the events of postwar depression and reform.

After the late 1940s a new and unprecedented array of political forces arose. On one end of the political spectrum was a group of conservative voters. They represented the old-line rulers, the business and agricultural communities, and the Toyota enterprise leaders. Ranged against them on the other end of the political spectrum were labor unions representing organized workers in the city's factories. They were joined on some occasions after 1955 by fractious farmers in the newly incorporated village areas. Undermined by social changes after the 1930s and postwar reforms in the 1940s, community solidarity gave way to an environment more fragmented socially and competitive politically than any before in Kariya's history.

A new phase of change began in the 1950s which brought the period of radical politics to an end. Chapter 7 illustrated how, after the early 1950s, the Toyota enterprise adopted a new political posture in the community. Abandoning its old practice of covert operation, the enterprise threw itself into local politics through the efforts of Ishida Taizō. Ishida's purpose was simple: to make local government responsive to big business. To achieve his ends, Ishida had to reduce the influence of progressive unions in the city by forcing workers in the Toyota enterprise to conform with his political desires. By instituting a new system of labor relations in the enterprise, he eventually secured their compliance. Takada Ichirō's victory as mayor in 1959 symbolized Toyota's success. Owing his position to Ishida's influence and to electoral support from Toyota workers, Takada worked obediently to guarantee government's service to industry. The city of Kariya remained divided into a complex of contending political groups. But it witnessed a remarkable intervention by the Toyota enterprise which shifted the balance of power strongly in favor of a conservative coalition supporting local industry. Most of the city's organized industrial workers were an indispensable part of that coalition.

Thus, at the end of the century, the distribution of power in the community assumed a complex, constantly shifting form. The dominant single force in local politics was the Toyota enterprise. Relying on the electoral strength of perhaps as many as three in four of its workers, who acted in concert with management's wishes, the enterprise exercised pervasive influence over the city's political life. Several thousand organized workers employed in manufacturing and transportation made up another important force in local politics. They maintained a political position independent of the Toyota bloc, despite the fact that some of them worked in Toyota firms. By judiciously aligning with others, this group was sometimes able to determine issues in local politics. A third force—the largest numerically—was a body of conservative voters whose loyalties lay with the Liberal Democratic Party. Some Toyota enterprise workers, perhaps 10 to 15 percent of the total, were a part of this group, but they were a minority among the farmers from the old village areas and the businessmen from the old town area who comprised its majority. Finally, there were many unstable groups of political participants made up of those who worked in small factories or in commercial or service establishments. These groups sprang up suddenly, and disappeared just as quickly, in accord with the fate of minority parties such as the Japan Community Party and the Clean Government Party. By 1972 these four groups formed coalitions so casually that it was often impossible to predict how any electoral campaign or political issue in the city would be resolved. Only one thing was certain. A large minority in the community was disposed to cater to the wishes of the Toyota enterprise.[3]

This review of the structure of community power in Kariya between 1872 and 1972 has identified three major periods in the community's history. The first, stretching from the mid-nineteenth century into the 1940s, was a period during which leaders from prestigious local families dominated a community characterized by its solidarity. Between 1946 and 1959 Kariya's political system underwent substantial change. Organized industrial laborers became a considerable political force and injected a note of radicalism in local politics. More importantly, they fragmented the distribution of power in the community, ending a long period of consensual behavior. A third and final period of political change in Kariya began in the 1950s and continued into the 1970s. In this period an ever more complex distribution of power emerged. Its central feature was the predominance of the Toyota enterprise in local politics. Toyota's ascendancy took place because its leading manager assumed a direct role in local affairs, and because organized workers gave their enterprise the electoral support needed to buttress its position. Despite its power, however, Toyota was not always able to dictate the course of local events, as Miyata's election to the mayoralty in 1967 attested.

Preceding chapters have viewed Kariya's political evolution alongside

[3] One of the shortcomings of this book is its inability to deal in any depth with issues in local politics in the postwar period. The lack of salient issues of community-wide importance, and of adequate data to analyze them, has forced this study to deal primarily with electoral politics. Future research on Japanese communities would profit by empirical investigation of the decision-making process—both formal and informal—in local politics.

the history of several Japanese cities, but it would be valuable to assess changes in the structure of community power in Kariya in the broader light of an international comparison. The availability of data on power structures in American communities readily facilitates this task. One of the seminal works in the field, Robert Dahl's study of New Haven, Connecticut, has already been mentioned. There are numerous others.[4] Surprisingly, in view of their number, few of these works were written in a historical context; most were synchronic studies examining the distribution of power at a single point in time. There is one notable exception to this rule, however, which provides a fitting case for comparison.

Robert O. Schulze has investigated historical changes in the structure of community power in the city of "Cibola." Actually the industrial community of Ypsilanti, Michigan, that city was a center for the manufacture of auto products when Schulze undertook his study in the 1950s. It had a population of about twenty thousand, and most of its factories were large ones affiliated with General Motors. Bearing several features in common with Kariya, Ypsilanti provides an excellent case-study against which to compare the uniqueness of Kariya's history.[5]

Schulze developed the following set of hypotheses to describe the evolution of a community power structure. He felt that in isolated, self-contained communities, the power structure "tends to be monolithic, that is, that the persons who have greatest power in its economic system tend to be the same persons who have greatest power in its socio-political system." As such a community industrializes and urbanizes, "the local community loses control over its economic system." This occurs as outside firms buy old local firms, which then become a part of a regional or national organization managed from outside the community. The new managers, mobile executives in a giant corporation, take little interest in local affairs because they are economic specialists who do not identify with the local community. At this point, the community adopts what Schulze calls a "new localism." A new breed of community leader appears "who refers most of his behavior to local community groups, who has developed a wide core of local interpersonal and organizational relationships, and who maintains a sustained and active interest in local community affairs." The upshot of this development is a "bifurcation of power" in the community, characterized by "ever-widening social, psychological, and physical distances" between new local leaders (who tend to be small businessmen) and economic dominants (executives in the largest firms).

---

[4] A recent bibliography is Willis D. Hawley and James H. Svara, ed., *The Study of Community Power* (Santa Barbara, California, 1972).

[5] Schulze's findings appear in two publications: "The Role of Economic Dominants in Community Power Structure," *American Sociological Review* 23:1 (February 1958), pp. 3–9; and "The Bifurcation of Power in a Satellite City," in Morris Janowitz, ed., *Community Political Systems* (Glencoe, Ill., 1961), pp. 19–80 (hereafter abbreviated as "Bifurcation").

Schulze suggests that in the wake of bifurcation "a considerable measure of autonomy would accrue to the public leaders in the initiation and direction of community action." [6]

The events of Kariya's history affirm many of Schulze's hypotheses. First, during the period in which Kariya was an isolated, self-contained community the power structure was "monolithic," as foregoing discussions of rule by old-line families indicated. Second, Kariya did lose local control over its economic system as industrialization progressed, due to the closed nature of ownership and direction in the Toyota enterprise. Third, Miyata Ichimatsu represented what Schulze terms "the new local leader." He was a community native with a "wide core of local interpersonal and organizational relationships" in youth groups, the PTA, and neighborhood affairs. He was also a small businessman who was somewhat distant from the leaders of the Toyota enterprise. While they generally belonged to the Rotary Club, Miyata was only a member of the less prestigious Lions Club. Finally, one could see in Miyata's election to the mayoralty some marks of "autonomy" which Schulze felt would accrue to a community if its economic dominants divorced themselves from local politics. In these four important ways, the structure of community power in Kariya changed in a manner comparable to Ypsilanti.

However, in other important ways Kariya's experiences diverged from those in Ypsilanti. Most significantly, unlike executives in American communities, business managers in Kariya did not divorce themselves from local affairs as the community urbanized and industrialized. Instead, they threw themselves into local politics with vigor, installing local officials who were sympathetic and obedient to their wishes. They did not possess a greater sense of civic duty or community responsibility than their American counterparts. On the contrary, their motives were the same as those of managers in Ypsilanti: to maximize business opportunity. Ypsilanti managers felt they did that by avoiding participation in local politics, thus preventing the company from making enemies and thereby contributing to its economic success. Ishida Taizō, on the other hand, believed he would maximize Toyota's economic opportunities by doing the opposite, by actively engaging in local politics. In summary, therefore, industrialists in Kariya maintained a far more overt interest in local politics than economic dominants in Ypsilanti did.

Five reasons help to explain the distinctions between Ypsilanti's political history and that of Kariya. One of the most important is the sequence of economic change. When Ishida Taizō intervened in Kariya politics in the mid-1950s, the Toyota enterprise was undergoing the most rapid expansion in its history. It was building new factories and drawing thousands of

[6] Quotations are from Schulze, "Bifurcation," pp. 21–23.

new workers to Kariya annually. Managers felt cooperation from local government was essential if corporate expansion were to continue apace. The enterprise could not grow if provision of schools, roads, sewer lines, etc., lagged too far behind. Convinced that Socialist-influenced governments could not do the necessary job, Ishida and other economic dominants in Kariya threw themselves actively into local politics to insure the election of conservative mayors.

It is noteworthy that bifurcation occurred in Ypsilanti when economic growth in the community had levelled off. By the 1940s industrial concerns in Ypsilanti were mature business organizations which were being absorbed by large, outside corporations. After consolidation, local firms did not expand. Rather, they underwent an organizational change as they were drawn into a larger, nationwide network of production. That network grew during the 1940s and 1950s, but growth bypassed Ypsilanti as the corporate center established new productive facilities in faster-growing areas of the United States. Economic dominants in Ypsilanti, therefore, did not confront the same need for local cooperation which Kariya dominants did in the 1950s, and their political behavior was markedly different as a result.

Corporate absenteeism is a second factor accounting for distinctions in the political history of Ypsilanti and Kariya. There was a clear difference between the two cities on this count. By the 1940s the largest manufacturing concerns in Ypsilanti were part of a giant auto firm headquartered in a nearby city. As ownership of the city's largest firms passed into the hands of outsiders, a gap emerged between non-resident managers and owners and hometown businessmen and professionals. Schulze refers to this as bifurcation. The industrial managers lived outside the city and eschewed participation in local affairs. They failed to establish the close ties with local bankers, businessmen, and professionals which had promoted interlocking directorships and a close identity with community progress during an earlier period in Ypsilanti's history. As a result, economic dominants came to view Ypsilanti as merely a factory site. They did not view it as a community in whose progress they should participate.

Kariya, on the other hand, was headquarters for four of the seven large Toyota factories in the city. Rather than fret about living in a rustic rural city, Toyota managers were proud to be with their "company in the boondocks" (*inaka zaibatsu*) and did not hesitate to live in Kariya. This brought them into intimate contact with the community. As leading citizens, they were quite apt to be drawn into local disputes, as Ishida was drawn into the school crisis in the 1950s. Having once participated in a public controversy, Ishida's restraint quickly broke down. By the mid-1950s he was taking an active interest in local politics.

Toyota managers did not always play an overt role in local politics.

Both before the 1950s and after 1967, economic dominants in the Toyota enterprise avoided overt political participation in Kariya. It is significant that in both those periods the central figures in the enterprise lived outside Kariya. Toyota Sakichi and his two sons, Risaburō and Kiichirō, all lived in Nagoya (or China) during the years before 1950 when they led the company. Toyota Eiji, the leading figure in the auto firm after Ishida withdrew in the late 1960s, lived in the neighboring city of Toyota. These observations endorse the critical importance which absenteeism plays in determining the political behavior of economic dominants.

A third factor which accounts for distinctions in behavior between economic dominants in Ypsilanti and Kariya is differing career patterns in American and Japanese corporations. Executives in American firms tend to be quite mobile. They often win promotions in the form of transfers to other offices in a far-flung national enterprise. Thus, for many industrial managers in Ypsilanti, their assignment in the city was just a brief stopping point on the road to a better job elsewhere. They felt their task was to keep things running smoothly, and, above all else, to avoid a controversy which might taint their personal careers. This clearly bred what might be termed excessive timidity on their part. They looked almost with horror on involvement in a conflict which threatened to stain their reputations or endanger promotion. The American career pattern thus fostered constraint among economic dominants in Ypsilanti which caused them to shrink from participation in local affairs.

The Japanese career pattern was markedly different. As chapter 7 indicated, Toyota executives nearly always joined the enterprise on graduation from college and remained until their retirement. Since virtually all the factories and offices in the concern were located in western Mikawa, they usually settled in a town near their work and expected to remain there for the rest of their professional career. This undoubtedly bred a different attitude toward community participation than that held by their American counterparts. It made them realize they would have to deal with the local community, because they would be a part of it for thirty years or more. Consequently, economic dominants from the large Toyota firms were active members of local social organizations, such as the Rotary Club and the Chamber of Commerce, and some eventually became political activists as well.

A fourth factor which promoted differences between Ypsilanti and Kariya was the structure of industrial organization. Ypsilanti was the site of small manufacturing concerns which had become subcontractors for a nationwide corporation. In the context of the corporation, Ypsilanti was simply another factory site, and a modest one at that. It was no more than a dot on a corporate map which spanned the country with its factories, personnel, and operations. Consequently, Ypsilanti did not deserve significant attention from either the corporation or its managers. It was a minor part of a giant organization and far less important than corporate offices in Detroit and New York or assembly plants in Michigan and California.

The structure of industry in Kariya was entirely different. All production facilities in the Toyota concern were heavily concentrated in western Mikawa. Perhaps that was due to economies of scale achieved by producing in a single location. Perhaps it was sensible in a concern which exported a third of its output. Whatever the reason, the Toyota enterprise was deeply entrenched in Toyota and Kariya. In Kariya alone there were seven large factories. Most of them encompassed both production facilities and corporate offices on the same site. Corporate executives were already disposed by the economic needs of the enterprise, their place of residence, and their career patterns to play a role in community affairs. The concentration of the Toyota enterprise in Kariya reinforced that tendency.

Different conceptions of corporate imagery provide a fifth and final explanation for the behavior of economic dominants in Ypsilanti and Kariya. Ypsilanti executives liked to think of themselves as part of a corporation which was trying to be a good neighbor. The corporation was just another house on the street, perhaps a bit larger than the others, but certainly not intending any ill will as a result. It just wanted to avoid making trouble, or exposing dirty linen. It would be glad to help if anyone needed assistance, of course, but for the most part it would prefer to go quietly about its own affairs. The tense, hands-off attitude which Ypsilanti's economic dominants adopted toward community affairs derived in part from the image their corporation wished to project.

If the "good neighbor" label identifies corporate imagery in Ypsilanti, the metaphor of paternalism describes its Japanese equivalent in Kariya. The rather plutocratic *noblesse oblige* which lay behind Ishida Taizō's participation in Kariya politics stemmed from three sources. It was first a product of Ishida's personality. He was a brash man who liked to take command. Second, paternalism aimed at the community was in part a product of self-confidence nurtured by the unprecedented importance which the industrial community assumed in Japan in the 1950s. Ishida's attitudes, in fact, were somewhat reminiscent of the plutocrats of America's nineteenth-century business community, a group in which he might have found hearty fellowship. Finally, the Toyota enterprise had long behaved paternalistically toward its employees. It was inevitable that such paternalism would eventually project itself on the community, too.

These five factors are by no means exhaustive, but they help to explain why Kariya's economic dominants played an overt role in local politics which differed so much from that played by their counterparts in Ypsilanti. It is essential to realize, however, that in important ways

Kariya's economic dominants relied on proxy representatives to implement their power. Ishida Taizō *did* personally mediate local school disputes, campaign for his candidates, and negotiate for the technical high school. But he never stood for office himself. Instead, he relied on Takada Ichirō, Fujii Seihichi, and others like them to assume formal office as Toyota's political servants.

Takada and Fujii could win office for the crucial reason that most organized workers in the Toyota enterprise supported the political views of their managerial superiors. Had those workers not done so, had they pursued the oppositionary stance which they adopted briefly in the decade after the war, Kariya's political history would have followed a much different course. To fully explain, therefore, how Kariya's economic dominants were able to capture power in the community and exercise it for the benefit of the Toyota enterprise, it is essential to understand why organized workers in the community behaved politically as they did.

An explanation for their political behavior rests importantly on the role of Kariya's—and Japan's—heritage of social values. The term is used in a special sense. It does not mean "traditional values," as that phrase is so loosely used. Rather, the heritage of social values refers to a pattern of attitudes shaped by historical events. The patterns are often molded by the values indigenous to a society. To the extent that indigenous values have a decisive influence on forming the heritage, it has persistent features, but not *static* features as "traditional values" tend to have. The heritage of social values is also shaped by the timing and quality of particular events, so it is a dynamic phenomenon. It is subject to constant change which is dictated by events but constrained by indigenous values.

The heritage of social values has had a critical influence on Japan's modern history, a statement true of virtually all spheres of life. In fact, much of the recent literature on Japan deals either directly or indirectly with the problem of continuity and change which is implicit in the definition of this concept. One subject which has received considerable attention from this perspective is Japan's system of industrial relations.[7]

The most penetrating and original study of Japan's labor practices is Dore's comparison of electrical factories in Britain and Japan. Dore asserts that Britain and Japan have nationally diverse labor systems. He characterizes the former as market-oriented; the latter, as organization-oriented. British workers find employment by responding to market opportunities, shifting jobs as new openings at better pay crop up. By contrast, Japanese workers (in large firms) seek ties with organizations which retain them for life, paying increased salaries as seniority accrues.

[7] Three major works are James Abegglen, *The Japanese Factory* (Glencoe, Ill., 1958); Robert E. Cole, *Japanese Blue Collar* (Berkeley, 1971); and Ronald Dore, *British Factory—Japanese Factory* (Berkeley, 1973).

On these basic distinctions rest industrial relations systems which are unique to each country.

The following pages illustrate how national diversity characterizes the auto industries of Britain, the United States, and Japan, and how such diversity has affected the political behavior of organized auto workers in the three countries. The purpose of these comments is to explain the comparative significance of worker behavior in Kariya in order to round out this analysis of its political history.

By the 1960s the automobile industries in Britain, the United States, and Japan were structurally quite similar. Put briefly, auto firms were big and few. In Britain two major firms produced about 70 percent of all autos. In the United States four major firms dominated the market, with the two largest producing about 70 percent of the total. In Japan, also, two giant firms produced approximately 70 percent of all autos in the late 1960s. In short, the auto industries of all three countries were structured in a common fashion. They also operated on the basis of a similar technology.[8]

Despite these similarities, there were marked differences in the auto industries of the three countries. In each country union structures and worker behavior differed noticeably. Wage bargaining practices, strike activity, and political preferences were just three areas conspicuously lacking in uniformity, as the following comments reveal.

Workers in the British auto industry, like British workers in general, belonged to a multi-union structure of organization. In a given enterprise, it was common to find the work force divided among three or more unions. In 1965 three major unions embraced 86 percent of all organized auto workers in Britain, but no single union had a membership surpassing 35 percent of the total.[9] In the United States, by contrast, virtually all auto workers (over 90 percent) belonged to a single international union popularly known as the United Auto Workers (UAW). Finally, most Japanese automobile workers were organized in two national unions, one focused on the Toyota enterprise and the other on the Nissan enterprise. Despite a common structure of auto production, union organization in the three countries diverged considerably.

Reflecting this diversity was a significant difference in labor practices. Patterns of wage bargaining offer one illustration. The complex, multi-

[8] For the British auto industry see: H. A. Turner, et. al., *Labour Relations in the Motor Industry* (London, 1967); B. C. Roberts, ed., *Industrial Relations,* rev. ed. (London, 1968); and John H. Goldthorpe, et al., *The Affluent Worker* (Cambridge, 1968). For the American auto industry see: John B. Rae, *American Automobile Manufacturers* (Philadelphia, 1959); Keith Sward, *The Legend of Henry Ford* (New York, 1972); Wyndham Mortimer, *Organize!* (Boston, 1971); Ely Chinoy, *Automobile Workers and the American Dream* (Garden City, N.Y., 1955); and Bennett Berger, *Working-Class Suburb* (Berkeley, 1960).

[9] Turner, p. 195.

union structure of British auto firms placed great power in the hands of shop stewards who were chiefly responsible for basic problems at the workplace. Since meaningful wage agreements occurred on that level, the unions which engaged in wage bargaining at the enterprise or national level exerted relatively little influence on the wage determination process. American practice differed almost diametrically from British. In the United States one large union determined wages in negotiations conducted at the national level with each major firm. These agreements were subject to adjustment at the local level, but they exerted the decisive influence on wage rates. In Japan yet another pattern prevailed. Bargaining there took place between two major unions and their respective employers in two geographically-focused enterprises. Auto workers at Toyota negotiated with their firm in the Aichi area; Nissan workers with theirs in the Yokohama region.

As a result of these different patterns of wage bargaining, workers in each country adopted different views of their employers. The British worker found his wages determined by rates prevailing in a local market and depended on shop stewards, not union officials, to secure satisfactory compensation. He perceived the bargaining process as an intense competition between workers on one hand and their implacable adversary—the management—on the other. American workers, by contrast, relied on leaders who had organized one of the most effective unions in the country. UAW leaders and auto company executives both sought to foster an image of competitive bargaining, but behind the facade a "civilized relationship" developed between the two parties.[10] It led to rising material rewards for workers and fostered a climate of cooperation between the union and the companies on economic issues, although not on political issues. Still another orientation toward one's firm developed among Japanese workers. Since their wage rates depended on the financial condition of their enterprise, and less on prevailing local, industrial, or national rates, they felt constrained to shape their demands to the company's ability to respond. This produced an unusually strong identity of interest between workers and their employers.

These labor practices resulted in different levels of worker activism among the three countries. British workers were the most strike-prone. One observer attributed this to "a failure of organizations—trade unions, employers' associations and management structures—to accommodate themselves." [11] The institutional complexity of the British system made it difficult to respond to worker expectations and to resolve labor conflict. By comparison with their British counterparts, American auto workers were far less strike-prone, especially after the difficult years of organization drew

[10] See William Serrin, *The Company and the Union* (New York, 1973).
[11] Turner, p. 356.

to an end around 1950. Major strike activity in the American auto industry coincided with periods of contract re-negotiation and was regulated by pattern-bargaining in a highly centralized system.[12] Following the activist days of the early 1950s, Japan's auto workers became unusually passive in their strike behavior as they reaped material rewards from rapidly expanding enterprises. They were the most cooperative auto workers among the three countries. Any complete explanation for these differences would require consideration of many factors, but one claim seems warranted. Worker dissidence was a function of labor relations systems unique to each country. These created organizational patterns that led workers to perceive their employers in divergent ways, and to modulate their behavior accordingly.

To express their political demands, auto workers in the three countries affiliated with political parties which represented the interests of organized workers. The Labor Party in Britain gave voice to the political demands of the English auto worker. It was a party created by the labor movement to serve its purposes. In the United States auto workers lent their political support to the Democratic Party, which was an important—but not the exclusive—political instrument of organized labor. Auto workers and their union leaders were faithful Democrats because the party had aided their organizational efforts during the 1930s and because many auto workers were from the South, where support of the Democratic Party was a family tradition. In both Britain and the United States, therefore, auto workers had formal, enduring ties to political parties which represented organized labor.

Japanese auto workers also supported parties which represented the laboring classes. But there was a marked difference in the history and durability of the bonds between Japan's Socialist parties and organized auto workers. The history of the bond in 1972 stretched back only a quarter-century, less than in either Britain or the United States. Moreover, the bond was hardly durable. When unions first organized after the war, auto workers affiliated with leftist elements in the Japan Socialist Party. Their ties were short-lived, however. Within less than a decade organized auto workers dissolved their national union and cut their ties with the JSP.

In the wake of those changes, auto workers in Japan adopted flexible political ties. As chapter 7 illustrated, workers in the Toyota enterprise eventually reorganized a union which had no affiliation with a national center. The union assumed a local, enterprise-oriented posture and mobilized its membership politically in numerous ways. For many years it supported a candidate for the Japan Socialist Party in Diet elections. But

[12] Ibid., pp. 295–306.

at the same time it often threw its electoral support behind conservative candidates for the prefectural assembly or for the mayoralty. Underlying support of conservative local candidates was a tacit—but tangible—acceptance of the guidance of corporate managers. By the late 1960s worker acceptance of managerial guidance took concrete form in the *jiban* of Watanabe Takezō. His was an electoral base tied politically to a rather conservative Democratic Socialist Party and founded on the unity of workers and managers in the Toyota enterprise.

As a consequence of their party affiliations, auto workers in Britain and the United States usually found themselves in political opposition to their employers and managers. At national and local levels, they supported parties whose political goals were directed toward the benefit of organized workers, in competition with the parties which owners and managers tended to support.

The political economy of Japan's auto industry was notably different. As this study has demonstrated, workers and managers alike supported the same candidates to achieve common political goals. In Kariya the tendency could be traced as far back as 1955, when Fujii Seihichi won votes from Kariya's industrial workers to gain a seat in the prefectural assembly. In subsequent years workers and managers provided the indispensable electoral support for mayors (in both Kariya and Toyota cities) and, in 1969 and 1972, for a Diet member from the Fourth District. Kariya's political history thus evidenced not competition between organized workers and industrial managers but unity and cooperation which extended well beyond the production process deeply into the political arena.

This pattern of political behavior derived in large part from a heritage of social values. Shaping those values were attitudes indigenous to Japanese society, especially deference to superiors and in-group solidarity. Workers in Kariya had demonstrated such values clearly in the prewar period. Their cooperativeness was a mark of deference to their managerial superiors in the Toyota enterprise. It also signified their acceptance of the claim that the enterprise was a "family-like" collectivity in which the individual benefitted by working for the good of the group.

Events in the period immediately after World War II severely tested worker allegiance to those values. Depressed economic conditions created a climate in which material rewards did not match worker expectations. As a result of such conditions management carried out sometimes arbitrary acts which sparked worker unrest and provoked disavowal of customary behavior. For several years workers assumed an unusually contentious attitude in both their economic struggles and their political activities. But there was always resistance to such activism from some in the labor force who remained loyal to the values of deference and familism.

The persistent loyalty of those workers encouraged managers in the Toyota enterprise to find inducements that would expand and deepen support for indigenous values. They strived to create an organizational environment in which such values could flourish. Chapter 7 described the nature of their efforts. Managers were aided in their task by a virtually continuous period of economic prosperity which provided real affluence for many industrial workers. Amidst their prosperity, workers accepted anew the claim that deference to managerial policies and loyalty to corporate goals would benefit them more than contention. They accommodated themselves to a corporate structure which promised comfortable wage increases and guaranteed job security. They also adopted a pattern of union organization which assured stability for that corporate order, if it did not indeed foster its growth.

By the 1960s most organized industrial workers in Kariya had thus reverted to a pattern of behavior reminiscent of the prewar era. They did so in a social environment substantially different from that of the 1930s, and for reasons based on shrewd economic calculations. But the key point in this: industrial workers in Kariya adopted a pattern of behavior which was congenial to their heritage of social values. It secured their aspirations for material reward and conformed with the indigenous values of deference and in-group solidarity. Those values, operating in an era of economic prosperity, helped to produce a vertically integrated economic organization and political bloc which was distinctive among industrialized societies.

The findings of this book require no further elaboration. Simply put, modern societies are not converging. The social and political consequences of industrialization are not characterized by their predictable uniformity. Rather, they are notable for their diversity. Citizens in industrial societies may share common goals, but they strive to achieve them in cultural settings where values, events, and institutions mediate human behavior in unique ways. The history of Kariya is one case which illustrates the remarkably distinctive social and political consequences to which Japan's industrialization has given rise.

BIBLIOGRAPHY

With the exception of titles published in Kyoto and Tokyo, all Japanese works in this bibliography were published in Aichi Prefecture. For a critically annotated bibliography of sources available for the study of Japanese urban history, the reader should refer to: Gary D. Allinson. "Modern Japan: A New Social History." Historical Methods Newsletter 6:3 (June 1973), pp. 100–110.

JAPANESE SOURCES

Adachi Muneharu. *Aichi ken Kariya chūgakkō kaikō jisshūnen kinen* [Tenth Anniversary of the Opening of the Kariya Middle School]. Kariya, 1928.

Aichi ken. *Aichi ken shi* [A History of Aichi Prefecture]. 4 vols. Nagoya, 1938–1939.

———. *Aichi ken tōkei gaihyō* [Statistical Outline of Aichi Prefecture]. 7 vols. Nagoya, 1877–1883.

———. *Aichi ken tōkei nenkan* [Statistical Annual of Aichi Prefecture]. 23 vols. Nagoya, 1950–1972.

———. *Aichi ken tōkei sho* [Statistical Handbook of Aichi Prefecture]. 51 vols. Nagoya, 1884–1893, 1907–1942, and 1946–1949.

Aichi ken, Hazu gun nōkai, ed. *Aichi ken, Hazu gun, Nishinomachi mura sonze* [Village Conditions in Nishinomachi, Hazu County, Aichi Prefecture]. Nishio, 1903.

Aichi ken, Kariya shi. *Kariya no jinkō* [Kariya's Population]. Kariya, 1970.

———. *Kariya shi sōgō keikaku: 1968–1977* [Comprehensive City Plan for Kariya: 1968–1977]. Kariya, n.d.

Aichi ken, keikaku ka. "Kōgyōka ni tomonau chiiki shakai no keizaiteki shakaiteki hendō ni kansuru chōsa: Nairiku kōgyō chitai to shite no Kariya shi" [Survey of the economic and social changes attending industrialization in a local community: Kariya, an inland industrial area]. Nagoya, 1966.

Aichi ken, keisatsu bu, kōba ka. *Aichi ken kōba yōran* [Factory Manual for Aichi Prefecture]. Nagoya, 1933.

Aichi ken, Nukata gun, Fujikawa sonze chōsa [Survey of Village Conditions in Fujikawa, Nukata County, Aichi Prefecture]. n.p., 1902.

Aichi ken, rōdō bu, rōsei ka. *Rōdō kumiai meibo* [List of Labor Unions]. Nagoya, 1954.

———. *Aichi ken rōdō undō nempyō (kō):1945–1950* [Chronology of the Aichi Labor Movement (Draft): 1945–1950]. Nagoya, 1963.

———. *Aichi ken rōdō undō nempyō: 1951–1960.* Nagoya, 1964.

Aichi ken, sangyō bu. *Aichi ken fukugyō jōtai chōsa* [Survey of Agricultural By-employments in Aichi Prefecture]. Nagoya, 1923.

263

Aichi ken, sōmu bu. *Shichōson tōkei ichiran* [Outline of Village, Town, and City Statistics]. Nagoya, 1938.

Aichi ken chihō rōdō iinkai, ed. *Aichi ken rōdō nempō* [Annual Report on Aichi Labor]. Nagoya, 1959.

Aichi ken gikai jimu kyoku, ed. *Aichi ken gikai shi* [History of the Aichi Prefectural Assembly]. 7 vols. Nagoya, 1953–1973.

Aichi ken Kariya kōtō jogakkō. *Kinen shashin chō* [Commemorative Photo Album, Kariya Higher Girls' School]. Nagoya, 1924.

Aichi ken keizai kenkyūjo. "Tōkai chiku ni okeru jidōsha buhin kōgyō no kōzō henka to zaihensei" [Structural Change and Reorganization in the Automobile Parts Industries of the Tōkai Area]. Nagoya, 1966.

Aichi ken Kinugaura chiku tōkei kenkyū kai, ed. *Kinugaura no tōkei* [Statistics of the Kinugaura Bay Area]. no. 4., n.p., 1972.

Aichi ken kyōiku kai. *Aichi ken ijin den* [Biographies of Eminent Aichi Personalities]. Nagoya, 1934.

Aichi ken nōkai. *Aichi ken dokuannai* [Self-guide to Aichi Prefecture]. Nagoya, 1899.

————. *Aichi ken no fukugyō* [By-employments in Aichi Prefecture]. Nagoya, 1920.

Aichi ken shōhin chinretsu kan. *Aichi ken shōkōgyō tōkei* [Commercial and Industrial Statistics for Aichi Prefecture]. Nagoya, 1915.

Aichi ken senkyo kanri iinkai, ed. *Aichi no senkyo 20-nen* [20 years of Aichi Elections]. 2 vols. Nagoya, 1965–1966.

————. *Aichi ken senkyo kiroku: 1966–1967* [Aichi Election Returns: 1966–1967]. Nagoya, 1967.

————. *Aichi ken senkyo kiroku: 1969* [Aichi Election Returns: 1969]. Nagoya, 1970.

————. *Aichi ken senkyo kiroku: 1970–1971* [Aichi Election Returns: 1970–1971]. Nagoya, 1972.

Anjō shi shi hensan iinkai, ed. *Anjō shi shi* [History of the City of Anjō]. Anjō, 1971.

Arisaka Takamichi, and Fujimoto Atsushi. *Chihōshi no kenkyū to henshū: tsuketari zenkoku chihō shishi mokuroku* [Research and Compilation of Local History, with an Index to Local Histories in Japan]. Kyoto, 1968.

Asahi shimbun [Asahi News] (Nagoya). 1960–1972.

Asahi shimbun sha, ed. *Shiryō Meiji hyakunen* [Historical Documents of the 100 Years since Meiji]. Tokyo, 1966.

Chihōshi kenkyū kyōgikai, ed. *Nihon no machi: Sono rekishiteki kōzō* [Japanese Towns: Their Historical Structure]. Tokyo, 1958.

————. *Nihon no machi: Bakumatsu-Meijiki ni okeru toshi to nōson* [Japanese Towns: City and Village in the Late Tokugawa and the Meiji Periods]. Tokyo, 1961.

————. *Nihon sangyōshi taikei* [An Outline of Japan's Industrial History] 8 vols. Tokyo, 1959–1961.

Chōjō Tomichika, ed. *Aichi ken shichōson jinshi roku* [Biographical Dictionary of Eminent Local Figures in Aichi Prefecture]. Nagoya, 1929.

Chūbu keizai shimbun [Chūbu Economic Journal] (Nagoya). 1958–1972.

Chūkyō shimpō [Chūkyō News] (Nagoya). 1899–1905.

Chūnichi shimbun [Chūnichi News] (Nagoya). 1945–1972.

Fujita Keizō. *Nihon sangyō kōzō to chūshō kigyō* [The Japanese Industrial Structure and Small and Medium Enterprises]. Tokyo, 1965.

Fukutake Tadashi, ed. *Gappei chōson no jittai* [Actual Conditions in an Amalgamated Community]. Tokyo, 1958.

Furushima Toshio. *Chihōshi kenkyūhō* [Research Methods in Local History]. Tokyo, 1955.

Handa shi. *Handa shi shi* [History of the City of Handa]. 3 vols. Handa, 1969–1972.

Hayashi Hideo. "Kinsei makki ni okeru Bisai men orimono no hatten katei" [The Development of Cotton Weaving in the Bisai Region during the Late Tokugawa Period]. *Shakai keizai shigaku* 22: 5 and 6 (April 1956), pp. 44-74.

Hayashi Tōichi. *Nagoya shōnin shi* [A History of Nagoya Merchants]. Nagoya, 1966.

Hosoi Wakizō. *Jokō aishi* [The Sorrowful History of Textile Operatives]. 1925. Reprint. Tokyo, 1954.

Ikeda Masaji. *Saigō no daibantō: Ishida Taizō no sekai* [The Last Manager: The World of Ishida Taizō]. Tokyo, 1971.

Ishida Taizō. *Jibun no shiro wa jibun de mamore* [Protect Your Castle!]. Tokyo, 1968.

————. *Jinsei shōbu ni ikiru* [Living for Life's Challenges]. Tokyo, 1961.

Itō Gōhei. *Chihō toshi no kenkyū: Atarashii Toyohashi* [Studies of a Local City: The New Toyohashi]. Tokyo, 1955.

Itō Jissei. *Toyota ke no shinwa* [Myths of the Toyota House]. Tokyo, 1972.

Iwanami shoten, ed. *Kindai Nihon sōgō nempyō* [Comprehensive Chronology of Modern Japan]. Tokyo, 1968.

Jinji kōshin sha. *Zen Nihon shinshi roku* [Who's Who in Japan]. 10 vols. to date. Tokyo, 1951– .

Jinji kōshinsho, ed. *Jinji kōshin roku* [A Who's Who Directory]. 38 vols. to date. Tokyo, 1903– .

Jisshūnen kinenshi henshū iinkai. *Rōdō kumiai sōritsu jisshūnen kinen shi* [Commemorative History of the First Decade of the Labor Union at Toyota Motors]. Okazaki, 1956.

Kajinishi Mitsuhaya. *Toyota Sakichi* [Toyota Sakichi]. Tokyo, 1962.

Kariya chō shi [History of the Town of Kariya]. Kariya, 1894.

Kariya machiyakuba. *Kariya chō shi* [History of the Town of Kariya]. Kariya, 1932.

Kariya Rotary Club. *Jūgonen no ayumi* [Fifteen Years' Progress]. Kariya, 1969.

Kariya seinen kaigisho. *Akarui yutaka na Kariya shi no tame ni* [For a Brighter, Richer Kariya]. Kariya, 1967.

————. *Kaiin meibo: 1970* [Junior Chamber of Commerce Membership List: 1970]. Kariya, 1970.

————. *Rōdō jittai chōsa* [Survey of Actual Labor Conditions]. Kariya, 1965.

Kariya shiyakusho. *Kariya shi shi* [History of the City of Kariya]. Kariya, 1960.

————. *Kariya shisei yōran* [A Survey of Kariya City Conditions]. 23 vols. Kariya, 1950–1972.

Kariya shōkō kaigisho. *Kaiin meibo* [Chamber of Commerce Membership List]. 6 vols. Kariya, 1947–1972.

Katō Bunzaburō. *Aru shōgai* [A Life]. Kariya, 1968.

Kichiji Shōichi. *Okada Kikujirō den* [Biography of Okada Kikujirō]. Anjō, 1954.

Kijō dōsō kai. *Sōritsu rokujisshūnen kinengō* [Sixtieth Anniversary Commemorative Issue, Kijō School]. Kariya, 1935.

————. *Sōritsu hachijisshūnen no kinenshi* [Eightieth Anniversary Commemorative Issue, Kijō School]. Kariya, 1953.

Kimura Hitoshi. *Ogasawara Sankurō sensei kaisō roku* [Recollections of Ogasawara Sankurō]. Nishio, 1967.

Kinenshi henshū iinkai, ed. *Aichi kenritsu Kariya kōgyō kōtō gakkō sōritsu goshūnen kinen shi* [Fifth Anniversary History of the Prefectural Higher Industrial School of Kariya]. Kariya, 1967.

Kōjunsha. *Nihon shinshi roku* [A Directory of Eminent Japanese]. 56 vols. to date. Tokyo, 1889–

Kōmei senkyo remmei, ed. *Shūgiin giin senkyo no jisseki* [Results of General Elections for the Lower House]. Tokyo, 1968.

Kumai Yasumasa. *Mikawa chimei jinshi roku* [A Biographical Dictionary of Eminent Mikawa Figures]. Tokyo, 1939.

Mainichi shimbun sha, ed. *Ikiru Toyota Sakichi* [The Living Toyota Sakichi]. Tokyo, 1971.

Meiji yōsui shishi hensan iinkai, ed. *Meiji yōsui* [The Meiji Canal]. 2 vols. Anjō, 1953.

Mikawa hyōron [The Mikawa Review] (Okazaki). 1960.

Miyoshi Shirō. "Nihon Denmaaku chitai nōgyō kōzō ron" [An Essay on the Structure of Agriculture in the Japan Denmark Area]. *Aichi daigaku chūbu chihō sangyō kenkyūjo kenkyū hōkoku*, no. 6. Toyohashi, 1961.

Mombushō. *Gakusei nanajūnen shi* [Seventy-year History of the Educational System]. Tokyo, 1942.

———. *Nihon teikoku mombushō daiyonjūkyū nempō* [Forty-ninth Annual Report of the Imperial Japanese Ministry of Education]. Tokyo, 1921.

Murase Masayuki. *Gaun Tatsuchi* [Gaun Tatsuchi]. Tokyo, 1965.

———. *Bakumatsu-Ishin no Kariya* [Kariya in the Late Edo and Early Meiji Periods]. Kariya, 1969.

Nagoya joseishi kenkyūkai, ed. *Haha no jidai: Aichi no joseishi* [Mother's Era: A History of Women in Aichi Prefecture]. Nagoya, 1969.

Naikaku tōkei kyoku. *Kokusei chōsa hōkoku: 1920, Aichi ken* [National Census Report: 1920, Aichi Prefecture]. Tokyo, 1925.

———. *Kokusei chōsa hōkoku: 1930, Aichi ken.* Tokyo, 1933.

———. *Kokusei chōsa hōkoku: 1935, Aichi ken.* Tokyo, 1937.

Nakamura Takafusa. *Senzenki Nihon keizai seichō no bunseki* [An Analysis of Economic Development in Prewar Japan]. Tokyo, 1971.

Nakane Chie. *Tate shakai no ningen kankei* [Human Relations in a Vertical Society]. Tokyo, 1967.

Nakashima Yokichi, ed. *Aichi ken, Hekikai gun, Hitotsuki sonze* [Village Conditions in Hitotsuki, Hekikai County, Aichi Prefecture]. Nagoya, 1906.

Nihon jimbun kagaku kai. *Gijitsu kakushin no shakaiteki eikyō* [The Social Effects of Technical Innovation]. Tokyo, 1963.

Nihon keizai shimbun sha, ed. *Watakushi no rireki sho* [My Vitae]. Tokyo, 1959.

Nijūnen shi henshū iinkai, ed. *Nijūnen no ayumi: Toyota jidōsha rōdō kumiai* [Twenty Years' Progress: Toyota Motor Company Labor Union]. Toyota, 1966.

Nippon Densō. *Nippon Densō jūgonen shi* [A History of Fifteen Years of Nippon Densō]. Kariya, 1964.

Nōgyō hattatsu shi chōsa kai, ed. *Nihon nōgyō hattatsu shi* [History of the Development of Japanese Agriculture]. 7 vols. Tokyo, 1955.

Nōshōmu shō, shōkō kyoku. *Shokkō jijō* [Conditions Among Factory Workers]. 1903. Reprint. Tokyo, 1967.

Nozaki Seiichi, ed. *Toyota shiki bōshoku kabushiki kaisha sōritsu 30-nen shi* [Thirtieth Anniversary History of the Toyota-style Spinning and Weaving Corporation]. Nagoya, 1936.

Ogasawara Sankurō. *Jiden: Jinsei wa mijikai* [Autobiography; Life Is Short]. 2 vols. Tokyo, 1967.

Okado Buhei. *Tōshi no ōkan: Ishida Taizō den* [Crown of Battle: The Biography of Ishida Taizō]. Nagoya, 1965.

Okamoto Tōjirō, ed. *Toyota bōshoku kabushiki kaisha shi* [History of the Toyota Spinning and Weaving Corporation]. Nagoya, 1953.

Ōkōchi Kazuo. *Sengo Nihon no rōdō undō* [Japan's Postwar Labor Movement]. rev. ed. Tokyo, 1961.

Okumura Sakae. "Toyota no hatten to Toyota shi" [Development of Toyota Motors and the City of Toyota]. *Toshi mondai kenkyū*, no. 186 (June 1966), pp. 54–70.

Ōkura shō. *Yūka shōken hōkokusho sōran* [A Compendia of Reports on Negotiable Securities]. Tokyo, various dates.

Ōno Ichizō. *Kariya to Ōno ke* [Kariya and the Ōno House]. Kariya, 1965.

———. *Kariya ga shi ni naru made no hatten shi* [A History of Kariya's Development Before It Became a City]. Kariya, 1955.

———. *Kiju ni mukaete watakushi no ashiato* [My Experiences on Approaching Seventy-seven]. Kariya, 1961.

———. *Toyota Risaburō kun to Kariya shi* [Toyota Risaburō and the City of Kariya]. Kariya, n.d.

Ōtsuka shigakkai, ed. *Shimpan kyōdoshi jiten* [Revised Dictionary of Local History]. Tokyo, 1969.

Ōtsuka Takematsu. *Hansei ichiran* [A Guide to Domain Administrations]. 2 vols. Tokyo, 1928.

Ozaki Masahisa. *Toyota Kiichirō shi* [A Biography of Toyota Kiichirō]. Tokyo, 1955.

Ozawa Yūrin. *Aichi ken shinshi roku* [A Biographical Dictionary of Eminent Men of Aichi Prefecture]. Nagoya, 1914.

Rōdō jōsei [Labor Conditions]. Library, Aichi kinrō kaikan, Nagoya. 1948–1957.

Rōdōshō, ed. *Shiryō rōdō undō shi: 1953* [Documentary History of the Labor Movement: 1953]. Tokyo, 1955.

———. *Shiryō rōdō undō shi: 1954*. Tokyo, 1955.

Sakamoto Shin'nosuke. *Kamiya Dembei* [Kamiya Dembei]. Tokyo, 1921.

Sakano Kenjirō, ed. *Aichi ken kaisha sōran* [Guide to Aichi Corporations]. Nagoya, 1935.

Sanage chō shi hensan iinkai, ed. *Sanage chō shi* [History of Sanage Town]. Toyota, 1968.

Sangyō kenkyūjo. *Watakushi no ayanda michi* [The Road I've Walked]. Tokyo, 1965.

Sawada Hisao. *Nihon naichi gaichi shichōson betsu jinkō* [Population of the Cities, Towns, and Villages of Japan and the Japanese Territories]. Tokyo, 1942.

Shashi hensan iinkai, ed. *Nagoya tetsudō shashi* [A History of the Nagoya Railroad Corporation]. Nagoya, 1961.

Shashi hensan iinkai, ed. *Toyota shatai nijūnen shi* [A Twenty-year History of the Toyota Chassis Company]. Kariya, 1965.

Shashi henshū iinkai, ed. *Aichi seikō sanjūnen shi* [A Thirty-year History of Aichi Steel]. Tōkai, 1970.

Shashi henshū iinkai, ed. *Toyota jidōsha 30-nen shi* [A History of 30 Years of Toyota Motors]. Toyota, 1967.

Shashi henshū iinkai, ed. *Toyota jidō shokki seisakusho 40-nen shi* [A History of 40 Years of the Toyota Automatic Loom Works]. Kariya, 1967.

Shirai Taishirō. *Kigyō betsu kumiai* [Enterprise Unions]. Tokyo, 1968.

Shūgiin jimu kyoku. *Shūgiin giin sōsenkyo ichiran* [Handbook of Lower House General Elections]. 30 vols. Tokyo, 1904–1973.

Sōrifu tōkei kyoku. *Kokusei chōsa hōkoku: 1955, Aichi ken* [National Census Reports: 1955, Aichi Prefecture]. Tokyo, 1958.

———. *Kokusei chōsa hōkoku: 1965, Aichi ken*. Tokyo, 1966.

———. *Kokusei chōsa hōkoku: 1970, Aichi ken*. Tokyo, 1972.

———. *Nihon no tōkei: 1967* [Statistics of Japan: 1967]. Tokyo, 1968.

Suzuki Kiyosetsu, ed. *Mikawa kensei shiryō* [Materials on Constitutional Government in Mikawa]. Nagoya, 1941.

Takayama Fukuyoshi, ed. *Kobayashi Kanae sensei* [Professor Kobayashi Kanae]. Toyota, 1963.

Takekasa Keisuke. *Aichi kenritsu Kariya kōtō jogakkō jisshūnen kinen* [The Tenth Anniversary of the Prefectural Higher Girls' School of Kariya]. Nagoya, 1931.

Tamaki Hajime. "Meiji chūki ni okeru Aichi ken no sangyō" [Industry in Aichi Prefecture in the Mid-Meiji Period]. *Aichi daigaku chūbu chihō sangyō kenkyūjo kenkyū hōkoku*, no. 15. Toyohashi, 1966.

———. "Mikawa chihō ni okeru sangyō hattsushi gaisetsu" [An Outline of the History of Industrial Development in the Mikawa Area]. *Aichi daigaku chūbu chihō sangyō kenkyūjo kenkyū hōkoku*, no. 1. Toyohashi, 1955.

Tanaka Keizaburō. *Aichi ken Hekikai gunkai shi* [History of the Hekikai County Assembly of Aichi Prefecture]. Kariya, 1923.

Teikoku himitsu tantei sha. *Taishū jinji roku* [A Who's Who Directory]. 27 vols. Tokyo, 1925-1973.

Tokiwa Yoshiharu. *Ogasawara Sankurō den* [Biography of Ogasawara Sankurō]. Tokyo, 1957.

Toyota kōki nijūnen shi hensan iinkai, ed. *Toyota kōki nijūnen shi* [A Twenty-year History of Toyota Machine Tools]. Kariya, 1961.

Toyota Sakichi ō seiden hensanjo, ed. *Toyota Sakichi den* [A Biography of Toyota Sakichi]. Nagoya, 1933.

Tsuchiya Takao. "Meiji shonen no jinkō kōsei ni kansuru ichi kōsatsu" [An Investigation of Population Structure in the Early Meiji Period]. *Shakai keizai shigaku* 1:1 (May 1931), pp. 158-167.

Tsukamoto Manabu, and Arai Kikuo. *Ken shi series: Aichi ken no rekishi* [Prefectural History Series: History of Aichi Prefecture]. Tokyo, 1970.

Uda Hajime. *Hekikai gun no nōgyō to sono kyōiku* [Agriculture and Education in Hekikai County]. Tokyo, 1935.

Uno Yukio. *Kariya han ni kansuru kenkyū* [Researches on Kariya Han]. Nagoya, 1959.

Waga nōsei Yamazaki Nobuyoshi den kankō iin kai. *Waga nōsei Yamazaki Nobuyoshi* [Biography of Our Teacher Yamazaki Nobuyoshi]. Anjō, 1966.

Waseda daigaku shakai kagaku kenkyūjo, ed. "Tokushū: Chihō sangyō toshi no kenryoku kōzō" [Special Issue: The Power Structure in a Local Industrial City]. *Shakai kagaku tōkyū* 11:1 (June 1965).

Yamaguchi Kazuo. *Meiji zenki keizai no bunseki* [Analyses of the Early Meiji Economy]. Rev. ed. Tokyo, 1963.

Yasui Jirō. *Sen'i rōshi kankei no shiteki bunseki* [A Historical Analysis of Labor Management Relations in the Textile Industry]. Tokyo, 1967.

Yunoki Manabu. *Kinsei Nadazake keizaishi* [An Economic History of the Nada Sake Industry in the Tokugawa Period]. Kyoto, 1965.

Zenkoku shichō kai. *Nihon toshi nenkan: 1969* [Municipal Yearbook of Japan: 1969]. Tokyo, 1969.

ENGLISH SOURCES

Abegglen, James C. *The Japanese Factory: Aspects of Its Social Organization.* Glencoe, Ill., 1958.

Allen, G. C. *A Short Economic History of Modern Japan.* London, 1963.

Allinson, Gary D. "Kariya, A Japanese Community: Economy, Society, and Polity, 1870-1970." Ph. D. dissertation, Stanford University, 1970.

Allinson, Gary D. "Modern Japan: A New Social History." *Historical Methods Newsletter* 6:3 (June 1973), pp. 100–110.

Baerwald, Hans H. *The Purge of Japanese Leaders under the Occupation.* Berkeley, 1959.

Beardsley, Richard K.; Hall, John W.; and Ward, Robert E. *Village Japan.* Chicago, 1959.

Beasley, W. G. *The Meiji Restoration.* Stanford, 1972.

Bendix, Reinhard. "Tradition and Modernity Reconsidered." *Comparative Studies in Society and History* 9:3 (April 1967), pp. 292–346.

Berger, Bennett. *Working-Class Suburb: A Study of Auto Workers in Suburbia.* Berkeley, 1960.

Berger, Gordon M. "The Search for a New Political Order: Konoe Fumimaro, the Political Parties, and Politics in the Early Shōwa Era." Ph. D. dissertation, Yale University, 1972.

Chinoy, Ely. *Automobile Workers and the American Dream.* Garden City, N.Y., 1955.

Clark, Terry N., ed. *Community Structure and Decision-Making: Comparative Analyses.* San Francisco, 1968.

Cole, Robert E. *Japanese Blue Collar: The Changing Tradition.* Berkeley, 1971.

Coser, Lewis A., ed. *Political Sociology: Selected Essays.* New York, 1967.

Curtis, Gerald L. *Election Campaigning Japanese Style.* New York, 1971.

Dahl, Robert A. *Who Governs? Democracy and Power in an American City.* New Haven, 1961.

Dahrendorf, Ralf. *Class and Class Conflict in Industrial Society.* Stanford, 1959.

Dore, R. P. *City Life in Japan: A Study of a Tokyo Ward.* Berkeley, 1958.

————. *Land Reform in Japan.* London, 1959.

————. *Aspects of Social Change in Modern Japan.* Princeton, 1967.

————. *British Factory-Japanese Factory: The Origins of National Diversity in Industrial Relations.* Berkeley, 1973.

Eisenstadt, S. N. "Post-Traditional Societies and the Continuity and Reconstruction of Tradition." *Daedalus* (Winter 1973), pp. 1–27.

Embree, John. *Suye Mura: A Japanese Village.* Chicago, 1964.

Gerth, H. H., and Mills, C. Wright, eds. *From Max Weber: Essays in Sociology.* New York, 1946.

Goldthorpe, John H., et al. *The Affluent Worker: Industrial Attitudes and Behaviour.* Cambridge, 1968.

Gutman, Herbert G. "Class, Status, and Community Power in Nineteenth-century American Industrial Cities—Paterson, New Jersey: A Case Study." In *The Age of Industrialism in America,* edited by F. C. Jaher, pp. 263–287. New York, 1968.

Hall, Ivan P. *Mori Arinori.* Cambridge, Mass., 1973.

Hall, John W. *Japanese History: New Dimensions of Approach and Understanding.* Service Center for Teachers of History Publication No. 34. Washington, D.C., 1966.

————. "The Castle Town and Japan's Modern Urbanization." *Far Eastern Quarterly* 15:1 (1955), pp. 37–56.

Handlin, Oscar, and Burchard, John, eds. *The Historian and the City.* Cambridge, Mass., 1963.

Hawley, Willis D., and Svara, James H., eds. *The Study of Community Power: A Bibliographic Review.* Santa Barbara, Calif., 1972.

Henderson, Dan F. *Foreign Enterprise in Japan: Laws and Policies.* Chapel Hill, N. C., 1973.

Hout, T. M., and Rapp, W. V. "Competitive Development of the Japanese Automobile Industry." In *Pacific Partnership: United States-Japan Trade—Prospects and Recommendations for the Seventies,* edited by Jerome B. Cohen, pp. 221–240. Lexington, Mass., 1972.

Ito, Hiroshi, ed. *Japanese Politics: An Inside View.* Ithaca, N.Y., 1973.

Kawai, Kazuo. *Japan's American Interlude.* Chicago, 1960.

Knights, Peter R. *The Plain People of Boston, 1830–1860: A Study in City Growth.* New York, 1971.

Landes, David. *The Unbound Prometheus: Technological Change and Industrial Development in Western Europe from 1750 to the Present.* Cambridge, 1969.

Laslett, Peter, ed. *Household and Family in Past Time.* Cambridge, 1972.

Lockwood, William W., ed. *State and Economic Enterprise in Japan.* Princeton, 1965.

Marshall, Byron K. *Capitalism and Nationalism in Prewar Japan: The Ideology of the Business Elite, 1868–1941.* Stanford, 1967.

Michels, Roberto. *First Lectures in Political Sociology.* New York, 1965.

Morley, James W., ed. *Dilemmas of Growth in Prewar Japan.* Princeton, 1971.

Mortimer, Wyndham. *Organize! My Life as a Union Man.* Boston, 1971.

Ohkawa, Kazushi, and Rosovsky, Henry. *Japanese Economic Growth: Trend Acceleration in the Twentieth Century.* Stanford, 1973.

Polsby, Nelson W. *Community Power and Political Theory.* New Haven, 1963.

Pyle, Kenneth B. "The Technology of Japanese Nationalism: The Local Improvement Movement, 1900–1918." *Journal of Asian Studies* 33:1 (November 1973), pp. 51–66.

Rae, John B. *American Automobile Manufacturers.* Philadelphia, 1959.

Roberts, B. C., ed. *Industrial Relations.* rev. ed. London, 1968.

Rosovsky, Henry. *Capital Formation in Japan, 1868–1940.* Glencoe, Ill., 1961.

———. *Industrialization in Two Systems.* New York, 1966.

Schnore, Leo F. "Social Mobility in Demographic Perspective." *American Sociological Review* 26 (July 1961), pp. 407–423.

Schulze, Robert E. "The Role of Economic Dominants in Community Power Structure." *American Sociological Review* 23:1 (February 1958), pp. 3–9.

———. "The Bifurcation of Power in a Satellite City." In *Community Political Systems,* edited by Morris Janowitz, pp. 19–80. Glencoe, Ill., 1961.

Serrin, William. *The Company and the Union: The Civilized Relationship of the GM Corporation and the UAW.* New York, 1973.

Smelser, Neil. *Social Change in the Industrial Revolution.* Berkeley, 1959.

Smith, Robert J. "Aspects of Mobility in Pre-industrial Japanese Cities." *Comparative Studies in Society and History* 5:4 (July 1963), pp. 416–423.

———. "Small Families, Small Households, and Residential Instability: Town and City in 'Pre-modern' Japan." In *Household and Family in Past Time,* edited by Peter Laslett, pp. 429–472. Cambridge, 1972.

———. "Pre-industrial Urbanism in Japan: A Consideration of Multiple Traditions in a Feudal Society." *Economic Development and Cultural Change* 9:1, part II (October 1960), pp. 241–257.

Smith, Thomas C. *Agrarian Origins of Modern Japan.* Stanford, 1963.

———. *Political Change and Industrial Development in Japan: Government Enterprise, 1868–1880.* Stanford, 1955.

Steiner, Kurt. *Local Government in Japan.* Stanford, 1965.

Sward, Keith. *The Legend of Henry Ford.* 1948. Reprint. New York, 1972.

Taira, Koji. *Economic Development and the Labor Market in Japan.* New York, 1970.

Thernstrom, Stephan. *Poverty and Progress: Social Mobility in a Nineteenth-century City.* Cambridge, Mass., 1964.

Tilly, Charles. "The State of Urbanization." *Comparative Studies in Society and History* 10:1 (October 1967), pp. 100–113.

Tönnies, Ferdinand. *Community and Society.* Translated and edited by Charles P. Loomis. East Lansing, Michigan, 1957.

Turner, H. A.; Clack, Garfield; and Roberts, Geoffrey. *Labour Relations in the Motor Industry: A Study of Industrial Unrest and an International Comparison.* London, 1967.

Tussing, Arlon. "The Labor Force in Meiji Economic Growth: A Quantitative Study of Yamanashi Prefecture." *Journal of Economic History* 26:1 (March 1966), pp. 59–92.

U. S. Strategic Bombing Survey. *The Effects of Air Attack on Japanese Urban Economy: Summary Report.* Washington, D. C., 1947.

———. *The Japanese Motor Vehicle Industry.* Washington, D.C., 1946.

Vogel, Ezra. *Japan's New Middle Class: The Salary Man and His Family in a Tokyo Suburb.* Berkeley, 1963.

Wylie, Laurence. *Village in the Vaucluse: An Account of Life in a French Village.* Cambridge, Mass., 1957.

Yoshino, M. Y. *Japan's Managerial System: Tradition and Innovation.* Cambridge, Mass., 1967.

INDEX